Tudor Autobiography

TUDOR
AUTOBIOGRAPHY
Listening for Inwardness

Meredith Anne Skura

The University of Chicago Press
Chicago and London

Meredith Anne Skura is the Libbie Shearn Moody Professor of English at Rice University. She is the author, most recently, of *Shakespeare the Actor and the Purposes of Playing*, published by the University of Chicago Press.

The University of Chicago Press, Chicago 60637
The University of Chicago Press, Ltd., London
© 2008 by The University of Chicago
All rights reserved. Published 2008
Printed in the United States of America
17 16 15 14 13 12 11 10 09 08
1 2 3 4 5
ISBN-13: 978-0-226-76187-9 (cloth)
ISBN-10: 0-226-76187-8 (cloth)

Library of Congress Cataloging-in-Publication Data

Skura, Meredith Anne, 1944–
  Tudor autobiography : listening for inwardness / Meredith Anne Skura.
    p. cm.
  Includes bibliographical references and index.
  ISBN-13: 978-0-226-76187-9 (cloth : alk. paper)
  ISBN-10: 0-226-76187-8 (cloth : alk. paper)
  1. Authors, English—Early modern, 1500–1700—Biography—History and criticism. 2. English prose literature—Early modern, 1500–1700—History and criticism. 3. Autobiography. 4. Self in literature. 5. Identity (Psychology) in literature. 6. Biography as a literary form. I. Title.
  PR756.A9S58 2008
  820.9′353—dc22
                                2007050132

♾ The paper used in this publication meets the minimum requirements of the American National Standard for Information Sciences—Permanence of Paper for Printed Library Materials, ANSI Z39.48-1992.

For my family

Contents

List of Figures, ix | Acknowledgments, xi

CHAPTER 1
Autobiography—What Is It?
Issues and Debates
1

CHAPTER 2
Lyric Autobiography: Intentional or Conventional Fallacy?
The Poetry of John Skelton (1460–1529) and Thomas Wyatt (1503–42)
19

CHAPTER 3
Identity in Autobiography and Protestant Identification with Saints
John Bale and St. Paul in The Vocacyon of Johan Bale *(1553)*
49

CHAPTER 4
Autobiography: History or Fiction?
William Baldwin Writing History "under the Shadow of Dreames and Visions" in A Mirror for Magistrates *(1559)*
73

CHAPTER 5
Sharing Secrets "Entombed in Your Heart"
Thomas Whythorne's "Good Friend" and the Story of His Life (ca. 1569–76)
98

CHAPTER 6
Adding an "Author's Life"
Thomas Tusser's Revisions of A Hundreth Good Points of Husbandry *(1557–73)*
126

CHAPTER 7
A Garden of One's Own: *Isabella Whitney's Revision of [Hugh] Plat's* Floures of Philosophie *in Her* Sweet Nosegay *(1573)*
149

CHAPTER 8
Erasing an Author's Life: *George Gascoigne's Revision of* One Hundreth Sundrie Flowres *(1573) in His* Poesies *(1575)*
168

CHAPTER 9
Autobiography in the Third Person: *Robert Greene's Fiction and His Autobiography by Henry Chettle (1590–92)*
197

CHAPTER 10
Autobiographers: Who Were They? Why Did They Write?
220

Appendix: *The Portraits*, 229 | Notes, 233 | Index, 285

Figures

FIGURE 1. "Skelton Poeta," *Garland of Laurel* (1523), 26
FIGURE 2. Skelton, *Against a Comely Coystrowne* (152?), 26
FIGURE 3. Wyatt, "What rage is this?" (n.d.), 35
FIGURE 4. Bale, from *Three Laws* (ca. 1548), 50
FIGURE 5. Bale, from *Catalogus* (1557), 50
FIGURE 6. Bale, *Vocacyon* (1553), 57
FIGURE 7. Bale, *Illustrium* (1548), 63
FIGURE 8. Bale, from *Illustrium* (1548), 63
FIGURE 9. Baldwin, *Mirror for Magistrates* (1559), 77
FIGURE 10. Whythorne, oil portrait (1569), 113
FIGURE 11. Whythorne, woodcut portrait (1571), 114
FIGURE 12. Tusser, *Husbandry* (1573), 137
FIGURE 13. Whitney, from *Nosgay* (1573), 162
FIGURE 14. Gascoigne, "Hemetes" (1575/76), 191
FIGURE 15. Gascoigne, *Steele Glas* (1576), 194
FIGURE 16. Greene, *Never too late* (1590), 207

Acknowledgments

I am grateful to the libraries and institutions that have given permission to reproduce their material here: *English Literary Renaissance* granted permission to reproduce an essay that has become part of chapter 4. The British Library provided images for the reproductions of the portrait of John Skelton from *Garland of Laurel* (1523), the representation of George Gascoigne and Queen Elizabeth from the manuscript of "Hermetes the Heremyte" presented to her (1575/76), and the woodcut portrait of Thomas Whythorne (1571); the Huntington for the portrait of John Skelton from the 152? edition of *Agaynst a Comely Coystrowne*, the portrait of George Gascoigne from a 1587 copy of *The Steele Glas*, and the title pages from John Bale's *Vocacyon* (1553), Thomas Tusser's *Five Hundreth Points of Good Husbandry* (1573), and Robert Greene's *Never Too Late* (1590); ProQuest for digital reproductions of the last two; and the Bodleian Library at Oxford for the portrait of John Bale from *Three Laws* (1548) and two representations of Bale and King Edward VI from *Illustrium* (1548).

I would like to thank the Folger Shakespeare Library for its fellowship support during the beginning year of this project, the Rice University Center for the Study of the Humanities for a semester's leave that allowed me to finish a final draft of the project, and grants from Rice deans facilitating summer research. The Folger staff were extraordinarily generous with their time and expertise, for which I am truly grateful, as I am for the ongoing human fellowship among the readers there.

I am much indebted to those who read and commented on earlier versions of various chapters—Lois Potter, Robert Patten, Logan Browning,

Russ Macdonald, George Pigman III—and to those who endured and helped with entire drafts: Carol Neely, Dorothy Haskell, Anne Goble, two anonymous readers for the University of Chicago Press, and, most of all, Marty Wiener, who provided patience, advice, and support through many drafts. Several graduate students—some of whom have by now become professors and authors themselves—provided invaluable help with research: Lloyd Kermode, Ronit Berger, Kara Marler-Kennedy, Jill Delsigne. Discussions with them, and with Beth Womack and others in seminars, have helped develop my understanding of the autobiographers. Terry Munisteri contributed her eagle-eyed assistance with editing as she typed chapters. Vivian Wiener's copy editing helped polish the final draft. To all of them, heartfelt thanks.

An earlier version of chapter 4 was published as "*A Mirror for Magistrates* and the Beginning of English Autobiography," *English Literary Renaissance* 38, no. 1 (Winter 2008): 25–56.

CHAPTER I

Autobiography—What Is It?
Issues and Debates

> Autobiography hardly exists in sixteenth-century England, and what there is, like Thomas Hoby's *Travail and Life*, relates deeds and opinions, not inward thought and emotion. It is not until the seventeenth century that the keeping of diaries and the framing of memoirs begin in earnest. And even then, selfhood is in abeyance. It is revealing that astrologers and Calvinists—men seeking less to pursue the vagaries of inwardness than to confirm the working of a metaphysical order in the individual life—should figure so prominently among our first autobiographers.
> JOHN KERRIGAN, introduction to William Shakespeare's
> *The Sonnets and A Lover's Complaint*

> Birds probably started flying millions of years earlier than scientists previously thought. It is just that fossils of those first flying birds—predecessors of Archaeopteryx—have never been found.
> JOHN NOBLE WILFORD, "Ancient Bird Had a Brain"

Histories of autobiography in England often assume that it hardly existed before 1600.[1] On the continent Augustine had been followed by Dante, Petrarch, Abelard, and many later life-writers. John Kerrigan, among others, argues, however, that autobiographical writing would not appear in England for another hundred years or more, long after men and women like Cardano and Cellini and St. Teresa were recording their life stories in Italy and Spain.[2] Yet there were at least a dozen sixteenth-century writers in England who found ways to incorporate their lives into a sermon, a saint's life, courtly and popular verse, a history book, a traveler's report, a husbandry book, and a supposedly fictional "adventure" suspected of hiding its author's secrets and slandering worthy personages. The writers came from the court, the country, and the city; one was a Catholic bishop, two were dedicated Protestant reformers, and the others held positions between those extremes; they include scholars and musicians as well as some of the first Englishmen to call themselves professional writers.

That I find more autobiographies than Kerrigan does is partly a matter of definition. Scholars have looked in past literature for texts like today's autobiographies, a practice institutionalized by Philippe Lejeune's 1973 definition of *"autobiography"* as "a retrospective prose narrative produced by a real person concerning his own existence, focusing on his individual life, in particular on the development of his personality."[3] Such a strict definition ruled out a good deal of early self-writing because it was too allegorical or because it appeared only in scattered passages and was incidental to other purposes. Most of all, as Kerrigan argues, such writing was "less concerned to pursue the vagaries of inwardness than to confirm the working of a metaphysical order in the individual's life."[4] In other words, it didn't seem to be in the line of development toward modern inward-looking self-reflexive autobiography, and so it was not considered.[5]

I am less interested in uncovering the forerunners of today's autobiographies than in finding out how and why people talked about themselves before the modern "autobiography" or "self" was culturally encoded.[6] The only requirement for inclusion in this discussion is that an author be writing about his or her experience—whether outward events or "that within," as Hamlet calls it—looking back over the experience and organizing it into a narrative of some sort.[7] In the early modern period, when it was not particularly interesting or appropriate to talk about "inwardness" or the "development of personality," writers—not surprisingly—hardly ever pursued the topic.[8] Indeed, outside the courts, early modern narrative was not usually organized to record causal development of anything; the inherited forms had been designed rather to illustrate a point.[9] Narrative coherence often depended on unifying ideas or concerns rather than on mimetic reproduction of history, just as the Armada portrait of Elizabeth shows the "development" of that battle by picturing two different stages simultaneously. Nonetheless, people did write about themselves, and they included material that they thought was important, in the way they thought appropriate. My goal in what follows is to retrieve all the information I can from what people did say, as well as from what they may have revealed inadvertently. Who were these writers, publishing their stories when almost no one else did? What were they expecting from publication? Who did they imagine as readers? What does their writing reveal about their mental world?

Adopting a looser definition also means that I don't try to distinguish between "true" and fictional autobiographies. Of course, in a number of texts the problem of distinguishing never arises. Some early autobiographies are clearly fictional, like Robert Copeland's pamphlet about Jyl of Braintford (1527), who bequeathed twenty-six and a half of her famous farts to the knaves and fools gathered at her bedside. At the other extreme, others, like Bale's *Vocacyon of John Bale* (1553), seem to be so dependable that they have been accepted as sources for modern histories of the period. But many, like Isabella Whitney's personally revealing although fictional "will," based partly on "Jyl of Braintford," are mixed enough to make separation problematic. Richard Helgerson finds a whole category of Elizabethan "fictional" narratives that are recognizably autobiographical.[10]

Separation is also anachronistic. The sixteenth-century habit of reading allegorically and looking for contemporary allusions in stories about the past often obscures the boundary between truth and fiction. Many writers in this period did distinguish between true "history" and feigning "poesie." But as Philip Sidney argued in his *Apologie for Poesie* (1579), the distinction was not necessarily between "truth" and "lies." William Baldwin could praise the poet who "feyneth well but never lyeth," whose fiction was not, as it is often said to be today, a lie.[11]

Factual verification is often beside the point in early autobiographical writing. One of this book's most important assumptions is that the development of "true" autobiography and of fiction have been too closely entwined to separate them clearly. It has always been through "fiction" that the significance of a life has been understood, and the deepest roots of Western autobiography lie in the ambiguous literature written before the modern divide between history and fiction. Augustine's *Confessions*, the first truly individual autobiography, drew on Ovid's mythology as well as Genesis.[12] The "pseudo-autobiographies" of the great introspective writers of the fourteenth century—Dante, Petrarch, Chaucer—all elude the binary classification.[13] In England too, from early Tudor to late Elizabethan times, texts are situated tantalizingly in the borderland between history and fiction.[14] The "personal voice" we associate with contemporary autobiographies has no precedent in official humanist autobiography or in

Caesar's *Commentaries* or, in England, Edward VI's journal. But it was a powerful aspect of Langland's "feigning" dream vision, *Piers Ploughman*, and more generally in the vision form that continued to serve sixteenth-century autobiographers like John Skelton, William Baldwin, Isabella Whitney, George Gascoigne, and Robert Greene.[15] There is almost always "fiction in the archive" of early autobiography, as Natalie Zemon-Davies has argued for trial records.[16] Fictional picaresque tales like *Lazarillo de Tormes* (1554; English trans. 1576), for example, shaped Benvenuto Cellini's "true" autobiography just as Jyl Braintford's will shaped Isabella Whitney's.

One of the most fascinating aspects of the history of autobiography is that truthful autobiographical texts so quickly produced fictional versions. Hares and a "Hawthorne Tree" left wills long before Isabella Whitney and George Gascoigne used the form. Years of fictional confessions preceded Robert Greene's famous "deathbed confession," *Groatsworth of Witte, Bought with a Million of Repentance*. By 1631, John Taylor the "Water Poet" noted ironically, dying confessions were so numerous that if a man told his life story you knew he was going to be hanged.[17] First-person foreign travel narratives were more or less transparently fictionalized, from Thomas More's *Utopia* to Francis Godwin's tale about his moon voyage. Thomas Harman fictionalized travel to an alien subculture at home in his *Caveat or Warning for Common Cursetors*, which included not only his testimony but also that of the "walking mort" whom he exposed.[18] Reports of visionary experiences like Margery Kempe's were greatly outnumbered by avowedly fictional dream visions written or, like Langland's *Piers Ploughman*, revived during the century.[19]

For much of the century, personal revelation had no place in serious discourse and was tolerable only in youthful toys like amorous lyrics or in wanton fictions. The association of lyric with private experience was one likely source for the well-known sixteenth-century elitist bias against the genre. The supposed aristocratic "stigma of print" was hardly that; it was more a stigma of youthful self-revelation.[20] It reflected a disinclination to make public one's youthful indiscretions, rather than a concern to avoid publication itself. Elite authors, Thomas Sackville and Thomas Wyatt among them, willingly published translations and discourses. What they did not publish were lyrics, especially love lyrics.[21]

Given the sixteenth-century restrictions on self-revelation in England, anyone interested in the "vagaries of inwardness" will find more in poesie than in official "lives" and official *res gestae* accounts. Indeed, to omit lyrics and other "fictional" writing when exploring the history of self-writing—and then to claim that there was no record of inner life before 1700—seems almost perverse. It may not even be possible. Lejeune's formal definition of autobiography was itself influenced by the fictional model that it tried to exclude, the nineteenth-century bildungsroman, any given example of which might fit Lejeune's definition exactly except that it is not "true." He too eventually gave up his restricted definition.[22]

Lejeune had formulated that definition at a time when it was thought that a witness's memory could describe the past as it really was. At that point, the author's stated intention was all one needed to tell fact from fiction; and the resulting division of autobiographies from fiction made more sense. Today, however, we know how difficult it is to establish authorial intention.[23] It has also become clearer that even with the best intentions, autobiographical memory can be unreliable, or "fictional," in many other ways. As Ernest Renan writes in his memoirs, "What one says of oneself is always poetry."[24] Yet such fictions can be revealing, just as the testimony at early modern witch trials can be revealing even if it is not "true." Oral historians no longer assume that the data they collect are factually true, but they find them useful for other reasons.[25] The life stories that Luisa Passerini heard when she asked Turin workers about their experience of fascism sound more like cultural legends than twentieth-century accounts of individual development. But the mere fact that people fell back on such legends—in which, for example, character is fixed until a sudden dramatic change—suggests something about their state of mind and about what needs the form may have fulfilled. Borrowing tactics like Passerini's and Zemon-Davis's, rather than eliminating fiction I have found it useful to identify "fictional" elements in the texts and see what role they play.

There is a second factor, in addition to the strict definition of autobiography, that has distracted attention from the available autobiographical documents. A number of the autobiographical texts discussed here have been treated before, but they have almost always been considered as examples of larger cultural and historical phenomena rather than as inherently interesting documents. The most striking example of this tendency is the assumption everywhere that the history of autobiography is inseparable from the history of self-consciousness (or "individuality" in older studies and "subjectivity" in recent ones). This assumption is what brought autobiography into the academy in the first place. Georg Misch began his study of the genre because he saw autobiography as a window into the individual consciousness of its author and, at a general level, into the emergence of the modern self.[26] Similar assumptions shape the posthumanist claim that early modern authors are products of technologies of power, knowledge, and discourse. This claim does not escape Misch's equation but simply reverses the causality: it is no longer authors that create texts but texts that create authors. In 1965 George Kane warned against the "autobiographical fallacy" of interpreting the pilgrim narrator "Chaucer" as the author's representation of himself. Chaucer, Kane warned, was not telling the truth about himself when he named the narrator; he was merely following a literary convention.[27] Within three years authors were not only separate but dead, mere "effects" of the prior text. So Paul Zumthor argued of the medieval troubadours who sang in the first person, Stephan Greenblatt argued of Wyatt's lyrics, and Thomas Webster of early modern diarists. The "technology" of autobiography (or song or lyric) was said to produce the self. "Self-identities," says Michael Mascuch, "take shape in the modern West as objects of representation in autobiography."[28] Throughout, the emphasis has been on tracking the emergence of modern subjectivity in general—a notoriously elusive goal.[29] The wider focus has discouraged close attention to individual texts and what they might reveal about their individual authors.

The result is that the pool of autobiographical texts in English before 1600 has been doubly limited: critics dismiss not only texts that lack "the vagaries of inwardness" but also texts that seem to describe inwardness but are "really" fictions or that are produced by literary conventions, prevailing "cultural codes," or common rhetorical tactics. So, for example, John Skelton's eccentricities are said to tell us less about himself than about conventions of goliardic satire; the seemingly autobiographical Wyatt is simply "a superior performer of cliché"; John Bale's vision of his calling is not his own but is instead "subjected" to the reformist model of St. Paul; and Thomas Whythorne's narrative is "a product, not of seventeenth-century [i.e., later] attitudes toward the self, but mid-sixteenth attitudes toward poetry."[30]

On the contrary, to read these texts there is no need for any a priori assumption about whether "the self" produces the text, is produced by the text, or exists quite independently of the text. Nor is there any need to assume that conventional language and belief are always at odds with individual self-expression or that cultural construction is always incompatible with autobiographical truth. Conventions, whether discursive or behavioral, always play a role in autobiography, but they are often vague, tacit, ambiguous, or even opaque. It is not easy to predict what role they will play in each case.[31] Although they affect everyone, they are always mediated by a writer's friends, her family, her religious practice, her work, her reading, and her past. What matters is the particular balance in each case. Theoretically all sonnets are alike in following conventions of meter, length, rhyme, and so on, but in practice it is not hard to distinguish Surrey's translation of a Petrarchan sonnet from Wyatt's or to tell Sidney's sonnets from Shakespeare's—and to learn from the difference.

A third factor that has discouraged appreciation of early autobiographical texts is a preoccupation with questions about content: does the author make statements about the "development of personality"? the "vagaries of inwardness"? Of course a writer's explicit statements about what he, or others, thought and felt are important. The presence of such overt statements is probably why many studies of early modern subjectivity gravitate toward the period's theories about subjectivity or inwardness rather than toward more reticent personal documents. Even the history of religious belief during the period, argues historian John Morton, tends to stress the stated contents of belief rather than the more indirectly implied dimension of how religious experience felt.[32] Because overt statements are the most directly available form of evidence, they have been given more weight than they may deserve. Other factors have been overlooked.

It would seem almost too obvious to mention, were it not so often forgotten in studying these early texts: what makes autobiography more than just a subdivision of biography is the author's presence as narrator, not only as the hero of his narrative. The author is both the "I" and the "me"; he is the *autos* as well as the *bios* of the text, as James Olney puts it; in Roy Pascal's formulation, he negotiates between the "design" he imposes and the historical "truth" of his past.[33] He is doing something as well as saying something about himself.

The author of a biography, of course, is also doing something, but his work is intended to be self-effacing; we read the book for information about its subject, not its author. But in autobiography, as George Gusdorf first argued, the author's effort to make sense of his subject is itself the "subject" of the book. "The truth [about the past] is not a hidden treasure already there that one can bring out by simply reproducing it as it is," writes Gusdorf. "No one can revive the dead." A writer can only "call up the past in the present and for the present."[34] I would add that the called-up past is shaped by the writer's present way of seeing himself and the world.

The distinction between the autobiographer's two roles as narrator and narrated is essential if we are curious about anything like inwardness. In this period, as Kerrigan says, autobiographical content provides little information. Even today, when writers intend to talk about inwardness, the most conscientious and self-involved leave things out. No one can tell everything she knows about herself, and she may well conceal or distort things even without realizing it. But however little they say about themselves, authors almost always reveal themselves by what they do—by the act of writing itself and by the linguistic and narrative choices they make as they shape their stories. As A. C. Spearing says of medieval narrators, they not only describe themselves but also encode themselves in the narrative.[35] Even in a "drab" poem or another text less concerned with inwardness, as Kerrigan might say, than with the working of a metaphysical order in her life, a writer's choices can yield new information about her feelings about metaphysics, order, and life, if put in context and given the sort of attention we used to accord only to literary texts. The writer's personal voice, as Judith Anderson calls it in her study of William Langland and Edmund Spenser, is part of his unique "way of organizing and conceiving experience." It can reveal him "exploring the self while searching for [metaphysical] Love and Truth." Kerrigan emphasizes the autobiographer's interest in the "working of a metaphysical order in the individual life," rather than in inwardness. Anderson, however, reverses the relation between self and metaphysics. The metaphysical order, or "fundamental concerns of philosophy and theology," she argues, "become progressively more personalized.... Their truths become more subjective and relative to one person than before."[36]

Close reading of personal voice, or style, may seem like an old-fashioned approach to documents embroiled in their cultural context, but a writer's way of telling a story can be at least as revealing as direct statements about herself. It helps us understand her relationship to the world and to what she says about it. Scholars in the relatively new field of affective linguistics, even more than literary critics, have explored subtle and numerous dimensions of language, variations of which characterize their author.[37] Using the linguist's methods to examine what a writer is doing as well as what he is saying—which do not always coincide—makes it more possible to tease inwardness from an otherwise reticent text.[38]

For example, simply reading John Bale's *Vocacyon* for its content, we come away with the sense that his life has mirrored St. Paul's and that he has subdued himself entirely to his religious model. If we look also at what Bale does, things are not so simple. He frequently stutters out his Pauline claims through negatives and double negatives that call attention to what they deny, raising questions about the motives Bale attributes to himself. A writer's stylistic choices can imply more "vagaries of inwardness" than pages of statements in propositional form. The secrets he decides to tell can be supplemented with the secrets he does not mean to betray.[39]

The emphasis on what an author is doing as well as what she says is especially useful for readers today, because it reminds us that "autobiography" implies an act as well as a text. Recent theorists of the genre now usually speak of autobiography in general as an "autobiographical act" rather than a text.[40] Tudor autobiography in particular is occasional. It emerges from an act defined by a particular setting and a specific audience. Today that scene has all but disappeared.[41] Writing an autobiography now needs no particular occasion, or rather it provides its own. Its intended readers constitute a large and mostly impersonal audience, who read the book more in the context of textual tradition than in the context of the particular conditions that produced it. Readers with this in mind approach early texts by trying to find *some* textual tradition that must have been available to early autobiographers, and they have cited a range of possibilities from Ovid and Plutarch to Joachim du Bellay and Edward VI.[42]

But although textual examples were important in the sixteenth century, what mattered to autobiography as much as any single text was the expectation that on certain occasions you would tell your story to other people. It is safe to say that talking about yourself was part of the stuff of daily life long before personal accounts were first written down, then printed and codified as a genre. Even after people had begun to publish autobiographical texts, these were written not for themselves but to serve some other purpose. Only gradually did autobiography separate from its contexts in sermons, letters, prefaces, and testimony to stand on its own. Like painting, which began as adornment of sacred spaces and only later was practiced independently, autobiographical writing was always part of some other occasion. One reason that Kerrigan and others assume there was so little autobiography before the sixteenth century is that we have overlooked most of these occasions, with the notable exception of religious confession and, more recently, secular trial testimony.[43]

But there were other situations that prompted "confession" in Augustine's sense of "bearing witness" rather than "admitting guilt." Some, like

Augustine's, mark momentous occasions and constitute what Gusdorf calls a personal justification, or apologia, or a task of personal salvation.[44] Death produced some of the earliest recorded autobiographical writing in wills and testaments that could expand into life accounts. Lighter occasions prompted confessional moments too: a nurse telling her small charge a story might add something about how and where she learned it; or a minstrel might tell about the composition of his ballad, as Richard Sheale does in a ballad that opens with a preface about having been attacked by highwaymen on his way to perform.[45] One of the most common occasions for autobiography was simply the occasion of writing something—anything. The first poem in the early poetic miscellany, *Court of Venus* (ca. 1538), speaks not only about love but also about the experience of writing about Venus:

> My penne take payne a lytle space
> To follow the thing that doth me chase
> And hath in hold, my hart so sore
> And when thou hast this brought to passé:
> My pen I praye the wryte no more.

Like cave artists leaving handprints beside their drawings, or like Italian Renaissance painters including cameo self-portraits in their works, Thomas Tusser added "Thomas Tusser made me" to his introductory poem in his husbandry book.[46] Jasper Heywood, Barnabe Googe, John Hall, and Richard Robinson wrote about themselves in prefaces to translations, miscellanies, and dream visions. Skelton included himself as a character in pageants, and Bale's plays incorporated Baleus as authoritative Prolocutor. Whythorne's life story began as a commentary on his poems. Gascoigne's miscellany was designed to advertise his gifts as a writer, and some of Greene's most autobiographical passages are found in the prefaces and letters introducing his texts.

Other passing events—births, accidents, separations, birthdays—produced a "vast, vanished repertory" of private, often autobiographical, verse commenting on them.[47] In personal letters as well, people who would never have considered publishing their experiences shared them with intimates, telling about recent household events, as many women did when their husbands were away on business.[48] Letters were everywhere in a world without newspapers or technology, constituting their own "culture of epistolarity," as it has been called.[49] Narration too was everywhere because so much experience had to be narrated in order to be shared with absent friends and family.

Most of the resulting performances and manuscripts, like Elizabeth Holless's composition of "the passages of her whole life" (<1578), have been lost. The practices that produced them, however, left traces on the somewhat later works studied here.[50] In particular, the habits fostered by intimate exchange helped generate texts and modulate print's formalities. Ordinary letters to friends, for example, fleshed out the model of classical epistolary verse for midcentury poets like Isabella Whitney, half of whose autobiographical miscellany consists of letters to friends and relatives. Thomas Whythorne's entire "life" is cast in the form of a letter exchanging "secrets of the heart" with his friend. Thomas Tusser's husbandry book (1557) is prefaced by a dedication to Thomas Lord Paget, and it emerges from the ease of familiar interchanges during ten years of service as much as from the model of traditional dedications.[51] Whether as friend or in some other role, for many of these writers the audience's immediate presence, real or imagined, is at times a precondition for writing at all.[52]

Even if a text is extant, then, it remains incomplete. Like a letter that once accompanied a gift, it lacks the original framing context—the gift, the recipient, the occasion—that a reader needs to understand it.[53] Later in the century, as writers came to take print conditions for granted, they began to include the contexts that readers needed, and texts became more self-sufficient. We have recognized this compositional change as a major influence on the movement from Tudor "drab" to "golden" Elizabethan verse, but we have failed to see its effect on the development of autobiography.[54]

The occasions for autobiographical acts were located temporally as well as geographically, and as Erik Erikson has argued in his biography of Martin Luther, they should be read in light of both the writer's past and his culture's history up to that moment.[55] More so than today, the earliest autobiographers often produced different—and sometimes differing—accounts of themselves at different times, creating what Karl Weintraub calls an "additive autobiography."[56] John Skelton's verse portrays his poetic career at different stages, for example, and John Bale left several sketches of his life among the bibliobiographies that he compiled first for the Carmelites and later for all England's writers. Other texts can be additive in a different sense, if, like Thomas Whythorne's narrative of his life, they were composed in parts over a period of time, although the final draft may have been compiled all at once later. Thomas Tusser's husbandry book went through several editions, changing not only as he changed but also in response to his audience. The fourth edition of Tusser's book in 1573, with its newly added "Authors Life," can seem self-contradictory unless it is read in the context of its publication history. Rather than a snapshot of his 1573 farming wisdom, the book is an album of snapshots from fifteen years of farming and writing. Though odd to a modern reader who is accustomed to autobiographies written from a single retrospective point of view, Tusser's book is as characteristic of his age as the many Tudor paintings that ignore single-point perspective and realistic space to include objects seen from different points of view at different times.[57]

To summarize, this book is not an intellectual history of concepts of the self but rather an exploration of what people said about themselves, in whatever terms or forms they used. The method has been determined in large part by simple curiosity about individual texts and their writers in this period. I begin with a very loose definition of autobiography so as to include as many different kinds of texts as possible, and with similarly loose expectations about the writers. Some of the texts illustrate what we know abstractly, but others can expand and refine existing generalizations about "the" early modern subject. The range of material offers fascinating glimpses of the variety of lived—and imagined—experience, in great houses, at court, on a tenant farm, in London rooms and streets.

However, one thing these different texts and writers all had in common should be noted at the beginning. They—unlike many other autobiographical texts—were in fact printed, or on the way to being printed. Their uniqueness lies not in being early autobiographies but in being published. This puts them in a very different category, a distinction to keep in mind when thinking about their place in the history of autobiography. When Whythorne asked his friend to overlook lapses in his manuscript, he explained that "a man cannot always speak in print."[58] What he meant, of course, is that he could not be sure he was perfectly proper and accurate in every word. But the fact that such perfection is figured as "speaking in print" suggests that Whythorne saw a difference between speaking in print and other kinds of speaking. For him, "speak in print" was still something of an oxymoron.[59] It is easy to forget that printed autobiographies—like printed lyric—were not the first ones produced in English, or that their sudden multiplication may be explained in part by print itself rather than by a change in the nature of authors.

The writers too were in some ways unique. Not surprisingly, even the earliest of them were unusual in their access to print. All of them were educated, and most had formal training in the rhetorical skills that would help produce the great dramatists and poets at the end of the century. Some of the writers, like William Baldwin, worked in printers' shops, or they printed their own books, as Bale did on occasion. Their careers made them writers, whether they were politicians, musicians, or clergymen. Many of their names would appear on any list of the century's important authors: John Skelton, Thomas Wyatt, William Baldwin, John Bale, George Gascoigne, Robert Greene. All were not merely literate but also immersed in texts and surrounded by other writers. Even Isabel Whitney, who probably had no access to formal schooling, was familiar with the latest literary styles, and she knew her printer well enough to mention him in her mock "will." All took for granted the kind of audience that print made possible. Once the idea occurred to any of them to tell his or her story, it would have been far easier for them to think of publishing it than it would have been for other less literary (or less literate) peers.

In other words, the turn to autobiography among this early group seems to be associated less with something so fundamental as a change in subjectivity than with something instrumental, like the availability of means and models for circulation. Even before the early modern period there had always been men (and a very few women) among the literate—both clerical and secular—who wrote their own histories in some form, intended for an audience that mattered to them. With the spread of print culture, means and models multiplied.[60]

For purposes of tracing its earliest manifestations in English, printed autobiography might be seen as an innovation—like a new farming technique or a new Continental poetic technique—that spread according to rules of its own and depended on a variety of factors such as contact, print, and other communication networks, usefulness, ability, materials, and general receptivity, apart from any deep change in those who adapted it.[61] Its growing practice within Britain, like the spread of autobiographical writing from Italy northward, need not imply anything about the writer's "subjectivity" rather than her more specific characteristics. James Amelang's description of Europe's earliest artisan autobiographies in the period finds the same traits among them that are identified by diffusion theorists as marking "innovators" and "early adopters" in other fields: creativity, intelligence, independence, and so forth.[62]

The long sixteenth century of the Tudors, which is also the first century of the printing press, is a fascinating period for tracking the spread of autobiography in England. This book might have begun earlier, with the scattered individual Latin texts from the British Archipelago. A case could be made for beginning with Chaucer and those who learned from him: the Scots, Margery Kempe, and Chaucer's student Thomas Hoccleve, who influenced the writers treated here. Earlier autobiographical writing, however, is more like a series of isolated phenomena, about which, very often, too little is known.

At the end of the period, literacy and print had become common enough that autobiographers no longer needed special access to print in order to publish. In the early 1590s a reader could go to the stationer's and choose among poetic "complaints," dying confessions, traveler's reports, and prodigal son stories, as well as sonnet sequences (the first of which, Thomas Watson's, had appeared in 1580) by Sidney, Spenser, Shakespeare, Daniel, Donne, and others, letters between Harvey and Spenser, the pamphlet quarrels between Harvey, Greene, and Nashe, and the volley of personally directed insults in the Marprelate battles. When Greene died in 1592, the autobiographical format had been established, and Henry Chettle was only the first of several who forged Greene's supposed repentance and autobiography. Just the few years at the turn of the century saw Will Kempe's pamphlet about his dance from London to Norwich (1600), Simon Forman's "Life and Generation of Simon" (1600), Father Robert Parson's account of himself in his *Memorial for the Reformation of England* (1596), Sir James Melville's *Memoirs of his own Life* (ca. 1590/93; pr. 1683), his daughter Elizabeth Coleville's quasi-autobiographical poem *Ane Godlie Dreame* (1603), and Hugh Holland's autobiographical preface to his would-be epic *Pancharis* (1603), among other complaints, travel reports, confessions, and miscellaneous texts.

By 1656 Margaret Cavendish began her autobiography with a self-conscious review of the genre. Enough models were available so that she did not need to invent the genre—as Isabel Whitney did in 1573—out of a patchwork of other materials. Some of the models, like conversion narratives, in fact were becoming so codified that it is difficult to identify an individual author's contribution to a text. The sixteenth century is when the tipping point is reached, tumbling enough people into awareness of a form of writing activity to which few had had access before. During this relatively brief period, the balance between individual and cultural factors is most easily observed. The spread of autobiography is fast enough—but not too fast—to explore in detail. It is possible to separate incidents in the chains of influence across world and texts that would soon become networks too dense to sort out.

I sometimes refer to texts as "life writing," one of the terms introduced recently (like "self-writing" and "ego-documents") to emphasize the difference between early writing and later codified "autobiography," as it came to be called about two hundred years ago. But all terms are anachronistic, because the texts here would not have been recognized as a separate category. I have tried not to use any term exclusively, and if I refer mostly to "autobiographies," that is only because other terms are so awkward.

"Autobiography" is not a clear category today either. There is no all-purpose definition; there have been too many historical forms of autobiography and too many overlapping genres, like memoir, diary, psychomachia, and autobiographical fiction. Critics will always debate at least three different dimensions of the material: First, how important is the writer's stated intention about whether the text is to be read autobiographically (let alone any unstated but implied intention)? Second, how important is it that what the author says be true (and what does "true" mean)? Third, are there restrictions, if any, on autobiographical format? The variables make definition almost impossible. But as Lejeune says in a somewhat different context, "in spite of the fact that autobiography is impossible, this in no way prevents it from existing."[63] Each critic simply chooses the most useful definition for a given project, as I have done here.

The following autobiographical examples are offered in an order roughly corresponding to the spread of sixteenth-century autobiography in England from court to city, from upper to lower gentry, and from performance-based to made-for-print texts. The book begins with writers from the Tudor courts of Henry VII and Henry VIII: John Skelton (ca. 1460–1529) and Thomas Wyatt (1503–42). They are followed by early reformist authors, John Bale (1495–1563) and William Baldwin (ca. 1515–63). The discussion then moves to a group of writers among the growing numbers of landless gentry in London: Thomas Whythorne (ca. 1520–95), Isabella Whitney (fl. 1566–73), Thomas Tusser (ca. 1524–80), and George Gascoigne (ca. 1539–77). It ends with two somewhat later Elizabethans who tried to make their living by writing: Robert Greene (1558–92) and Henry Chettle (ca. 1560–ca. 1607).

Although the writers are introduced in chronological order, I have discussed them primarily in relation to issues raised in recent critical debates that have either ignored them or judged their work lacking as autobiography. Chapter 2 challenges views that reduce Skelton's and Wyatt's apparently autobiographical verse to the conventions of goliardic satire, in Skelton's case, or in Wyatt's, to a special skill in manipulating clichéd rhetorical convention. Chapter 3 argues against the reduction of John Bale's feisty self-presentation in his *Vocacyon* to a simulacrum of St. Paul. These two initial chapters also establish the book's twofold approach to autobiography, demonstrating why it is so important, in listening for what is distinctive about a text, to distinguish between what the writer says about his past self and what he reveals about himself as he says it now, in the present. Skelton, Wyatt, and Bale provide three examples of an increasing—and increasingly revealing—distance between the "I" who is writing and the "me" who is being written about.

Chapter 4 moves from arguments about literary and discursive convention to debates about the place, if any, of fiction in autobiography. One of the most important unrecognized texts in the history of autobiography is William Baldwin's *A Mirror for Magistrates* (1559). *Mirror*, a collection of first-person fictional monologues by "ghosts" of fallen English princes, is framed by Baldwin's own first-person tongue-in-cheek account of how he and his coauthors composed the monologues. *Mirror*'s unique combination throughout of outward-looking history and inward-looking "poesie," rather than disqualifying it for a place in the history of autobiography, inspired later autobiographical writing by both its contributors and its readers.

The writers discussed in chapters 5–8 were all impoverished gentry centered in London, all writing at the same time in the 1570s, and therefore subject to similar social and economic pressures. But their remarkable differences are better understood in terms of the particular situation each writer faced, the particular characteristics he or she brought to it, and the existence of a particular someone else who could be counted on to read about it. Chapter 5 argues for the tremendous importance of friendship and epistolary exchange in producing autobiography. The friend's role is most explicit in Thomas Whythorne's case but can be seen in others as well. The chapter also suggests that although Whythorne is preoccupied with living up to externally imposed codes of behavior and although he speaks in ready-made generalities about the "seasons of a man's life" and the humors that dominate them, he is more independent than he has seemed before and more preoccupied with inward as well as external pressures. Chapter 6 treats Thomas Tusser, musician-turned-farmer, whose verse "Life," added to the fourth edition of his *Book of Husbandry* (1573), has either been passed over as one more unremarkable tale of hardship or taken merely as a sign of economic individualism among sixteenth-century English tenant farmers. But the genealogy of Tusser's odd little poem reveals much more about how a "Life" emerges, in stages, from the context of one man's experience and his network of relationships. Chapter 7 discusses Isabella Whitney, the first woman in the sixteenth century who is known to have published original secular poetry. Her quasi-autobiographical *Sweet Nosgay* (1573) has been treated primarily as a valuable source of information about women of her class in service in London when she was there, but she deserves closer attention as an inventive autobiographer as well. Like an "outsider" artist today, she drew on popular literary forms of representation as well as elite, and she put together an engaging and effective structure to convey her life story.

Chapters 8 and 9 discuss George Gascoigne and Robert Greene, who have been doubly displaced from histories of autobiography: they have been seen as writers of fiction rather than of autobiography, and their work has been thought to be shaped more by the economic crises from which they wrote than by the intent to record their lives truthfully. But although what Gascoigne and Greene tell readers about their past life cannot be factually verified, we can locate each text in its human context as well as its economic context. Information about what a writer was doing, as well as what he was saying, can suggest why he chose autobiographical form—there are many other ways to sell books—and what his choices might reveal about the story he tells. Even a distorted account of a writer's past experience can be informative. Indeed, in Greene's case, *Greene's Groatsworth of Wit* (1592), the pamphlet that has been accepted as Greene's autobiography because it seemed accurate, turns out to have been written by someone else. But his *Never Too Late* (1590), dismissed as fiction, adds more than *Groatsworth* can to an understanding of how and why Greene wrote and how he saw himself and his writing.

That a variety of people left such accounts suggests how compelling it could be for individuals to tell their own story even in a period when the genre of autobiography had not been recognized. By gathering information about other individual people who talked about themselves as these writers did, we will be better prepared to think about something so general as "early modern subjectivity." Chapter 10 offers some suggestions that I hope can serve as a starting point for further study.

CHAPTER 2

Lyric Autobiography: Intentional or Conventional Fallacy? *The Poetry of John Skelton (1460–1529) and Thomas Wyatt (1503–42)*

The poetry of John Skelton (1460–1529) and Thomas Wyatt (1503–42) makes a good starting point for thinking about early English autobiography. Readers have been struck by each poet's apparently autobiographical speaker, who seems to be talking about his own experience rather than repeating the commonplaces found in other courtly verse. Both writers created personas whose fame lasted beyond the poet's life: Skelton, the rogue and jester; Wyatt, the ideal poet-courtier. The popularity of each was revived by twentieth century critics admiring his toughness, plain speaking, and sincerity and comparing him favorably to the artifice of earlier aureate and later golden poets.[1] Each was praised for writing poetry that was less a statement about the world than an enactment of the mind attempting to understand it.[2] But, as poets, they have been excluded from histories of autobiography that are restricted to prose narratives. More recently, their use of literary and rhetorical convention has led to questions about whether each is autobiographical at all.

The following discussion examines the relation between convention and individuality in poems by Skelton and Wyatt before discussing each as an example of one of two roles for the writer in autobiography: the narrator (Wyatt) and the central figure in the narration (Skelton).[3]

The two poets are not usually considered together. Skelton, a priest from an undistinguished family in the north, looks backward and inland to medieval Catholic England. Wyatt, from a rising family at court, looks forward and outward to the Continent (and even to colonialism, Roland Greene argues).[4] But they were near contemporaries, and both were accomplished performers appreciated by the same community (Skelton served Henry VII, Henry VIII, and possibly Edward IV; Wyatt served Henry VIII). In addition, different as their styles can be, both had benefited from a similar humanist education, and both had the combined resources of native and Continental literary convention to draw on. Both made use of commonplaces about the flattery, hypocrisy, and fatal deception at court. Skelton adds to these familiar topoi medieval complaints against the clergy, and Wyatt adds the Renaissance commonplaces of Petrarchan courtship—the cruel lady, the rejected lover.

In Skelton's case the bias against convention helped fuel early debates about whether his poetry was "medieval" (i.e., highly conventional and impersonal) or "Renaissance" (i.e., spontaneous and naturalistic). If some readers find a "freshness, vigor and density of realistic detail" in Skelton, others point out his "scarcely to be exaggerated reliance on very limited and definite portions of" Chaucer and Langland. These debates are by now largely spent and the categories retired.[5] But a number of recent readers have questioned the authenticity of Wyatt's verse for similar reasons. Because Tudor court poetry was so often read or sung aloud for courtly gatherings, at times to music, H. A. Mason has argued that the study of verse written for courtly love-games is a job for the sociologist and not the literary critic.[6] C. S. Lewis famously dismissed Wyatt's songs as "a little after-dinner entertainment," and Stephen Greenblatt added a Foucauldian twist, arguing that a lyric by Wyatt is like a "diplomatic mission, sent forth to perform the bidding of its creator . . . to manifest and enhance his power at the expense of someone else."[7] Mason's initial doubt about some of Wyatt's amorous lyrics was ultimately generalized and applied to all his verse.

It has also been argued that Wyatt's plain style is as much an artifice as is the aureate: "seductive as a voice of inwardness and confession may be, it is no more the 'real' voice of the poet than any other."[8] If this is true, none of the poems should be read autobiographically. But there is no need to choose between the individual significance of Wyatt's verse and its conventional social function.[9] Just a decade or so after Wyatt died, the music instructor Thomas Whythorne, who entertained the lady of the estate and her guests as part of his service, seems to have taken it for granted that he could have both. His songs were carefully composed, he explains, so that he could reveal his feelings but later dismiss them as mere entertainment should they prove embarrassing.[10]

In fact, it is difficult to imagine any poem completely free of convention and still using language. Rhetoric becomes conventional only because it works, because it provides a useful model for navigating and communicating experience at that moment. The supposed "clichés" in Wyatt's poems are found also in "sincere" letters between husbands and wives at the time.[11] The modern impression of Skelton's or Whythorne's conventionality is a function more of temporal distance than of discursive difference. Poems that now seem conventional to readers looking back through five centuries of writing may have seemed quite radical when they were read in the context that Wyatt would have known. Today's reader has a dictionary to define Wyatt's words but lacks the familiarity with a living language and its use in different contexts that Wyatt took for granted. To reconstruct the nuances of Wyatt's phrases we would need an anthropologist's thick description of amorous discourse in the first part of the sixteenth century in order to know, for example, how loosely was the word *kindly* used? In what circumstances? Only after answering these questions could we say that one of his phrases was merely a cliché.

Besides, conventions are always in flux. There was no genre for "autobiography" in the sixteenth century and certainly no term for it. Writers had to work with what they had; they cleared discursive space by revising or recombining old forms. In doing so they recognized dead conventions as well as we do, and they made fun of anyone who did not. When Bottom chose the tired old ballad form to report his dream in Shakespeare's *Midsummer Night's Dream* (ca. 1595), he revealed his bad taste, but Shakespeare knew what he was doing. Today's focus on originality—in poetry, in film, in dress, in scholarship—makes it easy to forget how necessary convention is in organizing even the most individually inventive texts. What we take to be spontaneous confessional narratives in our own best-sellers follow conventions that happen to work for us now. These autobiographical conventions remain invisible until someone succeeds in deceiving readers—and even prize committees—by using convention to disguise an inauthentic "autobiography."[12]

The problem of autobiographical truth is best addressed more closely and in individual cases. On this level it becomes clear that even a conventional poem is seldom entirely conventional. In lyric there is always tension, no matter how imbalanced, between convention and its embodiment in particular experience. Almost no one can write without drawing on experience, just as no one can write without convention. Lyric's dichotomy of convention and embodiment has been described in different ways: conventional versus personal experience (G. K. Hunter); song versus speech (Alicia Ostriker); eye versus ear (Joel Fineman, who, unlike other theorists, attributed the duality to no one before Shakespeare); or ritual versus fictional dimensions (Roland Greene).[13] Individual lyrics create different balances between the two. Some of Skelton's and Wyatt's poems are almost entirely conventional. But part of the autobiographical effect in their other poems is the narrative fecundity that individualizes and locates convention.

Indeed, part of what makes these two poets unusual is their unconventional treatment of convention. Skelton sets up surprising juxtapositions between the formal aureate style and his "helter-skelter" Skeltonics. At times he alternates a liturgical format with scatological satire, as in describing a bloody hawk hunt inside his church on a holy day: "Sed non secundum Sarum, / But like a March harum / His braines were so parum."[14] He is inspired by conventional goliardic impropriety, but he filters it through his own modern, classically trained perspective. Wyatt similarly pairs disparate poetic conventions, most notably to invent a new sonnet form to accommodate two different ways of thinking about a topic, expansive in the body and epigrammatic in the final lines.[15] Setting up conventional expectations only to break them is part of what helped both Skelton and Wyatt convey the individuality of experience.

The mention of a listener's expectations raises an important issue often overlooked in debates about authorial intention. For the history of autobiography, audience response is at least as important as the author's intention. Skelton and Wyatt gave their audiences powerful and popular new models for talking (whether truthfully or not) about their own experience. Even in the unlikely case that nothing either poet wrote was autobiographical in the factual sense, the models they created were available from then on to be used autobiographically by others.

If there is an implied question about "real" people here, it is not "Does this poem's persona express Wyatt's real feelings about himself?" but "Why was Wyatt the only one to produce poems in which he *seemed* to be expressing his own feelings?" Where did such an innovation come from? How did he manage it? What can we learn about him from it? But there is no reason to dismiss the additional possibility of biographical interpretation for the poems. Other Tudor poems drew on their authors' experience. Nicholas Grimald (1519–62), who, after Surrey and Wyatt, contributed the largest number of poems to Richard Tottel's 1557 anthology, refers to his life in his verse, most famously in a poem about his mother's death. In the 1560s George Turberville wrote about his ambassadorial experiences in Russia; beginning in the 1570s some of Thomas Churchyard's poems reported on his war experiences, as did George Gascoigne's; and Robert Baker's verse account of his voyage to Africa (1562) was included in Richard Hakluyt's first collection of travel accounts in *Principall Navigations* (1589).[16]

Skelton and Wyatt pose the same difficulty about verification that literature and introspective writing always do. But apart from external facts, cumulatively the poems themselves can reinforce one another and suggest degrees of possibility. Was Wyatt's "Whoso list his wealth and ease retain" as the content implies, written from prison as he watched Anne Boleyn's beheading "out of a grate"?

> The bell towre showed me suche syght
> That in my hed stekys day and nyght;
> Ther dyd I lerne out of a grate,
> Ffor all vaulore, glory or might,
> That yet *circa Regna tonat*.[17]

No one knows. But we do know that his contemporaries linked Wyatt and his imprisonment to Boleyn, and that Wyatt wrote at least one other poem while in prison ("Syghes ar my foode, drynke are my teares," [CCXLIV, 1–2]), as did Henry Howard, earl of Surrey, and others.[18] There is not enough evidence to base a biography on the verse, but together the period's poems reveal what Wyatt and others thought was a plausible account of how it felt to be in prison. Compared to one another they can also make it easier to see what makes Wyatt's account different.

Both Skelton and Wyatt wrote about themselves in different forms, designed for different occasions. But each presents a coherent vision of the world and himself throughout the scattered individual texts. Each also speaks consistently like himself throughout. It is always possible for a poet to disappear into his verse, sounding like any other narrator and leaving a listener or reader alone to focus on his story. But the speakers in both Wyatt's and Skelton's poems compel attention in their own right. It is not only that they use odd grammar, intrusive rhymes, and choppy meter and make outrageous or self-contradictory statements. Each, like an autobiographer, also seems to be working out what he has to say about his experience while he is saying it. The interest lies not only in the experience itself—Wyatt has been rejected again, Skelton meets another stupid priest—but in what he makes of it.

The following discussion of Skelton emphasizes the first dimension, Skelton's "me," or what he says about himself. The section on Wyatt emphasizes the second, the poet's "I," his narrative voice. The emphasis could easily have been reversed. But the speaker of Skelton's verse—whose voice is so unique that it has become adjectival—has been described before. Skelton's full contribution to autobiographical writing can be better appreciated by noting the consistency of his story. Wyatt's story, his vision of his world, is relatively familiar from the works of other court poets. It is rather his voice, his way of describing and responding to that world, that most exploits lyric's potential for autobiography. The discussion here suggests that he does so more thoroughly and in even more ways than we have recognized before.

"Skelton Poeta" in His World

Much is obscure in Skelton's background, but what we do know suggests he had a powerful sense of himself as a writer. Skelton was proud of the skills that his education had given him. He wore "Calliope's livery" ("Calliope," 346); he was England's "phoenix" ("Ware the Hawk," 101); he imagined himself thunderously applauded in the Palace of Fame ("Garland of Laurel," 347). Scholars have worked out a probable life story from the few facts we have, and it, too, centers on his writing.[19] Born sometime in the early 1460s, Skelton came from an undistinguished family in northern England and was trained as a chorister. Like the two other sixteenth-century autobiographers with similar musical training, Thomas Tusser and Thomas Whythorne, he went on to Cambridge, his "alma parens that first lovingly suckled me with her paps of wisdom."[20] He was made laureate at home (Oxford, by 1489; Cambridge, by 1493) and abroad (University of Louvain, by 1523).

He was closely associated with the powerful Howard family from as early as 1482, the date of what may be his first known poem, *The Bouge of Court*.[21] Connections to the Howards may have secured his role as poet at the funeral of Edward IV (1483). By 1492, after his laureations, he was part of the group of humanists at Henry VII's court and was made tutor to Henry, duke of York, then preparing to become archbishop. Ten years later when the crown prince died, the new heir, Henry, was assigned a new tutor. Skelton left court to assume the rectorship of Diss in East Anglia. By 1512 or 1513, however, he was back at court serving as *orator regis* to his former pupil, now King Henry VIII, and by 1516 he had begun his bold poetic attacks on Cardinal Wolsey. He was probably granted sanctuary at Winchester, where he died in 1529.

Throughout his life, whether servant to the Howards or to the king, in his own parish church or resident at Winchester, Skelton never let go of his identification with learning and with poetry. Once he achieved the status of laureate, few poems failed to mention that honor, and many flaunted his learning at length. He oversaw the publication of his works and took care in selecting the portraits added to his text (see figs. 1 and 2). As his additions to "Philip Sparrow" suggest, he took pains to make sure he was understood. Referring to readers who objected to an earlier version of that poem, Skelton says, "But Philip, I conjure thee / ... show now unto me / What the cause may be / Of this perplexity!"[22] Skelton's claims at times go even beyond mere excellence and assert divine inspiration. One of his earliest works, the prelaureate 1483 "On the Death of the Noble Prince, King Edward IV," devotes eight of its thirty-two stanzas to the invocation and description of his poetic powers, including a demurrer that even if all nine Muses had breathed influence divine into him and even if he had the eloquence of laureate Phoebus, it would be too little to praise Edward. Though he had not yet earned them, Skelton was already trying on those honors that he would spend much of his later poetry parading. His last poem, "The Replycation" (1529), makes Skelton's most extravagant claims for the power of poetry and its origin in divine inspiration.

When C. S. Lewis argued, with good reason, that Skelton "has no real predecessors and no important disciples," he was speaking largely of Skelton's style.[23] It was first a dramatic style. Skelton may have been concerned with ideas and morals, but he embodied them in dramatic encounters between a particular good person (usually himself) and a particular bad person. His flyting poems are typical: "Against a Comely Coistrown" (1495–96), "Against Dundas" (n.d.), "Poems against Garnesche" (1513–14), and "A Replication against Certain Young Scholars Abjured of Late" (1528). But combat was also incorporated into his other lyrics and dream visions.

Figs. 1–2 "Skelton Poeta," *Garland of Laurel* (1523), portrait on title page verso (© The British Library Board. All Rights Reserved [82.d.25, title-page]); Skelton, *Against a Comely Coystrowne* (152?), title page portrait (this item is reproduced by permission of The Huntington Library, San Marino, California [RB 59200]). Skelton helped choose the first and perhaps the second himself.

One source of the poetry's autobiographical effect was that the drama is often internal. As John Holloway says, "To read [Skelton's lines] is to find oneself in almost total contact with the movement of a living mind."[24] It's a mind in the act of both thinking (Stanley Fish describes Skelton's drama of moral choice) and feeling (Robert Graves argues that in Skelton's verse "intuitive thought reigns supralogically, and personal rhythm subdues meter").[25] In this Skelton was different from most other poets at the time. The aureate poems of Stephen Hawes, one of Skelton's most admired contemporaries, for example, was typically composed of rational statements. Skelton's satires respond passionately and more roughly to a world that defies such assured statements.[26]

But much of Skelton's autobiographical effect depends also on its content, on what is being described. Skelton's world is vividly pictured. He typically anchors his verse in specific places and events, whether a royal funeral (the partly aureate elegy for King Edward the Fourth), activities at a local tavern (the Skeltonic "Tunning of Elinour Rumming"), or confrontation with an enemy, of whom, the poems indicate, Skelton had many. Accordingly, while Holloway, Graves, and Fish praise Skelton's inward-looking drama, W. H. Auden calls Skelton the most outward looking of poets, and he praises Skelton's visual and auditory precision.[27] With an eye (and ear) toward the divine, Skelton nonetheless directed a "camera eye" to the grubby details of a teemingly secular world.[28] He trained it mercilessly on Garnesh's body odor ("Ye wot what I think— / At both ends ye stink" [155]), at Jane's pet sparrow inside her clothing ("Upon my naked skin. / Got wot, we thought no sin: What though he crept so low?" [65]), and even at the elegant details of an aristocratic hall that intrude into an otherwise allegorical dream in "Garland of Laurel" (*Complete Poems*, 372–74).

What will be emphasized here, however, is an autobiographical aspect of the texts that deserves more attention: his continued analysis of his own struggle for professional and spiritual achievement, together or separately. Skelton's three most autobiographical poems, *The Bouge of Court* (1482?), *The Garland of Laurel* (1495), and "Ware the Hawk" (1503–05?), were composed on different occasions and in different genres. Two of them are dream visions; the third is a typically Skelton anticlerical satire. But they all trace the progress of a very Skelton-like speaker through his world. The sequence is chronologically coherent as well, charting Skelton's poetic and secular progress from initiation to triumph.

Skelton's world is conventional in many ways; its central locations are the familiar institutions of court, church, and worldly "Fame," and Skelton's disillusionments are traditional. But it is a world noticeably skewed by Skeltonic values and concerns. The dream visions in the first two poems sketch its landscape. It is a black-and-white world, divided into good (friends) and bad (enemies). Friends are powerful and intelligent enough to welcome Skelton into their grand palaces and halls. Enemies are rude, ignorant, noisy, and often ugly; they come from dirty taverns or hovels and try to invade Skeltonic territory or to chase him out of it. (Even the birds that Skelton inherited from medieval and Continental tradition are segregated: the parrot from paradise and the regal phoenix together balance the brutal hawk, the vulgar daws and pigeons, and the lecherous sparrow.)

The earliest of the three, *The Bouge of Court*, set in 1582 and perhaps written close to that date, comes from Skelton's prelaureate and precourtly experience, though probably after he had become attached to the Howards. Skelton chose the closest form to autobiography that was available to him, the dream vision. Although the genre was already old-fashioned, by using it Skelton signaled his membership in poetic literary tradition, and by updating made it his own.[29] The narrator is troubled by poetic rather than by more typical amorous failure; he longs to join the distinguished "poets old" who could touch a moral truth and cloak it subtly, but (as Ignorance tells him) he lacks the requisite "connyng." He falls asleep on an autumn night in a seaside inn (Powers Key, probably owned by the Howards), rather than in a springtime landscape. The opening of his dream may seem like a traditional allegory of love: the dreamer, whose name is Drede, must find his way to the beautiful Dame Sanspeer, negotiating a path between the figures of Desire and Daunger who beset traditional lovers. But this lady's favor is the "bowge of court" (rewards or maintenance granted to courtiers), not the rose of love, and once Drede wins it, the dream suddenly shifts into a comically realistic court satire.[30]

Dame Sanspeer's "bowge of court" is a "ship, goodly of sail," piloted by Fortune, and the dreamer must press his way past a crowd of vulgar merchants also seeking Fortune's commodified Favor. On board he meets seven deadly courtiers, whose allegorical names hardly prepare us for Skelton's naturalistic portrayal of the flattery, deceit, and envious disdain of those who have no respect for the hesitant scholar-dreamer. What follows is a psychologically realistic nightmare, as Drede slowly begins to understand the dark side of the courtier's ability to "cloak truth." He realizes that he is caught, friendless, in a crowd that pretends to know and admire his "connyng" but is secretly conspiring to kill him. Finally, terrified when they close in on him, he jumps overboard. Waking suddenly, he starts to record what we have just read.

Although hardly autobiographical in the sense of recording an actual voyage on *The Bouge of Court*, the dream offers an inner truth, not the facts but the experience.[31] It shows how Drede makes sense of the betrayal and humiliation that always lie in wait at court. It also provides a comically nightmarish analogy for the narrator's poetic self-doubt before he fell asleep. The dreamer's dread of lacking a true poet's cunning and ability to "cloak" a truth is transformed, within the dream, into a vision of despicable courtiers who can cloak the truth but whose distortions the dreamer disdains as much as the courtiers disdain him. However, he triumphs by dreaming and recording the dream, one whose "cunning" mastery in teaching moral truths proves that his initial fears were unfounded.

The Garland of Laurel (1495), Skelton's second dream vision, revisits the autobiographical saga of his poetic ambition, but this time as wish fulfillment rather than as nightmare.[32] It is the same world with the same concerns, but since writing *Bouge* Skelton had secured his three laureations, the Howard family's patronage, and his own poetic identity.[33] This time the specific location is Gaultree Wood outside Sherrif Hutton, the Howard estate, just as *Bouge* had been set in the Howards' inn. Here Skelton is free of poetic self-doubt when he falls asleep, but the dream itself is devoted entirely to his poetic occupation. In *Bouge* he had to win the favor of Dame Sanspeer, who owned the ship of court; here it is the "peerless" Queen of Fame into whose Palace of Fame he asks entrance. In *Bouge* he had to woo Fortune before he could board Sanspeer's ship. But now it is wisdom personified, Pallas, who argues his case to Fame. *Bouge*'s Drede despaired over his own Ignorance and lack of cunning, but wisdom had already favored this speaker before the dream began.

Crowds of rude candidates rush the gates of Fame, just as the vulgar merchants had in *Bouge*. The Queen of Fame seems to favor the merely famous riffraff over true achievers like Skelton—as did Sanspeer. But at this point *Garland* leaves the trials of *Bouge* behind and leads Skelton Poeta toward a more literal—and more triumphant—trial of his poetic worthiness. The noisy crowd is replaced by a parade of poets led by Apollo, starting with "old Quintilian" (*Complete Poems*, 348) and culminating in the great English poets to whose company the speaker had not dared aspire in *Bouge*. Gower, Lydgate, and Chaucer welcome Skelton, and they call Occupation to guide him into the Palace of Fame, where the trial will be held.

Occupation represents Skelton's identity as a writer, exactly what had been in question in *Bouge*. Here she greets Skelton like an old friend and reminds him that she had rescued him "when broken was your mast / Of worldly trust" and "Your storm-driven ship I repaired new" (*Complete Poems*, 364). It is as if she has transformed the allegorical shipboard adventure in *Bouge* so that its doom-bound ship, now "new-repaired," has now become a figure for his poetic calling.[34] Occupation takes Skelton Poeta through the palace gates, into its grounds walled against the pressing crowds, and further inward to an enclosed "herber." Here he finds the poet's delight, a paradise that brings "new comfort of sorrows escaped" (*Complete Poems*, 370, 368). In the center of the herber, the nine Muses and Flora, queen of summer, dance in a circle around a "goodly laurel tree" whose fragrance preserves against all "Infections" and "rancour" (*Complete Poems*, 369). Virgil's Iopas sings about creation, and a phoenix of Araby nests at the top of the laurel. Skelton discovers the only serpent in this paradise, Envious Rancour, a figure in "yonde pile," who, like Drede's shipmates on *Bouge*, is most dangerous when speaking most sweetly (*Complete Poems*, 371–72). He is a reminder that even the laurel flowers cannot keep Rancour out. But for the moment at least, he is harmless.

At last Occupation leads Skelton from the garden up a winding stair and into "a goodly chamber of estate, / Where the noble Countess of Surrey" sits with her ladies in waiting. They are busy embroidering a garland of laurel for him, and they welcome his arrival. Their domestic scene is safe from vulgar crowds and envious rancor, as well from any demand that Skelton prove himself. But freely reciprocating their gift, he sings his own "garland" of special songs, one for each of the twelve as they work, and the secretary records it all. The poems more than answer Fame's earlier complaint that Skelton had not written enough poetry "to purchase / The favour of fair ladies" (*Complete Poems*, 349). They are a tour de force of metrical calisthenics, and their lyrical charm is unlike either the poet's usual aureate or his "Skeltonic" verse. Skelton's move into the palace and up the stairs is also a move from allegory to a more naturalistic portrayal of how and where he created his *Garland*. The portrait of his affectionate exchange with the countess and her waiting women—the poet reading, the ladies sitting on chairs in a circle around the countess as they embroider their separate pieces, and the secretary recording all—provides a glimpse of the poet's role as a familiar entertainer in a noble household.[35]

Finally, armed with their embroidered garland as well as with the extraordinary poetic garland he has just created for them, Skelton is led back by Occupation into the allegorical Palace of Fame, where she reads his comically long, detailed curriculum vita. When she comes to the most recent item, the *Garland of Laurel*—the very poem we are reading—the audience of "A thousand thousand" poets and orators cry "*Triumpha, triumpha!*" and the "starry heaven...shoock with the shout," ending Skelton's dream. He wakes to find himself outside in the forest surrounding Sherrif Hutton, where he began. Looking at the stars, he places his vision in a larger historical and astrological frame. Two-faced Janus tells the poet to look both "behind and before" as the god does himself, with his "double chere" (*Complete Poems*, 393). The poem's astrological specifications mark the moment as Skelton's thirty-third birthday and, like Janus, point not only backward to Skelton's birth but also forward to the promise of a stellar future. Skelton anticipates that future in the several poems at the end that proclaim him Briton's Catullus, Adonis, and Homer (*Complete Poems*, 394).

The third of Skelton's autobiographical poems, the satirical "Ware the Hawk," is hardly a dream vision, but it is as concerned with his occupation. "Hawk" was written after Skelton's first period of court service and before his return, an interlude spent as rector of the church at Diss, during which he wrote his most outspoken attacks on Wolsey. The poem describes a neighboring cleric who used Skelton's parish church to exercise his hawks. Skelton, the speaker, tells us that he had complained to the authorities about the episode but they had done nothing. Now he brings the case to his captive audience:

I shall you make relation,
By way of apostrophation
Under supportation
Of your patient toleration
How I, Skelton Laureate,

Devised and also wrate
Upon a lewd curate.
>   (*Complete Poems*, 102)

The intruder, having loosed a pigeon to his hawks and locked the church doors, urges them on to the kill. Skelton, glancing in and then finding a secret way to get past the lock, describes the hilariously indecorous scene that follows, with the hawk not only mangling the bloody pigeon at the altar but dropping excrement on the altar linen:

The blood ran down raw
Upon the altar-stone;
The hawk tired on a bone;
And in the holy place
She dunged there a chase.
>   (*Complete Poems*, 102)

All the while Skelton races after the cleric shouting judgment. Finally, he challenges the uneducated man to read Skelton's Latin inscription and then triumphantly proclaims his own superiority when the priest cannot do it.

The poem draws heavily on conventional clerical satire of priests who know no Latin and spend time hunting or otherwise defecting instead of performing their pastoral duties. Like Skelton's attacks on Wolsey, it is very funny. But at the same time Skelton keeps the sacred before us by organizing the narrative as if it were a sermon, with sections entitled "Observate" (*Complete Poems*, 103), "Considerate" (104), "Reformate" (106), and so on.[36] He makes the most of words like *blood*, *altar*, and *sacrifice* that allegorize his fleshly mishap, and he specifies the Feast of St. John as its date. Skelton thereby elevates his comic rage into a lesson and turns the cleric's misdeeds into blasphemy. In the final, most scathing section, Skelton questions the cleric as if he were hearing confession and gleefully exposes his ignorance.

The exposure of the reality beneath clerical pretense leaves "Hawk" as energetically naturalistic as the two earlier poems were allegorical. But different as it is in both form and substance, its narrative links it closely to the dream visions, and, like *Garland*, it announces Skelton's phoenix-like poetic achievement. Skelton is the protagonist again, and his world centers on one special enclosed space. Skelton's church is an idealized locus like the grander *Bouge of Court* and Palace of Fame, and it too is beset with crude and threatening invaders. The difference is that in the earlier poems the speaker had been trying to get into what seemed (the court in *Bouge*) or really was (the Palace of Fame in *Garland*) an ideal space. He had been impeded by merchants shoving aboard in *Bouge*, by the rabble of "dawcocks" outside Fame's Palace, and by the "dawcock" Envious Rancour lurking at the edges of the palace herber.

Here the action is simply reversed. The sacred space, the church with its holy altar at the center, is already Skelton's. This time the "dawcock" priest has sneaked past the gates and threatens to turn Skelton's church into the antichurch, with his dogs biting and barking and his hawk dropping its dung with its blood on the altar, as if this were Elinour Rumming's alehouse, where pigeons dropped their contributions into her ale (*Complete Poems*, 117). But Skelton triumphs over the invader by proving his poetic skill and his cunning, precisely what was at stake in both dream visions. By challenging the priest to read his Latin message, Skelton not only cleanses the hawk from the altar but installs there the phoenix, his own laureate version of the dove that should hover above it. His Latin claim makes him into "England's phoenix" and transforms his church into Fame's "herber," where the phoenix can roost, keeping this priest, like all "Envious Rancour," at bay.

Skelton's texts, whatever else prompted them and whatever more immediate function they served at court or for him, record parts of an individual view of the world and his place in it. The self-doubting and ignorant poet Drede fails to board the ship of court, but his failure proves to be the proof of his value and the means of his success. Then Skelton's Wisdom, along with his lifelong Occupation, gain him entry to the contentment of the Duchess of Howard's chamber and from there to the Palace of Fame, where he is no longer Drede but "Skelton Poeta." In "Hawk," since he has left court, Skelton's concerns are limited to protecting the small sacred space he does have, his church, from the dawcocks who had once competed with him for entrance. Again, he is spectacularly successful. One may doubt the literal truth of the poems, even the nonvisionary "Hawk," but not their consistency and coherence of vision. And anyone in Skelton's original audience thinking about reporting his own vision of experience could hear or read these poems and learn how he might do so.

Thomas Wyatt's Voice

Language most shewes a man; speake that I may see thee.
BEN JONSON, Discoveries

Skelton's role at court as laureate was valued, but he was nonetheless a servant. Wyatt lived closer to the political center, where love as well as politics was vulnerable to public scrutiny, and self-revelation could be dangerous.[37] But many of Wyatt's poems, even more than Skelton's, trace the experience of an individual mind as it navigates that dangerous territory.

Born in 1503, Wyatt came from a family that had risen to power at the court of Henry VII. He was probably educated at Cambridge, and he held important positions both in the court of Henry VIII and abroad as its representative in France and Rome. He translated Plutarch for Queen Catherine and was present at Anne Boleyn's coronation. He was arrested in 1536, along with Boleyn's suspected lovers, but he survived to become an even more successful and admired courtier if also a subject—as he is still—of rumor and guesswork about his relation to Boleyn.

Wyatt was a courtier first; he never boasted about his writing as Skelton did. But throughout his career, whether home or abroad, his writing suggests a sense of himself not only as a master of language and an "orator" or ambassador but also as a writer. Many of his poems refer to writing, whether in the guise of "speaking" or of lute playing, and if "lament my losse, my labor, and my payne" (CCXIV) is by Wyatt, he there addresses a "Redre."[38] Wyatt kept his own copy of his poems and took care to rewrite them, possibly preparing them for publication. *The Court of Venus* (154?), the earliest known printed miscellany, may include poems by Wyatt, obtained with or without his permission (see fig. 3).[39]

His vision of the world, like Skelton's, remains consistent across the collection.[40] For him everything is disturbingly unstable. There is no safe Palace of Fame or duchess's chamber.[41] Those in power—the king and the beloved—are fickle and do not reward service as they should, although they demand ridiculous courtly observances from their servants. Wyatt, drawn almost against his will into intrigues, inevitably chooses to withdraw from chaos and betrayal into the "quiet of mind" or the "thing in the mind."[42]

However, rather than examining the content of Wyatt's verse I will focus more on how Wyatt sees and conveys it. Wyatt's education and mastery of rhetoric, like Skelton's, made him familiar with classical, Continental, and native literary conventions, and he was skilled at using them. He is

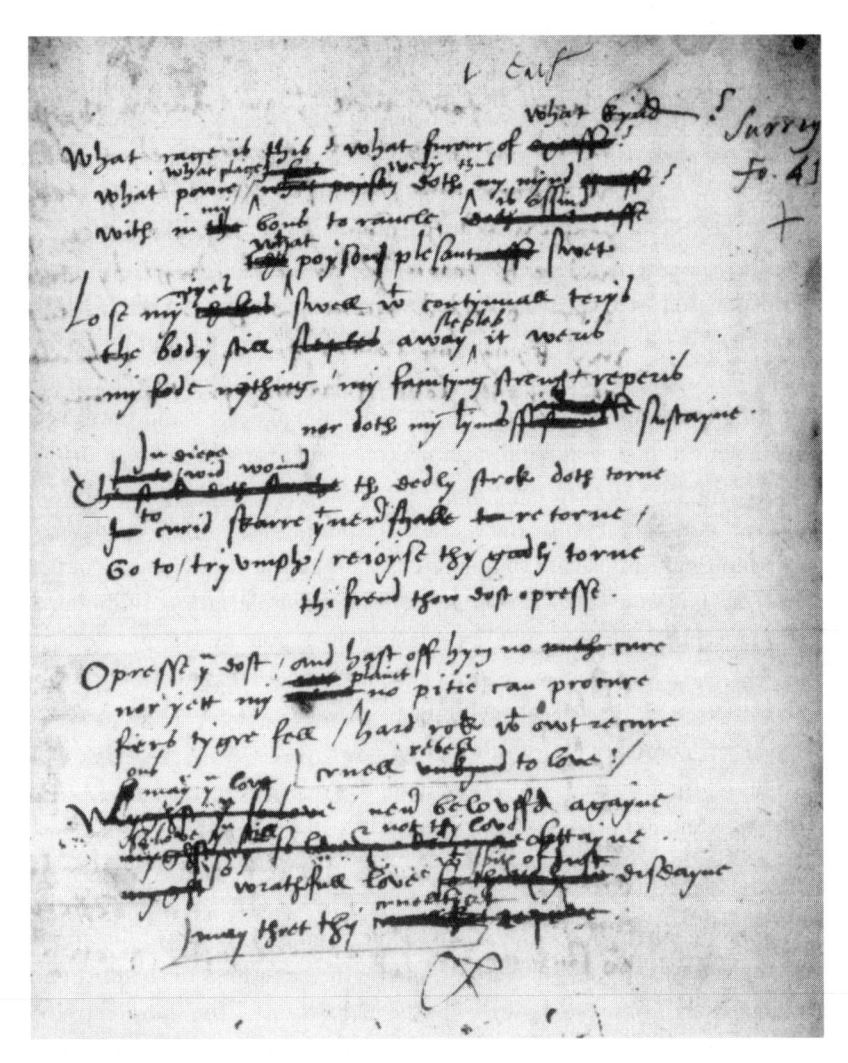

Fig. 3 Page from Egerton Ms., in Wyatt's hand, with his "What rage is this?" (CI) and corrections.

indebted to Chaucer, and even more so to poets whose work he almost certainly got to know during his trips abroad. Wyatt was the first to translate Petrarch into English, and his versions of twenty-five Petrarchan sonnets demonstrate his sympathetic reading of the originals. The young English poet learned from Petrarch's self-reflexivity in his autobiographical *Rime Sparse*. But Wyatt's uniqueness depended, like Skelton's, on his ability to reconfigure existing material, which he did even in his "translations."[43]

In particular, Wyatt, like Skelton, had a "dramatic touch" that moved his verse toward dialogue rather than toward impersonal exposition.[44] Even more than Skelton's, Wyatt's drama was internal. His poems return to the same courtly forms, like the lover's plaint, but rather than repeating the commonplaces about them, he makes each the occasion for examining the speaker's often conflicted uncommon response. He barely describes the external world—even his beloved—except as it affects him.[45] In the debated "bell towre" poem quoted above, for example (CLXXVI), Wyatt translates "public" experience—"The bell towre showed me suche syght"—into private experience—"That in my hed stekys day and nyght." What he learns "out of a grate" is not what anyone else could have seen outside, but rather what he himself makes of it: "Ffor all vaulore, glory or might, / That yet *circa Regna tonat.*"

Wyatt does not describe the speaker's response to what he sees but does something more unusual. His poems enact the speaker's "movement of the mind," as if he were "thinking out loud."[46] For example, after a disappointment one speaker asks his wretched heart why it goes on living:

Most wretchid hart most myserable,
Syns the comforte is from the fled,
Syns all the trouthe is turned to fable,
Most wretched harte why arte thou nott ded?
        (XCI, lines 1–4)

But immediately, at the beginning of the next stanza, he changes direction: "No, no, I lyve and must doo still." And by the beginning of the third, he changes again, "But yete thow hast bothe had and lost." The stanza refrains alternate between defeat ("most wretched harte") and resolution to bear it ("For he is wretched that wenys hym so"), until the poem reaches a balance of sorts at the end.

Yet can it not be thenne denyd,
It is as certain as thy crede;
Thy gret vnhap thou canst not hid:
Vnhappy thenne why art thou not dede?

Vnhappy, but no wretche therfore,
For happe doth come again and goo;

> For whiche I kepe my self in store,
> Sins vnhap cannot kil me soo.
> (XCI)

You cannot deny your seemingly fatal misfortune, he tells himself, but by now you also cannot deny that it hasn't killed you. Since happiness comes and goes, I won't mourn it but wait for it to return.

This movement of the mind, reproduced in the movement of the lines of verse, is recognizably Wyatt's. Although readers may disagree about whether a particular poem (like "wretched harte") refers to political or amorous events, no one doubts that Wyatt is the one who is reacting.[47] Wyatt's larger dramatic gestures are the most visible, but every detail at every level of Wyatt's language works as well to express the speaker—even down to the usually overlooked choices among parts of speech or the balance between active and passive verbs.

Wyatt provides a usefully exaggerated example of the subjective language that can be seen, to a lesser degree, even in the prose autobiographies that will be discussed later. Linguists have shown the ways in which a speaker's everyday language, especially language as eccentric as Wyatt's, can reveal his attitude toward what he says. The linguist's "subject" is simply the marker for the "I" who speaks, defined in contrast to the "you" or "it" that is spoken about.[48] A phrase borrowed from linguistics, "subject position," is often used as if the subject were only a camera lens, a pure point of view. But a speaker's use of pronouns is only the first of many informative details about him. Wyatt's way of subordinating clauses and connecting sentences can tell us what he feels, and even his choice of verb tense and mood helps convey information. A camera may be pure point of view, but *someone* chooses where to put the camera and how to focus it, and chooses lights, sound, rhythm, attention span, mood, and so on. Someone decides what to include in his view, when to include it, how long to focus on it, and how clearly and objectively to do so. That someone is the speaker Wyatt creates, revealed as much by his linguistic choices as by what he says. "*Language* most shewes a man," Ben Jonson said; "speake that I may see thee."[49]

At his most extreme, Wyatt's speaker, with his rough metrics, casual diction, and condensed grammar, speaks a version of mentalese, a language so rooted in private thought that it can be difficult for an outsider to understand. His poetry records the effects of impulses, doubts, and "motions" and passions of the will that interrupt the sequence of logical thought and conventional poetic structure. In "Som tyme I fled the fyre that me brent" (LIX), for example, it is difficult to know whether the speaker is flying from desire or seeking it:

> Som tyme I fled the fyre that me brent
> By see, by land, by water and by wynd;
> And now I follow the coles that be quent
> From Dover to Calais against my mynde.
> Lo! How desire is both sprong and spent!
>   (LIX, lines 1–5)

Without knowing the historical context it is impossible to know whether the speaker has recovered from desiring or not. It seems so: "How desire is both sprong and spent." But if so, why does he now *follow* the "coles... *against*" his mind? Who is making him follow against his mind?

Richard Tottel edited the poem to clear up the confusion. He substituted "with willing mind" in the fourth line for "against my mynde," so that his speaker follows willingly. But that is not what Wyatt meant; he wanted the contradiction. The final three lines of the last stanza make things worse: first, by jumping without transition to a new metaphor and, second, by changing from "I" to "he" without letting us know who "he" is:

> And he may se that whilome was so blynde;
> And all his labor now he laugh to scorne.
> Mashed [meshed] in the breers [briars] that erst was al to torne.
>   (LIX, lines 6–8)

Nonetheless, although Wyatt's speaker does not provide all the information a listener needs to understand quite what he is saying, his linguistic choices reveal a good deal about him and why he says it that way. Wyatt does not announce his new distance from desire, but he indicates it when he moves from "I" at the beginning of the poem to "he" at the end. His ambivalence is further suggested by the way he moves undecidedly between past and present ("whilome," "now," "erst"), or from one claim about his desire (it began, but now it is dead) to a slightly different one (it used to tear me up, but now it only catches me in its mesh). We may not hear a clear summary statement of the speaker's position. But we watch a man clearly caught in the briars of his contradictory thoughts and feelings.

Wyatt's idiosyncratic speaker cannot be reduced to his mastery of rhetorical "decorum," although many have argued that it can.[50] To observe decorum was simply to make the speaker's style consistent with his persona, so that audiences would be convinced by him. The trouble with seeing Wyatt's achievement as mere "decorum" is that, in general, rhetorical personas were stereotypes: old man, silly man, lover, pedant. When Erasmus invokes decorum in his *The Praise of Folly*, it is to note that he makes "Folly" herself speak like a fool.[51] Defending his playful decision to speak in the person of Folly, Erasmus assures the reader that "since I have feigned her [Folly] speaking, it was necessary to observe decorum in her character." If Erasmus were arguing in his own voice, he would speak differently. For example, to argue in his own voice that "in a sense, folly can be useful," Erasmus would make the double, yet still rational, claim that (1) although old people are foolish to believe they are young, yet (2) in another sense they are not foolish, because the belief makes them happy. But foolish Folly, obeying decorum, just speaks "foolishly." She simply says that she should be praised for making old people believe they are young, and she leaves the audience to infer the rest. In other words, Erasmus uses the speaker Folly to explore the contradictions in the abstract concept of folly.[52] He is not interested in portraying any particular foolish person.

Wyatt does exactly the opposite: he uses abstract ideas to explore the speaker. The idea in "Som tyme I fled" is, roughly, that once desire wanes, its torments seem distant and puzzling. But the poem emerges from the speaker's own contradictory expressions of that idea. Wyatt was not interested simply in speaking like a typical lover or like a personification of an abstract trait like "Love." Instead he showed what it felt like to think and feel like a particular lover. He gave "decorum" a new meaning by extending its reach inward, from explicit statements about familiar truths to private, implicit, and often uncommon thought and feeling. He used eccentric language as he used eccentric rhythm, to express individual feelings.

The eccentricity of Wyatt's voice stands out when he is compared to the period's other famous Petrarchan poet, Henry Howard, earl of Surrey. Like Wyatt, Surrey wrote poems that were autobiographical in content, most famously during his confinement in Windsor Castle. But although Surrey's affection emerges from the praise in his epitaphs for Wyatt, otherwise his style does not usually reveal a specific, individual personality as Wyatt's does. Surrey's well-known sonnet "The soote season," although at one extreme of Surrey's poetry, is still a good example:

> The soote season, that bud and blome furth bringes,
> With grene hath clad the hill and eke the vale;
> The nightingale with fethers new she singes;
> The turtle to her make hath tolde her tale.
> Somer is come, for every spray nowe springes;
> The hart hath hong his olde hed on the pale;
> The buck in brake his winter cote he flinges;
> The fishes flote with newe repaired scale;
> The adder all her sloughe awaye she slinges;
> The swift swalow pursueth the flyes smale;
> The busy bee her honye now she minges;
> Winter is worne that was the flowers bale.
> And thus I see among these pleasant thinges
> Eche care decayes, and yet my sorow springes.[53]

Surry's subject is more poetic than Wyatt's usually are: springtime and love, gently qualified by the lover's "sorrow" in the last half-line that nonetheless integrates the lover back into the happy landscape through its rhyme. The sonnet is also more musical, more visual, and more predictable than Wyatt's. Surrey's metrical regularity, immediately noticeable after one reads Wyatt, is an example of what George Puttenham praised in *The Arte of English Poesie* (1589) as the "sweete and stately measures and stile of the Italian Poesie." But it is more "sweete" than it is expressive of Surrey's unique attitude. The sweetness characterizes Surrey's surroundings, the external visual world that he—unlike Wyatt—portrays in unambiguous detail, with its buds, blooms, nightingale, hart, and brake. Surrey's animals are all exactly what readers expect: the turtle has her "make" (mate), the fishes float, the adder sloughs her skin, the bee is busy and the swallow swift. Compare Wyatt's dreamlike deer-women in "They fle from me that sometyme did me seke" (XXXVIII), who are characterized not by Surrey's predictably deer-like traits, such as "old head" and "winter coat" in a "pale" or in a "brake," but rather by the wholly unexpected "naked foot." Surrey's birds sing but Wyatt's are "restles": "Off the restles birdes they have the tune and note" (XXXIII, line 13).[54] Wyatt's lines constantly surprise. The only surprise in Surrey's poem enters gently, unstressed, unambiguous, and undisturbing, in a metrically expected last part of the last line.[55]

Surrey's sweetness, more than Wyatt's rough style, was popular in mid-century Tudor verse, or so Richard Tottel seems to have thought when he edited the poems he chose for his collection, *Songes and Sonnetes*. One of the best ways to understand what made Wyatt Wyatt is to compare his most famous poem, "They fle from me" to Tottel's edited version of it in *Songes and Sonnetes* (1557).[56] Tottel is famous for having regularized Wyatt's meter, but along with Wyatt's odd metrics Tottel regularized other aspects of Wyatt's subjective language. He thus transformed Wyatt's idiosyncratic speakers into conventional spokesmen for the period's rhetorical norm; he moved the poetry back toward "commonplace means of expressing commonly accepted truths."[57] Kerrigan's complaint that sixteenth-century autobiography emphasizes general truths rather than the "vagaries of inwardness" does not fit Wyatt's original verse, but it describes Tottel's edited versions nicely.

I should note that recent discussions of Tottel have made the opposite claim. His editing has been blamed for mistakenly creating, rather than undermining, Wyatt's autobiographical force. That claim is based on Tottel's practices: he invented titles for Wyatt's poems, making it seem as if the separate poems were all written by a single "lover," thus reducing the distance between poet and persona.[58] Similarly he often mistook oblique political ironies for autobiographical love plaints, sometimes even adding details to make the "lover's" experience more concrete. All this is true. But it makes Wyatt more autobiographical only in objective content, and only in the limited sense that Tottel's speaker gives a fuller description of his adventures in love. But Wyatt's original poems are more autobiographical in the more important sense that they record the speaker's subjective reaction to what he describes.

Tottel wanted poetry that, like Surrey's, appealed to established taste. The first thing Tottel did was to change the content of Wyatt's verse to bring it closer to the cultural ideal of romantic love. He omitted Wyatt's most negative poems, damped the irony in the poems he did select, and rewrote them so that Wyatt's rebellious, unchivalric courtier emerged sounding like a selfless, devoted romance hero. But more than changing the content, Tottel foregrounded and clarified it, largely by eliminating the indirections and difficulties of Wyatt's style.

That is, he normalized Wyatt's language. He valued elevated language and sentiment, so he eliminated semantic impropriety ("dung" replaced the vulgar "turd"). He also disliked ambiguity. He reconciled Wyatt's contradictions, as in "Som tyme I fled the fyre," and ruined his riddles. Readers of the manuscript poems wondered whether Wyatt was referring to his forbidden love for King Henry's Anne Boleyn, in the poem whose first three lines are "What wourde is that that chaungeth not, / Though it be tourned and made in twain?"/ It is myn *aunswer*, god it wot" (L). Tottel left no doubt. He simply changed the third line to "It is mine *Anna*, god it wot." And just to be sure, he titled the poem "Of His Love Called Anna." He also rewrote other perfectly proper but surprising, unfamiliar, or irregular expressions, so that the un-Surrey-like "restless" birds were domesticated into "singing" birds.[59]

Tottel's sense of decorum led him also to rewrite innocent passages like the last lines of "Tagus farewell" (XCIX), a verse eagerly anticipating Wyatt's return to court from his duties abroad, apparently because their sentiment was too emotionally extreme. Tottel is known for reading Wyatt's political or ambiguous poetry as if it were purely amatory, ignoring politics. But in this case Tottel moves in the opposite direction; he edits the love out of politics. What he did not like, it seems, was any confusion between the two. Wyatt's impassioned speaker in the original had called longingly, like a lover, to "My kyng, my Contry, alone for whome I lyve," and asked that "Of mighty love the winges for this me gyve." The speaker is extreme—he lives only for king and country:

> Tagus, fare well, that westward with thy stremes
> Torns vp the grayns off gold alredy tryd:
> With spurr and sayle for I go seke the Tems
> Gaynward the sonne, that shewth her welthi pryd
> And to the town which Brutus sowght by drems
> Like bendyd mone doth lend her lusty syd.
>   My kyng, my Contry, alone for whome I lyve,
>   Of myghty love the winges for this me gyve.

He was too extreme for Tottel. Tottel's revised speaker also seeks his king, but he is not so excessive as to live for king "alone." He says, more conventionally, "My king, my country, I seek for whom I live." And he asks unerotically for "winds" from "Jove," instead of "wings" of "love": "O mighty Jove! The winds for this me give."

In short, Tottel's changes accord not only with propriety but also with a distrust of imaginative freedom, ambiguity, and unpredictability. He prefers plain statements to questions or exclamations, and certainty to what we might call Wyatt's signature "subjunctivity." Tottel wants to know "how it is," but Wyatt's speaker is always digressing into "how it was" or "how it might have been." Tottel prefers the clear sunshine of the present, but for Wyatt's speakers their shadowy dreams or memories are more real than reality. Tottel demands one single truth, but in poesie, as Blake wrote, "anything possible to be believed is an image of truth." As a result, it is no heresy to paraphrase one of Tottel's revised poems; some of them can even be summed up by their titles.

The difference between the original and edited versions of Wyatt's best-known poem, "They fle from me" (XXXVIII), shows how Tottel could change an extremely subjective lyric into something more like conventional narrative. For Wyatt the paraphrasable content hardly matters. The speaker summarizes the whole thing in the first line of the poem: "They fle from me that sometyme did me seke." He then proceeds to restate, reenact, and rethink that claim about his experience with courtly love encounters, wrestling with it all through the poem. He describes the change in the women (presumably) who now flee; he then focuses on one particular woman and stops to dwell on their happier past, hardly noticing, it seems, the imagery of stalking and preying that he uses. Then he returns to the present, puzzled, to question himself and wonder at her unkindness in rejecting the gentleness he thought she expected: "All is tourned thorough my gentilnes" [and] "Syns that I so kindly ame served, I wonder what she hath deserveth." He did everything he was supposed to do, he implies, but yet she wanted something else. By this point the reader (and perhaps the speaker as well, although not quite consciously) may have come to realize that the speaker had broken the rules, just as "she" did.[60] His eager "gentilnes" was no more innocent and ritualized than her naked stalking. Both should have known what the chase had in view.

Tottel keeps the substance of what Wyatt's lover says, but he changes not only the metrics but also the smallest linguistic details that root the poem's movement in the speaker's mind. As a result Tottel's speaker has the experience but misses the meaning.

Wyatt's lover, as his language shows, is turned inward. Memory and fantasy more than reality are important. For him it is the external, public reality that is vague, while inner memory is in perfect focus. In the opening line, for example, reality is dreamlike: "They fle from me that sometyme did me seke." "They" are vaguely described in metaphorical terms that

Lyric Autobiography: John Skelton and Thomas Wyatt 43

make them difficult to visualize concretely. "With naked fote," "stalking in my chambre," "take bred at my hand": Are they deer? Women? Are they naked above the foot too? How did they get into his chamber? Are they really just eating bread? Even the timing is vague: "They fle" in a generalized continuing present (we might say "these days") and are compared to a vaguely located nostalgic past ("sometyme").

By contrast, the speaker's memory in stanza 2 is physically vivid and very realistic: he describes a specific, unmistakably human woman ("she") and a concrete erotic encounter that is quite easy to visualize ("she," "loose gown," "arms long and small," "kissed"). The chronology is exact: the remembered event happened only "once in special," just as the word *ons* itself occurs only once in the poem, separating the memory from everything else. The special memory is so powerful that the speaker is distracted from his statement for the length of an entire stanza.

Tottel's version, however, makes reality as powerful as the memory. He clarifies Wyatt's chronology and reduces that special memory to just one more past event like all the others. Where Wyatt's external reality is vaguely located in a continuous "sometyme," Tottel chops his into discrete events: once this, once that, once the other thing. Not "I have seen them" but "*Once* have I seen them," and they "do not *once* remember," "*once* especiall." The result is that Wyatt's "ons in special" is no longer special, either in diction or in metrical emphasis. For Tottel's lover, in other words, nothing is special. The present is just as important as the past.[61]

Wyatt's original language also suggests the speaker's extreme passivity along with his inwardness. Wyatt brilliantly exploits the grammatical passive voice so that it becomes an attribute of the speaker rather than his grammar. In his version of the story, which is of course the only one we hear, the speaker merely watches and thinks. "They" and "she" are the only actors. In the first stanza, for example, it is always someone else who acts:

1 They fle from me that sometyme did me seke
2 With naked fote stalking in my chamber.
3 I have sene them gentill tame and meke
4 That nowe are wyld and do not remember
5 That sometyme they put themself in daunger
6 To take bred at my hand; and nowe they raunge
7 Besely seking with a continuell chaunge.
           (line numbers added)

In the present they are active: "They *fle*," (2) "[they] *are* wyld," (4) "[they] *do* not *remember*" (4), and "they *raunge*...seking" (6–7). In the general past "they" were also active, although in the opposite way: "[they] *did* me *seke*...stalking," and "they *put* themself in daunger to take bred at my hand." But while "they" are doing all this, the weakly verbed speaker does nothing active. He merely describes them: "I have sene them." He is simply the passive object of their actions: "they fle from *me*," "[they] did *me* seke...stalking in *my* chamber," "to take bred at *my* hand."

Even the shifts in time, from present to past in stanza 2, and back again in stanza 3, are recorded with a weak subjunctive ("Thanked be fortune" [8]), a limp copulative ("hath ben" [8]), and a passive verb ("is tourned"): "Thanked be fortune it hath ben otherwise" (8); "But all is tourned thorough my gentilnes" (16). The speaker might have said something more active, like "I changed all" or "I ruined all." But instead, according to him, he has nothing to do with the sequence of events in which "all is changed." He is not even present when it occurs—except in the possessive form, "thorough *my* gentilnes."[62]

The parallel between the speaker's linguistic choices and his extreme passivity is nowhere more manifest than in that one special remembered past event in stanza 2. Here is a vision of erotic passivity so complete that the speaker nearly disappears from his own account of it. His grammar imitates him. Almost three whole lines go by without any verb at all (lines 9–11). All action is suspended and even the actor is hidden until at last "she" emerges from her loosened gown:

  8 Thanked be fortune it hath ben otherwise
  9 Twenty times better but ons in speciall
10 In thyn arraye after a pleasant gyse
11 When her loose gown from her shoulders did fall—

At that point "she" takes over the action, and suddenly the verbs are frequent and specific—but all hers: "she me caught" (12), "did me kysse" (13), "softely said" (14).

12 And she me caught in her armes long and small;
13 Therewithall swetely did me kysse,
14 And softely said "dere hert, how like you this?"

She is the one who acts. Her power is conveyed not only in the events themselves but also in Wyatt's careful choice of words to convey it. The concrete verbs ("did" [13], "said" [14], "did...kysse" [13]) make her the most active character not only here but also in the whole verbally flaccid poem.[63] In contrast, he exists only as the pronominal object of her enchanting question: "how like you this?"[64]

The speaker is as silent as he is passive; he doesn't even answer her question. He is left with no more than an unmetrical stutter of amazement: "It was no dreme: I lay brode waking" (15).[65] Continuing with similar amazement, the speaker then returns to the present:

15 It was no dreme: I lay brode waking.
16 But all is tourned thorough my gentilnes
17 Into a straunge fasshion of forsaking;
18 And I have leve to goo of her goodenes,
19 And she also to use newfangilnes.

He doesn't understand. His sole action here at the end is to be dismissed passively ("I have leave to goo"; "I so kyndely ame served") and to wonder subjunctively ("I would faine knowe"). He doesn't even judge. The ironies of his wide-eyed description emerge only indirectly, through ambiguous words like "straunge" (unusual? alien? or perhaps cold, distant, or like a "strange woman" or harlot)[66] and "kyndely" (literally? or ironically, "unkindly"?). He has finally begun to question things, but answers are left to the reader:

20 But syns that I so kyndely ame served,
21 I would faine knowe what she hath deserved.

We do not even know whether he is serious or ironic when he says that she treated him "kindly." Wyatt thus leaves the speaker at the end of the poem hovering between innocence and responsibility, just as we first found him hovering at the beginning between past and present.

Tottel's version, while preserving much of Wyatt's, eliminates the narrator's doubting, confused, contradictory point of view that makes a res gestae account of things done into subjective autobiography. He transforms Wyatt's passive, puzzled lover into a crisply objective reporter, less ironically out of tune with the events he narrates. Tottel begins by adding a title that makes his lover active and assertive even before the poem begins. "The lover sheweth how he is forsaken of such as he hath enjoyed." Already Tottel's lover is different from Wyatt's. As we have seen, Wyatt's lover "sheweth" very little; at most he suggesteth.[67] The original line in Wyatt on which Tottel based the title is subtly but importantly different. Wyatt's speaker says, "All is tourned thorough my gentilnes / Into a straunge fasshion of forsaking." He mentions his gentleness but backs away from saying anything about who is forsaking whom. Is he the one forsaken? Or is it she? Or is it perhaps just a strange fashion of forsaking out there unrelated to anyone? By contrast, Tottel's phrase "how he [the lover] is forsaken" implies a specific action at a specific time: someone (he) was forsaken by somebody (her). End of story. (Tottel also rewrote the original line to make its timing and its judgment less ambiguous. Wyatt's line is not clear: "all is tourned [*when?*] ... / Into a straunge [*strange?*] fasshion of forsaking." Tottel's lover says more helpfully and less ambiguously, "But all is torned now into a bitter fashion of forsaking.")

Tottel's simplification in the last stanza is especially destructive. In the original, the speaker's ambiguous closing question reveals a continuing internal debate about her behavior and perhaps his too: "But since that I so kyndely [*meaning?*] ame served / I would faine knowe what she hath deserved." In Tottel's version, however, the ambiguity is clarified and the debate settled. The lover knows that she is unkind. He asks a rhetorical question with only one answer that shows him to be as clueless about his behavior as Tottel is: "But sins that I so unkindly am served..."

Finally, Wyatt's speaker had been talking to himself. Tottel rewrites Wyatt's interior monologue as one side of a locker-room exchange between two men. He makes Wyatt's inward-turning speaker into a regular guy. When Tottel's lover asks his buddy "how like you this?" not only does he know the answer to the question, but he also crassly repeats the exact words that "she" had used in her erotic teasing. His memory of her words is not special at all.

Autobiography depends not only on what a speaker says about his inner life but also on how freely he encodes his own point of view into his speech as he says it. When Tottel rewrote Wyatt, he added and subtracted seemingly unimportant words: "once," "now," and so on. But in doing so he obliterated the nuances of expressive discourse and the linguistic clues that reveal the speaker's subjective stance toward events. He turned

Wyatt's subjectively fuzzy account into a more neatly chronological sequence of concrete separate events that could as easily have been described from the outside by someone else. By normalizing Wyatt's autobiographically revealing voice, Tottel eliminated its "vagaries of inwardness" and moved the poem back toward an account, however concrete, of outward actions.

CHAPTER 3

Identity in Autobiography and Protestant Identification with Saints: *John Bale and Paul* in The Vocacyon of Johan Bale (*1553*)

> Sanct Paule also rejoyced.... Whie shulde I than shrinke or be ashamed to do the lyke?
>
> JOHN BALE, *The Vocacyon*

In the summer of 1552 rumors of King Edward VI's death reached Ireland and contributed to a long-simmering rebellion in the northern bishopric of Ossory. The recently appointed bishop, John Bale (1495–1563), scholar, playwright, and avid reformer, had been trying to move his reluctant flock closer toward the English Protestant norm. Not long after, when Queen Mary was proclaimed, Bale narrowly escaped an ambush in which several of his servants were killed. He managed to get to the Continent, refuge for exiles fleeing Mary's reign, and within a year he had published his account of the events, *The Vocacyon of Johan Bale to the Bishopric of Ossorie in Irelande* (1553).[1] Its forty-nine folios, addressed to Bale's brethren, establish a parallel between his trials in Ireland and St. Paul's travels. Bale likens himself to Paul: "Sanct Paule also rejoyced.... Whie shulde I than shrinke or be ashamed to do the lyke?" The text is intended to praise God for saving him and to comfort others by his example as they undergo the trials of Mary's reign. It treats only a year in Bale's life, but Donald Stauffer calls it the first separately printed prose autobiography in English.[2]

Bale's engagingly choleric *Vocacyon* has never been read widely and seldom sympathetically.[3] As with Skelton's and Wyatt's, the text's conventional

Fig. 4 Bale, from *Three Laws* (ca. 1548), portrait (The Bodleian Library, University of Oxford [Mal. 502, G2r]).

Fig. 5 Bale, from *Catalogus* (1557), portrait "aetatis suae anno 62."

aspect has been overemphasized, and its evidence as vivid life writing in the midsixteenth century has not received the attention it deserves. Bale's text has been used to illustrate the belief that group identity, such as Bale's strong identification with Protestant saints, erases individuality. But in fact, Bale's career suggests the opposite. It was in part due to the security of belonging to a group of like-minded believers and seeing himself as the product of a line of predecessors that Bale could speak out about himself and hold so stubbornly to his beliefs. Bale's texts are part of the Reformation legacy, but they also convey his unique vision well enough that we can learn even more about him than he probably intended to reveal. The following discussion first sketches Bale's background, then examines the discrepancies between *Vocacyon* and its theological models, and ends by reading his text's internal discrepancies in the context of Bale's other autobiographical writings.

John Bale

Vocacyon was in part a product of Bale's troubled times. In 1552 religious turbulence reached a crisis that affected the other autobiographical writers in this study. Bale may have been more extreme than most in his reactions: the confrontations that Thomas Wyatt saw as a courtly duel of wits or ritual hunt, Bale saw as Armageddon. He had also endured more of the Reformation's upheavals than most, but his writing is rooted in the same Reformation context. Born during the reign of Henry VII, he lived through four reigns and as many religious changes. Unlike fellow reformer William Baldwin, Bale held tenaciously to the old belief until he joined the reformists and dug in on their side. Unlike his flexible compatriot, therefore, Bale was twice forced into exile.[4]

Vocacyon was also in part a product of reformist belief. Traditional worshipers had always identified with Christ's suffering, but the reformers outlined a more directed return to biblical origins in order to cleanse papist distortions from the Word. Sixteenth-century devotees were encouraged to model their faith on that of the early Christians, whose example included their own emulation of still earlier Christians. Paul's life in particular had been a model for biblical martyrs in talking about their lives.[5] In more recent times, John Wycliffe's follower Willard Thorpe (d. 1407) was one of many who had compared himself to Paul. Bale's friend William Tyndale, before he was burned for heresy in 1535, had advised contemporary saints to "play Paul."[6]

Bale's sense of himself was always as part of a religious community, whether Catholic or Protestant. As a Catholic, he had created a genealogy of Carmelite heroes culminating in himself, and after his conversion Bale began to trace a new genealogy of Protestants, singling out a line of predecessors extending from Wycliffe through Thorpe and Tyndale to himself.[7] In his *Summarium,* Bale literally presented himself in Wycliffe's image. The text includes portraits of only two men, Wycliffe and himself, their stance and facial attributes almost identically portrayed in the two woodcuts.[8] From Tyndale Bale took an ideology whose sentiments (and at times exact words) he reproduced in his own texts.[9]

Given *Vocacyon*'s foundation in the period's common Protestant rhetoric and belief, some readers have hesitated to call it autobiographical in the modern sense. Bale's biographer, Leslie Fairfield, even while pointing out aspects of *Vocacyon* that belong to "a nascent tradition of autobiography," suggests that Bale's life "has meaning only insofar as it represents a type"—the "few faithful in each age." It lies "squarely within the tradition of hagiography," he says, and he cautions against overemphasizing the "hints of modernity" in *Vocacyon* rather than its fundamental medievalism.[10] Recent readers have described a "Bale" constructed by his Pauline text or "subjected" to his Pauline sources: for Bale, "an 'already read' scriptural authority constitutes the subjectivity of the individual; there should only be a repetition of this original text, not a simulacrum.... [Bale's] identity is produced as a 'readerly text,'" one that reproduces the original rather than responds to it.[11] To these readers, in other words, Bale seems like another writer interested less in his individual experience than in the general form of Christian virtue embodied in Paul.

But *Vocacyon* is unmistakably the product of the man known as "bilious Bale," no matter how much it depends on shared belief, other texts, and its Pauline model. If Bale was a product of his age, he had helped shape the age; if Bale modeled himself on Paul, it was a Paul remade in his own image. Although William Tyndale had already written about creating Protestant "saints," Bale was instrumental in providing two of the most important saints—Sir John Oldcastle and Anne Askew—and in authorizing a new role for them as models rather than as intercessors.[12] Bale also influenced John Foxe's *Acts and Monuments* (1563), the book that was to become something like a second Protestant bible.

Like the other autobiographers, Bale was devoted to the scholarship that drove his career as antiquary and, even more, to the oratorical skill that his education gave him. He was hardly suited to use his talent in politics as Wyatt had. But he had an abiding sense of himself as a writer. Like Skelton, he came to associate his calling as a writer with his religious calling. Born the first of ten children in a poor family, Bale was brought to the Carmelite Brotherhood when he was twelve. There he began the education that gained him access to the fringes of the courtly culture that nourished Skelton, Wyatt, and Baldwin as well. From the time he joined the brotherhood, Bale lived among texts—almost literally so for the first thirty years of his life. He saw the world through books, and his life's work was to survey the world's history in his own books. He was almost obsessively thorough. Anyone who writes, Bale says in the motto he chose for his edition of John Leland, "fyrste, muste with hys understandynge gather the matter togyther, set hys wordes in ordre, and dylygently seke out on every parte."[13] The first history he wrote (like his early verses to saints) traced the Carmelites back to biblical times. The convent sent him beyond its walls to Cambridge, but he ignored the reformist movement there, lived with Carmelites, and continued his Carmelite history. Even after Bale had begun to preach doctrine reformist enough to get him in trouble, he kept writing traditional Carmelite history. He simply accommodated his new perspective by confining his praise to the Carmelite's Edenic past.

Bale finally converted from Catholicism to the new religion in the mid-1530s, but he never gave up his devotion to writing. His reputation as a playwright attracted Thomas Cromwell's attention; under the vice-regent he spent the rest of the decade staging antipapist drama like *King John* throughout the countryside. When Cromwell's fall in 1540 drove Bale into exile, he resumed writing history, albeit from a polemical stance opposite to the one he had taken earlier. His *Image of Both Churches: After the Reuelacion of Saynt Johan the Euangelyst* (1545) encompassed a history of the Christian world from creation to the crack of doom. He had also begun to collect information for the catalogs of British writers collected in *Summarium* (1548) and expanded as *Catalogus* (1557, 1559), which still remain the sole evidence for many lost texts. He personally supervised the preparation of his manuscripts, and he may even have printed and sold some himself.[14]

For Bale, writing was a way not only to represent himself but also to wage the battle between Good and Evil in which he had enlisted himself. Writing and life had too early been entwined for him to separate them, and in his case it is particularly appropriate to emphasize the autobiographical act rather than the text itself. *The Vocacyon* was one more move in his fight against the papists. Battles appear in the titles of his early (lost) Catholic plays about the harrowing of hell and the debate between Vices and Virtues.[15] Much of his later work took the same form: the story of an isolated antagonist in the thick of apocalyptic battle.

Bale saw life as dramatic conflict, and he had a real histrionic gift. He wrote plays for Lord de Vere, earl of Oxford, in the early 1530s, and the last part of that decade was dedicated to the writing and performance of his polemical Protestant plays.[16] Even Bale's nondramatic works are built on conflict. His antiquarian bibliographies, rather than listing all authors and titles together, sorted literary sheep from goats. Before Bale began his martyr biographies, the inherent drama of martyrdom had already been realized in Willard Thorpe's own account of his heresy trials, cast in the form of Christ's examination by Caiaphas.[17] Bale's saints' lives similarly took the form of "forensic biography,"[18] so that he theatricalized the sources for Sir John Oldcastle's life, for example, and even added an audience for the scenes.[19]

Bale's dramatic writing drew also on offstage human drama. His writing gravitated toward scenes and dialogue. His texts, like his sermons, came from a particular speaker and were directed to a particular audience, whom he usually addressed directly, as he does in *The Vocacyon*. His life may have been dedicated to abstract belief, but his texts are full of people. His martyrologies are obviously organized around individual figures, but so are his formidable surveys—of the Carmelite order, of England's writers, of the Christian religion, of the universe. The magisterial *Catalogus* of British authors is divided into "centuries" that consist not of one hundred years or even of one hundred texts but of one hundred lives, with a brief biography to accompany the list of his texts for each author.[20] Bale's goal was to catalog the numerous manuscripts that he feared would be destroyed along with the nation's monasteries. Yet in his lists all texts were connected to their authors; anonymous texts were separated or omitted. Later he would describe his rescue of manuscripts as a rescue of potential human martyrs, and he implied a parallel between his action and Queen Elizabeth's protection of reformers.[21]

The autobiographical first-person format did not come as often or casually to Bale as it did to Skelton and Wyatt. But he spoke for and through many people just like himself, especially after the Reformation had given him a voice and a stage. In the pulpit he spoke for himself as well as for God. On stage he cast himself as prolocutor in four of the five extant plays he wrote during this period, and he may have played God and the Vice figure as well. "Baleus Prolocutor" introduces each play by telling the audience what they are about to see and reappears at the end to summarize its meaning. Baleus speaks with the commanding authority that his author spent his life trying to establish offstage by other means.[22]

Even the saints he writes about have a Balean cast, so that Askew's self-confidence, though not quite bilious, is more "high stomached" than it is in other accounts.[23] The reformist martyrological pattern established by Thorpe and Tyndale had already substituted verbal for physical heroism, but Bale changed the saints further into writers. Thorpe and Askew, who wrote accounts of their own lives, were obvious subjects for him. But even John Oldcastle, not known for his writing, was made to fit the pattern. The latter, according to Bale, was persecuted for a poem that he wrote against the bishops, an activity more typical of Bale than of Oldcastle.[24]

As Bale's experience changed over the years, his heroes changed with him. So long as he had been fully supported by Cromwell, Baleus the Prolocutor had spoken with patriotic authority. After Cromwell's fall left Bale vulnerable and eventuated in his exile, he wrote a commentary on Revelation, the vision recorded by St. John in exile on Patmos, and he began to describe himself as if he were John: "I, John Boanerges, an earnest thunderer out of the gospel, and a stirrer up of men's minds to heavenly things."[25] Then, while compiling his biographical bibliographies of British authors, Bale glorified earlier collective biographers with whom he identified, such as Eusebius and Bede. Back in England and chafing against Northumberland's restraints at the end of Edward's reign, Bale published ad hominem dialogues between himself and particular "rank" or "frantick" papists. He was debating theological fine points by telling about his experience fighting for them. Quoting his enemy's attack, for example, Bale interrupts one narrative to assure the reader of his first-person knowledge: "No man knoweth this to be more true than I do upon whome he not only bestowede these uncomlye names, but also ... sette hys one hande upon my Bearde and bosame, and hys other hande sometyme on hys Dagger."[26]

Bale and the Saints

In *Vocacyon*, published in the following year, Bale wrote overtly about himself and his own experience, the first time he had done so at such length.[27] But although his central figure was John Bale instead of someone like King John, Bale presented his experience as a reenactment of someone else's, in this case as a parallel to Paul's during his last journey from Rome to Jerusalem. Modern readers have accepted the validity of Bale's presentation. The standard histories of the period use his narrative as a primary source, although noting his eccentric bias.[28]

Similarly, literary critics accept Bale's claim that he saw himself as another St. Paul. It would be incompatible with everything we know about Bale to doubt the sincerity of his claim. But there are contradictions in his narrative that raise questions not only about how much like Paul Bale actually was but also about how much he believed that he was. One of Bale's contemporary enemies openly questioned his account. James Cancellar, chaplain to Queen Mary, published a condemnation of the reformers in which he attacked Bale's comparison between himself and St. Paul in *Vocacyon*.[29] Cancellar's religious position, of course, predisposed him to deny whatever Bale said about his relation to God. Nonetheless, Cancellar's attack shows that even at the time there was more than one way to read Bale's text.

As Cancellar sees it, Bale's citation is mere self-aggrandizement. Bale, he says, "not a litle triumpheth of hys daungerous travailes... not shaming to compare himself with holy saincte Paul in troubles, in perill of shippe wracke, in perill of the sea.... This [i.e., Bale] whilest he is comparing himself with the holy Apostle lyke a mad harehead beginneth to say why shoulde I shrinke or bee ashamed to boste as the Apostle hath?" "Friar Bale beginneth craftely to perswade the poore christians that GOD hath delivered him from peril of death by miracle as though he were called of god in these daies to set up a light in his churche." Bale may claim that God saved him by a miracle, Cancellar says, but he is more like "a false disciple, to put forth himselfe and to tread downe in these our dayes the true light."[30]

Cancellar is also suspicious about Bale's ultimate escape. Bale attributes it to God's intervention on behalf of his faithful servant, but Cancellar suspects a more worldly explanation. "If you had been as you saye a tre disciple of Christ and as fellow lyke with Saint Paule... when you by chaunce of wether were dryvyn into Dover rode would lyke as Paule did a[t] Phillus have set youre fote on lande and preached Criste but contrary wuyse... you were more desirous to sette your hand to a bill of fifty poundes more than you were able to pay to that end that you myghte be set on launde in flaunders."[31] If Bale were really imitating Paul, says Cancellar, he would have preached to the heathen when he found himself in dangerous territory, instead of rushing to buy his escape by promising fifty pounds that he did not even have.

Fig. 6 Bale, *Vocacyon* (1553), title page (this item is reproduced by permission of The Huntington Library, San Marino, California [RB 56275]).

Cancellar's reading is obviously biased. But the differences between Bale and Paul are real. They begin on the title page, where Paul's words are quoted as if they describe Bale's Irish adventure ("If I must nedes reioyce / I wil reioyce of myne infirmytees [2 Cor. 11]"). But there is nothing Pauline about the visual image accompanying them. On its left an "English Christian," a clean-shaven innocent, stands in front of a flowering plant with his hands clasped in prayer or supplication and his head bent docilely toward the enemy. A lamb hides behind his legs like a bashful child. Lunging toward the Christian from the right is "the Irish Papist," snarling as he draws his long sword. The papist's side of the landscape is barren, and his mustachioed face is almost as doglike as that of the dog (or wolf) at his

Identity in Autobiography: John Bale 57

side, lunging with fangs bared. The image conveys how Bale felt in Ireland, but it is hard to see Paul as a cowering childlike Christian.

Bale's text is divided into three parts: a central account of the year in Ireland, based on a saint's life, and a Pauline frame preceding and following it. At first glance the text supports Bale's pastoral claim, its three-part structure a reminder of Pauline epistolary form.[32] In the preface (pref. 33–38), Bale, like Paul, identifies himself and addresses the brethren. Like Paul, he announces his purpose for writing: "For thre consyderacyons chefely (dere bretherne) have I put fourth thys treatyse: that men should know true vocation of a Christian Bishop, that they should understand that persecution not bodily wealth follows this godly office, and that they might behold how graycyously our most mercyfull God... finally delivereth them in most depe daungers." Again, in the conclusion, Bale explains that, like Paul, "I wryte this unto the / thu sorrowfull churche of Englande / that in the middes of thy afflictions thu shuldest not despayre" (1775–77).

But any superficial resemblances between Paul and Bale are outweighed by differences. Even the passage always cited as evidence of Bale's "subjection" to the apostle is in fact one of the least Pauline elements in the text. This is Bale's Fluellen-like citation of specific parallels between Bale and Paul in the preface to *Vocacyon*. If Paul ever compared himself to others it was humbly: "Be imitators of me, as I am of Christ" (1 Corinthians 11:1). Bale's long list, by contrast, boasts about "resemblances" in order to show how much like Paul he is. Adding to the discrepancy, Bale focuses on the letter, not the spirit, of their shared experience. He cites tangible similarities to Paul's experiences but ignores their spiritual significance. One of these, for example, is the parallel between the desperate methods used in both Paul's escape from Damascus and Bale's escape from Ossory: Paul resorted to a basket let down from a window, and Bale to mariner's apparel. "He [Paul] in the cytie of Damascon / beinge layde waite for / by the liefe tenaunt of Kinge Aretth / was lete downe at a window in a basket / & so escaped [Acts 9]. I in the cytie of Dubline / beinge assaulted of papists / was convayed awaye in the nyght in mariners apparell / & so escaped that daunger by Gods helpe" (346–51). But the ultimate significance of the escapes is never mentioned. Bale's list finally ends with an unwitting anticlimax in which even the letter is not quite parallel: "Thus had I in my troublous journaye from Ireland into Germanye all those chaunces in a maner that S. Paul had in his journaie of no lesse trouble / from Jerusalem to Rome," he concludes—"saving that we lost not our shippe by the waye" (213–17), as if a missing shipwreck were a minor detail.

The rest of the preface is modeled on a very uncharacteristic selection from Paul's writing. Bale draws most heavily on the special case of 2 Corinthians, primarily to justify boasting about his vocation. That text was written during a difficult period for Paul, when the Corinthians had been listening to false or "superfluous disciples" and had gone so far as to attack Paul himself during a recent visit.[33] Here Paul, angry, is atypically brusque and boasts about his superiority to the false prophets who had tried to displace him.

Paul's sarcastic boasting counters the impostors in their own terms: "Whatever anyone dares to boast of—I am speaking as a fool—I also dare to boast of that. Are they Hebrews [the rival disciples]? So am I" (2 Corinthians 11:21–22).[34] Only fools boast, he says. But Paul does it now in order to expose the vanity of the newcomers' boasts: "Accept me as a fool so that I too may boast a little" (11:16), and "I am become a fool in boasting myself; ye have compelled me" (11:11). Even so, Paul is still careful to distinguish between the impostors' boasts and his. They claim physical powers; he claims only the power of faith. They boast that God answers their prayers; Paul boasts that God did not answer his prayer but instead "said to me, 'My power is made perfect in weakness'" (12:9). Bale's boasting shows no such epistemological subtlety. He simply boasts: "Neyther am I ashamed to tell my bretherene / what God hath most graciously done for me / nomor than s. Paule was for hymselfe in hys owne Epistles…and thus maye we wele do / and boast of it also without offense / for so did the aforenamed S. Paule [2 Cor. 11]" (65–67, 84–86).[35] The difference between the two kinds of boasting can seem comic to anyone other than Bale.

The most important difference between Bale and Paul is their attitude toward their congregations. Paul always addressed members of communities he had personally converted and taken into his care, and he wrote to them about his concern for their welfare. Paul's pastoral concern is easily observed: he calls himself a father to the believers; he sends his letters to comfort and guide them when he cannot visit; he wants them to them know they are not alone in their troubles. Even in 2 Corinthians, the anger he expresses derives in part from his concern for the future of the community endangered by false prophets. In contrast, although Bale is certainly concerned about his community, he seems to want to have a father more than to be one. He says he writes to prove that *he* is not alone in his trials, almost as if comforting himself. To this end he cites not only Paul but—unlike Paul—an entire genealogy of his predecessors from biblical times to his own.

Bale's rewriting of Paul is foregrounded when read beside Martin Luther's 1539 preface to 1 Corinthians 15, which also cites Paul as precedent. Luther identifies with Paul's pastoral responsibilities. Like Paul, he says, he is faced with a congregation that has split into factions and "deteriorated to such an extent that it is terrible to recall." Both are trying to save their communities. Luther's citations go to the heart of the same theological dilemma that troubled Paul. His point is Paul's point: although self-assertion like his is often wrong, someone must bear witness in a time when competing voices all claim to witness the one truth. Finally, although Luther likens himself to the apostle, he never loses sight of the distance between himself and Paul: "What might we who are preaching now expect when the holy and exalted apostle, compared to whom we are nothing, experienced this at the hands of his disciples?"[36] The holy apostle suffered; I who am nothing to him must also expect to suffer. By contrast, Bale cites personal parallels with Paul and uses them to elevate himself to Paul's status: the holy apostle suffered; I suffer too, so I am as justified as he.

Finally, even the limited Pauline resemblance ends with the preface. The central section of *Vocacyon*, with its own frontispiece, is visually (as well as conceptually) separated from the preface and conclusion. It may even have been written first, before the Pauline frame was added to it.[37] The topic here is solely Bale—his spiritual genealogy, his travels to and through Ireland to Ossory, his preaching, the Irish attack on him after King Edward's death, his escape to Dublin, and his kidnapping by pirates on the way back.

The model here, at least at the beginning, is the Protestant saint's life, as Bale had established it in his martyrologies.[38] The frontispiece seems to be based on the one in Bale's editions of Anne Askew that shows the Woman Clothed in the Sun (Revelation 12:1) holding the Bible and treading on the papist dragon.[39] Bale's frontispiece shows a similarly posed woman, holding a volume marked *verbi dei* and stepping on a serpent smaller than Askew's dragon but clearly a member of the same satanic family. Bale's section closes, as the Askew text does, with a quotation from Psalm 118. The genealogy of martyrs that glorifies Askew in her text is here recalled by the genealogy tracing Bale's vocation to its "first foundations" in Adam. It extends into a six-page list culminating with King Edward VI, who appointed Bale to the bishopric of Ossory, as if all history had been leading to that single moment. In Bale's telling, his appointment to the bishopric was a miracle in which Edward raised him from the dead.[40]

> As concerning the fornamed Kynge Edwarde I will recite here what hys wurthinesse ded for me his most unwurthie subject / that I shuld among others be a collectour [or] a caller togyther of the christen flocke in thys age. Upon the.15. daye of August / in the yeare from Christes incarnation 1552 beynge the first day of my deliveraunce / as God wold / from "a mortall ague / which had holde me longe afore. In rejoyce that hys Majestie was come in progress to Southampton…I toke my horse about .10 of the clocke / for very weakness scant able to sitt hym.…The Kynge havynge informacion that I was there in the street / he marveled therof / for so much as it had been tolde hym a lytle afore / that I was both dead and buried. With that hys grace came to the wyndowe / and earnestly beheld me a poore weak creature / as though he had upon me so symple a subject / and earnest regard / or rather a very fatherly care. (592–617)

"And to conclude," Bale says, "thus was I called / in a manner from deathe / to this office without my expectacion or yet knowledge" (645–46).

Bale's claimed humility seems incompatible with the tacit claim to sainthood. He says that he was called from his sickbed and that he accepted only out of a sense of duty: "Yet was not my rejoice so muche in the dignite therof / as doinge for the time / the office thereunto belonginge" (101–3). But at the same time he emphasizes the glory of the appointment. From what Bale says, God himself delivered him from a mortal ague so that he might come before King Edward, who then looked on Bale with "a very fatherly care" and called him (in a manner) from the dead.[41]

At times Bale's account seems incompatible with the facts as well. Bale's claim that the appointment to Ossory shows King Edward's concern, for example, is hard to reconcile with the fact that William Turner of Cambridge had just declined the position, apparently because it was so undesirable; Edward was finding it a difficult post to fill.[42] Again, Bale says that he was called to this position "without my expectacion or yet knowledge therof" (646–47). Yet he had been desperately seeking patronage and

Identity in Autobiography: John Bale 61

had given King Edward a presentation copy of his *Summarium* (1548), almost certainly with some "expectacion." *Summarium* included not one but two pictures of himself making the presentation: one kneeling humbly before the king's throne, on the title page, and a second of him standing like an instructor before the king, who is seated like a student at a lectern (figs. 7 and 8). In the latter, Bale dominates the image. Bale had also sought patronage from Northumberland just the year before and made him the dedicatee of "An Expostulation to a Frantik Papist."[43]

Bale's passionate narrative is very different from lives written by the martyrs themselves. Willard Thorpe and Anne Askew both balance gracefully between self-assurance and modesty, able to convey a sense of humor as well as utter seriousness. Askew, interrogated in prison, makes a theological point by citing biblical images with gentle wit. Responding to her questioner's claim about Communion, she says, "Ye may not here (sayd I) take Christ for the materyall thynge that he is sygnyfyed by. For than ye wyll make hym a verye dore, a lambe, and a stone."[44] In contrast, Bale tells the Irish who oppose his innovations that the priest's Communion wafer is a gilded turd.

Bale is also more vocal about himself and his own suffering than Anne is. Her description of her torture is notable for its reticence: "Then they ded put me on the racke, because I confessed no ladyes nor gentyllwomen to be of my opynyon, and theron the kepte me a longe tyme, And bycause I laye styll and ded not crye, my lorde Chauncellour...toke peynes to racke me their owne handes, tyll I was nygh dead."[45] Bale, in contrast, keeps us informed of his various illnesses ("sycke agayne / so egerly / that noman thought I shulde have lyved" [757–58]), about his enemy's compelling power ("In the meane tyme was I poore sowle compelled / to set my hande to a false bylle" [1672–73], "against my will" [1677]), and about his suffering ("tossed to and fro upon the seas....And I was by that time / so full of lyce / as I coulde swarme" [1679–80]).[46]

Unlike the martyrs—or Paul or Luther for that matter—Bale often appeals to his own human argumentative skill rather than to God's word. Just as his claim to reenact Paul's journey is bolstered by references to tangible objects and to external rather than spiritual similarities, Bale's arguments are supported by logic, not faith. Where Luther turns "from all disputation and tutelage of reason" to invoke faith in things "not in man's competence and power," Bale says, "I wryte not this without a cause" (1118).[47] Addressing his Irish enemies, he lists their sins of whoredom, idolatry,

Figs. 7–8 Bale, *Illustrium* (1548), title page, presenting his book to King Edward; Bale, *Illustrium*, another image of the presentation (The Bodleian Library, University of Oxford [Douce B subt. 165 title page, and fol. 12v]).

drunkenness, and murder—"as I am able to prove by a thousande of your lewd examples," he adds, citing none (1194–97).

Bale remains at the center of his text—not Paul, not the brethren, not God. The battle between good and evil revolves around him alone. Other people are not so much "good" and "evil" in themselves as "good for Bale" and "bad for Bale." Whatever their valence, they exist almost entirely in their relation to him and not to one another. At one point, for example, Bale is brought to the house of "a man fearinge God / and his wife a woman of muche godlynesse also / which was to me [a] careful creature / a singular comfort provided by God" (1683–85). The couple are married ("and his wife"), but we never see them interact with each other, only with Bale. The woman, in fact, is almost entirely subsumed into the category of "a singular comfort provided by God" for Bale. Bale himself is described in much fuller detail. We know the exact hour at which he took horse to see the king pass in Southampton (595); we hear about his two agues, about the way Walter "searched us both to the very skinnes / and toke from us al that we had in moneye / bokes / and apparell" (1363–65), and about his being "so full of lyce / as I coulde swarme" (1680).

Bale shows no curiosity—and so we get no information—about what the other people he describes were thinking, and he cannot understand why the Irish clergy are so upset when he condemns the Mass and tells them to take wives. Nor does Bale seem to be thinking much about his readers, who might need an overview of Irish geography or politics in order to understand events (nothing like "It had been a cold season" or "The previous bishop had already left"). All we hear is what Bale thought from moment to moment in each new encounter.

Unlike the martyrs, he attacks enemies more than he praises God or reassures others. His satiric descriptions of the clergy mix uneasily with a saint's life. Bale's enemies, outnumbering his friends, swarm like the lice that infest him on the ship. The emblematic representatives of Antichrist may be the ultimate enemy, but far worse are those specific individuals who cross him in person. Bale tells about Thomas Lockwode ("Blockheade he myghte wel be called"), the "asseheaded" dean of the cathedral church (720–22, 747) who opposed the new form of Communion because it would "hindre his kychin and bellye" (728–29). He reports on "the drunken bishop of Galwaye" (1124), who went gadding from town to town, baptizing children for twopence apiece without even examining their Christian beliefs. This "beastly bishop" (1131–32) happily confirmed a "dogge wrapped in a shete with .ii. pens about his necke" that was brought in among a neighbor's children (1131–40). Even in his framing conclusion, where Paul would have offered a general lesson for the faithful, Bale rails instead against the whole lot of Mary's Catholic "pelting preses / knightes of the dongehill / though they be Sir Swepestretes / maistre doctours / and lord bishoppes," whose "most filthie buggeries in the darke / with their other prodiguous whoredoms / holden a most pure state of livinge" (1789–91, 1881–83). His brethren now forgotten, Bale goes on about his enemies: "Though they now are busily spisinge and paintinge of a toorde (their ydolatrous massee)," he says, "yet will a toorde be but a stinking toorde" (1876–78).

Similarly the three concerns announced at the beginning of *Vocacyon*—Bale's calling, persecution as God's reward, and comfort for the brethren—often give way to more mundane, material concerns: finding a place to stay, arranging dinner, making sure his chest of goods is not stolen, and so on. His is a material world, and while serving God Bale was also negotiating relations of power, profit, and status. His narrative begins with an account of all the stops between his English parsonage and Ossory, less like a saint's life than an ordinary list of grievances. Bale stresses the papists' secular crimes, particularly as they affect him and his income. Here he attacks the "greate Epicure the Archebishop," not because of religious malpractice but because he "went about to diffarre the daye of our consecration / that he might by that means have prevented me / in takine up the proxyes of my bishopricke to his owne glottonouse use / and in so depryvine me of more than halfe my lyvynge" (714–19). Sir Richard Routhe, church treasurer, and Sir James Joys, Bale's chaplain, hired Irish kerns to kill Bale, not for religious reasons but because "they were so desierouse of my landes" (1059–68). It is hard to imagine Paul making ad hominem attacks like these.

The last ten of the thirty-seven pages in the central section of *Vocacyon* are dominated by Bale's attempted escape not only from Ireland but also from the secular forces in his own (now Catholic) England. His enemy is Walter the pirate, whose connection to religion lies only in Bale's nickname for him ("a cruell tiraunte of helle ... being Pylate [Pilate] as the call them" [1356–57]). Walter arranged to have Bale kidnapped and held for ransom. Once the crew had secured Bale's money, they tried to get him arrested during a weather-forced landing, and they went ashore in another town in hope of earning a bounty by accusing him of treason. But Bale managed to raise enough money to bribe his way to Flanders, an act that, as noted earlier, made Cancellar suspicious.

Identity in Autobiography: John Bale

With the end of Bale's adventure in the central section of the book, the narrator turns from satire to the Pauline frame and its theological concerns, to which we will return later.

Bale the Narrator versus Bale the Character

The discrepancy between Bale's text and the saints' lives it imitates points to a discrepancy between the saintly "Bale" described in the narrative of the past and the cannier Bale who writes in the present. *Vocacyon* may sometimes seem like the single-minded attempt of a narrow and humorless man to prove himself another Paul. But it is better understood as a compromise. On the one hand Bale wanted to represent his apostolic experience. But he also brought to the writing of *Vocacyon* his un-Pauline drive to expose the clergy, just as he had brought it to Ossory the year before. For Bale the two motives were compatible, as were his saintly and self-serving statements. Bale was not, as Cancellar claims, lying. He wanted to comfort fellow believers and to praise God. But he was in a difficult position. He had just failed in his royally assigned duty to preach to his endangered flock. Although he had always praised heroic behavior and had presented the lives of saints as models, in Ossory he himself had run from his pastoral duty. At one point he had even been accused of treason. Bale may have felt that he had to defend himself against claims like Cancellar's, or even against internal doubts about whether he ought to have chosen martyrdom over ignominious escape. If so, then emphasizing the Pauline parallels could help prove that he was not a failed bishop of Ossory. Bale would not have been the first to make strategic use of his narrative, whether consciously or unconsciously.[48]

Even if Bale meant to present his case objectively, no one can be sure of remembering the past as it "really" was. Memories are not static objects stored for retrieval but traces, combined and reshaped during recall. Modern cases of "false memory" have called attention to the fallibility of witnesses. Similar examples can be found among witnesses at early modern witch trials, who were often certain about the supernatural phenomena they saw. Bale's bias probably affected his original perception of the Irish papists, along with the later memories of his traumatic year among them.

Inga Clendinnen points out a contemporary example of unwittingly distorted memory, in the "curiously selective amnesia" that she sees in Diego

De Landa's *Relacion de la cosas de Yucatan*. Landa, a missionary living among the Maya at about the time of Bale's tenure in Ireland, wrote his detailed and sympathetic account of the Spanish conquest without ever explicitly reporting that after their conversion the Mayans had reverted to human sacrifice.[49] From analysis of Landa's situation as well as the *Relacion*, Clendinnen teases out the possibility that Landa's painful ambivalence about the reversion—and about his own role in the subsequent trials, confessions, and punishments—may have led him unwittingly to avoid recalling the events in much detail.

Like Landa, Bale never acknowledges any ambivalence or any contradiction in his presentation of himself and probably felt none. Bale almost never records any inner conflict. He does not mention any personal struggle with his thirty years of celibacy, for example, although his accounts suggest one when they report that his conversion coincided with his marriage or when they concentrate their antipapist bile on the vow of chastity and clerical abuse of celibacy.[50] Nor does Bale report any conflict about conversion.[51] He seldom mentions conversion at all, and if the topic does come up, he describes it as a coolly rational choice: the example of his friend Thomas Barrett in one text and, in another, the combination of Lord Wentworth's leadership and Henry VIII's dissolution of the monasteries.[52] Again, a comparison with Bale's contemporary Luther, who describes the difficulties and self-doubt that he suffered as he gave up one set of beliefs for another, is striking. "Here, in my case," Luther wrote, "you may see how hard it is to struggle out of and emerge from errors which have been confirmed by the example of the whole world and have by long habit become a part of nature, as it were."[53]

Although Bale's text never mentions conflict, its rhetoric suggests ambivalence throughout. Bale's claims about himself often have to make their way past denials that call attention to what they deny. Two of these appear early in his preface. The first is "*I am not alone* in these 3. matters of vocacion / persecucion / & deliveraunce / but have on my side an infinite nombre of examples" (61–64, italics added). The second follows almost immediately: "*Neyther am I ashamed* to tell my brethrene / what God hath most graciously done for me / nomor than s. Paule was for hymselfe in his owne epistles" (33, 65–68, italics added). Concluding, Bale tells his readers something else he is not doing: "I write not this rude treatise / for that I woulde receyve praise therof / but that I wold God to have all the prayse" (244–45).

Negative claims recur throughout: after his neighbor attacked him, for example, Bale says, "I sent my servaunt unto him / not as one desierouse to be revenged / but to knowe what cause his grome had" (1077–78).

It is as if Bale knows what he ought to think—and to a large extent he does think it, but he cannot forget what he does think. He declares that he is not alone, not boasting, not glorifying himself; but the multiplied denials suggest that loneliness and pride are not easily put aside. One wavering double negative in particular suggests the conflict: "I speake *not thys for myne owne part only / but nether utterly exclude I myselfe / but* I utter it also for my exiled bretheren" (223–25, italics added). The identification with Paul is an effort, as if it were in conflict with other tendencies. Henry Peacham, in the *Garden of Eloquence*, calls double negatives like Bale's "Leptotes" (litotes), the figure that states by denying. Peacham could have been describing Bale's application of the figure when he explains that it is used to commend oneself or dispraise another, and he warns that the misuse of the figure shows arrogance or malice.[54]

Few writers show less interest in the "vagaries of inwardness" than Bale does. All his drama is external. He is rarely self-reflexive even about expressed attitudes, let alone any, like arrogance or malice, that he might not have expressed. The contradictions in the text, however, can express it for him.

Bale's Several Lives

Bale wrote several other short accounts of his life that can suggest what else he brought to the writing of *Vocacyon*. They provide another context, in addition to the historical and theological contexts, for *Vocacyon*. The details in the longest of these, Bale's entry for himself at the end of the first volume of his bibliography of British authors, *Catalogus* I (1557), make it particularly useful here. Written after five years of exile following his escape from Ossory, the *Catalogus* passage has a quieter tone.[55] But Bale's vision of the world and his place in it has changed very little since *Vocacyon* in 1553:

> I John Bale, a Suffolk man in origin, born to my parents Henry and Margaret in the village of Cove, three miles from Southwold, five from Dunwich, have brought this present work on the writers of Britain from the disposition of the islands among the sons of Japhet

and their heirs up to this year 1557 after the birth of Christ, some 3618 years. For I, a boy of twelve years, was thrust by my parents, who were both weighed down by numerous offspring and deluded by the tricks of pseudo-prophets, into the abyss of the Carmelite order in the city of Norwich so that by means of the faith in Christ I might travel to the contemplation of the mountain (of Sion) in peace, and that in turn I might be a disciple of the mountain. There and at Cambridge I wandered in complete barbarism of scholarship and blindness of mind, having neither mentor nor Maecenas: until, with the word of God shining forth, the churches began to be recalled to the purest springs of true theology. But in that splendour of the rise of the New Jerusalem, called not by monk or by priest but by the distinguished Lord Wentworth, as though by that Centurion who said that Christ was the Son of God, and earnestly aroused, I saw and acknowledged my deformity for the first time. And immediately I was carried by divine goodness from the arid mountain to the flowery and fruitful valley of the Gospel: where I discovered that all things were built not in sand but upon solid rock. Thence I scraped away from there the magic sign of the most wicked Antichrist and threw far away from me all his yokes so that I might be given to the chance and liberty of the sons of God. And lest henceforward in any way I might be a creature of so bestial a nature I took the faithful Dorothy to wife, listening attentively to this divine saying: let him who cannot be continent seek a wife. After this, at once, trouble followed and it has not left me to this time. Deprived of all possessions I was soon dragged from the pulpit to the courts of justice, first under Lee at York, and then under Stokesley at London: but the pious Cromwell who was in the confidence of King Henry always set me free on account of the comedies I had published. After his death I remained an exile through the tyranny of the bishops for eight years in lower Germany where I wrote many works in the English tongue.[56]

Here, where Bale is free from both Pauline and martyrology models, he presents his life story as a recurring, almost biblical, cycle of being "thrust" out of a protected world into a "wilderness," "having neither mentor nor Maecenas." Again and again, he finds another haven, but each time he is only thrust out and exiled again. The repetition and the sentiment it evokes suggest that on some level Bale sees himself as an abandoned child. His

Identity in Autobiography: John Bale   69

goal is to return to that earlier protected world he once knew, the home where he belongs but that he cannot reach.

Bale was first "thrust" out of his home, "a boy of twelve years," into the Carmelite order and Cambridge. He was rescued from this wilderness by Lord Wentworth and converted, but then he was cast out again, this time from his vocation: "dragged from the pulpit to the courts of justice." Cromwell rescued him, but a third ejection came when Cromwell died and "the bishops" exiled him, until "recalled by the most pious King Edward VI, and made Bishop of Ossory in Ireland I bore witness to Christ crucified." The fourth exile, from Ossory and England is the one portrayed in *The Vocacyon*.

The *Catalogus* associates the 1553 flight from Ossory with a past lifetime of lonely exiles, including the first one in childhood. In *Vocacyon* Bale never likens his current experience to the earlier exiles. But given that he saw all history as repetition, it is not surprising that traces of them remain. It certainly makes the emotional force of Bale's opening claim in the *Vocacyon* ("I am not alone") more understandable. The *Catalogus* emphasis on having "neither mentor nor Maecenus" in his youth helps explain the adult sense of isolation in Ireland that Bale describes. The lack of good people to balance the bad gains emotional as well as satiric force. Good people, if present at all in Bale's world, are distant and hard to reach. Even King Edward VI makes his one silent appearance high above Bale, in a window looking out over the crowded street, and communicates only later and indirectly by letter. Bale also mentions the good (i.e., Protestant) archbishop of Armach, Hugh Goodacer, who might have helped him after the ambush on Bale's household. But the archbishop had by then been poisoned at Dublin by "certen prestes of his diocese" (869). The "worst of all" his troubles at the time, he says, is that he "had no English deputie or governour within the lande to complaine to for remedies." It was the abandonment, not the attack itself, that led to his flight. So, he says, "I shoke the dust of my fete against those wicked colligyners ... accordinge to Christes commandment" (1289–92).

Bale's sense of abandonment and exile may also suggest the appeal to him of his habitual genealogies—two of which are included in *Vocacyon*. He sought not only individual figures with whom to identify, like Paul, John the Baptist, St. John of Patmos, King John. So often exiled from a community, Bale also sought a lineage, a family, whether Catholic or Protestant, and then, within the latter, a line of personal predecessors, stretching like an umbilical cord through Tyndale and Wycliffe back to his spiritual "mentors." Bale's deep affiliative loyalty to admired friends and their ancestors is the other side of his biliousness toward others. It seems to have given him the remarkable energy it took to be as bilious as he was. Bale has been seen as subjected totally to his identity as a Protestant and to his identification with Paul. Jacob Burckhardt's argument in *The Civilization of the Renaissance in Italy* (1945) famously opposed all such group identity to the development of individuality. But identifications, as Natalie Zemon Davis has argued, often nurture rather than hinder autonomy and self-expression. Bale's role as spokesman first for the Carmelites and later for the reformed church seems to have given him the strength to speak out on his own and in his own way.[57]

Bale's uniqueness here can be seen in his difference from the equally vituperative Skelton. Both men railed against heretical and stupid enemies—Bale, in fact, borrowed some tactics from Skelton—but whereas Bale bestowed praise generously on his predecessors, Skelton's praise was usually reserved for Skelton himself or the Howards, as if he had no ancestors.[58] Since Skelton had the Howards to praise, perhaps he did not need any.

Bale's stubborn insistence on seeing Edward VI's "very fatherly care" in appointing him to the thankless bishopric of Ossory also makes more sense in light of the image of himself as an abandoned child. In the concluding section of *Vocacyon* he again emphasizes the fact of abandonment before salvation. Paul's language returns here, but not Paul's stance as father to his followers. Instead, Bale switches models to identify with brethren now seen as "a flocke of orphanes / which beinge destitute of father and mother / are in this worlde subject to manye sorrowfull calamitees" (199–201). He calls on God to protect them all and invokes Psalm 26: "Though my father and mother have left me / yet hath the lorde taken me up / for his" (2011–12). His communal address does not mention his own "deluded" parents who first thrust him into the wilderness "out of ignorance and poverty." But he identifies with the brethren, who, he says, have all been failed by parents and adopted by God. He tells them to be grateful that God, "after the sinne of our first parentes," received the church to grace and preserved it. Christ, he concludes, "will not leave us as orphanes / or fatherless and motherlesse children without comfort [Joan. 14]" (2038–41). Not only King Edward VI but God himself will rescue Bale and fill the gap that so many had refused to fill before, beginning with his parents.

The emotional dimensions of Bale's self-image help explain a curious passage in *Vocacyon*. It follows after Bale has described the worst of his sufferings in Ireland: the fierce resistance from many clergy and laymen, the verbal humiliations, and the physical attack on his household that left several servants dead. Bale then goes on to liken Ossory, the scene of his suffering, to an oddly attractive Babylon: "I thought my self now of late / for the cares of this lyfe / wele satteled in the bishoprycke of Ossorye in Ireland / and also wele quieted in the peaceable possession of that pleasaunt Euphrates / I confesse it. But the lorde of his mercye / wolde not there leave me.... By violence hath he yet ones agayne / as ye in this treatise have redde here / driven me out of that gloryouse Babylon / that I shulde not taste to muche of her wanton pleasures" (1740–45, 1747–49). He had thought himself settled in pleasant Ossory, now free of cares in life.

"Babylon" is traditionally the epitome of all evil, sometimes embodied in hellishly papist Rome. But this "gloryouse Babylon," the "pleasaunt Euphrates," seemed to Bale almost the Eden of Genesis, fed by the Euphrates (Genesis 2). Not a Babylon in the traditional sense of a place of exile, Ossory was to him an Eden that he had once possessed and was exiled *from*. Bale rewrites his disastrous tenancy and near-fatal failure at Ossory and makes it into respite in a peaceful haven. He transforms his fortunate escape from murder into a difficult "crosse" that God's chosen few must bear. This is hardly a historically accurate record of what happened in Ireland, nor is it taken from his Pauline model or a saint's life. It is another chapter in Bale's own cyclical history of repeated exile, a scene from his inner world, not Paul's or Ossory's reality.

Vocacyon is conventional in many ways: its religious stance, its citation of authority in the approved manner, its imitation of Paul's epistolary format and Bale's martyrologies, and Bale's effort in it to see his life as an example of moral principles. He spends no time exploring the development of his individual personality or expressing the self-awareness that we look for today in autobiography. But while striving to submit to the doctrine, Bale—wittingly or, more likely, unwittingly—gives his individual attitudes and his unique sense of himself free rein in choosing how and what to say. He does not talk about his inner life, but his narrative is shaped so that a modern reader can find its traces everywhere.

CHAPTER 4

Autobiography: History or Fiction?
William Baldwin Writing History "under the Shadow of Dreams and Visions" in A Mirror for Magistrates *(1559)*

It is hard to imagine a less likely site for autobiography than a book so politicized that it was suppressed in 1554/55 and was not actually available in print for another five years.[1] *A Mirror for Magistrates* (1559), edited by Protestant William Baldwin, was addressed to Mary's repressive Catholic regime. *A Mirror*, much reprinted, enlarged, and imitated for nearly one hundred years, was a collection of monologues by the ghosts of Britain's fallen leaders. Each told his story as a warning for magistrates who ignore their obligations.[2] *A Mirror* has been read most often as historiography because, like the chronicles that were among Baldwin's sources, it recounts the lives of powerful figures who shaped British history.

Nonetheless, Baldwin's *Mirror* is one of the most important unrecognized texts in the prehistory of autobiography. It is a remarkably extensive repository of detailed and opinionated first-person narratives—not only by the ghosts but also by Baldwin in his account of how the collection was made. Like the verse in Richard Tottel's similarly popular *Songes and Sonnetes* (1557), the *Mirror*'s monologues were widely imitated in first-person verse and life stories, beginning almost immediately with lyric "complaints" and posthumous monologues, extending to book-length imitations (e.g., Anthony Munday's *Mirror of Mutability* [1579]) and later broadsides "by" the ghosts of Richard Tarlton, Robert Greene, Gamaliel Ratsey, and others.[3] *A Mirror* provided models for its writers as well as for its readers; two of the original writers (Thomas Sackville and Thomas

Churchyard) were among the earliest English writers to publish autobiographical texts, as were one of its earliest imitators (Munday) and the editor who succeeded Baldwin (John Higgins).

A Mirror's relevance for life writing derives partly from the fact that, unlike other histories, it draws on a tradition of first-person English "poesie" or fiction as well as on historiography. Indeed its influence on subsequent historiography was small, and it is remembered now rather for its literary legacy—most famously in drama but in other forms as well. Combining two different kinds of writing, the *Mirror* encompassed both public and private worlds. It combined both historical truth and a "personal voice," as Judith H. Anderson calls it, a speaker's unique way of and conceiving and organizing experience.[4]

William Baldwin and *A Mirror for Magistrates* (1554/5–1563)

To a degree *A Mirror* was a group project, but Baldwin was at the group's center, and he was responsible for the autobiographical frame that held the book together.[5] The "preeminent imaginative writer of the English reformation," as John King calls him, Baldwin was one of the most gifted of those who produced the steady flow of texts from Protestant printers under Protector Somerset during the reign of Edward VI.[6] The *Mirror* itself was generated during the period of restraint that followed under Northumberland's protectorship and then Queen Mary's reign.

Those were the years that led John Bale to rail autobiographically against the English clergy in 1551 and 1552 and then to the report on his disastrous attempt to reform the Irish. The first abortive version of *A Mirror* emerged at almost the same moment as Bale's *Vocacyon*. Like Bale, Baldwin wrote about the true poet who spoke from divine inspiration. After editing two editions of *A Mirror* he joined the clergy, "called to an other trade of life," as he said in the 1563 *Mirror*. But otherwise, although the times were the same, the men and their responses were distinctly different. While the monomaniacal Bale pressed toward apocalypse, the more chameleonlike Baldwin rode the waves of change by coaxing his readers instead of bludgeoning them. According to John Stowe, Baldwin himself was capable of attack and wished to see a gallows set up at Paul's Cross "and y[e] old byshops othar papestis to be hangyd thereon."[7] But the *Mirror* frame is held together by a cosmopolitan wit that contrasts strikingly with Bale's vituperation.

Baldwin was also more oriented toward the written word than was Bale. Bale kept the printers busy in two countries, but his model for writing was oral presentation. His polemical pamphlets reproduce the effect of face-to-face confrontation in a sermon, a stage play, or a dramatic monologue. Baldwin was deeply involved in the world of stationers and printers. He worked with Protestant printer John Whitechurch under Edward and stayed on when Catholic John Wayland took over. He was a charter member of the Stationer's Guild. At home in the new medium, Baldwin was not only in touch with popular taste but also adept at manipulating the visual resources like typeface and placement that print had made available.[8] Its print orientation was one of the important differences between Baldwin's *Mirror* and its model in John Lydgate's *Fall of Princes*.

Baldwin's mastery of printing formats gave free rein to the perspectival play that his humanist training encouraged. Even before *A Mirror* he had experimented with multiple frames for his texts and the interplay among author's and printer's perspectives. Other printers like Robert Copeland had grown expansive and even somewhat self-referential in the introductory material they provided for texts like *Jyl of Braintfords Testament* (ca. 1535) and *The Seven Sorowes That Women Have When Theyr Husbandes Be Deade* (ca. 1526).[9] But unlike Copeland, Baldwin extended his prefatory letter into a continuing commentary throughout the book and foregrounded it with a larger typeface. Combining the printer's license to frame with the author's, Baldwin's introductory letters expand into a spacious account of his own experience creating them.

The printer, Baldwin says, had asked him to supplement a new edition of Lydgate's *Fall of Princes* (ca. 1432–38). Lydgate, following Boccaccio's original, had ended his account with Richard II, and Baldwin was to "have the storye contynewed fromm where as Bochas lefte, unto this presente time."[10] The seven scholarly men whom Baldwin asked to help him were a formidable crew of the most learned and respected scholars of the time. Of these, two are named in the 1555 or 1559 texts along with Baldwin (George Ferrers, Thomas Chaloner) and six more in later editions (Thomas Sackville, Thomas Churchyard, Dolman, Seagar, Cavyl, Thomas Phaer). Although not all were noble or even gentle, most were associated with one or more of the influential coteries attached to the court (Sackville and Ferrers), to courtly military service (Ferrers and perhaps Chaloner and Baldwin), to Oxford (Ferrers and perhaps Chaloner and Baldwin), and to the Inns of Court (Baldwin, Chaloner, Ferrers, and Sackville). All were eminent scholars with impressive combined experience reading, writing, translating, and making public the most important documents of the day. Critics have speculated that members of the Privy Council had suggested Baldwin's name to the printer and were counting on his help in furthering the Protestant cause. The men Baldwin chose to help him were all sympathetic to that cause.

John Wayland began printing the original text in 1554 or 1555. But as Baldwin says in the preface, the print run was "hyndred by the lord Chauncellour [Stephen Gardiner]" (66, 63). The only trace left from that first edition is the canceled title page at the end of some copies of Lydgate's *Fall*. Thomas Sackville intended to reorganize the project under his own editorship, probably soon after the cancellation. But in the end it was Baldwin's *Mirror* that appeared in 1559. Even then, four of the original tragedies from the table of contents in the aborted edition were left out, not to appear until the 1578 edition.[11]

The 1559 edition of *A Mirror* as it finally appeared in separate publication was a collection of nineteen English "tragedies," narrated by the magistrates' ghosts and framed by Baldwin's narrative about the composition of the work. The title page (Fig. 9) reads, "A Myrrour for Magistrates. Wherein may be seen by example of other, with howe grevous plages vices are punished: and how frayle and unstable worldly propertie is founde, even of those, whom fortune seemeth most highly to favour" (62). The book opens with Baldwin's dedication, "To the nobilitye and all other in office" (63), followed by his preface to the reader that begins the frame, and then by the sequence of tragedies. The latter range in length from slightly more than one hundred verse lines ("Richard II") to about four hundred ("Clarence") and are written in various meters.

In 1563 Baldwin edited a second edition in which he added eight new, mostly longer tragedies (Sackville's "Buckingham" runs to about eight hundred lines) and rewrote some of the earlier frame to facilitate narrative continuity between the two parts. Both internal and external evidence suggests that most of the material in the second edition had been completed by the time the first part was published, although the later ghost monologues are not only longer but also more literary. Further editions, rearrangements, expansions, and revisions were published in 1571, 1574, 1575, 1578, 1587, and 1610, but my interest here will be limited primarily to the two that Baldwin edited.

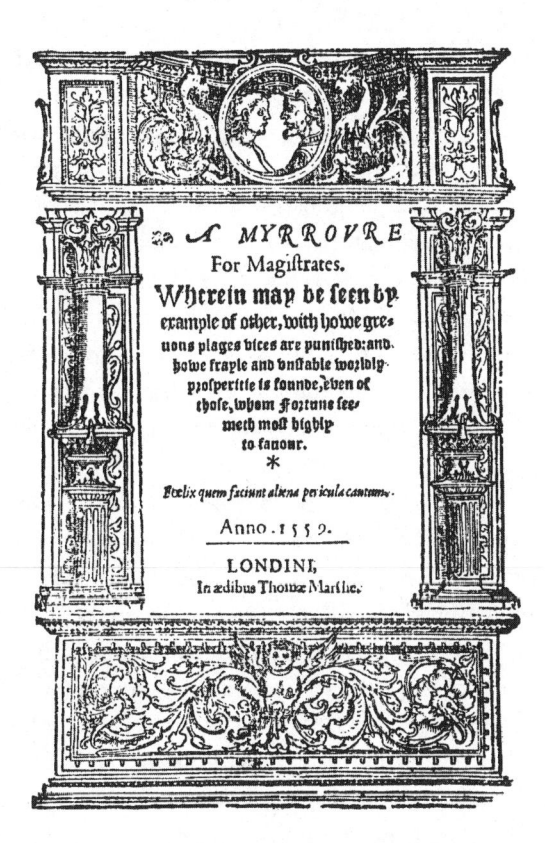

Fig. 9 Baldwin, ed., *Mirror for Magistrates* (1559), title page.

History and Poesie

Baldwin would probably have categorized the *Mirror* as history. He and his cowriters display far more historiographical self-consciousness about their relation to the past and how it can be known and used in the present than did Lydgate or any of his successors. By the time Baldwin began work on the *Mirror*, writers were increasingly concerned with separating true "historia" from the "invention," "conjecture," and biased judgment that had made it unreliably like poesie. Others had updated Lydgate with single complaints before Baldwin: More's "Ruefull Lamentation" (1495?), "King Edward the Forth" (attributed to Skelton and included in 1559), "The Lamentation of King James IV" (ca. 1513 dream vision later included in the 1587 *Mirror*), and David Lyndsaye's "Tragedye of Father David" (ca. 1546). George Cavendish's nearly contemporary *Metrical Visions* (1552–54) collected a number of such complaints by recent political figures. But

Baldwin goes further than the others to make the genre into history rather than poesie. However "medieval" their roots, Baldwin and his cowriters were far more modern than any of their *de casibus* predecessors. Most tellingly, unlike any others, Baldwin's fallen magistrates (apart from the one in his own dream vision) were not ghosts or visions but texts. Baldwin's is a post-Reformation, postpurgatorial world, and unlike Boccaccio's it has no room for ghosts. Baldwin and the others created the ghosts themselves. He tells us how the group read through the chronicles and took turns offering to "take uppon me the person of Richard Plantagenet" (138) or to speak "in the kinges behalfe" (111): they were, urbanely, composing a play rather than seeing ghosts, and they talk about the experience with notable self-consciousness.[12]

In addition, Baldwin and the other writers, like other historians in England's developing "culture of fact," were concerned to be accurate.[13] They used only trustworthy sources (34–62) and included no legendary or mythological figures among the ghosts. They were careful about chronology (getting the figures in correct order [71]), about national identity (is Scottish James properly part of this history? [154]), and about details that a poet like Shakespeare would later pass over (which Mortimer? [81]; which Earl of March? [131]). They make a point of trying to transcend the confusion they find in the chronicles, complaining about conflicting sources (Hall and Fabyan disagree about Mowbrey [110; cf. 267]) and scrupulously excusing their recourse to conjecture (267). The earl of Worcester's ghost complains that "divers writers" have misreported his story because of "Affection, feare, or doubtes" (198). These concerns were all part of a newly developing historiographic process, and although Baldwin never claims outright that he is more reliable than the flawed chronicles, his criticisms support that conclusion. Similarly, *A Mirror* negotiated between the old *de casibus* tradition that attributed the falls to Fortune and a more up-to-date concept of history in which the great men brought on their punishment.[14] On occasion the ghosts themselves call attention to the problematics of causality, as when Jack Cade begins his complaint by wondering which of two explanations for his fall might be correct: "Shall I call it Fortune or my froward folly / That lifted me, and layed me downe below?" (171). The saintly Henry VI, who wants to attribute his fall to Providence, nonetheless asks why Providence could let a good man fall: God "doth know how sore I hated sinne, and after vertue sought" (214).

But for all Baldwin's effort to be historically correct, his assignment was to continue Boccaccio's poetic account of princely falls as Lydgate had translated them. Baldwin's text is thus partly what Philip Sidney would call "poesie" or "fiction." Boccaccio's *De casibus* belongs to the long line of vision literature, including Dante's *Comedia* and ultimately Virgil's descent to the underworld in the *Aeneid*. The historical truth about such works was being debated, but their poetic truth could be defended. In addition, Baldwin's frame narrative was influenced by native dream visions known to be fictions; one of the ghosts cites "Pierce the Plowman's dream" [95]). Langland's poem (1360s–80s) had special import for midsixteenth-century Protestants and was reprinted four times in 1550–61.[15] Baldwin knew Chaucer's dream poems as well (although only the dream from the "Nun's Priest's Tale" appears in the *Mirror* [283]), along with Skelton's *Bouge of Court* (1482?) and *Garland of Laurel* (1525) and other texts that Tudor writers took as their national inheritance.[16]

Baldwin slyly signals his membership in the company of dream visionaries when he—alone among the *Mirror* writers—sees a magistrate's ghost in a dream.[17] Baldwin had been told to "note, and pen orderly" (71) the group's proceedings, but late in the afternoon, he says, after skimming over the stories of so many slain noblemen, he fell asleep. Then, "me thought there stode before us, a tall mans body full of fresshe woundes, but lackyng a head, holdyng by the hand a goodlye childe, whose brest was so wounded that his hearte myght be seen . . . his mercy cravyng handes all to bemangled, & all his body embrued with his owne bloud" (181).

Like other dreamers, Baldwin "waxed afeard, and turned away my face," but "there came a shrekyng voyce out of the weasande pipe of the headles bodye" commanding him to turn back and listen (181). Finally his colleague Ferrers, who had put him on secretarial duty, noticed him sleeping and had to shake him by the sleeve to wake him, noting sarcastically, "Belike you mind our matters verry much" (191). But Baldwin had been putting his dreaming mind to their business—like all visionary dreamers, he had been putting three minds to it: that of the author, that of the frame narrator awakened by Ferrers, and, finally, that of "Baldwin" in the narrator's dream. Such personas, unknown in the chronicles, are part of what readers would expect in works of poesie.

Baldwin had already gone on record declaring it "wonderfull" that writers should invent means to "publishe suche thynges as they thinke it necessary to be known, some under the colour of fayned histories, some under the persons of specheles beastes, and some under ye shadow of dreames and visions."[18] The *Mirror* incorporates other of these means as well as dream visions for conveying truth in fiction. Although he could have seen Italian and French narratives with informal prose links—like Boccaccio's *Decameron*, Castiglione's *Il cortegiano*, and perhaps Marguerite de Navarre's *Heptameron*—none had been translated when Baldwin first began work in 1554/55. Nor had any of the popular English collections like William Painter's or George Pettie's yet appeared. But from recent prose there were the humanist satires in Lucianic tradition, Erasmus's *Moriae Encomium* and Thomas More's pseudo-history *Utopia* (1551; trans. 1551), narrated by the straight-faced "More," as well as Baldwin's own parodic variation on *Utopia*'s comedy in *Beware the Cat* (1553; printed 1561).

The most immediate influence, particularly for the frame's narrator, "Baldwin," was Baldwin's own humanist predilection for frames.[19] Like his earlier narrators, "Baldwin" in *A Mirror* calmly reports both the ghosts' provocative claims and the debates among the writers. As in earlier texts, Baldwin creates multiple frames for the *Mirror*, each establishing a different point of view. Together they establish the distinctions between past and present, ideal and real, that are necessary for self-reflection in autobiography as well.

Baldwin was also influenced by Chaucer's frame in *The Canterbury Tales*. Like Chaucer's, Baldwin's narrator claims that the job assigned him "was a matter passyng my wyt and skyll" (68). He volunteers his first monologue only to show that he is not shirking ("Because you shall not say my masters but that I wyll in sumwhat do my parte") and humbly puts it "under your correction." He reminds us that he is merely the recorder, filling in only when "no man was readye with another" (101). Yet, like Chaucer's, Baldwin's authorial self-confidence is evident if the reader cares to look for it. His monologues, for example, are the only ones repeatedly praised by the company (110, 131, 170). Similarly, Baldwin's modest closing sentences about his secretarial duties may imply a more magisterial claim for his poetic power: "Whan this was sayde, every man tooke his leave of other and departed: And I the better to acquyte my charge, recorded and *noted* as they had wylled me" (240, italics added). Baldwin seems here to defer to his superiors again. But in the time since Ferrers had told him to "note, and pen orderly the whole process" (71), the word *note* has taken on a life of its own. Again and again the authors have reported creating the tragedies out of what they had "noted" in the chronicles: I "will shewe what I have *noted* in the duke of Suffolkes doinges" (161, italics added); "And as concerning this lord Clyfford...I purpose to geve you *notes*" (191, italics added); "the earle of Wurcester...ye shal heare what I have *noted* concerning his tragedy" (197, italics added); and so on. The implication is that just as the ghosts are fictions created by the *Mirror* group, the authors themselves are fictions. Although they may have historic counterparts, the other writers exist only because Baldwin has "noted" their actions and written them down, as they have "noted" and scripted the ghost monologues.[20] Like Chaucer, Baldwin gives his humble narrator more weight than it might seem.

Besides drawing on poetic sources, Baldwin, like many dreamers, concerns himself with the proper fashioning of poetry.[21] Introducing Warwick's story, for example, the text alludes to the constraints of the dramatic monologue format. There "one of the cumpany" (203), having jumped in as soon as the last tragedy was finished to speak for Warwick, slows down to indulge in a long introduction before getting to Warwick himself. He excuses his prolixity by explaining, "I have recounted thus much before hande for the better opening of the story, which if it should have bene spoken in his tragedy [i.e., in Warwick's monologue], would rather have made a volume than a Pamphlete" (204). This is not the voice of a historian trying to judge the veracity of his material but that of a poet trying to organize it into the fixed literary form of a monologue.

The group as a whole provides a running commentary on the literary value of their various contributions, they address problems of metrics and decorum (as in the "Tragedy of Richard, Duke of Gloucester" [371]), and they are as conscious of great poets they imitate—Cicero to Virgil and Dante to Lydgate and Chaucer—as they are of negative models in the fallen princes.[22]

Finally they make an ambitious claim for the role of poetry in the commonwealth. They welcome poetic sources for the *Mirror*. Baldwin spurns Merlin's merely "fayned rymes" in his tragedy of Glendower (127), but he makes no secret of the *Mirror*'s "allowed" poetic sources and their virtues (346). One of the group objects to Sackville's tragedy of Buckingham because it locates Buckingham in a suspiciously papist and purgatorylike hell. "That I am sure will be mislyked," he says. But another writer dismisses the objection as missing the point. "Tush [he said] what stande we here upon? It is a Poesie and no divinitye, and it is lawfull for poets to fayne what they lyst, so it be appertinent to the matter: And therefore let it passe" (346). It would be years before Sidney elaborated on the distinction between "Poesie" and genres like divinity.

The tragedy that follows this discussion is that of the poet Collingbourne, a magistrate's victim rather than a magistrate himself. Collingbourne was "cruelly put to death" by Richard III merely "for makyng of a ryme." He warns Baldwin and his fellows, "Beware, take heede, take heede, beware, beware / You Poetes you, that purpose to rehearce / By any arte what Tyrantes doynges are" (346–47). But at the same time, like Skelton and Bale before him, he claims divine inspiration for the "perfect Poete" winged like Pegasus, with "knoweledge of eternal thynges" and "Almighty Iove" in his breast (352–54). His listeners interpret the claim as a defense of their right to intervene in the real world of government and history. Baldwin's sympathy is obvious in his description of the ghost "holdinge in his hand, his owne hart, newely ripped out of his brest" (346). Another one of the company wishes "Gods blessing on his heart that made thys for specially reviving *our* auncient liberties." "Amen," says another. The "heart that made thys" was probably Baldwin's own, which, unlike Collingbourne's, was still inside his chest (359), because he wisely makes his claim only indirectly, through Collingbourne.

In the original summons to update Lydgate, Baldwin may have been given a tacit assignment as a spokesman for Protestants, but he took the opportunity to speak up for poets as well. The presence of a poet among Lydgate's princes underlines *A Mirror*'s declaration of poetic independence. In the *Mirror*, Lily Campbell argues, the poet for the first time took on the job of the historian, one that Sidney would only later claim the poet performed more delightfully and effectively.[23] I would add that Baldwin took on not only the job but also the authority of the historian, even when he talked about the private material traditionally reserved for poets. In doing so, he claimed a new importance for the poet's old territory of dreams, individual opinion, and narrative self-consciousness. He made room in history for the poetic "I" and placed the chronicle author in his text as blatantly as the dreamer steps into his dream. Appropriately, Baldwin and his colleagues conclude the first part of the *Mirror* by accepting as one of themselves "mayster Skelton," laureate to Henry VIII and a poet well known for self-dramatization. Skelton's "oracion" in the name of Edward IV, which one of them recites from memory, is used as the *Mirror*'s concluding tragedy (235).

Baldwin made a claim about veracity that few if any poets had made seriously before. "Chaucer" talks about his pilgrimage as if it were historical, but his account is marked as fiction by its genre. Dante, Boccaccio, and Lydgate spoke as historians and had included historical and even contemporary figures in their works, but these had been subsumed with the legendary figures into the poet's generic visionary landscape. For Baldwin, however, vision has been subsumed into history and Lydgate balanced with the chronicles. By combining history and poesie and claiming a poet's right to teach magistrates, Baldwin displays the laureate consciousness that Richard Helgerson has postulated only for later writers like Spenser and Ben Jonson who expanded the poet's subject matter to include the nation's past and the poet's role to include political adviser.[24] At this early date Baldwin legitimized the poet's self-consciousness about and freedom to focus on individual experience while writing a serious work. He took the freedom that only courtiers like Thomas Wyatt or Henry Howard, earl of Surrey, had glanced at before, and then only in a voice safely confined to brief verse outside the public sphere.

Baldwin's framed history thus brought together two vital components of autobiographical narrative: the narrative vitality of *The Canterbury Tales* and the truth claims of the chronicles, each now in the service of recounting individual experience. Writers may have produced and readers may have found one or another of these elsewhere. But the *Mirror* was unique in combining them and making them readily accessible for future autobiographers.

Seeing *A Mirror* as a generic mix helps resolve a much-debated issue in *Mirror* criticism. Whether critics deem the original *Mirror* to be conservative Elizabethan propaganda or a radical critique of government, all agree that its aim was strongly political and that later editions were less political.[25] Most critics agree that by 1610 the *Mirror* had degenerated from "ideologically aware poetic history into a sentimental historical poem."[26] Audiences, they complain, seem to have missed the point. But the *Mirror*'s dual nature meant that political ideology and poetic vision had been bedfellows from the first. If politics gives room to poetry, poetry makes politics resonant. Thomas Sackville's *Mirror* tragedy, argues Alan Bradford, attempts "to give cosmic resonance to what was otherwise merely a series of edifying political exempla."[27] What one critic sees as ideological decline another describes as a shift from a didactic to a dramatic mode, from morality to psychology. Certainly the history of letters shows that

Baldwin's collection had more influence on the poesie than on the historiography of the following century—and on the self-writing. Critics today, interested in ideology, may determine that texts like those collected in *A Mirror* and in Tottel's *Miscellany* (published only two years earlier) should be read politically.[28] But the *Mirror*'s readers, like Tottel and his readers, seem to have been more interested in reading for lives and individual experience.

Mirror and Autobiography

A Mirror is seldom considered in the context of autobiography and individual experience.[29] But readers could find in Baldwin's editions two powerful models for speaking about themselves: Baldwin in the frame and the ghosts in their tragedies, each more self-conscious about telling his story than were their models in Lydgate. The narrator's account of his experience is important here because it is unusual in historical discourse. But even the ghosts provide one of the most impressive collections of first-person narratives in the period, and their tragedies helped shape later drama. By contrast, Lydgate's *Fall* had been popular more for its framing commentary than for the ghosts themselves.[30]

With an irony that Baldwin would have appreciated, the ghosts are more charismatic than the writers who created them. Their originals were less striking. Although Boccaccio had presented the dead heroes as "real" people, his readers did not usually hear their actual voices. Boccaccio told their stories largely in indirect discourse and treated them in groups. His presentation of Mark Antony is typically undramatic. Boccaccio was about to end the current section of his text, he says, when he "was set upon by a crowd of clamoring people, and was unable to do so. I turned my attention to them and saw... [that] among them all it seemed that Mark Antony, the Triumvir, could best carry out the plan I had begun. He appeared with Cleopatra, but now his aspect was changed. Mark Antony was a nephew of Julius Caesar by his sister" (168–70).

Antony is one of the clamoring crowd that interrupts Boccaccio, and he is as real as the poet. But rather than stepping forward to talk to Boccaccio, he immediately melts back into the lesser reality of third-person narrative ("Antony was a nephew of Julius Caesar"), while Boccaccio maintains control of the story. Lydgate distances the ghosts even further. He refers even to Boccaccio in the third person, placing the poor ghosts at a double remove from the reader. In Lydgate the section opens when Boccaccio, "with penne in hond, casting up his eye," was interrupted by the spirits of Antony and Cleopatra, who "tofor hym cam pale of cheer & look" (6.3502, 3619). Further distracting the reader from Antony, Lydgate then digresses to retell Chaucer's version of the story before finally summarizing Boccaccio's. Antony by now has receded completely into the background.

Baldwin, by contrast, presents every ghost individually and lets them speak for themselves.[31] They often begin and end by addressing Baldwin directly, desperate for an audience and passionate in their regret. Sometimes Baldwin talks about them (albeit with a wink) as if they were real. After impersonating the ghost of Richard Plantagenet, for example, Baldwin continues his linking narrative by saying, "Whan stout Richarde had stoutly sayd his mind," rather than "When I had finished reading" (142). Or after another had spoken for the earl of Warwick, the rest respond as if to the earl himself instead of to the writer. As one of the group says approvingly, "I thinke the Erle...hath sayd no more of him selfe than what is true" (211). In addition, Baldwin, unlike Lydgate, is not squeamish, and his descriptions of the dead are mischievously ghastly. Lord Clifford, for example, appears "all armed save his head, with his brest plate all gore blood running from his throte, wherein an hedles arrow sticketh, thrugh which wound he sayeth thus..." (191); and Richard III's brother Clarence, of course, is "altobewashed in wine" (219)—an unfortunate condition that does not prevent Baldwin from wittily defending Clarence's sincerity by noting that "in vino veritas."[32]

Most important here, Baldwin's ghosts, whose flesh and blood are brought so literally to our attention, are more conscious of their unfleshly identities as narrators than any of their predecessors. They are not only talking about themselves; they are also aware of themselves as talkers, as the "I" who is telling the story now as well as the "me" who stars in the story. For example, Lord Rivers, the first ghost in the second part of the *Mirror* (1563), begins by telling Baldwin how the company "drave me to my dumpes" when they broke up last time without hearing his story, until he realized that they would return for another hearing later (246–47).

As much as Baldwin's ghosts model autobiographical acts, however, his own account of how the ghosts were created provides an even more important model for self-speaking and even more of a departure from Lydgate. Speeches by elite figures like the ghosts could have been found in the chronicles, but the framing narrative about their creation was unusual, as

E. M. W. Tillyard points out, in depicting ordinary people talking about their own experience. Here we can see the influence not only of poetic and humanist models but also of new forms of reportorial first-person writing like the chorography, or descriptive mapping, and travel literature that were then becoming more popular.[33] *A Mirror*'s account is one of the period's most self-conscious, tonally complex, and realistically detailed accounts of a text's own history and composition—and thus of its author's experience in the process.

Two aspects of Baldwin's narrative are important because they are associated with modern autobiography but are often said to be lacking in early life-writing. Baldwin portrays the "minutely discriminate spatio-temporal world" we associate with later prose fiction.[34] He specifies the social and psychological as well as the spatiotemporal locus of events. We know how he feels as well as where he is. He not only talks about himself but also talks *like* himself. His is a particular person at a particular moment, with a particular point of view. His attention to himself as recorder, to the "I" telling the story, will become as much a part of autobiographical writing as his taking himself as subject matter.

The multiple perspectives are apparent from *A Mirror*'s first pages. With Baldwin's opening dedication "to the nobilitye and all other in office" (63), the reader begins at *Mirror*'s outermost frame. This is the realm of medieval morality and truism that some readers see extended throughout *A Mirror*. But another perspective is immediately introduced with Baldwin's preface "to the reader" (68), the first installment of the *Mirror*'s inner frame and a different set of concerns. The contrast between the dedication and the prefatory letter is worth pursuing here because of its implications for autobiographical narrative: to suggest the ways in which Baldwin's narrative provides a model for talking about the self.[35]

The opening dedication locates the *Mirror* only in the ethereal nowhere of Plato's timeless sentences:

> Plato Among many other of his notable sentences concerning the government of a common weale, hath this: Well is that realme governed, in which the ambicious desyer not to beare office. Wherby you may perceive (right honorable) what offices are, where they be duely executed: not gaynful spoyles for the gredy to hunt for, but payneful toyles for the heedy to be charged with. You may perceyve also by this sentence, that there is nothing more necessary in a

common weale, than that officers be diligent and trusty in their charges. And sure in whatsoever realme such provision is made, that officers be forced to do their duties, there is it as harde a matter to get an officer, as it is in other places to shift of, and put by those, that with flattery, bribes, and other shiftes, sue and preace for offices. (63)

Baldwin presents unchanging truth about officers from Plato's time to his own, and in "whatsoever realme" they be found: a good officer is *always* diligent and trustworthy but *never* ambitious or seeking personal gain. Similarly, he speaks with unalloyed earnestness. Any rhetorical flourishes emphasize rather than complicate a statement that remains true from all perspectives as well as all times. Thus the nicely turned parallelism of "not gaynful spoyles for the gredy to hunt for, but paynefull toyles for the heedy to be charged with" reinforces rather than qualifies the contrast Baldwin makes. The only exception appears in a brief passage near the end, when Baldwin mentions the book's production.

From the formal dedication the reader moves immediately to the following chatty letter to the reader and the more human world in which the tragedies were written:

Whan the Printer had purposed with hym selfe to printe Lidgates booke of the fall of Princes, and had made privye thereto, many both honourable and worshipfull, he was counsailed by dyvers of theim, to procure to have the stoye contynewed from where Bochas lefte.... Which advyse lyked him so well, that he required me to take paynes therin: but because it was a matter passyng my wyt and skyll, and more thankles than gaineful to meddle in, I refused utterly to undertake it, excepte I might have the helpe of suche, as in wyt were apte, in learning allowed, and in iudgemente and estymacion able to wield and furnyshe so weighty an enterpryse.... Shortly after, dyvers learned men ... consented to take upon theym parte of the travayle. And whan certayne of thym to the numbre of seven, were throughe a general assent at an apoynted time and place gathered together to devyse thereupon, I resorted unto them, bering with me the booke of Bochas, translated by Dan Lidgate, for the better observacion of his order: whiche although we lyked well, yet woulde it not cumlily serve, seynge that both Bochas and Lidgate were dead. (68–69)

With Baldwin's opening allusion to "the Printer" in place of Plato, we have moved from humanist commonplaces to a historically specific "appointed time and place" where the authors met and wrote the book. The dedication had elided the centuries between Plato and Baldwin. It had hardly taken notice of the fact that Plato was dead. But the letter distinguishes carefully between the past and the present: since "Bochas" and "Lidgate" are now both dead, the new ghosts will complain to Baldwin instead.

The *Mirror* writers themselves seldom allude to secular or theological ideals, leaving those to the dedication ("justice") and to the ghosts ("providence"). But they pay close attention to the minutiae of composition. Because Baldwin's careful letter explains that he was following orders when he created *A Mirror*, it has been seen primarily as his disclaimer of responsibility for a dangerous text.[36] But it also serves to introduce a vividly detailed account of his experience writing. Baldwin describes how the seven learned men who had agreed to help him came together to begin "devysing" upon their task. He has brought a copy of Lydgate to the meeting as a model, and they begin leafing through the chronicles that they have on hand. Master Ferrers takes charge, appoints Baldwin to take notes, and offers to begin with the first story himself. "I wyll take upon me the miserable person of syr Robert Tresilian," he says (71), and he not only takes on at least two others but intervenes often during the rest of the meeting recorded in the *Mirror*'s frame. He instructs Baldwin to take note of figures they do not have time to discuss together; he ensures that the magistrates are addressed in chronological order ("*Baldwin*, take you the Chronicles and marke them as they cum" [91]); and he ends the session by calling for a second meeting in seven days. In the second part of *A Mirror* the writers meet "according to our former appoyntment" (*Parts Added*, 243) and continue as if it were only a week later, although four years had passed in real time. Ferrers arrives late, so Baldwin takes over and starts the group off himself. This time Baldwin and the others have brought completed monologues with them, so instead of composing on the spot as they had before, they assign someone to read through the chronicles while Baldwin interrupts to insert the finished monologues where appropriate. Another day goes by.

Although the production schedule of a week and two days is not literally accurate, throughout both parts we are revealingly aware of time passing and of the messiness of a temporal sequence of writing in contrast to the retrospective order of the finished *Mirror*. We have to wait while the appointed chronicle reader finds someone else to hold the book before he can take his turn to speak. There are false starts (Ferrers had wanted them to begin with ancient British princes before going on to Richard II's time) and blind alleys (Lord Vaux had promised to undertake the tragedy of Edward IV's two murdered princes, but Baldwin has not heard from him since, so they have to do without it [70]). Even with the material they have there are interruptions, as when, for example, someone offers to "personate" a figure but needs time to read up on the details, and they must stop and wait for another to fill in while he is getting ready. Meanwhile time passes, night comes on, and Baldwin gets tired and nods off, as we have seen, to dream. Ferrers terminates the first meeting when "nyghte was so nere cum that we could not conveniently tary together any longer" (235); he promises to write and solicit more stories and asks them to do the same. This is no Platonic mirror but a book that could have turned out differently had other writers showed up or Baldwin not been so sleepy.

Along with locating the writers in time and space, Baldwin sketches their social and psychological locus. Again the contrast with the dedication is clear. But here the homogenous voice of the dedication is replaced by a more humanly ambivalent voice, punctuated by Baldwin's humility ("it was a matter passyng my wyt and skyll") and by complaints about the task ("more thankles than gaineful to meddle in" without help from other writers "able to wield and furnyshe so weighty an enterpryse"—that is, with more political clout [68]). Then the company disagrees about particular choices, argues about principles, gets distracted, and goes off on tangents. Baldwin exposes the banal as well as weighty motives that determine whom they write about: if one fallen hero gets included because he is too important to be omitted, the group leaves out other equally important figures once they notice that time is getting short. They choose one story because it makes a contrast with the last and another for the opposite reason: because it repeats and drives home the moral of the last ("What neede that?" someone objects at this prospect of repetition [178]). In other words, despite the Platonic blueprint for a collection of morally improving tales about fallen magistrates, the stories themselves escape the superimposed order.

We also hear about the men's varied reactions to the stories. *De casibus* falls are traditionally framed by moralizing passages. Baldwin follows this convention on occasion, for example, after Lord Clifford's tale: "O Lord [someone said]. How horrible a thing is division in a realme" (196).

But elsewhere the response is focused on the group's experience rather than the moral lesson they wish to convey. Sometimes the men empathize with the princes and feel bad about their falls. After the earl of Salisbury's tale, Baldwin reports that "this straunge adventure...drave us al into a dumpne." (Appropriately enough, the teller's motive for choosing the next story, he tells the group, is "to quicken up your spirits" [154].) On another occasion they seem paralyzed contemplating the many fallen heroes during Henry IV's reign, and Baldwin asks, "What my maysters is every man at once in a browne study?" (119). After a particularly satisfying story, by contrast, "every man reioyced to hear of a wicked man so marveylously well punished" (170). Finally, not only are they depressed or cheered by what they hear, but also, like any group of writers at a daylong session, they make jokes. Once, after Baldwin's unusually short monologue for Richard, earl of Cambridge, one of the group says, "Belike...this Rychard was but a litle man, or els litle favoured of wryters, for our Cronicles speake very litle of him" (142).

If the dedication suggests a world of Platonic virtue and the letter Baldwin's human perspective, the ghosts themselves provide a third point of view. Separated from the writers, the ghosts not only are fictions but also come from another time. Unlike Lydgate, who ignores temporal separation, Baldwin distinguishes between the present and the historical past. When "one of the cumpany" speaks for Richard II, he calls attention to the present: "Imagine *Baldwin* [he says] that you see him al to be mangled, with blew woundes, lying pale and wanne al naked upon the cold stones in Paules church, the people standing round about him, and making his mone in this sort" (110–11). "Blew woundes," "cold stones," "making his mone"—invoking the immediacy of the senses. But this sensory past is anchored in the present scene of narrating it: "*Imagine, Baldwin,* that *you* see him [now]." The importance of current experience is even clearer when another of the company also evokes St. Paul's Church, but it is Baldwin's sixteenth-century church as well as the dead earl's twelfth-century church: "Imagine that you see the Earle lying with his brother in Paules church in his coate armure, with such a face & countenaunce as he beareth in portrayture over the dore in Poules, at the going down to Iesus Chappell fro the south ende of the quier stayres, and saying as foloweth" (205).

Like a guidebook writer for sixteenth-century tourists, the presenter describes the landmarks, identifying not so much where the earl lived and died but where he can be seen represented now in stone and paint, as you walk down the aisle toward the Jesus Chapel from the south end of the choir stair. This direction assumes a sophisticated historical self-consciousness, the kind necessary to write one's own life story, to distinguish between the writing self and the past self, and to appreciate what the difference means.

Mirror Writers as Autobiographers

That *A Mirror* encouraged its writers to reflect on their own experience is demonstrated not only by Baldwin in the text but also by the text's effect on its other contributors. No fewer than three of the other *Mirror* authors went on to use the *Mirror* model to write autobiographies of their own: Thomas Sackville and Thomas Churchyard, each of whom wrote one tragedy for the 1563 edition, and John Higgens, who took over after Baldwin died and wrote the 1574 prequel, the "First Part" of *A Mirror*, a mission Sackville had intended but never carried out. In addition, Anthony Munday, one of the early *Mirror* imitators, went on to write one of the earliest printed autobiographies in English. Munday had tried to profit from the *Mirror*'s success by titling his first published work *The Mirour of Mutabilitie, or Principall Part of the Mirrour for Magistrates* (1579). But although modeled closely on *A Mirror*, Munday's *Mirour* was neither "principal" nor any other part of the original, and it was never incorporated with the rest. Nor was his autobiography, as the others' were, modeled on *A Mirror*. Even without him, however, Baldwin and the others account for a significant proportion of the recognizably autobiographical writing in the sixteenth century.[37]

Sackville's and Churchyard's contributions to the 1563 *Mirror* are by all accounts the most accomplished, although among the least political. The autobiographical texts written by these poets seem to be modeled on the ghosts' complaint format. To be sure, the authors drew on the related poetic traditions available to any serious writer in the period. But the *Mirror* influence is striking. Each poem is not only the occasion for moral instruction, spoken by an old man facing death, but also echoes of the writer's earlier *Mirror* verse.

In Sackville's case, the autobiography ("Sacvyles Olde Age" [1566?]) may literally have been a close rewriting of his own *Mirror* contribution.[38] That contribution had included a long, ruminative "Induction" to the complaint Sackville wrote for Henry, duke of Buckingham—an unusual feature to which one of the company objects: "What meaneth he thereby, seeing that none other hath used the like order?" (*Parts Added*, 297). Baldwin explains that Sackville had written the "induction" as part of a planned new version after the 1554 *Mirror* had been censored. Sackville's induction lends itself to poetic rewriting in that it is even closer to its poetic (rather than chronicle) heritage than Baldwin's, and less political.[39] Baldwin's *Mirror* was a communal effort to influence contemporary magistrates; Sackville's was one man's lonely vision of cosmic mutability spoken to no one in particular.[40] While Baldwin's frame had distanced his group of writers from the world of the ghosts, Sackville entered the underworld himself. The atmosphere, too, is different from that in the other tragedies: more *ubi sunt*, as Bradford describes it, than *de casibus*.[41]

In his *Mirror* "induction" the melancholy Sackville, overcome with thoughts of mortality, walks through a barren winter landscape. There he comes upon the pitiful figure of Sorrow, who leads him to the jaws of hell. After he has entered hell itself, the ghost of Henry, duke of Buckingham, King Richard III's onetime supporter, comes toward Sackville and tells his story. Buckingham confesses that he was implicated in Richard's bloody crimes but complains that although he repented and went on to fight against Richard, Fortune still treated him badly. He was betrayed by a man he had once helped. Overcome by the memory of this betrayal, his own (not dissimilar!) crime forgotten, Buckingham is first rendered speechless and then driven to a passionate outburst unmatched elsewhere in the *Mirror*.[42] As Sackville had pitied Sorrow earlier, now he pities Buckingham: "And I the while with spirites wel nyye bereft, / Beheld the plyght and panges that dyd him strayne" (*Parts Added*, 339).

Sackville's autobiographical verse, "Sacvyles Olde Age," although not discovered until 1989, was probably composed in 1566, three years after "The Induction" and "Tragedy of Buckingham" appeared.[43] It is part of an unpublished addition to Sackville's *Mirror* contribution, apparently made some time after the *Mirror*. That manuscript text provides not only many lines but also the occasion, the rhetorical stance, the seasonal imagery, and the three-part structure for "Sacvyles Olde Age." Just as Buckingham had told his tale to warn magistrates about pride, Sackville in 1566 writes to counter a famous physician's hubristic claim that the art of medicine can prolong human life. On the contrary, Sackville says, medicine can neither cure old age nor bring back youth: "no arte may once renewe the passed dayes / off freshe grene yeres."[44]

Like the *Mirror* ghosts bewailing Fortune's turns, the speaker in "Sacvyles Olde Age" looks back on a happy past that had seemed eternal and compares it to the decline that he now realizes he must follow. The poem echoes the induction's affective weather to convey a sense of mortality. It parallels the induction's frozen winter landscape with a turning point in Sackville's life when his "freshe grene yeres" must yield to "[cruell] wynter" and his "lyvely bloud is dead / frosen wt cold and com is wynters woe."[45] In both poems such thoughts lead to a vision. But now, instead of seeing the fallen Buckingham as he had in the *Mirror*, Sackville sees himself grown old and changed into "an other man":

profe profe alas hathe made it all to true
lo me how late this sackevile did you see
flowrynge in youthe so gladsome and so green
now chaunged an other man and now not he
that erst appered when youthefulnes was seen
now felethe he the burden off his yeres
and now hys cowrse he bendes an other waie
now failes his strenghe now drouppen all his cheres
his chynne is whit now all his lockes ar graye.[46]

He sees himself as he will be in the age that follows a misspent youth: failing, weak, gray.

In the *Mirror* addition, when Sackville saw Buckingham he was struck as helpless and speechless as the duke. Words failed him. Comparing his poor skills to those of admired models like Chaucer and Wyatt, Sackville broke off in despair, leaving the poem unfinished. The last part of the "Sacvyles Olde Age," however, takes a more positive turn. It is still focused on a warning vision, but this time the vision spurs the poet to mend his life. Having seen the future, he refuses it; he is not yet too old to redeem his youthful carelessness and to make his remaining years valuable:

now slepe no more what Sackevile now awake
wt myght and mayne whyle as yet thy paur is suche
. . . .
but in the porche off sad and wofull age
while yet thy hore is grene and not increste
and while the lust yet dothe not hole aswage.[47]

Urging himself to repent ("slepe no more") while he still has a little lusty greeness left, Sackville resolves that he will forsake youthful "trifles," trifling love poetry most of all. He bids farewell to the poets he had invoked in the manuscript and farewell to his own "lusty rymes." From now on his pen will serve only to praise the Heavenly King. With this, Sackville reconceives the poetic failure that had silenced him in the manuscript and presents it as a willed renunciation. In the manuscript he had not been able to describe Buckingham as Chaucer could have, but now he triumphs over mutability by choosing not to write about such passion at all.

Besides the *Mirror*, there were not only literary influence on "Sacvyles Olde Age" but also practical ones.[48] The poem's editors argue that it may record Sackville's response to the process of assuming the tasks, titles, and responsibilities of the head of a powerful family. But the poem nonetheless bears traces of Sackville's many-sided encounter with *A Mirror* as an author, a would-be alternate editor, and a reviser of his own contribution. It points to the connection between Sackville's writing about someone else's life and his going on to write about his own.

The same is true of a second *Mirror* contributor, Thomas Churchyard. Churchyard's autobiographical "A Tragicall Discourse of the Unhappy Mans Life" (ca. 1572/73; printed 1575) is not, like Sackville's "Olde Age," a literal rewriting of his *Mirror* contribution, but it comes as close to the general format of a *Mirror* monologue as it is possible for a living man to do.[49] Churchyard's *Mirror* contribution, "Shore's Wife" (373–86), like Sackville's, was more emotional and sympathetic than didactic. King Edward IV's notorious mistress might easily have been presented as an opportunist greedy for the good life a monarch could offer her. But Churchyard's Shore is an attractive victim rather than a villain, who accepts her guilt for the fall. In addition, she reminds us about her vulnerability as a commoner, about her efforts to use her elevation to "do some good" for "the common weale" (*Parts Added*, 380), and about the dangers of court, where people admired her while Edward lived but deserted her when she "was by king Richarde despoyled of all her goodes, and forced to do open penance" (*Parts Added*, 373). As with Buckingham, the reader pities her.

"A Tragicall Discourse of the Unhappy Mans Life" draws not only on Churchyard's *Mirror* tragedy, "Shore's Wife," but also on Churchyard's "Tragedie" of Sir Simon Burleigh, which directly precedes it in the text where it appears. Burleigh is a ghost and would-be *Mirror* magistrate who claims that he was omitted unfairly from Baldwin's collection.[50] The anonymous "unhappy man," following the *Mirror* speakers almost exactly, addresses those gathered around what is apparently his deathbed, warning them to heed his example: "Com, courtiars all, draw neer my morning hers; / Come heer my knell ear corps to church shall go / Wyesly waye my thriftles fortune throwe, / And print in brest eache worde that heer is said."[51] Like Shore, the unhappy man warns about the dangerous illusions of court life and tells how those swept up into its glittering world of wealth and power will be abandoned by former "friends":

Yea thear wheremost my hope and haunt hath bin,
Where yeares and dayes I spent apon the stocke,
And divers doe good, hap and frendship win....
I skarce may moist, my mouth when thirst is great,
And hart is cleane consuemde with skalding heat.[52]

Hazy enough on the chronology of separate events to have confused many biographers, the poem is nonetheless quite clear in its overall presentation of a restless life spent alternating between going off to war ("My shues wear maed of running leather suer")[53] and then returning home hoping to find his fortune at court. This, as we know from other documents, was an accurate portrait of Churchyard's own life, and the point in "Unhappy Man" is that he gained little in either realm. There were moments of excitement, to be sure, and even occasions for pride. Churchyard tells of his rhetorical prowess and the generous use to which he put it, just as Shore had acknowledged her beauty and the power it gave her to do good for the "common weale" (*Parts Added*, 380). Taken prisoner in Scotland, for example, he talked the enemy into giving him lavish accommodations and freeing his fellows:

...on my band, I sent hoem sondry men
That els had peyned in, prison pyncht with cold.
To French and Scots so fayr a taell I tolde
That they beleevd whyt chalk and chees was oen.[54]

But there were many more disappointments than triumphs, and in the end he was left, like Shore, old, poor, and "forsaken cleane."[55] Toward its end, the tragedy slows for a meditation on mutability, fortune, providence, and human error, and it culminates in a *Mirror*-like vision of decrepit old age. The "unhappy man" then calls for death, bids the world farewell, and expires.

As for "Sacvyles Olde Age," whatever other influences shaping the poem, the *Mirror* ghosts had first provided Churchyard with a precedent and procedure for reviewing his life. Once he had written someone else's tragedy, Churchyard could go on to compose less *Mirror*-like autobiographical poems, but before the *Mirror* he had attempted none.[56]

John Higgins (ca. 1544–?), the third of the *Mirror* group who turned autobiographer, did not even wait until he had finished work on the *Mirror* before taking himself as subject; he included his story in the *Mirror* itself. Higgins, a friend of Churchyard and employee of the *Mirror* printer, took upon himself the task that Baldwin had first suggested in the original *Mirror* and that Sackville had begun but never finished: "to search & dyscourse oure whole story from the fyrst beginning of the inhabityng of the yle." His 1574 *First Part of the Mirroure* included tragedies of seventeen early British princes. It was quickly absorbed into the canon, perhaps because, as Lily Campbell says, Higgins seems to have been widely accepted as Baldwin's "apostolic successor."[57] And thus, she adds disapprovingly, began the *Mirror*'s downhill slide into an apolitical and purposeless collection of bad poetry. I would add that Higgins, even more than Baldwin, also made the *Mirror* into a medium for autobiographical display. Higgins's greater preoccupation with himself in the frame is immediately visible. Baldwin's ironic modesty in his letter to the reader is replaced by Higgins's self-serving defense of his own sources, methods, and motives. Higgins omits reference to any coauthors and adds a new "Author's Induction," identifying his *Mirror* as a dream-vision unified only by his own consciousness. Similarly, Higgins pauses at a point equivalent to the break between the two parts of Baldwin's enlarged 1563 *Mirror*. But while Baldwin had then opened the *Mirror* to as yet unknown other authors by asking for contributions to a second part, Higgins uses the break to add more about himself. Continuing the defense begun in the "Author's Induction," he says:

> . . . if you thincke I miste my marke,
> In any thinge whilere but stories tolde:
> You must consider that a simple clarke,
> Hath not such skill th' effect of things t'unfold.[58]

In taking possession of the *Mirror* authorship Higgins brought to it an even more overtly self-scrutinizing authorial stance.

With Higgins the direct connection between the *Mirror* and English autobiographers ends, except, as noted earlier, for Munday's maverick autobiography. But by the time the last edition under Higgins's control was printed in 1587, the *Mirror*'s influence had spread widely. By that year "a good many hopeful poets were apparently writing poems in the manner of the *Mirror* tragedies," as at least some poets had been done almost since *A Mirror* first appeared.[59] The sudden popularity of the complaint genre at this time has been linked to George Turberville's translation of Ovid's *Heroides* (1567), but the translation itself may have been prompted by the *Mirror*'s success. All were thriving on the mixture of history and poesie circulating in the *Mirror*'s many editions.

A Mirror's tragedies had been offered as negative examples of behavior: "Don't do what I did!" But they had also, perhaps not inadvertently, served as positive examples for autobiographical writing, and they generated sympathy for their speakers that had little to do with their moral function. *A Mirror*'s many readers could have found in it not only enlightenment but also a model for speaking about themselves and, perhaps, permission to do so. It was not an entirely new model, but it had been given a modern, rationalized, and Protestant turn that made it acceptable again even though it derived from an increasingly scorned medieval belief in ghosts.

Both Baldwin's 1559 *Mirror* and the similarly popular 1557 Tottel's miscellany made new models available for autobiographical writing. The difference between the two collections only underscores the variety of sites, occasions, and media that individuals could now employ to talk about themselves. The results led ultimately not only to the golden age of Elizabethan literature but also to the rapid growth of English autobiography that should more often be seen as a part of it.

CHAPTER 5

Sharing Secrets "Entombed in Your Heart"
Thomas Whythorne's "Good Friend" and the Story of His Life (ca. 1569–76)

> My good friend, recalling to mind my promise made unto you, I have here sent you the copies of such songs and sonnets as I have made from time to time until the writing hereof. And because that you did impart unto me at our last being together some of your private and secret affairs past, and also some of the secret purposes and intents the which have lain hid and as it were entombed in your heart, I to gratify your good opinion had of me, do now lay open unto you the most part of all my private affairs and secrets.
>
> THOMAS WHYTHORNE, *Autobiography* (ca. 1569–76)

Thomas Whythorne's "book of songs and sonnets" was completed in the mid-1570s although not published until 1961. In the decade and a half since Tottel's 1557 *Miscellany* and Baldwin's 1559 *Mirror*, life writing had spread. John Foxe's *Acts and Monuments of the Christian Church* appeared in 1563 and again in 1568, soon becoming one of the most widely read books of the century. The *Book of Martyrs*, as it was known, not only included stories about ordinary individuals but also reprinted many of the martyrs' stories in their own voices. During the same decade, England was inundated by a flood of Continental fiction about less heroic but still ordinary people. The easy availability of so many models, historical and fictional, had an inevitable effect on first-person writing. The 1570s were almost as remarkable in England as the decade or so just preceding on the Continent, during which St. Teresa of Ávila, Benvenuto Cellini, and Gerolamo

Cardano produced their autobiographies. Thomas Churchyard, Thomas Whythorne, Isabella Whitney, George Gascoigne, Gabriel Harvey, and George Whetstone all wrote (and all but Whythorne and Harvey published) autobiographical texts in the 1570s.

Of all of these, Whythorne's "songs and sonnets" has been singled out as the first modern autobiography. Its ninety folio leaves of manuscript record more than two hundred of Whythorne's "songs" and frame them with an account of his life to explain "the cause why I wrote them" and "my secret meaning in divers of them."[1] "Songs and sonnets" is in many ways a conventional text. Whythorne's moralizing poems are typical of Tudor didactic verse and epigrammatic style. His placement of the poems within a framing commentary had precedent in Dante's and in Petrarch's collections, and Whythorne probably knew sixteenth-century examples as well: popular editions of the penitential psalms framed by the story of why David wrote them and fashionable poetic miscellanies like Richard Tottel's *Songes and Sonnetes* (1557) and its many derivatives.[2] In particular, George Gascoigne's 1573 *Hundreth Sundrie Flowres*, which incorporated one poet's verse in a playful tale of his "Adventures," has been suggested as a model.[3] But where Gascoigne's frame played new and sophisticated games with the reader, Whythorne's poems were incorporated into a more traditional narrative structured by the medieval "seasons of a man's life" and the related schema of humoral development.[4]

Whythorne's philosophical and religious concerns are similarly conventional, as Anne Ferry has noted. Like John Kerrigan citing the preference for metaphysics over the vagaries of inwardness in sixteenth-century autobiography, she points out Whythorne's "tendency to see himself not as a unique individual but as a particular instance of the general condition of man." Whythorne, she says, "equate[s] what is in the speaker's heart with the generalized experience of a representative 'he,'" and he therefore lacks a language of individual "inwardness."[5] Whythorne's social and economic anxieties, Andrew Mousley argues, were equally conventional. "Whythorne's elaboration of a text of his life," he argues, "should not be taken as an indication of a new concern with 'the self' so much as an intensified preoccupation with status and role."[6] Mousley sees the manuscript as Whythorne's commonplace book, where he compiled insights about how to get ahead. Other critics have offered similar arguments about even Whythorne's seemingly private concerns about masculinity and his image of himself. These, it is argued, are constructed by courtly ideals or by the bourgeois standards of behavior newly circulating in Tottel's miscellany and its imitations.[7]

But this is a complex book, put together from passages that Whythorne composed over a period of more than twenty-five years, and its determinants are not easily isolated.[8] Whythorne's manuscript does show the influence of literary convention, of religious belief, and of a position in service caught awkwardly between the roles of servant and friend to his employers. Indeed, Whythorne's pages detail the daily climate of social life in country estates, or in the colleges at Cambridge, as few other texts do: what was expected of a servant to a titled lady? of her suitor? of a man in the contradictory position of servant-suitor? But Whythorne also dwells on his personal collection of concerns, from the history of the musical profession, to the conduct of his courtships, to the effects of travel on a man's character (49–51), to the metaphysical status of gods like Venus and Fortune (25–26). And unlike almost any other writer whose work survives from the time, he was a remarkably thoughtful and self-reflexive observer. The book is compelling, finally, not only for its record of a particular society but also because it shows what one particular man made of that society. Whythorne's manuscript sets forth the secrets entombed in his heart. His unusual self-consciousness extended not only to the outside but also to the inner world. Throughout his life, he tells us, he battled with what he called "venereal" desire and with angry impulses, with Venus and Mars, Eros and aggression. The battle runs along like a subplot accompanying the story of his career and social life.

The work as a whole book escapes generic categorization, although a number of genres have been suggested. Its editor called it a "life," a description supported by the title and preface, which promise "discourses" of the child's, young man's, and old man's life. But the first part of Whythorne's title is "songs and sonnets," and the book has also been described as a sonnet sequence or poetic miscellany, with its life narrative as subordinate pretext or an add-on. Categorization is made still more complicated because it is not clear whether the carefully prepared manuscript had been intended for publication. The verse preface seems designed for the public. It promises an educational text for the young: "Wherein young youths are learned lessons large / By which they may, if like do chance them charge / That happened to me, the better know to deal." But the text itself begins as if it were a private letter to "my good friend." Rather than publicizing anything, it promises to "lay open unto you the most part of all my private affairs and secrets, accomplished from my childhood." Only at the end of the introductory section, as a parenthetical afterthought, does Whythorne mention the possibility of a wider audience: "(Also it may be for their good, who shall read this hereafter)" (1–2).[9] Was the introductory address to his friend, as some have suggested, merely a conventionally modest format, introduced only to excuse publication? Or was the occasion for the manuscript really a private exchange? Evidence for Whythorne's motives, as for his publishing plans, is unclear.

Because of the uncertainties, this text—more than earlier, more easily categorized courtly verse (John Skelton and Thomas Wyatt), self-defense (John Bale), or political argument (William Baldwin)—raises the central question of this book: why would someone write about himself at such length when there was no tradition for doing so? Resisting any one simple answer, Whythorne's manuscript provides an example of the multiple motives and the complex and often messy processes that can lie behind what now seems to be a seamless final text.

The following discussion begins with the introductory pages of Whythorne's text and what they suggest about the role that Whythorne's friend played during the manuscript's original occasion—or occasions. It then considers the two conventional schema that Whythorne used to organize his text, the poetic miscellany and the seasonal cycle, arguing that the narrative finally evolves independently of both, at times even contradicting or eluding them entirely. The last section discusses several representative passages about Whythorne's struggle with his emotions, in which his own language eludes his controlling schematic presentation and, as in the case of John Bale, conveys perhaps more of his "secrets" than he intended.

"My Good Friend"

Cultural codes of belief and group identities are inevitably important to the way people see themselves. But as in the case of John Bale's identification with St. Paul, group identity need not be opposed to a sense of individuality or independence, as Jacob Burckhardt's *The Civilization of the Renaissance in Italy* (1945) argued they were. Bale was more of a maverick than Whythorne; it is easy to see how the determined, eccentric priest might have shaped his own version of Paul to facilitate as well as subject his energies. But cultural schema, whether religious or social, are always mediated by local contexts of family, parish, neighbors, occupation. Natalie Zemon Davis's argument that local identities often nurtured rather than hindered autonomy and self-expression holds for Whythorne as well as Bale. In particular, Davis argues for the "strong pull of the family to the exploration of the self," and she cites examples such as Thomas Platter's memoirs that begin by addressing "My dear son Felix," who, he says, has "often asked me to describe my life."[10] Talking about oneself was part of a larger occasion that included an audience, often family, who wanted to hear what one said.

Whythorne's text provides evidence for expanding Davis's argument about nurturing environments for autobiography to friendly as well as familial exchanges. The wider significance of friendship in this period is well documented, but its generative role in early autobiography has not been appreciated. A letter to a friend, like a conversation, provided an occasion for gossip, secrets, and personal revelation.[11] Having someone who was interested in reading encouraged writers to write more about themselves. Friends exchanged verbal self-portraits in the same way they exchanged painted portraits of themselves. So Erasmus sent his portrait to Sir Thomas More (to "be always with you, even when death shall have annihilated us").[12] Similarly, Whythorne's contemporary Richard Maddox, in an apparently common gesture, commissioned a portrait to leave with his family in his place before he sailed on an Atlantic voyage. Whythorne had in mind a different, but still related, exchange when he ordered a copy made of his mistress's portrait, planning to have her see it hanging in his rooms (38).[13]

In the opening paragraph of Whythorne's manuscript, the epigraph for this chapter, Whythorne implies that he would not have written the book were it not for the friend: "Because you did impart unto me at our last being together some of your private and secret affairs past, and also some of the secret purposes and intents the which have lain hid and been as it were entombed in your heart, I, to gratify your good opinion of me, do now lay open unto you the most part of all my private affairs and secrets." The secrets are also necessary to explain the songs and sonnets he had promised to show his friend.

Readers have argued that the paragraph is simply Whythorne's version of a conventional modesty topos, an exchange invented to excuse what might otherwise seem an immodest publication of his verse.[14] Yet Whythorne felt no need for either convention or modesty when he published two volumes of music and accompanying "songs" in 1571 and 1590. Whythorne's version of the letter is, in fact, uncommon at this early date, although it was more common later, and there is no external evidence to justify dismissing the idea that Whythorne wrote for a friend. Even if he invented the exchange, as perhaps he did, he may have done so less to justify an already completed text than to imagine a congenial audience for whom he could write. An imaginary friend as well as a real one could foster the self-consciousness and self-confidence that autobiography demands. Even Petrarch imagined an Augustine to unlock his "secrets."[15]

In any case, Whythorne's address to his friendly reader—unlike those mentioned in the conventional modesty topos—continues throughout the book. After a digression he explains, for example, that, "I have stayed you somewhat long on choleric, angry, and sharp accidents, which was more of purpose than of oversight. Because that my biles and choler provoked me to say somewhat" (177). Again, excusing an interruption to his narrative in order to explain a poem, he says, "Now I must tell you of another matter than I have as yet not touched. The which, although it be not pertinent or pertaining to the story aforesaid, yet it is to the purpose of that which I must open, if I shall follow orderly that which I have had, and am now purposing to do concerning my songs and sonnets" (85).

The friend's presence is suggested even by what Whythorne chooses to say and how he says it. For example, he begins with childhood but says nothing of his family's origins or status, as one might expect he would at the beginning of an autobiography written for strangers rather than for someone who knew him well.[16] The silence is not due to any lack of pride on Whythorne's part. He included "gent" on the title page, and as he tells the reader, he wrote proudly about family connections in the book of music that he published in 1571.

Indeed a "friend" was the most appropriate audience for a book like this one so concerned with secrets. Being able to share secrets was one of the most valued benefits of friendship in the period. Books consulted by ambitious young men for information about appropriate behavior, from Baldassare Castiglione's *Book of the Courtier* (trans. 1561) to Thomas Wright's popular *Passions of the Mind* (1604) and John Cleland's *Institution of a Young Nobleman* (1607), all commended sharing secrets with friends, and all warned against entrusting them to anyone else.[17] Thomas Breme's *Mirrour of Friendship* (1584), for example, notes appreciatively that "to a true and assured friend, a man may discover the secrets of his heart, and recount to him all his griefes, trust him with things touching his honour, and deliver him to keep his goods and treasures."[18]

For Whythorne, friendship seems to have been the only unproblematic form of social life. He mentions friends often but only in passing, as if they were not remarkable enough to comment on. They invite him to their houses, meet him in London, serve as sounding boards for his plans, introduce him to eligible women, and write introductory poems for his music book. He had even engaged in autobiographical exchanges with friends before. The present book was partly composed, he says, from the texts written for those earlier occasions. The first of these was an early poem about his childhood written to "requite a friend" who did "declare unto me the state of his life for a certain time" (7), and later he wrote to a friend to report about his travels abroad (54). Just as Whythorne's life story was always part of his poetry, Whythorne's friends were regularly part of the process of reviewing his life.

Escape from Order

The material following Whythorne's epistolary introduction seems also to have sprung from multiple motives and models. It certainly takes account of separate narrative skeins, some perhaps begun earlier than others. Whythorne began to incorporate his existing verse into the manuscript sometime between 1569 and 1576, probably rewriting an additional final draft and translating it, at that point, into his unique system of orthography.[19] As he put the verse together, Whythorne explains, he composed "explanatory discourses" for individual poems, adding, however, that "part of the which discourses I made and wrote when I did make these songs and sonnets; and now as more matter hath come into my remembrance, so have I augmented the same... in print." In other words, the book reflects a process of collecting and commenting on bits and pieces written at a variety of times, as well as a process of creating a new narrative to integrate everything. Whythorne never quite finished the process. The manuscript's editor notes that bits of paper dated later than 1576 had been inserted between the pages of the manuscript, perhaps continuing the habit that had generated the book itself.

In a sense, Whythorne had been composing commentaries on his life in one form or another for years. Nothing had worked well enough by itself. He wrote didactic verse, and when that was not enough to convey what he meant, he simply added to it, filling in what it left out. What makes his work so unusual, and so rewarding, is the way it shows him in the process of patching and remaking, moving from the conventional model to his commentary on it—and as a result, coming up with his own new way of conveying a complex subjective point of view.

Whythorne's title announces the two schema intended to organize the book, the poetic miscellany and the traditional cycle of seasons in a life. He mentions the first of these, the collection of songs and sonnets, in his first sentence. But even before Whythorne sets out his first poem for explication, he announces a deviation from the miscellany format: "But or ever I do come to the body of my purpose, I will…declare unto you somewhat of my erudition and bringing up until I came to the time of my knowledge in making and writing English verse" (2). The miscellany has given way to the autobiographical narrative that envelops it.

Had Whythorne arranged his book like other poetic miscellanies, with poems presented either randomly or by topic, the separate poems would have stood out as the book's most prominent feature, each with its accompanying explanation. But by presenting his poems chronologically, as part of his life cycle, Whythorne shifts attention from individual poems to the narrative portrait of the artist who wrote them. The narrative always comes first, literally, with the poems precipitating out of each account just as they did out of the original experience.

The first section, on childhood, has nothing directly to do with the collected poems. Whythorne was born in 1528 to a wealthy family in Somersetshire, whose motto was derived from the asperity of a horn and thorn embedded in their name: "Sharp but not too much" (176–77). His narrative omits these facts and quickly reaches the period when, at the request of his Oxford uncle, Whythorne's father sent the ten-year old boy to live with the uncle. The uncle let him know that despite property and motto, Whythorne would have to earn his living. It is not clear that Whythorne would have been given musical training or prepared for university had he remained at home. With his uncle's support, however, he studied music and Latin and was well read enough to tutor a Cambridge student (101) many years later. Whythorne finally chose music.

It became clear early on, however, that although he was trained as a musician, called himself a musician, and published only musical compositions, Whythorne always thought of himself as a writer. The musical profession entailed more than it does today. Nicholas Grimald, Philip

Edwards, and Richard Mulcaster all engaged in musical productions as well as in writing plays or poetry. Whythorne could have known them, and he would have worked with others like them when he attended the Oxford choir school, whose performers collaborated closely with the university on productions.[20] The England of iconoclastic Protestantism had no claim to achievement in the visual arts; and its men of letters were just beginning to create a vernacular literature and drama that would be worthy of their classical and Chaucerian heritage. But musicians had begun to draw attention and admiration. Musicians carried the aura of learning and professionalism that clerics did in the upper reaches of their hierarchy, particularly if they were employed by the court or church. As musical appreciation and ability came to be a mark of gentility among socially conscious families, the increased desire for musical literacy also raised the demand for music tutors, and Whythorne benefited at times from the demand, as when he played two job offers against each other (43–48). Unfortunately, when times were bad, those like Whythorne who depended at times on the patronage of lesser nobility were often forced to enter the master's household as a "semi-professional dogsbody"—or as Whythorne put it, like "a water-spaniel" (28), poorly paid or offered terms more feudal than contractual.[21]

But whether in good times or bad, music for Whythorne was always associated with writing, as it was for John Skelton and Thomas Tusser, two other writers discussed here who had trained as musicians. Whythorne chose an apprenticeship with John Heywood, who not only taught him to play on the virginals but also was "such an English poet as the like, for his wit and invention...was not as then in England" (6). It was during his apprenticeship that Whythorne's future became clear to him. One of the tasks Heywood assigned Whythorne was to copy "divers songs and sonnets that were made by the Earl of Surrey, Sir Thomas Wyatt the Elder," and others (6). After making a copy for himself too, Whythorne immediately decided to "follow their trades and devices in writing as occasions moved me" (9). The first poem he records writing was composed during his time at Master Heywood's, and echoes of Wyatt may be heard in Whythorne's early verse.[22]

The rest of Whythorne's life as a tutor and music master was inseparable from his writing about it, usually in verse. Poetry was important to him long before he began collecting his verse for his text. It was part of everyday life. Like commissioning one's portrait, writing verse was a way of capturing a specific moment.[23] Popular metrical psalms and moral commonplaces allowed easy recall of important facts and lessons. Whythorne was in service with Heywood when the latter poet published his huge *Dialogue Conteyning the Nomber in Effect of all the Proverbes in the Englishe Tongue* (1546), a collection reprinted more often in the sixteenth century than Tottel's miscellany. Whythorne alludes to a number of similar collections, such as Erasmus's *Adagia* (trans. 1569), William Baldwin's *Treatise of Morall Phylosophie* (1547), and Lodovico Guicciardini's *Garden of Pleasure* (trans. 1576). His familiarity with (and sometimes memorization of) their contents no doubt contributed to his facility in inventing his own rhymed maxims "to print the substance [of an experience] deeper in my remembrance" (63).

At least as important for Whythorne, perhaps more so than for those who had other ways of socializing easily, verse was a means of social exchange. As noted above, he had already exchanged summaries of his experience with individual friends. Additionally, in the small society of the households where he spent many years as a music instructor, Whythorne, like court poets at another level of society, was called on for entertainment. Like Wyatt's, the members of his audiences usually knew each other well, and he could count on their friendly reception. He was known and respected for his songs and accompaniments, when he was visiting friends as well as when he was in service. The gittern he kept by his side "was an instrument much esteemed and used of gentlemen, and of the best sort in those days" (21). John Skelton's *Garland of Laurel* describes his performance for a circle of ladies surrounding the duchess of Norfolk. Whythorne's employers were lower on the social scale, but he too entertained them with songs made especially for the listeners (135–36). For a "bashful" man like Whythorne, poetry was more useful still for intimate exchanges between two people. One young woman who was too "shamefast" to speak in person left a note for Whythorne in his gittern strings, and he left one in return (20–22). Verse sung to music in private could also distance an intimate encounter enough to render it less dangerous, and, if necessary, it could later be disowned (40).

Most of all, poetry served for Whythorne "to ease my mind." Despite his pride in his profession, it was to writing he turned in distress, not to music.[24] In a few years Philip Sidney would claim that he wrote because he was "overmastered" with thoughts or because he was compelled to deliver "monsters" from his brain. With Sidney we have no way of knowing whether this was true, but Whythorne's explanations for his poems indicate that he meant it. Whythorne's apprenticeship with Heywood brought him to the brink of adulthood. Then he settled into living on his own in London and making a career, like Heywood's, of writing and giving music lessons. But a two-year bout with a terrible ague, to which I will return, depleted both his strength and his money, and the central section of Whythorne's narrative treats the long sequence of positions that he occupied in aristocratic households thereafter.

It was during this part of his career that Whythorne was most preoccupied with making his way in both the domestic and the larger social hierarchies that regulated his life as a private tutor. This section of his narrative reveals much about his daily life and his character. Apart from his private tutoring engagements, Whythorne and his immediate circle of family and friends were members of the professions. Osborne notes that two of his brothers-in-law were engaged in law (172), and the good friend who wrote an introduction for Whythorne's 1571 song book had been a tutor for Cambridge students, as Whythorne himself had at one point. We can now add Whythorne's good friend in London, "B. the P.," to the group, if he was, as I believe, the John Bettes who was a painter and son of the better-known court painter John Bettes.[25] Whythorne found he had much less in common with the London merchants he dealt with when he worked as an agent for William Broomfield.[26]

When Whythorne worked in aristocratic households, he was one of the hierarchy of servants. In some homes, however, he was treated as a friend as well as a servant, a distinction he enjoyed. His social ambitions during this period are easy to see. Whythorne recorded every social nuance that he observed as he moved between the worlds upstairs, downstairs, and (literally) in his lady's chamber. "I had been in the companies of those who be worshipful, right worshipful, and also honourable," he says, with some pride (138). Always discreet, Whythorne refers to people only by initials or nicknames, as with the anonymous member of the Privy Council (73) and the woman whose prior experience at court impressed him deeply (80–81). But we know that Lord Ambrose Dudley and the duchess of Northumberland were among his employers or would-be employers and that, like Bale and Baldwin, Whythorne was close enough to powerful circles to feel the political repercussions when Edward VI died.[27] Finally he served in the distinguished position of music master to Archbishop Parker at Canterbury.

The country estate was a claustrophobic world where people on different social levels depended on one another and lived under one roof, with not much beyond the household to distract them. Whythorne's relationships—whether with his fellow servants or, when he could arrange it, with his employers—were closely watched. Whythorne was always worried about how his betters saw and judged him. But others kept watch too. Small rivalries festered below stairs—a "place where Envie raines," as Walter Darell called it in his *Short Discourse of the Life of Servingmen* (1573)—and rumors thrived.[28] Shakespeare's Iago may have been "monstrous" when he invented gossip about a fellow soldier to make Othello jealous, but he was not an oddity. Many lesser Iagos must have sprung up from the fertile brew of half-knowledge and suspicion in a world where the classes were separated more by custom and manners than by physical distance.

Whythorne's concern with secrets is understandable, given the domestic arrangements for live-in servants, which guaranteed little privacy for anyone's secrets. His living space was always at the disposal of his employers. He did not even control his storage "chest," the one private space that servants might usually count on.[29] In one situation, for example, Whythorne's mistress—without consulting him—took the opportunity offered by his temporary absence to move his chest out of one room and into another one closer to her. In service to a woman like this, it is no wonder Whythorne was guarded, particularly about his encounters with the opposite sex.

Part of Whythorne's characteristic secretiveness in relationships with both superiors and equals, men and women, was typical of others. Isabella Whitney warned her young sisters in service not to talk too freely or leave themselves vulnerable to the "infection" that rumor can spread (*A Sweet Nosgay*, 1573). Even Thomas Tusser, out in the more sparsely populated countryside, wrote a poem warning about envious neighbors who spread slander (1570). In the same few years, George Gascoigne revised and retitled his 1573 *Hundreth Sundrie Flowres* because he was accused of circulating slanderous revelations thinly disguised as fiction.

Yet Whythorne was even more guarded than others. In an arrangement unusual enough for him to remark on it, he always kept private rooms in London, and he retreated to them when he could to escape from his work and his employers. Withdrawal was a "need," he says, not a luxury: "I kept always a chamber in London, because that home is homely, what chance soever should happen.... I have always a chamber of mine own in that city to resort unto, in my time of need" (38, 80). He often locked his thoughts away separately too. He kept watch on himself so that he would give nothing away by "blabbing," and he avoided the drunkenness, anger, trust, and closeness that might lead to loose talk. Whythorne was so careful that he went to the opposite extreme, hiding his thoughts entirely or secreting them in his poems. Poetry for him was another private chamber for his secrets; some of the poems in the manuscript were never intended to be seen by the people they address. Guarded about many things, Whythorne is, however, particularly sensitive about letting people know how he feels. He can talk easily about potential sexual encounters and getting "stiff" (33), but he tries to hide any need or vulnerability that someone could mock.

The body of Whythorne's narrative begins to wind down when, having found the life of service unsatisfactory in a number of separate households, he decides to give up tutoring and return to an independent career of teaching and practicing music. At this point in the story, Whythorne's two announced organizing schema, the poetic miscellany and his life story explaining it, come together; and the narrative about this period takes up a substantial proportion of the manuscript. Whythorne's life for the next two years will itself be dedicated to his poems, or songs, because he wants to begin his new career by publishing his music. Then, after the book is published, Whythorne discovers that it is not selling well enough, so he decides to offer another book. This one will publish his songs in order to lure buyers into seeking out the music for them (138–49, 172–81). Apparently the songs never reached print, although the collection may have influenced the manuscript we have. But the latter cannot be reduced to a book of songs. It is far looser and baggier and much more personal than any other surviving collection of verse.

The second conventional organizing schema that Whythorne had originally indicated for his book besides the poetic miscellany was the narrative of his progress through the seasons of a man's life. But just as the miscellany was absorbed into the story of Whythorne's writing life, the seasonal schema too leaves only faint markers on that story. It is true that the seasons are announced in the title and the preface. And other passages do appear at appropriate moments. So, for example, Whythorne marks the onset of childhood (2–3), which he says "continueth from the infancy until fifteen" (11), of "adolescency, which is "the first part of the young man's age" (11), and of the second part of youth, or "juventute," which lasts "from the twenty-fifth until forty years of age" (66–67). As he nears thirty he says farewell to youth (117). At times Whythorne also cites the received wisdom "touching the ages of mankind." He is clearly familiar with the humoral theory that had been integrated into the period's metaphysics, and he tells the reader "what humours have most domination in every age," such as blood in adolescency (12) and both blood and choler in "juventute" (66–67).

But Whythorne names the seasons at only four points in the 293 printed pages of his manuscript, and he calls his seasonal lessons "digressions," as if he felt that they were interruptions in the narrative flow of experience.[30] If the space the seasons occupy in his text is any indication, they did not preoccupy his thoughts. Whythorne no doubt did see life as a progress of seasons and his emotions as bodily humors, blood and choler. Indeed, Whythorne is one of those people who seem to have been born old and organized. Even as a young man he kept his end in view, as if he were simultaneously an old man looking back on the present. He seldom forgets the all-seeing eye of eternity. But he saw much else as well: immediate earthly sensation and contradictory points of view, experiences, and interpretations.

Contradictions do not bother him. For much of his narrative Whythorne analyzes his life in terms closer to actual experience than to metaphysics, referring to a period of time as "my careless years" as well as "adolescency," for example, or marking the turning points in his narrative by the significance of particular events, or by his relationship to his writing, rather than by the season. Sometimes he simply gets lost in detail and forgets to categorize at all. He moves in and out of many different perspectives, depending on what is appropriate at the moment. G. K. Hunter cites early modern mariners who alluded to the medieval allegorical maps of the world but followed more recent detailed guides when they actually set sail.[31] Whythorne is similarly open to contradictory maps of life and ways of navigating experience.

At times he reinterprets or contradicts part of a "map." General truths about the seasons of a life and social expectations like courtly codes of masculinity are almost always learned indirectly and in different or even contradictory forms. Not everyone is subject to them in the same way or to the same degree. The important point is not the conventions or conventional beliefs but how Whythorne used them and what he did with them. At times, for example, Whythorne invokes a general truth only to point out that he is different. Adolescence is dominated by Venus, he says, but not in his case (12). He knows that choler is the ruling humor in the last part of youth, yet he introduces discussion of his anger much earlier, long before medical theory tells him to suffer it, because that's when it was important to him (27).

One of the most striking indications of the relatively minor role played in the text by seasonal categories is that Whythorne's remarks about them often seem like afterthoughts imposed on his story, in the same superficial way that his eccentric orthography was imposed on a prior copy of his manuscript in ordinary spelling. The seasonal grid translates and rationalizes his story rather than serving as the perceptual or interpretive lens through which he first experienced it. Sometimes Whythorne actually gets ahead of himself in the narrative, so that he has to backtrack to insert the seasonal markers in the appropriate places.

For example, his narrative about the period that Whythorne will eventually categorize as "adolescency," and mark as the age of "blood," is not introduced that way. It begins with details (10). First Whythorne tells how he finished his apprenticeship, "became mine own man," took a chamber in London. There, to his surprise, he realized that independence brought cares and responsibilities as well as freedom. To ease his mind, he marked the experience with a poem (10). Only afterward does Whythorne pause in his narrative to categorize his experience as "adolescency": "into the same age *was I not many years entered* when I wrote the said sonnet" (10–11, italics added).[32] The entrance into adolescence is unnoticed and unmarked. Then another page goes by before Whythorne pauses to define adolescence and "speak somewhat again of the foresaid age named adolescency" (12). Before getting there, though, he is eager to tell about his new dancing, fencing, and music lessons and about his new bachelor's apartment in London, decorated with portraits of himself playing the lute and of Terpsichore, muse of music.[33] Whythorne describes what he does and what he sees, and only afterward does he remember to categorize it.

Even when he does remember the traditional categories, Whythorne's self-consciousness about how far they apply to him often makes the commonplace uncommon. His unrelenting self-scrutiny is what makes his otherwise conventional manuscript so unusual. He observes himself in writing just as he has himself painted in oils. Whythorne arranged to have a total of four portraits of himself painted and a fifth engraved for the frontispiece to his book of songs, in order to observe and capture his image at different stages of life (see figs. 10 and 11).[34] One of his first acts after completing his apprenticeship and "becoming my own master" in 1549 was to

Fig. 10 Whythorne, painter unknown (1569). One of four portraits he commissioned.

commission a portrait reminding him that, however young he is now, age will inevitably overtake him. *Vanitas* portraits like this were common. They were meant as a reminder that even this important moment would pass into insignificance.[35]

Whythorne carried this doubled perspective to extremes. As soon as the portrait was complete, he wrote a poem about it, to be inscribed on the painting. Soon afterward, he wrote a second poem about having written the poem for the painting. Now, still processing the experience some twenty years later, he records the entire sequence in his manuscript. Finally he comments on his own narrative (11–12). All autobiography demands a double consciousness—the observing "I" of the present and the experiencing "me" of the past. But Whythorne's book is actually a record of triple consciousness. For him that past self is also an observing self, whom he now observes observing.

Whythorne observed and analyzed not as a disinterested scholar of human nature but because he needed to know. The world for him was full of dangers, inside aristocratic households in particular but also in encounters anywhere with anyone, even fellow servants. He wanted to know what people were thinking about him. A domestic Machiavelli, he was never satisfied with what people said out loud. He wanted to understand what

Sharing Secrets: Thomas Whythorne 113

Fig. 11 Whythorne, woodcut taken from the painting for inclusion in his book of musical compositions (1571); also used in his 1590 book of music (© The British Library Board. All Rights Reserved [K.4.c.3 back page]).

they meant, what they wanted, and therefore how he might be able to control them. He scrutinized the mundane give-and-take of daily life: "she said," "I said," "I thought," "she thought," and so on. If he were writing today Whythorne might qualify as a classic neurotic, a Jerry Seinfeld more than a Machiavelli:

> The which presumptions and tokens made me to think that she did bear me some good will; the which, if she did dissemble, I, to requite her, thought that to dissemble with a dissembler was no dissimulation, and to play with her as the hunter doth who hunteth a hare: as much to see her subtle skips and leaps as to get her carcase. But an if she meant good will indeed, then I was not willing to lose it, because of the commodities that might be gotten by such a one as she, either by marriage or otherwise. And therefore I...made this song somewhat dark and doubtful of sense. (30–31)

In this game of second-guessing, poetry is Whythorne's weapon as well as his means of communication.

His ruminations suggest the complex, if usually unverbalized, inner reality that can lie behind the period's apparently conventional verse, as well

114 *Chapter 5*

as behind its conventional schema like the seasons. Most of that unverbalized complexity has been lost. But Whythorne's text preserves enough of it in his narrative to suggest what we have been missing. Whythorne's poems create one impression of the man. A very different impression emerges from the manuscript's alternation between its short moral epigrams and the longer, more passionate prose that surrounds them. The poems coolly categorize Whythorne's passions as part of an impersonal system ("venereal," "choleric"), but the prose often describes them in the vivid imagery of gossip and popular anecdote. The conflicting modes of description carry conflicting feelings, and the alternation suggests Whythorne's attempt to resolve the conflict. He uses the commonplaces to subdue or contain unpleasant thoughts. As Kerrigan says of early autobiographies, his verse confirms the "working of a metaphysical order" in his life. But Whythorne writes verse precisely because he feels life's disorder. The effort it takes to contain disorder suggests that he is a man too much, rather than too little, interested in the "vagaries of inwardness."

Doing Battle with Venus and Mars

On the whole, Whythorne's self-consciousness increases his understanding of himself. He is a more accurate self-observer than Bale or Skelton, more wide ranging than Wyatt, more assiduous about detecting his own flaws than Baldwin. He knows how much he depends on rationality and truthfulness. He acknowledges his plain-speaking bluntness ("sharp but not too sharp"). He admits freely that he was not very religious when he was young and that even now it is pragmatism rather than morality that keeps him from illicit affairs with his female employers. Most of all, he is aware of how important it is for him to be in control. He loves being his own master, free of male overlord or female mistress and wife. He resents natural as well as human incursions on his freedom and is enraged when the ague ends his "careless days" as an independent tutor after his apprenticeship. He keeps control of his manuscript too, noticing departures from his narrative plan and, of course, controlling the spelling so that it follows his own orthography in his final draft.

Nonetheless, there are times when Whythorne seems less in control than he says he is, particularly in describing his experiences with Venus and venereal desire but also in his dealings with anger. He is well aware of his battles with these two passions. But his claims to have his passions under control—and captured in verse—are sometimes belied by the rest of his narrative, so that a gap between his interpretation and the reader's begins to widen when he talks about his courtships or his quarrels.

Whythorne's account of his love life offers two particularly good examples of the conflicting currents tamed by his epigrams and narrative structure. The first example took place in adolescence, when Whythorne began his relationship with women by renouncing them (12–13). The last occurred much later and brought him full circle. Having suffered several unsuccessful encounters with potential wives, one last failure in courtship makes Whythorne vow to "turn over a new leaf" and resume his original distance: he will once again "estrange myself from all loving occasions" (170). In both incidents, Whythorne's summarizing commonplaces give no indication of the intensity of his feelings. But his surrounding prose explanations rehearse events in ways that begin to suggest the psychological probings of Jacobean drama rather than a mid-Tudor text.

The first passage begins with his move to London and the section on adolescence already quoted (12–13). Here Whythorne starts out with generalizations that distance him from adolescent hot "blood," but he ends more passionately involved. At first he keeps his experience at a distance by referring playfully (or as playfully as Whythorne can) to classical mythology. Cupid and Venus, he says, are "very busie to trouble the quiet minds of young folk" in adolescence. But he himself has them under control: "I had been sometimes dribbled at with cupid's golden shafts," but "I did put them by and would not suffer them to pierce me." He rejected Venus and instead worshiped Pallas, Apollo, and Terpsichore. He wandered chastely in the imagined walks of Diana, and even there he was careful to avoid Actaeon's fate.

But then the references to Diana's mythical and symbolic "woods and groves" change confusingly into references to an actual gentleman's house in the country with real "woods and groves to walk in" (13). From there on, with almost no narrative transition, reality intrudes even more forcefully. Whythorne reports the commonplaces he has heard from gentlemen at Oxford and London who "blab" about real women (19). Women, they said, are willful, slippery, contradictory, and carnally voracious; they will find a way to cuckold you. Trying to find one to marry, he was told, is like being blindfolded and trying to catch an eel in a pot full of snakes; even if you don't come up with a snake that bites, you've got nothing to show for your effort but a slippery eel.

Whythorne himself is careful never to "blab," but here—as elsewhere—he seems fascinated by what careless men can reveal (usually about women) when they do. Having dwelt on the gossip for a while, however, Whythorne regains control of his narrative by writing his own poem "to put me in mind to beware of those whom I had heard such evil spoken of." The poem turns anecdote into epigram. It speaks of beauty and virtue in the abstract but never mentions either Whythorne's discomfort or the beautiful women who cause it (18). But the women have already taken up far more than their share of the "adolescence" chapter, and the reader is left with a colorful image of a pot of snakes and slippery eels to balance Whythorne's marble statue of Diana in her grove.

In fact, the poem brings Whythorne no more than a moment's peace. As soon as he finished, he says, something else "came to my remembrance"—as if it were a free association to a dream or an uninvited thirteenth fairy at a christening. What he remembers is a story about what happens when men—even men (like Whythorne) who vow not to marry bad women—succumb to beauty. It describes an unfortunate man who, through "flattery," was "once brought into a fool's paradise by a subtle shrew, who fetched him in finely, and handled him so cunningly that she made him to love her a good pace.... And when she perceived that she had him fast bound by the beak, she afterward requited his liberal and costly gifts bestowed upon her with amiable looks and pleasant fair words. In the which time, he thought that he had gotten God Almighty by the little finger: whereas indeed he had caught the Devil by the great toe" (18–19).

Whythorne's point in this anecdote is that the man foolishly fell for a "shrew"'s flattery, realizing too late that she was the "Devil." The man's greatest mistake, according to Whythorne, was to trust her and give her everything, even his most private secrets. Not only did he bestow his money ("his substance") on her, but he also imparted "unto her the very secrets that were hidden in his heart, not only of things pertaining to their affairs, but also of all his other trades, mysteries, attempts and intents." Once the shrew found out "the bottom of his chests and substance, and also of his heart, she played with him a sluttish touch and part, giving him the slip." Even worse, the man's complaint had no effect on her. There was nothing he could do; he was helpless. When he "blamed her a little for her inconstancy," that only made it worse. She became enraged and "blazoned abroad that which he had told her to keep in secret." Had the poor man committed felony or treason, Whythorne says, she would have exposed that along with everything else.

This story, supposedly just an afterthought, unsettles Whythorne again. To regain control he writes another poem (actually three poems!) to settle his thought (19–20). The poems provide a perfect example of how writing works for Whythorne to "ease my mind." None of the three gives any indication at all of the dangerous material that prompted them. Not a single one of the three poems mentions women, let alone beaks or bodies or violent connections between the two.[36] The unsettling shrew anecdote that has been successfully banished from Whythorne's poems, however, dominates the rest of his narrative. Throughout the remaining pages Whythorne will either play out this man's story in each new household he enters or will fear that he is playing it out: a woman seduces (or tries to seduce) him; she takes his valuables—just as his mistress had moved his private chest closer to her bedroom—and then reveals his secrets.[37] So invested is he in the story that sometimes Whythorne, like the queen's spymaster, Richard Topcliffe, seems to half-create the opposition he fears, as when he second-guesses the employer who has as yet done nothing to deserve suspicion. At other times he sees danger when a reader sees none, for example when he keeps insisting that his neighbor Elisabeth, the head housekeeper, is only teasing when she calls him husband, or when he believes that she is trying to trap him when she falls "ill" after he refuses to see her. Always wary of women's duplicity, Whythorne remains unaware of his own biased expectations and defensive maneuvers, and he distances himself from them with platitudes.[38]

In the last of his courtships, the earlier anecdotal image of a woman as a container for poisonous vermin also reappears (166–67), this time a toad rather than eels. In this case Whythorne does not even try to write a summarizing poem to calm himself at the end. All we have is an unusually long (again!) narrative in language that reveals Venus's power, even as Whythorne claims to get it under control (150–81). Whythorne is courting a rich widow, and in a reversal that he seems not to notice, she has her own chest of gold that he wants to secure by his proposal. However, although she accepts his courtship and courtship gifts, the widow keeps postponing the wedding, and Whythorne wonders whether she is just trying to see how much she could get from him. Finally, he ends the relationship. He says nothing about how its termination made him feel, and he comments only that it was all for the best. But once again his cheerfully dismissive summary immediately brings something else to "remembrance."

What he remembers this time is "a pretty jest" that he offers as an allegorical lesson about why, after all, it is not a good idea to get married (165–67). The jest is about "a Jersey priest" who set snares "to catch wild fowl in the night." At first the priest was in control. The birds scratched him as he groped for his prey in the dark, but he took care of that by nipping off their heads with his teeth. Then, without realizing, he grabbed a toad, and it "offended" him by scratching even more than the others. Thinking to triumph over it, the priest "put the toad's head into his mouth, and did bite it as he did the other birds." But toads are poisonous, and so the offensive toad triumphed over the priest after all. From this story, Whythorne says smugly, you may see whether "many a one being blinded by blind Cupid, do not choose a toad among other fowls," which "by their poisoned conditions will infest and poison their husbands that way every day more, than the priest was poisoned" (166–67). Only stupid men like the priest hunt for wives, and they are punished by catching poisonous toads. Whythorne is glad he did not get a chance to bite the widow's head off—he might have gotten poisoned.[39]

For Whythorne, trying to find a wife is like trying to grab an eel from a pot of poisonous vipers or a bird from a game bag of fowl: you are likely to get bitten by a snake or poisoned by a toad, and if not, you still can't be sure of getting anything worth the danger ("yet he had but a slippery eel peradventure by the tail" [14]). Worse still, women themselves go fishing for men—they "fetch" men in and "handle" them—so that a man finds himself, willy-nilly, reaching out and catching "the Devil by the great toe." He may exult at first, but the truth is that she has *him* "by the beak." Once she gets a grip, she reaches into "the bottom of" *his* "chests and substance and also...his heart," as if to extract her pound of flesh, or semen, and empty him out (18–19). You must be always on guard. If you let go, women will literally take everything you have and everything you are, even your most secret physical and mental inner resources. Whythorne's emphasis in these anecdotes suggests a primitive vision of women and sex that would scare anyone into guarding his secrets and shoring up his resolve with platitudes.

To some degree the fear of women implied in all these passages might be seen less as a revelation about Whythorne than as rational caution, at least in cases where women's superior social status gave them real power over him. Involvement with a shrewish, "blabbing" woman without scruples might indeed endanger a man's wealth and reputation. If he were treasonous, it might even get him hanged. Insofar as Whythorne's fear is not rational, it is hardly unique. It reveals something about his world, in which women's lack of real political power belied their unacknowledged psychological power over men's sense of themselves and their self-worth. Women were proverbially deceptive and dangerous—the more attractive, the more dangerous. This common wisdom underlies the imagery of the hunt in Wyatt's verse, the cuckold humor in Shakespeare's plays, and the crude jokes and doggerel collected in young men's diaries and commonplace books.[40]

But Whythorne's particular version of the commonplace is revealing. He exaggerates, for example, the dangers of courtship in Wyatt's "They fle from me." For Wyatt the reversal of hunter and hunted is dreamily seductive rather than disgusting and physically dangerous. Robert Greene's warnings against "effeminate follies" repeat a similar warning about female tooth and claw, but in his case they trip off the tongue almost meaninglessly, lost in the narrative they decorate.[41] By contrast, Whythorne's prose gives them more structural weight. The stories about women are often longer and more vivid than surrounding accounts. Still more important, Whythorne presents these encounters as turning points, battles that mark both his entry into the world of courtship as a young man (12–20) and his withdrawal from it later (150–81).

Like his dealings with Venus, Whythorne's struggles with anger surface throughout his narrative but are not always reflected in his poems. As with misogyny, a male tendency to anger has been taken to characterize the period; but Whythorne's particular experience of it shows in detail exactly what part anger played in the way this young man saw himself, about where it came from, and about what effects it had. In addition, it suggests an unacknowledged dynamic relation among love, misogyny, and anger that complicates both sixteenth-century platitudes and scholarly generalization.

As he does with Venus, Whythorne talks about his battle with anger both early and later in his life. More explicitly than Venus, anger effects two important turning points in his narrative. Furious passion ushers Whythorne into service early in life, and another bout of anger sees him out of it many years later. Whether anger "really" caused the changes that Whythorne describes is something we cannot know. What matters is that, in reviewing his life, Whythorne attributes the change to his own feelings and active responses, at least as much as to passive endurance of Fortune or to the inevitable seasons and what they inevitably bring. His life story is driven as much by feeling and experience as by the application of general principles to them.

Anger is first mentioned in Whythorne's manuscript in the section on adolescence, after an illness that doomed him to many years as a live-in servant. During adolescence, despite Whythorne's more prominent encounter with Venus, his "carefree years," he says, were actually cut short "by another mean, and not by love." The mean was a recurring attack of ague that lasted over a year and depleted both Whythorne's health and his savings. The illness reduced him to seeking a job he hated as a private tutor in other people's houses. It also left him in an angry fury that he could barely control. The "cruel tyrant Sir John Ague," he says, keeps him in prison. Whythorne, who not so long before had exulted at "becoming mine own master," now realizes that he will have to serve other masters after all. He is caught, as the man in his anecdote had been caught by his shrew. Chafing against Fortune but helpless and too "timorous" even to show his anger, Whythorne can do nothing more effective than to write a poem about it (26). ("Though fortune frown on me always, / Turning my joy to pensiveness, / Yet still do I still hope for the day / That all my woe shall have redress," and so on [27]).

The poem's epigrammatic wisdom, however, conveys hardly anything of what Whythorne felt; it does not even mention the word *anger*. But Whythorne's prose explanation reintroduces the passion banished from the verse and gives individual immediacy to an abstraction like "choler": "In those days I would wreak mine anger altogether with pen and ink on paper.... (Much like as for example, a young shrewish maiden would do, who, when she was much angered, would straightways go into a cellar that her father had, and there would she with her teeth bite upon a post a long time, til she had digested the rage of her choleric humor.) And so, likewise did I" (27).

Like a powerless girl (or, as Whythorne calls her, "shrewish maiden") Whythorne has to push his unexpressed anger underground (as she is sent to her father's "cellar"). His astonishing image captures the experience of "gnawing rage" better than any of his poems. Like Whythorne's hunting images for courtship, this one also suggests why Whythorne tried so hard to control his anger. As he presents it, anger has teeth that can gnaw through wood. Francis Bacon would later say that the torment of keeping secrets is turned inward, like a kind of cannibalism.[42] But the seemingly helpless "maiden" Whythorne has in mind could cannibalize someone else if she let her anger loose. Eventually he "digests" his rage and accepts his fate, although Whythorne's perennial touchiness about his position might well have had something to do with the remnants of his anger.

Thus Whythorne's carefree days ended, and his career of service began in repressed rage. Many years later, his decision to leave service was similarly marked by a bout of barely controlled anger. That episode began when Whythorne was provoked by his master's argumentative houseguest, who made his provocative opinions known. At first Whythorne restrained himself in conversation with the man. He "said not one word unto him except it were once"; but that was all the visitor needed. Suddenly the man "bent all his ordinance at me, shouting at me, thundering shot with vehement words; whereat I, poor soul, was fain to retire for a time. But ... then I began to shoot at him as fast as he shot at me, so that we were like to have a hot skirmish, but that our betters were in place, who took on them to be moderators" (137). Despite the fact that Whythorne is only a servant, he fights with the visitor as an equal, and he describes his rage this time in martial rather than cannibalistic imagery. But he knows that he had been wrong to breach social boundaries in creating the disturbance, and he has to admit defeat. This time, however, Whythorne learns from the experience. Anger leads him, on analysis, to a rational solution. In fact, it changes his life. He sees that "the meaner sort (in comparison of their estates) were driven to put up quietly some injuries at their hands." Under such conditions, he would never find in service the life he had hoped for. He realizes that, after all, "I should not keep company with my greaters."

As usual, Whythorne closes this account of the battle with a poem. But as usual, it describes only the empty battlefield after the war, omitting the thundering shot and vehement words. The little sonnet he made does not mention anger at all: like the standard terminology of "Venus" or "choler," its words erase the lived experience of his passion and record only the general lesson about metaphysical order that Whythorne knows he should learn from it:

I have not only read, but eke by proof have tried,
How such who daily haunt their greaters' company

> Cannot shun great offence, on th'one or t'other side:
> Wherefor happy are they, who such an evil can fly.
> (138)

However, Whythorne soon describes something more like the "vagaries of inwardness" when he reports the self-examination that followed his momentous battle. The episode, he says, "caused me to call to my remembrance the whole discourse of all my former life" and all the "illusions of flattering and fickle fortune" (138–39). He alludes here to something he had not said openly before in his narrative: he had always expected to be able to "haunt [his] greaters' company" as an equal. Now he realizes that his expectation was just one of the many "illusions of flattering and fickle fortune" that he had suffered.

Whythorne's recourse at this point to blaming "fortune" for the quarrel and the "flattering illusions" is important, because it echoes his response to the earlier angry outburst in adolescence. It also suggests a link, one that Whythorne never addresses, between his anger and his attitude toward women. In adolescence, although it was "Mr. John Ague" who imprisoned him, Whythorne's rage was directed not at Mr. Ague but rather at "Dame Fortune, because she would not raise me from the bottom of her wheel and help me" (27). It is the female fortune who can help him and raise him and who is the target for his anger when he is helpless. So too it was the flattering shrew who undid the man in Whythorne's anecdote and her future avatars who make Whythorne's own life uncertain and miserable, whether they are his employers on the estate, or fellow servants, or visiting young women.

What is most interesting about this pattern is that Whythorne never says that he is angry at the women who hurt him, and at times he explicitly denies it—although he calls himself a choleric man and he does battle with other men. Among women, it is only Fortune whom he rails at. Although Whythorne describes several dangerous, predatory women who catch a man by the beak and take his heart, he never says anything about wanting to prey on them or even being angry at them. Similarly, the man in Whythorne's emblematic anecdote about the shrew may have been guilty of "felony or treason" (that the shrew will expose) but never of wreaking his anger on a woman. In Whythorne's manuscript, the only male aggression against women is contained inside other men's "blabbing" gossip—the sort of loose talk that Whythorne says he won't allow

Sharing Secrets: Thomas Whythorne 123

himself. For those men, getting married is like a savage hunt; if a woman, like a toad, bites back, they bite her head off.

Whythorne's carefully separate treatment of his venereal impulses and his choler isolates them safely from one another. He recognizes each but never their relationship. He hears gossip about men who get angry at women and bite their heads off. He doesn't do that. Whythorne's rhetorical tactics suggests that he gets angry too, but instead of feeling it, he projects his anger onto the women and winds up being afraid that women will clean him out and eat him up instead.

At one point, however, Whythorne does condense this aggressive dynamic between men and women into a single androgynous image of himself. When the ague undid all Whythorne's plans for a life being his own master, he did nothing about his fury at Dame Fortune. Instead he identified with—imagines himself as—another destructive female, the shrewish angry maiden eating her way through a wooden post. He is angry but doesn't act; she, only an alter ego, acts. Through her, he can be as harmless as a young maiden, even if she is a "shrewish maiden" who bites wooden posts.

Whythorne's example shows that it is worth looking in seemingly reticent texts like his for traces of "secret meanings," even when at first it seems there are none. No one reading Whythorne's verse apart from his manuscript could infer the depth of passion and conflict that his conventional epigrams manage to contain. Who could guess that for him writing poetry could be "much like" a shrewish maiden chewing on a post? Or that Whythorne, invoking that image, could describe poetry writing by saying, "I did wreake my anger with pen and ink on paper" (27)? Fortunately Whythorne not only wrote in conventionally generalized formats but also wrote around them. He includes not only his poems but also their "secret meaning." Whether wholly or partially by intent, he regularly manages to convey some of what experience felt like as well as what it was called, or how it was commonly categorized and explained. More important here, although his verse does not always record this, he thought about his experience and what it meant. An angry quarrel with a visitor makes him think, and the result, though it leads to conventional moralizing, also brings a larger self-consciousness: it "caused me to call to my remembrance the whole discourse of all my former life" (138)—perhaps helping to produce the manuscript we have.

Equally important in considering the development of autobiographical writing, Whythorne's self-consciousness itself may never have led to the manuscript were it not for Whythorne's good friend, real or imagined, who was there to read and receive what it produced. Whythorne's self-consciousness had produced poetry before, but not for a public. Often a poem was a site for storing his anger or other secrets without showing them to anyone, just as his private rooms in London were a retreat to which he withdrew from the houses where he worked. But although he did not publish his poetry or his secrets for everyone to see, he wanted to exchange them with one particular friend. The following chapters discuss other writers whose private exchanges with friends did lead to wider publication and seem to have been an important factor in publication.

CHAPTER 6

Adding an "Author's Life"
Thomas Tusser's Revisions of A Hundreth Good Points of Husbandry *(1557–73)*

> Wherein he doth discourse of his owne bringing up, and of the goodness of the saide Lorde his Master unto him, and the occasion of this his booke.
> THOMAS TUSSER, *Five Hundreth Good Points of Husbandry* (1573)

Thomas Tusser's metrical guide *A Hundreth Good Points of Husbandry* (1557) was so popular and so often reprinted that by 1585 it was parodied in (the lost) *Five Hundred Points of Evil Husbandry*, and it was reissued into the eighteenth century.[1] The wide appeal of books like Tusser's was due in part to the range of miscellaneous material they included, but in the much-expanded 1573 *Five Hundreth Good Points of Husbandry* Tusser added something no husbandry manual had included before: a final thirty-eight-stanza autobiographical poem, "Th'author's Life."[2]

Tusser's little poem, tucked away in the back of his farming manual, is unique among extant autobiographies in that the manual's multiple editions suggest traces of Tusser's composition process. The "Life" is best understood in the context of the entire 1573 husbandry book, which is itself only the final stage of a process that began at least sixteen years earlier. Even more than Whythorne's contemporaneous "songs and sonnets," Tusser's "Life" resembles an archaeological site more than a new built-from-scratch construction, with its origins in the 1557 *A Hundreth Good Points of Husbandry*.

Tusser, if read at all, has usually been studied for reasons other than his autobiographical significance. He has always been admired as a poet of homely commonplaces; an Amazon.com search reveals that he is still included in recent verse collections.[3] Among academics, however, his text has been treated more often as an example of social or economic trends. Andrew Macrae, for example, considers Tusser an example of the new economic individualism among middling tenant farmers during the sixteenth century. Tusser's ideal, Macrae argues, was "a steady, slightly secretive rise through the social order." Macrae traces a change in individualism he sees demonstrated by the successive editions; he explains Tusser's addition of the "Life" in 1573 as a marketing technique to attract more readers from the growing ranks of tenants by playing down his gentry status.[4] Elizabeth Heale recognizes the "Life" as autobiography but assimilates it to a loose category of other midcentury verse "narratives of experience."[5]

Certainly Tusser's book, like Whythorne's, cannot be understood apart from broader economic and political conditions or literary trends. Whythorne and Tusser were in service to men close to court, and the careers of both were disrupted when Mary Tudor succeeded Edward VI to the throne. Both men were deeply affected by the period's inescapable social hierarchy and the new possibilities—and dangers—of moving through it; both felt the painful contradiction between their status as gentlemen and their need to earn their living. But even more than Whythorne, Tusser was affected as well by more local upheavals that made his experience distinct. More than the long-term development of economic individualism in England, Tusser's individual economic ups and downs left their mark on the book. One constant throughout all the editions, even before Tusser added his "Life," was the husbandry book's connection to his own farming experience. Similarly, Tusser and Whythorne were affected by their immediate society, coworkers and friends, and by the particular path each took as he moved from country to city, from private service to independence, and from one manor or country estate to another. In particular, each depended on ties to friends or patrons who read what they wrote and cared what they said.

The following pages discuss both Tusser's own history and that of the book. They begin with his biography and the importance in it of Tusser's patron, William Paget. They then turn to the book's roots in Tusser's unusual stance between elite and popular traditions and between his two lives as musician and farmer, moving finally to the "Life" itself.

Thomas Tusser

In many ways Tusser resembles others who wrote about themselves. What makes him unusual is his connection to the land. He revised and expanded his 1573 *Husbandry* while resident in London, and he shared the problems of the generation of urban writers that included Thomas Whythorne, Isabella Whitney, and George Gascoigne. But he had permanent roots in the country, and he wrote from a deep sense of geographic place. He was born about 1524 in Rivenhall Essex, a county that John Norden called "Englande's Goshen, the fattest of land," for it contained some of the country's richest farming territory.[6] The great house on whose lands he lived was still standing in the nineteenth century.[7] Tusser identified with his county and the characteristics of its weather and soil. He spoke affectionately of the round of the agricultural calendar's occupations and holidays, noting in his first edition, "Old customes that good be, let no man despise" (st. 42). Throughout his peripatetic career he took care to mention, for each farm he worked, its location and what the location meant. His discussion of "champion versus several" in 1570, though probably responding to the recent popular uprising, is based on a comparison between his beloved Essex (whose fields had been enclosed early and peaceably) and the less happy division of land into "severals" that he had known elsewhere.[8]

Connections to the land may explain why Tusser had a love of "things to plough behoving," as he later said to Thomas Paget, looking back ruefully on his many agricultural failures ("To the right honourable ... Lord Paget" [1573, fol. 2r]). It was only with reluctance at the end both of his "Life" and his lifetime ("death drawing near" [st. 38]) that Tusser relinquished his yearning. The "Life" includes his reluctant and long-postponed acknowledgment that despite his family's status, he could neither expect to be given land nor to thrive by land acquired some other way.

Throughout, Tusser was tied as closely to his family as to their land, and his affection is apparent in the "Life," the primary source for the little we know about him. The Tusser family was recorded by the heralds, and Tusser was connected on his mother's side to Edward Seymour, later Protector Somerset, who may be the unnamed "friend" and benefactor who occasionally intervened to save him from desperate situations.[9] Tusser calls himself "gentleman" on his title page, and the third stanza of his "Life" notes that he was born "of linnage good, of gentle blood." But he always refers to his immediate family rather than citing their court connections. Later in the "Life" Tusser notes the deaths of both parents with sadness. In his poem about life's inevitable suffering, his heartfelt example is the need to move far from friends and acquaintances ("An habitacion enforced" [fol. 12v]). Despite his continued wandering, Tusser's farms, for whatever reason, were never far from his native country, and his last farm at Fairstead was very close to his birthplace.

The contrast between Tusser's and Whythorne's attitude toward their origins is telling. Whythorne notes only in passing that he was born in Somersetshire. Otherwise he hardly mentions his parents or the house where he was born, and when he speaks of his family it is abstractly— through the distant German origin of his ancestors and the symbolic meaning of the name it gave him. He passes over his first ten years with his parents, dwells a bit on his uncle who raised him and provided for his Oxford education, and mentions his mother only once, during his last courtship when he promises his potential bride a good living after his mother dies. But Tusser speaks affectionately of his early life and provides an unusual glimpse into family dynamics when he describes his mother's sadness when he was sent as a child, against his will, to music school and "no speech of tonge, / nor teares withal, / that often fall / From mother's eies, when childe outcries, to part hir fro: / Could pitie make, good father take, / But out I must, to song be thrust" ("Life," st. 4).

Nonetheless Tusser's education, painful as it was, became as central to him as to the other writers. Like Whythorne's, his experience shows what training and the right connections could do for an ambitious young man with musical talent. They helped him into the world of universities, the court, and a promising future. Tusser's father no doubt understood the opportunity such training offered when he insisted that the boy remain in the Wallingford Castle choir despite the hard work and mistreatment he suffered there. From then on "friends"—probably the Somerset connection—helped Tusser, first to St. Paul's school, then to Eton, and in 1543 on to Cambridge. It was probably the same friends who secured for him the position as music master with William, Lord Paget, Somerset's loyal follower.

Tusser's experience as a musician, like Whythorne's, almost certainly included experience writing lyrics to accompany music. He was taught by Nicholas Udall at Eton and John Redford at St. Paul's, both literary men as well as musicians. Paget's household was itself a center of culture in the

1540s during Tusser's years of service.[10] As Paget's servant, Tusser also became part of the court of King Edward VI, a vital center of intellectual activity during Somerset's protectorate. William Baldwin prepared court revels during Tusser's years at court. Thomas Sternhold was Edward's music teacher at the time, working on his metrical translation of the psalms into the easily memorized stanzaic form like the one that Tusser later used for his book of husbandry. Tusser remained at court for ten happy years that gave him as useful a literary background as that of almost any more courtly or urban writer treated here.

Then he left. It is not certain why or when. In his dedications to the Pagets Tusser cites his "yearning to farm" as the reason. But in his 1573 "Life" he implies that he was responding to the same political upheaval that affected Baldwin, Bale, and Whythorne: "When court gan frowne and strife in town, / And lordes and knights, sawe heavy fights, / Then tooke I wife, and led my life in Suffolke soile" (st. 28).[11] The marginal explanatory note, added in 1580, elaborated: "the nobilitie at variance in Edward the sixt daies." Sir William suffered in the collision between Somerset and Norfolk during King Edward's last days. Fined and even imprisoned, he may no longer have seemed a reliable patron for Tusser; or the gentle Tusser may really have been avoiding strife, as he says. He would do so again more than once.

Whatever brought it on, Tusser's departure from court initiated a series of wanderings and bad luck that were early associated with his work:

They tell me, Tusser, when thou wert alive,
And had for profit turned every stone,
Where'er thou camest, thou couldst never thrive,
Though here, best couldst counsel every one.[12]

Other writers found similar hardships in the country. George Whetstone tried and failed to make a living from the land. George Gascoigne reports that "when court had cast me off, I toyled at the plow," but he found "rente and all were falne in such disease, / As scarse could serve to mayneteyne cleanlynesse," and he turned elsewhere.[13] Tusser lasted sixteen years, but at last he too left husbandry altogether. Like his fellow musician Whythorne, he returned from his version of the trenches to the rarefied realm of pure music. "Since hap haps so, let toiling go.... Let Musickke win, let stocke come in" (st. 32).

What is striking in this unhappy record is the importance that writing had for Tusser throughout his career. Not every failed farmer publishes books or alludes to himself as a writer in doing so. But Tusser carried his identity as a writer from court to country and back at the end to Cambridge. His first book was written while he was working his first land in Catewald. He was still writing when he left his last farm and returned to London sixteen years later.

The Pagets

If one constant in Tusser's husbandry book is its connection to his own experience, an important part of that experience was his service to William, Lord Paget, and his lifelong connection to Paget's family. Tusser's relation to the elder Paget sounds closer and more satisfactory than any that Whythorne managed to establish. Of course, Paget was a source of funding, and economic necessity was probably the immediate catalyst for one of Tusser's new editions. Yet the informal and affectionate dedications, shaped like conversations with Paget, suggest that Tusser also looked to his patron for other kinds of support. Each new edition began with his apologia in the dedication to Paget for his way of life which was also a self-examination—a duality also present when Thomas Wyatt articulated his own philosophy by addressing his friend John Poynz and when Thomas Whythorne look backed over his life once he had written it down for his friend.

From what Tusser says in later marginal commentary to his "Life," the husbandry book most likely originated as an appeal to Paget for both financial and moral support. It was begun in Catewald on Tusser's first farm and was published just four years after he had left court. His wife's illness had by then forced the couple to leave farming for Ipswich, to "lie" awhile with friends. Tusser had not only begun to discover the hardships in his new life but also, in Ipswich away from the farm, he had more time for writing: "When wife could not, through sicknes got, / More toile abide, so nigh Sea side, / Then thought I best, from toile to rest, and Ipswich trie." If Tusser did need help, 1557 would certainly have been a good time to turn to Paget, who, after the change of reign, came back to favor at Mary's court and was at the height of his career.

The five-stanza dedication to Paget in this original 1557 husbandry book already contains the seed of Tusser's 1573 "Life." Written by a husband who has hardly shaken the court dust from his feet, it speaks nostalgically about his personal tie to Paget and to the life as a musician that he left behind when he left Paget's service. Offering his book, Tusser thanks Paget for his past help ("My serving you, thus understande, / And god his helpe, and yours withal: / Did cause good lucke, to take myne hande, / Erecting one, most lyke to fall" [fol. 3r]). Then he gives a brief survey of his life. His tone is rueful but resilient, as if to say, "It has been hard, but I have survived and I have made this book":

> Of court ten yeres, I made a say,
> No musicke then, was left unsought,
> A care I had, to serve that way,
> My joye gan slake, then made I chaunge,
> Expulsed myrth, for musicke straunge.
>   (fol. 3r)

Poignantly, at the end he describes his new career by using musical terminology that is no longer appropriate to it. The stanza momentarily becomes a reverse pastoral, as the ploughman pretends to be a courtier:

> My musicke synce, hath been the plough,
> Entangled with some care among:
> The gayne not great, the payne enough,
> Hath made me syng, another song.
> And if I may, my song avowe;
> No man I crave, to judge but you.
>   (fol. 3r)

Despite his country isolation, Tusser's continuing connection to Paget and to a writing life in his service is visible even in the layout of the page, with its three-part "signature" that appears above, below, and running vertically alongside the verse dedication. Master, servant, and author are linked around the poem that holds them together. The title above identifies Paget: "Lorde William Paget"; the signature below identifies "Your servant, Thomas Tusser"; and a vertical column to the left says "Thomas Tusser made me." Tusser's courtly connection is evoked as well in the cleverness of making his one hundred "poyntes" equal his one hundred verse paragraphs and in the elegant artifice of the final poem, in which every word begins with a *T*.

Later editions show the Pagets' continuing importance. By 1570 Paget had been dead for seven years, however, and although the dedication is reprinted in this edition, it is buried behind other introductory material. The book is addressed instead to the general public, and it sounds desperate for buyers. It begins with a new preface designed to catch the eye of a browser: "What look'st thou here to have?" it asks. This sounds more like an off-the-rack, all-purpose introduction by Tottel than like something by Tusser himself. It is not signed "By me, Thomas Tusser," as the opening verse was in 1557. It certainly aims at a practical audience with no time for literature, because its opening question is followed by three stanzas assuring the reader that here he will find no "trim verses" like "Surry's," no "grave sentences" like Chaucer's, no "rhetorike fine" of "makers of Englishe." Instead, "Looke nothing but rudenesse in these." No fine rhetoric but plain "good lessons for thee and thy wife," and "Things nedefull in tyme for to come." In the attempt to reach as wide an audience as possible, not only is literature slighted but "husbandrie" is not mentioned at all; the poem promises only "good lessons." It is odd that Tusser would have denied both his literary and country roots in this way, no matter how eager he was to sell.

Even if he did deny them in 1570, though, he changed his mind before the next edition three years later. In the expanded and near-final edition of 1573, Tusser restores the Pagets to pride of place at the beginning of the book, so that once again Tusser's advice is preceded by an account of his life for the Pagets. Tusser is still interested in selling books to a wider audience. But the crude huckstering preface of 1570 has been toned down and moved further back, and its disparaging references to "rhetoricke fine" are gone. There are now two separate dedications, a new one to the current Lord Thomas Paget as well as a reprint of the original to Thomas's father, Sir William.

These 1573 dedications evoke the same three aspects of life that had been most important to Tusser in the past: his service to the Pagets, his husbandry adventure, and his writing, symbolized by the book he offers as a gift. Both old and new dedications take roughly the same form. In the new one, Tusser addresses himself to Paget's son, "The right honorable & my speciall good Lord & Master, the Lord [Thomas] Paget of Beudefort" (fol. 1r). Like his first dedication to elder Paget, this one is modeled partly on a debate between court and country, between life with the Pagets and husbandry life. Tusser recalls his years at court with gratitude and happy memories of his service; then he takes the measure of what he has accomplished in the country since leaving. In a new revelation, Tusser adds that Paget had advised him against leaving court—advice he should have taken but didn't: "His counsel had I used, / and Ceres art refused, / I need not thus have mused, / nor droope as now I do." But he was stubborn: "But I must play the farmer, / & yet no whit the warmer, / although I had his armer [as his servant, wore Paget's livery], / and other comfort to" (fol. 1r). His love "of things to plough behoving," he says, blinded him. He adds excuses for the failures that followed: his ignorance, overreaching, and carelessness; his bad choice of servants (who "my gold away consumed"). Finally, "Great fines, so nere did pare me, / great rent, so much did skare me, / great charge, so long did dare me," that at last he gave up.

Certainly one reason for Tusser's pointed 1573 description of his failure after ignoring old Paget's advice is that he needed young Paget's support in order to return to the land. The appeal is quite explicit: "Yet will I not dispaire, / through Gods good gift so faire, / through friendship, golde & praier / in Countrey againe to dwell." He needs both God's gift and his friend's (fol. 2r). But both his account and its tone suggest that Tusser wanted friendship along with the "golde" that it might bring.

Tusser's pride in his new identity as a writer is also made clear, as if he wants Paget's recognition for that too. As in 1557, but with even more emphasis, Tusser counters the disappointments of husbandry with his writing achievement. Lest anyone think that he brought nothing away from his husbandry failures, he says, he offers the new husbandry book made out of them. If Paget will support him in a new husbandry endeavor, he promises that his repayment will be another book: the "gaine shall help maintain me, new lessons mo to tell" (fol. 2v). Whatever the future, however, as a proud author, Tusser insists that his book has always derived from his own experience, "and not by heare say, or reeding, / as some abrode have blowne" (fol. 2r). Writing is fused with husbandry, just as it had been in the 1557 dedication to Paget, where Tusser described husbandry in terms of the music he had just left behind at court: "My music synce, hath been the plough," and his husbandry book was a "song." Now he describes his new London book in terms of the husbandry he leaves behind in the country. The book is no longer a song but a "tree":

I have no labor wanted
To prune this tree I planted,

Whose fruit to none is scanted
>In house nor yet in fyeld:
Which fruite to saye (who haste of)
Though nere so much they taste of,
Yet can they make no wastye of,
>Such fruit this tree doth yield.
>>(fol. 2r)

Tusser's verse suggests how close the two forms of labor, planting and writing, were for him, particularly when reviewing his life for the Pagets. The association between the two can be seen in Tusser's new title for his reprint of the 1557 dedication. It neatly condenses all his interests—autobiography, authorship, husbandry experience, and grateful service to the Pagets: "The authors epistle to the late Lord William Paget, wherein he doth discourse of his owne bringing up, and of the goodnes of the saide Lorde his Master unto him, and the occasion of this his booke, thus set forthe of his owne long practice" (fol. 3r).

Husbandry Book?

Tusser's book draws on a variety of literary genres besides husbandry guides. His education, like Whetstone's and Gascoigne's, had familiarized him with classical literature, and the title of his book places it in the tradition of georgic writers from Xenophon to Cato, Varro, and Columella, who had praised honest labor as a moral and social good.[14] From the time of his contemporaries like Barnabe Googe (1577) through Henry Best (1641) and Walter Bligh (1649) in the following century to today's critics like Anthony Low and Andrew Macrae, Tusser has been treated as an agricultural writer like his only English predecessor, John Fitzherbert, author of *The Boke of Husbandry* (1523).[15]

Agricultural historians, however, have rightly emphasized the distance between Tusser's book of folk maxims and more professional treatises like Fitzherbert's.[16] Fitzherbert's family owned three large farms, and his *Husbandry* provided advice as technical as that in the book of legal advice about surveying that was bound with it. Fitzherbert addressed his book to educated gentlemen, and he elaborated philosophically on William Caxton's *Game of Chess* in the preface to his book. Although he wrote about yeomen, he wrote *for* land-owning aristocrats like himself, in whose library lists his book is found.[17] The landlord was expected to read aloud the relevant parts of the book to his illiterate tenants.[18]

Even a glance at Tusser shows why his book is not found in libraries of the wealthy noblemen for whom Fitzherbert wrote. Tusser carefully distinguished between such gentlemen and the husbandman he addressed:

> When gentiles use walking, with hawkes on their handes
> Good husbands, with grasing doe purchase their landes.[19]
>   (16v)

It is not clear whether "purchase" means literally to "buy" or simply to "secure" or "make full profit from," but the distinction between "gentiles" and husband needs no explanation.

Additionally, unlike Fitzherbert's, Tusser's book addressed both men and women. Fitzherbert described the ".x [10] properties of a woman" for his reader, inserting them between a paragraph on the properties of an ass and one on the diseases of horses.[20] He writes more about wives than for them, although later he does address several paragraphs to them. Tusser, however, spoke to women more directly, assuming a more equal working partnership, in "A Digression from husbandrie" (inserted after st. 72). Starting with the 1570 edition and possibly earlier, a handsome couple, each spouse with a child, stand on opposite sides of the title page frame (see fig. 12). This domestic group replaces the more usual architectural frame (like Fitzherbert's) or *Mirror*'s monumental arch upheld by personified abstractions on either side of its title page.

Fitzherbert opened his book with instructions for making a plow; Tusser began his with praise of domestic harmony and its rewards:

> Where couples agree not, is rancor and poysen.
> ...But contrary lightly, where couples agree,
> What chaunceth by wisdom, looke after to see.

Tusser's opening lines about couples voice the popular wisdom he is primarily known for; such advice plays a smaller role in Fitzherbert's book. Tusser's concerns ally him less with the classical husbandry tradition than with English domestic advice books. His verse about couples agreeing might have been taken almost directly from Richard Whitford's popular *Werke for Housholders* (1531), a mix like Tusser's of religious and house-

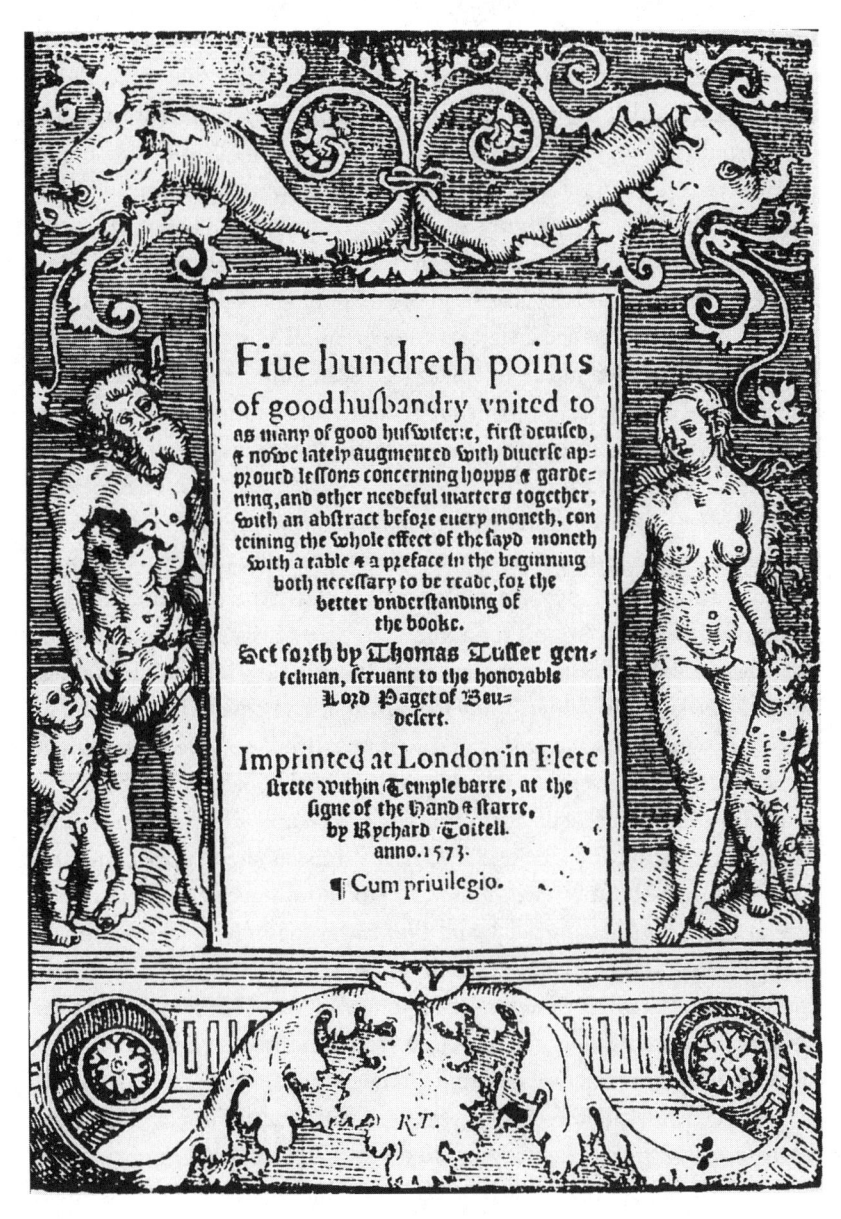

Fig. 12 Tusser, *Fiue hundredth points of good husbandry* (1573), title page (this item is reproduced by permission of The Huntington Library, San Marino, California [RB 69672]). Image published with permission of ProQuest. Further reproduction is prohibited without permission.

hold lessons. Whitford's final section, written "in the style of the proverbs of Solomon," opens with the instruction to "see first that peace be in your house," and it includes many lessons that readers of Tusser would recognize.[21]

Tusser's roots extend also to the extremely popular almanacs and calendars whose monthly progression identified the year's cosmic and agricultural as well as local events important in the ordinary husband's life. Fitzherbert's prose treatise had been organized logically, by topic. Tusser's easy-to-memorize metrical stanzas were organized pragmatically, like almanacs, month by month. Almanacs had been guiding rural lives for decades before any appeared in print; they derived from still earlier notations once notched into sticks for illiterate plowmen and shepherds. If gentlemen included Fitzherbert in their libraries, ordinary readers were more likely to turn to the popular English *Kalendar of Shepherds*, translated early in the sixteenth century from the French, one of the popular songs and books that Robert Laneham listed as part of "Captain Cox's library."[22] The *Kalendar* was soon known even to Londoners like Thomas Whythorne. It incorporated domestic with husbandry advice and was addressed not just to shepherds but to plowmen and their wives ("Peers go thou to plowe / and take with the thy wyfe"). The Master Shepherd who narrates the printed version gives lessons not only about astronomical and natural cycles that affect crops and cattle but also about the human seasons and about how to live "long and joyously."[23] His chapters move from how "the year goeth about by twelve months" to "how a man waxeth in twelve ages of his life" (*Kalendar*, 161), and they bring the individual life into accord with the cycles of the larger cosmos. People consulted the *Kalendar* to know when "is a good time for letting blood" (*Kalendar*, 12–13), what the "natural inclination" of a man was (150–55), or how to diagnose a family's diseases, both physical and spiritual (*Kalendar*, 27, 31).

The husbandry book's background in domestic and calendrical traditions helps explain why it nurtured autobiographical tangents while Fitzherbert's no-nonsense manual did not. The calendar format kept the entire cycle of the year in view for readers, but it also marked the progression of specifics in each "season." Keeping track of these prodded many readers into recording important moments in their own lives. Increasingly, owners of almanacs kept track of family events and business transactions in their margins. Extant family almanacs show that the daily guidebook became a daily record and linked the progress of the family's life to the progress of the weather, the crops, the church festivals. By 1565 the custom was so common that Hughbright's almanac included blank pages opposite each month for the reader to fill in.[24]

Tusser's "Life" is not organized by seasons as Whythorne's was, although some of his shorter poems are. Nonetheless, his linear progress through the years is informed by awareness of the larger cycle that both limited it and gave it meaning. The old calendar model was still a powerful means for the serious examination of life. In 1579, only six years after Tusser's collocation of "Life" and calendar, the period's most distinguished *Kalendar* derivative appeared when Edmund Spenser published his (anonymous) *Shephearde's Calender*. Whythorne had already shifted the story of "the seasons of a man's life" toward an account of the seasons of a writer's life. Spenser's Colin Clout, who "proportioneth his life to the foure seasons of the yeare,"[25] is a figure for Spenser as poet. Of course, Spenser's anatomy of a poet's development is part of larger political and religious as well as astrological cycles. But the *Shephearde's Calender* is nonetheless about Colin-Spenser in the same way that *The Faerie Queene* is about Arthur and, to a lesser degree, that Tusser's book turns out to be about Tusser.[26] The calendrical vision fits both Spenser's sophisticated and Tusser's more homely treatment of common concerns: What is the good life? What is the place of religion? Should one go or stay, visit the hills or the dales, lead the musician's life at court or the husband's life in the country?

Comparison between Tusser's metrical commonplaces and Spenser's inaugural literary achievement in the *Calendar* is not wholly inappropriate. One last context for Tusser's book is the literary tradition that he knew from his Cambridge and court years. *The Cambridge Bibliography of English Literature* pointedly includes him among the agricultural poets rather than the husbandry manual writers.[27] He was most admired among early readers for his verse. Henry Peacham praised his work, ordinary readers copied his poems into their commonplace books, and Gabriel Harvey cited him with others like Holinshed, John Heywood, George Gascoigne, and Samuel Daniel as "vulgar [vernacular] writers" among whom "many things are commendable."[28] He was one of the few writers before Philip Sidney on whom Samuel Johnson drew for illustrations in his *Dictionary*.[29] In its final form Tusser's book can be seen as one of the earliest single-author poetic miscellanies. From its first brief incarnation it revealed how close this particular husbandman was to the life of poetry and music he had never really left behind.

Tusser's husbandry book, then, is best described as a pastiche of his own experience and popular wisdom about whatever seemed useful to him, in whatever format happened to fit.

Tusser's Book

The book's variation over time was influenced by a similarly impromptu spirit. The first edition of *A Hundreth Good Points of Husbandry* appeared on February 3, 1557, followed soon after by its companion the *Hundreth Goode Pointes of Huswyferie* (1557), dedicated to Lady Paget as the former was to her husband.[30] Both were printed by Richard Tottel. *Husbandry* was a small book, its body consisting of the one hundred stanzas promised in the title, divided into twelve chapters. The brief prefatory material included the dedication to Lord William Paget and a short poem of domestic advice. The few pages after the calendar added seven couplets summarizing the monthly instructions and a two-line request for the reader's goodwill. The book ended with a final bravura poem, "A brief conclusion in which you may see / Each word in the verse to begin with a T," the sort of display that Whythorne enjoyed in his poem where all lines begin with *W*.

The book is aimed at people like Tusser, small farmers working alone with the help of a wife, a few servants, and extras at harvest time.[31] It comes out of the hard-earned wisdom of a new "husband" in both senses of the word, who had left his single life at court only three or four years earlier. Tusser advises hard work, temperance, thrift, and obedience to landlord and church, not without an eye to profit if possible but always with God's commandments in mind. What is most striking is the optimism and good cheer that characterize every part of the book. While acknowledging the hard work and disappointment husbandry entails, Tusser sees few other drawbacks or dangers in it. He all but romanticizes the husband's life and the human relationships it implies—husband and wife, master and servant, tenant and landlord. This guide for readers has been made into a nicely turned "song," as the dedication calls it.

Six more editions followed in Tusser's lifetime: 1561, 1570, 1573, 1574, 1577, and 1580.[32] Each was larger, covered more topics, and provided more detail as Tusser learned more about his calling, until the book took its final form in 1573 when he gave up farming. The short sequence of editions between 1557 and 1573, despite the accumulating collection of husbandry insight, record the sad epic of Tusser's husbandry failures and final defeat. The several editions provide an almost unparalleled opportunity to hear from a single individual repeatedly over the course of sixteen years, as he reviews his experience and reshapes it for his readers.

As Tusser's life changed, so did his book. For example, in 1561, after his first wife had died and Tusser married Amy Moon, the new edition published that year combined Tusser's first two 1557 books, *Husbandry* and *Huswiferie*, into one volume that was now titled *The marriage of one hundreth good points of husbandry with one hundreth good pointes of huswyferie*. The marriage also left its traces in a separate 1561 publication, Tusser's poem on "wyving and thrvying."[33] The union with Moon, as described in the 1580 "Life," marked the beginning of his first family, a momentous if somewhat ambiguous step: "Behold of trueth, with wife in youth, / For joy at large, what dayly charge, / Through childrens hap.... For pleasure rare, such endlesse care, / Hath husband wonne" ("Life," st. 29).

Later years brought further conflict between "pleasure rare" and "endless care," and starting with this second, 1561, edition, Tusser's infectious optimism in the book gives way to more subdued expectations. His resignation seems to be a response to the continued failures he records. As Tusser says in the introductory letter, the book's readers will learn from hearing about "my losses past / that ranne as fast / as running stream."[34] The third edition, *Five Hundreth Points of Good Husbandry*, appeared nine years later, in 1570, during the worst in his series of bad husbandry experiences. Having had to leave his previous holding because of illness, he had moved to a tenant farm in Fairstead and begun to raise a family. A son was born in 1568 and a daughter in 1570.[35] It was not easy, and the book's appearance at this point may mean that he was trying to eke out a meager living with book sales. His "Life" describes all the drawbacks of being a tenant. On the one hand Tusser has to endure the "tithing strife," the many "pays" (expenses) and "mirey ways" (st. 17) of an unsatisfactory holding, but on the other, he is still afraid of losing his claim, even to this unforgiving land, once the parson, the current landlord, dies and others get control of his lease: "charges grew, still new and new, / And that I spied, if parson died, / (All hope in vaine), to hope for gaine, / I might go daunce" (st. 17).

Not surprisingly, in this third edition Tusser's self-confidence is gone. He is more polemical about what to aim for and less optimistic about getting there. He promises less and exhorts more. The "thinges needful" he lists for readers turn out to be religion, morality, and acceptance of inevitable disappointment. Tusser's wary disillusionment is immediately visible in the introductory poem about domestic happiness, much revised since its first appearance in 1557. It had been titleless then but is now soberly offered as "xxiiii Lessons always to be observed."

The original poem had opened with a promise of the rewards that follow hard work, temperance, and marital harmony. But there are no promises now, only commandments: "Love God above al things" and "shew love to thy neighbor" (fol. 5v). Now for the first time we hear that the husband "trudgeth" and housewyf "drudgeth." A new note of disillusionment colors even Tusser's marital advice. "True wedlock," rather than being the foundation of good husbandry, is now advised merely for "avoidance of sin." Love is no longer enough: "Though love be in choosing far better than golde, / let love come with somewhat the better to holde" (fol. 5v). It never hurts to marry rich. Even so, no matter how much you start out with, you must remember that it can be lost through "ill usage, ill housewives, and such" (fol. 6r). Tusser for the first time mentions children but only as potential "trouble" if the husband cannot afford to "kepe house" (fol. 6r).

Similarly, the poem's several new stanzas consist of nothing but warnings: don't eat too much (fol. 6v); don't spend too much and don't "build for glory" (fol. 6v-7r); "delight not in parasites, harlots, and such" (fol. 7r); don't talk about politics ("Leave Prince's affairs" [fol. 6v]). Tusser also includes new and gloomy warnings about keeping books, making budgets, limiting expenses, and exercising discipline in borrowing and lending. For the first time the book provides minatory verse examples that illustrate the difference between "the good husband and his brother" and "good huswyferie and evil" (fols. 22v, 38v). The only comfort here is religion, and the book now culminates in poems titled "Principall Pointes of Religion," "The Husbandmans Beliefs," and the "Omnipotency of god and Debilitie of Man." Similarly the chapter on December now includes a lesson comparing a man's life to the seasons of the year ("all quickly forgotten as a playe on a stage" [fol. 12v]).

As Tusser retreats from his dream of farming life, however, he puts more of himself into his book. A new poem at the end, "For men a perfect warning," derives from Tusser's own painful experience of being forced into music school. It warns against pushing a child to learn music too early, too quickly, and with too much force ("Not rod in madbraines hand is that can helpe / But gentle skill doth make the proper whelpe" [fol. 37v]).

Finally, in 1573, Tusser published the fourth and largest edition of his husbandry book, in which he included "Th'author's Life." With this edition the book took the form in which, with minor changes, it was to be most widely known. Retitled *Five Hundredth Goode Pointes of Husbandry*, it more than doubled the size of the previous edition, not quite the eponymous five hundred in total but enough to make a hefty book. As advertised on the title page, it was "nowe lately augmented with diverse approved lessons concerning hopps and gardening, and other needeful matters together."

By 1573 Tusser had left his last farm in Fairstead and headed for London and "better chance." He had already been in London at least since March 1572, when his third child was registered in the Cripplegate parish.[36] The book's overt references to being "here" in London appear from the first to the last pages, suggesting that, like all but the 1570 edition, this one was written during a retreat from husbandry. As Tusser suggests in his new dedication, it was also to be his final retreat.

A life of husbandry, worthy as it is, cannot guarantee that a man will thrive. Tusser's quiet resignation sounds more like the medieval narrator's sense of mutability in the *Kalendar of Shepherds* than the ex-courtier's can-do enthusiasm in 1557. A line from a new introductory verse, "The Ladder to thrift," encapsulates the book's tone: "Bear thy crosses paciently / for worldly things are slippery" (fol. 7r). Details throughout help explain Tusser's final retreat from the land. He is even warier than he was in 1570 about family (a "mistress who scowls" [fol. 9r]) and the responsibilities that children bring. Along with treacherous servants (fol. 9r), Tusser now warns against "envious and Haughty neighbor[s]" with "mouth full of venom" (*Huswyferie*, fol. 25r), and he takes note of "slanderous tongues" (fol. 62r). For the first time Tusser describes the trials of being a tenant. His earlier books had incorporated reminders to tithe regularly, but now Tusser complains about landlords: "Good landlord who findeth is blesed of God, / to strip his poor tenant of ferme and of thrift" (fol. 8v). He still recognizes that one must "paye justly thy tithes," but he now knows enough to add, "though curat be bad, or the parson as evel" (fol. 52r).

Tusser's new sensitivity to social hierarchy suggests a man who has relinquished hope about the rewards of husbandry. In earlier editions he had been aware of social difference but hardly oppressed. He had advised generosity to those lower down and spoke benignly of those above, in part because he had been hopeful about his own "purchase" on the economic ladder: "While gentiles go hawking...husbands must work to purchase their land." But by 1573 he has given up on upward progress, and he is trying merely to avoid falling off the ladder. Like Thomas Whythorne after the sobering realization at the end of his narrative, he has accepted the realities of hierarchy: don't be rude to "hunters and hawkers" (who cut across farmland to pursue their game), and "take heed what you say...resist not with rudeness for feare of mishap" (fol. 11v). Where before he was intent on purchasing his land, now he focuses on avoiding "mishap."

But as Tusser relinquishes his dream of husbandry he takes fuller possession of his husbandry book. He identifies with the book's author now as well as its contents. The section that was once called "The Husband's Beliefs" is now "The Author's Beliefs," and Tusser adds poems about people as well as crops and cattle. One of the latter divides man's life "by prenticeships," or periods of seven years (fol. 5rv); the next offers "an other division of the nature of man's age" by dividing life into four stages marked by animals (apes for youth and asses for old age). These are paired with a "description of womans age by vi times xiiii yeares prenticeship" (*Huswyferie*, fol. 17v). Additionally, Tusser includes more short poetry about his own life. The earlier poem, "wyving and thriving," published separately in 1561, appears here for the first time, along with a poem about leaving court for the country and a touching sonnet about "The authors first vii yeares service" to his wife Amy Moon ("vii times the thirteen moones, have changed hew")—which ends, "Still yours am I, though thus time has past, / And trust to bee, so long as life shall last" (fol. 62v).

In this context "Th'author's Life" at the end of the book is not so odd an appendix to a husbandry book as it might have seemed. Its story of an ad hoc life seems almost an inevitable last chapter to Tusser's motley and increasingly personal collection of advice about everything. Its occasion, Tusser's farewell to husbandry, was an appropriate one on which to look back over his own life as well as his collected farming wisdom.

This autobiographical coda to the 1573 edition also rounds out the whole sequence of editions because it recalls the preface to the original 1557 *Hundreth Good Points*. Like that letter to Paget, the "Life"'s homely mixture of memory and moralizing has the ring of an intimate exchange with a friend who knows him well. When Tusser speaks from a particular but unidentified place, "here," and says unspecifically, "thus I live," he does not have to explain either "here" or "thus." The reader is as familiar with these as Tusser, although he may not be literally standing beside him. As in the Paget letter, Tusser writes to explain why he is "Full bent to spend my life to an end, / In this same place" ("Life," st. 2), now that "how through ye breers, my youthful yeres / have runne their race" (st. 2). In convincing his friend that he has come to terms with his country life, he can convince himself.

The twenty-eight-stanza review of his past is clear-eyed about suffering but upbeat, almost jaunty at times. As earlier quotes have indicated, Tusser comes from gentle stock and loves his family; he is grateful for his education and grateful to have been taken on by Paget at court. His years at court taught him about both the good and bad to be found there. He had a difficult career in husbandry, but he takes time to praise each benefactor who helped him along the way (friends in Ipswich, Southwell, Salisbury, Norwich), and he writes without bitterness about recurring illness and death that often destroyed his fortune. Finally, escaping the charges and uncertainty of his last farm, "away went I, / To London straight, to hope and waight, / for better chaunce" ("Life," st. 28). The review ends as Tusser greets London with hope: London, he says, "dost in deede, to suche as neede, much kindenes shew" ("Life," st. 29).

Like the Paget letter, the "Life" draws heavily on convention. The most obvious of these is the debate between court and country, as in Wyatt's epistle from the country to "John Poins" at court. The poem just preceeding Tusser's "Life" is a typical example of the genre. "Of th'authors departing from Court to the Countrie" (fol. 26), seems to have been written much earlier, on the occasion it describes (ca. 1553). Its formula is familiar. The speaker is contented with the country ("poore estate") that he knows the courtier hates: "Muse not my friend, to finde me here, / Contented with this poore estate, / And seeme to do, with willing chere, / That courtier, doth deadly hate." So too the beginning of Tusser's "Life":

Now gentle friend, if thou be kinde,
Disdaine thou not, although the lot
Will now with me, no better be,
    Then doth appear:
    Nor let it greeve, that thus I live,
    But rather guess, for quietness,
As others do, so do I to,
        Content me here.
           (st. 1)

But for Tusser this particular formula is no mere convention. In both poems it accurately reproduces his own departure from court and his accounts of it in dedications to the Pagets over the years. Most significantly, however, Tusser's 1573 use of the "formula" turns it inside out.

Insofar as it is conventional, Tusser makes use of the convention for his own ends. When Tusser says in the "Life," "[I] content me here," he uses lines that have always referred to the country (as he himself used them in the prior poem). Yet everything about Tusser's 1573 *Husbandry* implies that the book was written from London, the city, not from the country.[37] A poet like Gascoigne might have made much of this irony. But Tusser does not seem to care. It's what he knows, so he uses it. It does not quite fit, but it fits well enough, at least for the moment.

The same is true of another formula that Tusser uses at the end of his "Life," when he forgets the "gentle friend" of the opening lines and turns to a larger audience of "friends." He offers them a lesson from his experience, as he has been offering practical advice all through his book. The eight-stanza lesson takes familiar form, as if it were spoken by one of the ghosts in *A Mirror for Magistrates* or by Thomas Churchyard in his almost contemporary "The Unhappy Man's Life" (ca. 1573; printed 1575). "Thus friends," it begins, "by me, perceive may ye, / That Gentries stands, not all by lands, / Nor all so fest, or plentie left, / By Parents gift: / But now and then, of gentlemen, /The younger sonne, is deiven to ronne, / And glad to seeke, from creeke to creeke, / To come by thrift."[38]

The exhortation to "learn from my experience" was formulaic. But Tusser, unlike the *Mirror* ghosts, had real experience that he really wanted to talk about. Again, convention is an effective guide for what he is doing. He had been teaching lessons for years, turning his experience into books in order to make money and also to justify his life. Now he has still another reason to say, "Learn from my experience": his son. One of the last stanzas is directly addressed to the boy: "When all is done, learne this my sonne, / Not friend nor skill, nor wyt nor wyll, / Nor ship nor clod, but onley God, / doth alter all" (st. 35).[39]

Given Tusser's assumptions, modern readers need to remember that, congenial as it is, Tusser's casual attitude about distinguishing convention from experience can result in what seems like factual contradictions. For example, in the "Life" at the end of his book, London is a kindly, welcoming city, the relatively happy ending of Tusser's tale of hardship. But in the book's opening dedication to Thomas Paget, Tusser describes a different, "vaineful," and "greedy gaineful" city: "Citie seemes a wringer, / the peny for to finger, / from such as do there linger" (fol. 2r). Paget's London is part of a different story, told at a different time, for a different audience. In that story, Tusser is at heart a husbandman, and he needs help to escape from London's hardships back to the land.

But Tusser was not necessarily lying in either place. He was simply working with a different standard of truth, one more defined by a practical sense of what was most fitting for the moment. It was more like our standards for casual conversation than our expectations for print. ("Oh, did I say that before? It seemed right at the time.") Tusser can thus use the same convention in an old poem about taking up husbandry (ca. 1553), alongside a new poem about giving up husbandry (1573), and he does not worry about inconsistency.

That is certainly what he did in the following year, 1574, after living through events that took place too late to include in his 1573 "Life." Tusser had to leave London quite suddenly in 1573, probably because of an epidemic—one that may also have affected Isabella Whitney, as we shall see in the following chapter. He found safety in Cambridge. Once he was settled there in 1574, he issued a new edition of *Husbandry* with two new stanzas inserted into his "Life" (and little else changed in the book): When "death did crye, from London flye, / in Cambridge than, I found agen, / a resting plot" (st. 31). Here he reveals, surprisingly, that he is back at his musical career, a fact confirmed by Cambridge records.

> Since hap haps so, let toyling go,
> Let serving paines, yeld forth her gaines,
> Let courtly giftes, with wedding shiftes,
>   Helpe now to live,
> Let Music win, let store come in,
> Let wisdome karve, let reason serve,
> For here I crave, suche end to have
>   As God shall give.
>   (st. 32)

The result is that all later editions of Tusser's book, including the misleading and contradictory modern composite that is now most often cited, contain the expanded 1574 "Life" as part of the book otherwise dating from 1573. The new version of the "Life" once again changes the meaning of Tusser's opening claim, "I content me *here*... in this same place." Now the lines refer to Cambridge, rather than to either London or the country. There is no way, apart from comparing the original 1573 and 1574 editions, to tell that the added update was not part of the original poem. For Tusser, as long as he got in the new bit about leaving London, it didn't matter.

Tusser's "Life" is a reminder that early texts, at least the ones like Tusser's that grew along with the author's experience, cannot be read the way later more coherently conceived works are read. The "Life," like Tusser's whole book, is a palimpsest, like a manuscript diary with some lines crossed out or changed and others added, although it is unfortunately unlike a diary in leaving no separate traces of earlier entries. Both Tusser's husbandry manual and his "Life" may have begun with a blueprint, but both grew the way houses did when extra bits were needed, with a room here and more storage there, and no regard for an overall plan. The text and its immediate context in Tusser's life cannot be separated—not at any one moment nor over the years during which their histories mutually affected each other. In that way Tusser's ad hoc "Life" is more like his husbandry book than a modern "life" written to contemporary standards of consistency.

Tusser's easygoing attitude toward narrative, along with his assumption of an audience who knows him and doesn't need explanations as strangers would, leaves many factual questions open. What were the "courtly giftes" mentioned in the 1574 addition to his "Life"? Does his move to Cambridge mean that his 1573 dedication to Paget had been successful in soliciting those gifts? And what were the "wedding shiftes" also mentioned as part of the move?[40] But while the book thwarts a modern reader hot for factual certainties, the 1574 reissue of the "Life" suggests how important it was for Tusser to get it right by his rather different standards. He wanted his story known and available. His book suggests that by this time, rather then being unusual, the autobiographical impulse among the educated seems to have been growing stronger. What they wrote, although more reticent than autobiographies are now, conveys more about their lives than it might seem, so long as we consider the context of what people like Tusser were doing as well as what they were saying.

CHAPTER 7

A Garden of One's Own: *Isabella Whitney's Revision of [Hugh]* Plat's Floures of Philosophie *(1572) in Her* Sweet Nosgay *(1573)*

> Though they be of anothers growing, yet considering they be of my owne gathering and making up: respect my labour and regard my good wil.
> ISABELLA WHITNEY, *A Sweet Nosgay, or Pleasant Posy* (1573)

Isabella Whitney is the first woman known to have published original secular poetry in English. Her verse pamphlets, *A Sweet Nosgay, or Pleasant Posy: contayning a hundred and ten Phylosophicall flowers* (1573) and *The Copy of a Letter lately written in meeter, by a yonge Gentilwoman: to her unconstant lover* (1567), both printed by Richard Jones, have spurred comparison with women's writing in other times or places[1] and illuminated the underdocumented experience of working women in London when she was there.

But the texts are also interesting because they show how someone, male or female, who was outside university circles could construct an autobiography by taking advantage of the material that print made available. Whitney is not as extreme an example as, for example, Miles Hogarde, the London hosier who became a Catholic spokesman in midcentury religious debates (1553–58). Hogarde had no formal education, but he had read romances and dream visions that influenced his religious polemic. He knew the preface format, on which he modeled his own fleetingly autobiographical preface to "A Mirroure of Myserie" (1555), a manuscript presented to Queen Mary in 1557. There he answered critics who denied an uneducated man's right to join in religious debate and objected that

My calling is not bokes to write,
Nor no faultes to reprove,
But to follow my busynesse,
As wisedome would me move,
Before (say they) when men dyd preache
Which artificers were,
They were not calde thereto, say you,
Gods word wyl them not beare.
But now can ye suffer a man,
Which no learning hath,
Against his calling, as it were
To write upon our faith?
To them I do answere againe.
My selfe for to defende,
If Gods precept dyd me forbid,
No bookes I would have pende.[2]

But although Whitney was more privileged than Hogarde in regard to education, she too drew on her reading for her models. What makes her especially interesting is that she reused commonplaces and conventions drawn from her reading to convey specific personal details in her own texts.

Isabella Whitney (fl. 1567–73)

We know almost nothing about Whitney's life apart from her texts, but most scholars now believe that she was sister to Geoffrey Whitney, the author of *A Choice of Emblems* (1586), about whom more is known.[3] She came from a well-established family in Cheshire that displayed its own badge, the head of an ox. The Whitneys also spent time in London and in Smithfield ("my parents there did dwell"—"Wyll," 218), although judging from one of Geoffrey's poems in his *Emblems*, they were in Cheshire when he published that book.[4] As a child Isabella knew George Mainwaring, son of one of the country's influential families; in the *Nosgay* dedication she speaks of his kindness. Although Whitney says she "learning lackt" ("Auctor to the Reader," 3), she seems to have had access to some informal education, perhaps through Mainwaring or through Geoffrey, who had attended a nearby grammar school and may already have been writing poetry while he was still at home.

The earliest notice of Whitney herself appears in 1567 with the publication of *The Copy of a Letter by Is.W.* It was about this time that Geoffrey went up to Cambridge; Isabella may have been either still living with her family or already in service in London. The pamphlet contains four verse letters, organized as a contribution to the popular *querelle des femmes*, to which Thomas Tusser had also contributed before he wrote his own verse life.[5] The first two letters are from "Is.W.," one berating the lover who jilted her and a second letter warning other young women about men in general. The last two letters are from men, one who had been jilted and a second who offers a warning against women. The printer's "preface" teasingly hints that the verse is partly autobiographical when he says that it includes both "trifles that are trew" and "fables that be fained," but there is no reason to take him literally.[6]

The pamphlet itself is not particularly remarkable, and its use of convention is straightforward. But two aspects are worth noting because they suggest dimensions of Whitney's writing that become important in her longer and more autobiographical 1573 *Nosgay*. First, the author's persona, Is. W., is a clever, sophisticated writer. Recounting her lover's betrayal from an amused distance, for example, Is.W. turns her complaint into a playful show of fashionable learning: Will you "be of SINON's trade?" (*Copy*, 29); "Take example by ENEAS who dyd poore DIDO leave" (*Copy*, 34) and suffered "perpetuall shame" (*Copy*, 72); "would God I had CASSANDRAES gift" (*Copy*, 114), and so on. At the end of the letter, she reemphasizes her authorial identity even while acknowledging the loss of her marital prospects. Calmly proposing to send her ex-lover no more letters, she adds that if he wants to know why she sent this one, he should "peruse the rest" (*Copy*, 140). Second, because Whitney's suggestion that the man peruse "the rest" refers him to her next poem, "The admonition by the Auctor, to all yong Gentilwomen," she links her two separate lyrics into a single argument. That is, she creates narrative structure to unify her separate poems. Whitney's manipulation of structure will be as important to the autobiographical dimension of her later *Nosgay* as its content, and to later autobiographies as well.

There is no information about the period between the publication of *Copy* and *Nosgay* in 1573. By that year Geoffrey was probably in London at the Inns of Court. Four other Whitney siblings were there as well: a second brother, "B[rooke].W.," and a married sister, "A.B.," as well as two others in service. Geoffrey, Isabella says, was her "chiefest staffe that I shal stay on heare" ("To her brother G.W.," 8), apart from her parents, and he may have helped her establish her circle of literary connections in London, including her printer, Richard Jones, and her friend Thomas Berrie, whose verse is included in the *Nosgay*. Geoffrey may even have known Hugh Plat, a student recently come down from Oxford to Lincoln's Inn, whose 1572 collection of verse was a major source for Isabella's 1573 *Nosgay*. Geoffrey was to weave an impressive patronage network among Protestant aristocrats like Leicester and Sidney, and Plat was part of the same network. He could have introduced Isabella to the book if not to Plat himself. Her casually humorous reference to Plat, in *Posy*'s "Farewell to the Reader," may imply that she knew him.[7] Whether through her brother or not, Whitney had established a tie to the world of reading and writing, and she spoke of herself as a writer: "till some household cares me tie, / My books and Pen I will apply" ("To her Sister Misteris. A.B.," 27–28). Her texts reveal a familiarity with current literature like Plat's book, George Turberville's recent translation of Ovid's *Heroides* (1567), Tottel's *Songes and Sonettes* (1557), and Barnabe Googe's (1563) and Turberville's (1567) miscellanies.[8]

As Whitney implies in *Nosgay*, shortly before writing she had been dismissed from her position in service to a "virtuous Ladye, which / tyll death I honor wyll" ("G.W.," 15), and she was left without the means to live. While writing, she was living in Abchurch Lane, a short street between Cornhill and King William that extended from London Bridge Street as it left the poorer districts on the Thames shore and turned northwest. But the complaints in her letters to friends make it clear that she needed help in order to remain there.

A Sweet Nosgay (1573)

Whitney had published before. Like others in her situation, she probably turned to writing in hope of earning enough by another book to ease her current financial straits. She based her pamphlet on Hugh Plat's *The Floures of Philosophie With the Pleasures of Poetrie annexed to them, as wel pleasant to read as profitable to be followed of all men* (1572), one of the newly fashionable poetic miscellanies. She dedicated the text to her countryman George Mainwaring, but she may also have been writing for (though not directly to) her former mistress, hoping that the book's contents would help defend and perhaps reinstate her into the gentlewoman's graces.[9]

The seventy-four-page *Nosgay*, extant in only one copy that has no title page, is divided by printer's font and ornaments into two parts, first, the "Nosgay" of "phylosophicall flowers" and, second, "Certain familier Epistles and friendly Letters by the Auctor: with Replies."[10] Whitney's originality in the pamphlet is clearest when it is read in comparison to her model in Plat. In fact Whitney, like John Bale, encourages the comparison. She tells both reader and patron that she has taken material from Plat: "I did step into another's garden for these Flowers"—although they are "of my owne gathering and makeing up" ("To . . . George Mainwaring, Esquier," 30). Her somewhat exaggerated modesty about her debt to Plat might mislead a reader into thinking the two poets more alike than they are. After all, Plat himself, as he says without much ado, took material from Seneca. But Plat's flowers look entirely different in the autobiographical context Whitney constructs for them. Despite superficial similarities, Whitney's book is more original in ways that show why Plat's first-person verse, though a fine instance of the miscellany genre, has little to do with the development of autobiography, while Whitney's, along with Whythorne's and Gascoigne's, illustrates its move toward representing concrete individual experience.

Plat's book is almost entirely governed by the typical miscellany format, which even at this early date was becoming an independent although not quite standard genre.[11] He seems to have had no interest in individualizing detail. The book, as its title indicates, has two parts, a section of moral epigrams or "Floures of Philosophie," and a section of miscellaneous "Poetrie" annexed to them. The generic division is familiar from collections like Googe's *Eglogs, Epytaphes, and Sonettes* (1563). Plat's introductory material also follows convention. His dedication to Lady Anne, countess of Warwick, moves smoothly and impersonally from topos to topos: the anthology as a gathering of flowers, an apology to the countess for offering so poor a gift, a citation of sources, a suggestion that she apply one of the flowers to her heart as remedy to the "noysome smell of vice," and his praise of and good wishes for her. He frames the whole with similarly conventional letters to the reader. The introductory letter describes his arrangement for the posies (a "maze") but says nothing about himself or the reader. The farewell letter merely distinguishes conventionally between friendly and other readers, and it closes with conventional wishes.

The body of the book itself is equally impersonal. The 885 moral epigrams in the first part are organized randomly, offering no indication of Plat's attitude toward them. The poems in the second part are academic exercises, ranging from love poems to moral poems, to friendship exchanges, to an imitation of the *Mirror* ghosts.[12] As a result, despite a number of first-person occasional poems, a reader has no sense of a unifying speaker, theme, or argument.

Whitney's book is similarly divided into an opening section of epigrams selected from Plat's and a second section of verse, together introduced by the dedication to George Mainwaring and Whitney's address to the reader. But there the resemblance ends. Whitney makes the epigrams more thoroughly her own than the epigraph suggests by saying that they are of her "owne gathering and making up." They are indeed of her own gathering; she selects only about one-eighth of Plat's collection, and while Plat offered random advice, she emphasizes epigrams about friendship's cure for fortune's disappointments. But she also expands epigrams, sometimes adding a new emphasis, as in her version of Plat's epigram 880. He wrote, "Seeke not to please all men, for that is more than God himselfe doth." Whitney specifies which men are worth pleasing: "the best" (*Nosgay*, 1008 [108]).

Whitney's dedicatory letter too is more tailored to her book than Plat's was. His had politely flattered a woman he did not know. Whitney writes to a childhood acquaintance, George Mainwaring, and she alludes to "benefits, which I have from time to time (even in our Childhood) hitherto received of you" ("Mainwaring," 8–9). Instead of Plat's conventional request for protection against envious readers, Whitney describes a particular spiteful person who knows her and Mainwaring and wants to come between them: "vouchsafe to be a protector of [her Flowers] from the spightful, which (perhaps) will env[y] that I either presented you, or gathered them be[fore] they had done one, or both: and so might spoyle thi[s] Nosgay, and not let it come so happily into your handes, as I wish it may" ("Mainwaring," 32–36).[13] Whitney then signs herself "your Countrywoman" ("Mainwaring," 51), evoking their shared space outside her present London address, just as she had evoked their shared past in childhood.

By far the most original adaptation of Plat is to make the epigrams part of her own story.[14] They are not, like Plat's, simply part of a timeless anthology of commonplace advice. Plat's reader has no sense of when or where wrote his book. By contrast, Whitney frames her epigrams with an explanation of how and why she came to publish them. Her letter to the reader and the epigrams that follow it function more like a dream vision than like prefatory material for a miscellany.[15] Whitney begins her "vision" by establishing time and place, a particular autumn day (October 23, 1573) in London. Like John Skelton in "Bouge of Court" or *The Garland of Laurel*, she describes an isolation that reflects her troubled mind.

> This harvest time, I harvestless,
>   And serviceless also:
> And subject unto sickness, that
>   Abroad I could not go.
>   ("Reader," 1–2)

She has no role in either the country's harvest or the city's households, nor can academic pursuits help her. She tries: "I straight were weary of those Books, / and many other mor[e]" ("Reader," 11). She tries scripture, history, the classics, but they only "maze" her muse and "bruise" her brain ("Reader," 13). Unhappy, she walks outside—not into the dreamer's traditional spring landscape but rather into the nightmarish "infected" lanes of the city. There she meets a friend who warns her to go back home. By this point, the dreamer in a conventional vision would have fallen asleep. Instead Fortune appears to Whitney and brings her "to Plat his Plot... where fragrant Flowers abound" ("Reader," 29). There she "reposed one hour," and, as in a dream, Plat's "plot" reveals the answer to Whitney's problem ("Reader," 30). His flowers become her "defense" and keep her "safe" from the "stinking streets, or loathsome Lanes" ("Reader," 37). Relieved, she returns home. She conveys her gratitude to Plat, describes his book ("take hed it is a Maze" ["Reader," 10]), and recommends that readers visit Plat's plot themselves. Meanwhile she offers readers the nosegay she gathered from Plat, i.e., her epigrams, just as Skelton had offered his recorded dream in *Bouge*.

Ironically, it may have been one of Plat's own poems that gave Whitney the idea for revising his model by embedding the epigrams in her story. Plat's "A dossen of pointes sente by a gentlewoman to hir lover for a New-yeares gifte," a poem in the second part of his book, tells about a young woman at a fair, looking for a gift to bring back for her friend. None of the trifling toys she sees is suitable. Then, like Fortune leading Whitney to Plat's book, "Dame Vertue doth display hir booth / My hastie feete to stay," and there the speaker finds the perfect gift: "I found a knot or peereless points / Besette with posies neate. / These pointes in number twelve / Did shew themselves to be, / The sense whereof by Poets skill I will declare to thee." The poem's speaker then goes on to quote Virtue's twelve points for her reader, just as Whitney follows her explanatory letter with the gift of her epigrams. If Plat's poem is her source, the fact suggests how Whitney worked by combining pieces of different texts, using the lyric's miniplot to restructure the larger miscellany sequence.

Besides moving Plat's prefatory letter toward personal narrative, Whitney refashions Plat's conventional language into specific description by literalizing his figurative language. She follows his lead in offering a conventional floral nosegay against infection, but in doing so she literalizes his imagery to startling effect. Whitney's claim that she was "subject unto sickness" has always been read as reference to her own, probably spiritual, disease, as the infection is in Plat. But a more literal interpretation is suggested by the likelihood that she was describing an outbreak of deadly disease. Thomas Tusser describes what sounds like a threat of plague, earlier that same year, that had driven him from his Cripplegate lodgings in the city: when "death did crye, from London flye, / in Cambridge than, I found agen, / a resting plot."[16] Modern studies argue that the plague was endemic during many years, and there is specific reference to it in the records for 1573.[17] Whitney was writing at "harvest-time" or high summer, a common season for plague, even in years without newsworthy epidemics.[18] Infectious diseases broke out most often in ports and riversides, and the more crowded districts, like the one on which hers bordered, suffered most.

Threat of an epidemic provides a better explanation than individual illness for the exchange with her friend that Whitney reports after she does go outdoors and meets him on the street:

> I walked out: but suddenly
>   A friend of mine me met:
> And said if you regard your health:
>   out of this Lane you get.
> And shift you to some better air
>   for fear to be infect:
> With noisome smell and savors ill.
>   ("Reader," 15–18)

Unless she heeds her health more, he says, "you may: So make a dye [you may die]." He himself "was hastyng out of Town, / and could no longer byde" ("Reader," 25). Later Whitney uses her nosegay as a "defence" against "stynking streets, or lothsome Lanes / which els might mee infect" ("Reader," 37), a relatively straightforward reference to disease. At this point, however, Whitney is so upset at her "luckless life" apart from infection that she almost wishes for death anyway:

> I thanked him for his carefulness,
>   and this for answer gave:
> I'll neither shun, nor see for death,
>   yet oft the same I crave.
> By reason of my luckless life,
>   Believe me this is true.
>   ("Reader," 21–23)

As the reference to her "luckless life" implies, Whitney's situation is bad enough to drive her from London even without the added threat of infection. But if "infection" does, as it seems to, refer to a deadly epidemic, then Whitney's last will and testament at the end of the book is knit even more tightly—and autobiographically—than it might seem into her overall structure. The will likens her to "those which heere, no longer tary may" ("Wyll," 295–96): among them, we can infer, people like her friend who was "hasting out of town," as well as Tusser who had just fled and, of course, those who had succumbed to infection. "No longer tary may" is a chilling understatement for flight from the city, equating poverty, her stated reason, with the "infection" of mortal disease.

Thomas Nashe's "Sommer's Last Will," also set in autumn, is a more compelling work as it moves from the 1592 plague epidemic to a reminder of all human mutability and mortality. But although Whitney does not reach as far for cosmic themes, she does revitalize Plat's abstract figures of posies and moral "infection" by drafting them to describe her own concrete "loathsome lanes" and literally "infected air." Rosamund Tuve describes a similar tendency toward literalizing allegory in the fifteenth-century illustrations for the *Roman de la Rose*. The interpretive drift, as new audiences (like Whitney) gained access to books like Plat's miscellany, opened new possibilities for autobiography as well as traditional literary forms.

Having revised the first part of Plat's text to suit her narrative, once Whitney finishes the last of the epigrams in her nosegay and reaches the end of her text's first section, she deviates even more radically from Plat. His farewell letter had come at the end of his entire book, uniting the poems in the second part to the epigrams in the first. But Whitney instead says farewell to the reader here, just after the last epigram. The dream vision has ended. "Good Reader now you tasted have, / and smelt of all my Flowers." She hopes that the poems will help readers, that "He for whom I gathered them [Mainwaring], / take pleasure in the same, and that "he [Plat] who ought the plot" is not angry at her borrowings. Then she says goodbye—to Plat's model as well as to the reader—and closes her collection here as if it were the end of her book.

Plat had introduced the second part of his book with an appropriate verse. But Whitney gives neither introduction nor any other guide for the reader. Instead she disappears as organizing narrator. The second section of her text has only a title, "Certain familiar Epistles and friendly Letter by the Author: with Replies" (*Nosgay*, 8). If the first part of *Nosgay* was a dream vision, the second is a brief epistolary novel. It consists of a series of verse letters to and from Whitney and several friends, and it ends with a final letter to London containing her last will and testament. Plat had included verse letters, some with replies, among his collected poems. But they were scattered among his other verse and presented more as poetic exercises than as functioning letters. Once again adapting convention for self-revelation, Whitney presents her letters as actual correspondence, and they sound relatively spontaneous, or as spontaneous as such letters could sound at the time. There is little indication that they were even intended for public eyes. It is almost as if the letters, rather than being planned as part the same book, were simply appended afterward by someone else.[19] Whitney's friend Thomas Berrie actually describes Whitney's text as two separate works in his commendatory verse: "The smelling Flowers of an Arbor sweete, / An Orchard pickt presented is to thee: / And for her *second worke*, she thought it meet, / sithe Maids with loftie stile may not agree: / In hoape thereby, some thynge to pleasure thee" ("T. B. in commendation of the Author"; italics added). The first "worke" contains emblems "in lofty stile," but the second, less lofty, is more likely to "pleasure" young maids.

Although neither T. B. nor Whitney comments further on the dual structure, the shift from miscellany to epistolary format can be read as a narrative distancing that is itself part of Whitney's story. Thus two old conventions join to create something new—and newly autobiographical. The shift in format is the first indication that Whitney has now moved into the more complicated reality outside Plat's "garden," where his literary cure is no longer enough and where there are no omniscient guides. In fact the second part of Whitney's text contradicts nearly everything in the first. Earlier Whitney had found comfort and a cure for infection in Plat's teaching about friendship and its power against Fortune. Now it seems that Whitney has never heard of Plat, epigrams, or cure. Plat's epigrams about friendship had comforted before. Now when she resorts to her friends for help during this period of "Fortune fell," they all fail her.

Whitney's continuing troubles are taken for granted in most of the letters, although not mentioned overtly in every one. They set the scene in this part of the book. With this as their common context, her several epistolary appeals are carefully distinguished from one another. Their well-organized sequence outlines a narrative, in which Whitney begins by asking her family for help, moves further outward to cousins and friends, and ends by appealing to London itself before she realizes that there is no help to be had. (There are only two letters whose origin and date do not fit into the tight plot suggested by the others; these may have been written earlier.)[20]

The opening two letters are addressed to her brothers, Geoffrey and Brooke, on whom she depends ("my chiefest stay"). They are apparently out of London, probably between legal terms ("vacant time" ["G.W.," 1]). Here Whitney seems most concerned simply to get in touch with them. To G[eoffrey] W. she writes, "Cannot I once from you heare / nor know I how to send: Or where to harken of your health," ("G.W.," 3–4), and "graunt / me when that you ar here: / To se you ofte and also hence, / I may have knowledge wheare / A messenger to harke unto / that I to you may write" ("G.W.," 9–11). The letter to her second brother, Brooke, sounds even more urgent: not knowing "where you do sojourn," she says, makes her "dread, that you are dead" ("To her Brother. B.W.," 4, 7). These are the most direct and least literary-sounding of the letters and also the most passionate. Histrionic passion was common in the period's verse complaints. But in these letters Whitney sounds more upset than in the *Copy* letters, written six years earlier when Is. W.'s fiancé deserted her.[21] The contrast suggests how different *Nosgay* is from the earlier pamphlet, possibly because Whitney's actual situation now was more desperate. But perhaps a brother's abandonment was more threatening to her than a lover's?

In any case, Whitney seems to collect herself as she moves on to write to her sisters. These letters are quite different. If she looked to her brothers

A Garden of One's Own: Isabella Whitney 159

to take care of her, Whitney takes the nurturing role with her sisters. She has no fear that they will leave her. Indeed she seems more concerned with abandoning them by her own impending departure, and she instructs her two younger sisters in service how to behave "when I / shal further from you dwell" ("A modest meane for Maides," 1). She doesn't mention her troubles but instead sends her good wishes, and to the younger girls Whitney passes on her own hard-earned wisdom. She warns them to protect themselves from slander and the sort of accusation that brought her own dismissal: "God shyld you from all such, / as would by word or Byll. / Procure your shame, or never cease / tyll they have wrought you yll" ("Modest meane," 21–22). She warns them against being a "rolling stone," presumably because without her job she herself will now have to start "rolling," and she promises to provide a better example in the future: "Henceforth my life as well as Pen / shall your examples frame" ("Modest meane," 38). Even in the letter to her married sister, who has done Whitney good ("To her Sister Misteris. A[nne].B.," 9) and is willing to bestow "expense" (spend money) for her ("Misteris A.B.," 6), Whitney sends "blessings" and writes as if she were the one doing a favor "ere I parted hence" ("Misteris A.B.," 3).[22]

None of Whitney's siblings respond. In the rest of her letters she turns to friends, none of whom can help her either, although some do reply. The exception is C. B., to whom Whitney had written asking for "sound advice" about penitence ("To C.B.," 1). C. B. reassures Whitney that she is not entirely to blame and does not have that much to repent: "T'is not altogether sin, / that makes you sorrow this: / It is because that Fortune she, / doth frown on you iwis." Otherwise, even Whitney's friend T. B., author of the poem "in Commendation of the Author," disappoints her. In "Commendation" Berrie had promised Whitney that he "restes always at your call." Yet when she does as he suggests and calls on him (in "A careful complaint"), Berrie's answer is that he cannot help, because he suffers even more than she does: so "be content / and rip [reveal] no more, thy wrongs in such excess" ("In answer to comfort her, be showing / his haps to be harder").

Whitney writes back supportively about Berrie's harder "haps." But by the end of the sequence Whitney's strength flags. She is even betrayed by Fortune, one "whose painted speech, professeth friendship still / but time betrays the meaning to be ill" ("A Replye to the same [C. B.]"). Finally, "G.W." answers one of her appeals by complaining that he himself has nothing to give—although he does add, politely but not too helpfully, that "[my] wealth / I would to God were such, / as might your ease amend" ("Another letter sent to Is. W.").[23] At this point Whitney gives up. She simply replies (as she had earlier in the *Copy* letter) that she will stop writing until she feels better: "For now I wyll my writting cleane forsake / till of my griefes, my stomack I discharge" ("Is.W. beying wery of writing, sendeth This for Answere," 10–11).

The last letter in the collection suggests that Whitney never quite discharged her stomach of griefs, although she now writes from an ironic distance and, she says, "in no angry moode" ("A communication which the Auctor had to London, before she made her Wyll," 27). She writes to the entire city of London, accusing it of cruelty, although she admits wryly that she, like many women who fix their fancy on an undeserving lover, is nonetheless sorry to leave (fig. 13). You never pitied me, she says, never helped me in distress, never relieved me—"no, no, thou never didst me good" ("Communication," 25). Only "time" has pitied her by showing her the truth about London, by putting her "in mind, / of thy great cruelness: / That never yet a help would find, / to ease me in distress" ("Communication," 17–20).[24] With that she ends: "Now stand aside and give me leave / to write my latest Wyll" ("Communication," 33–39). With all those who could or would not help her, Whitney had remained remarkably patient and understanding. In fact her earlier letters had collectively demonstrated Whitney's devotion to family, her sympathy for friends, her willingness to accept blame for the "sinne" that presumably cost her her job ("Is.W. to C. B.," 9), and her patience and courage in the face of misfortune and abandonment.

But now she speaks more frankly, especially in her will. Here Whitney surveys different parts of London, just as she had written to a range of friends in the previous letters. The will is Whitney's final addition to the miscellany model. There is nothing like it in Plat's book or in her other predecessors.[25] For her last words Whitney turned to popular complaint literature instead of Plat's elite miscellany. Like her earlier switch midway into the text from epigrams to letters, this change from elite to popular format in itself contributes to Whitney's narrative of her declining fortunes. Models for complaints would have been easy to find. One that has been overlooked, for example, is John Lydgate's popular "London Lickpenny" (or "Lackpenny"). It is narrated by a poor man searching for a lawyer to plead his case. Tracing a map of disappointment across Westminster

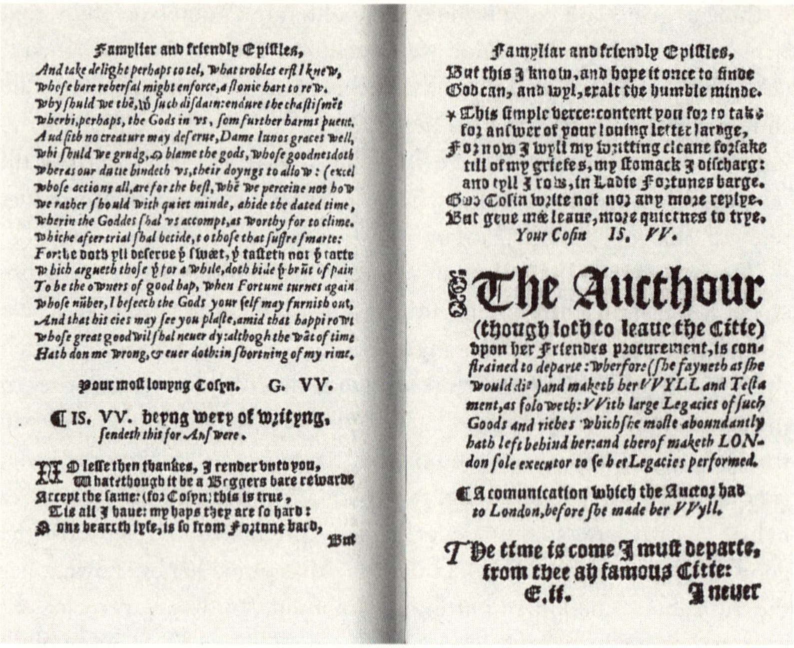
Famylier and friendly Epistles,
And take delight perhaps to tel, what trobles erst I knew,
Whose bare rehersal might enforce, a stonie hart to rew.
Why should we thē, wt such disdain: endure the chastismēt
Wherbi, perhaps, the Gods in vs, som further harms puent.
And sith no creature may deserue, Dame Iunos graces well,
Whi should we grudg, & blame the gods, whose goodnes doth
Wheras our dutie bindeth vs, their doyngs to allow: (excel
whose actions all, are for the best, whē we perceiue not how
We rather should with quiet minde, abide the dated time,
Wherin the Goddes shal vs accompt, as worthy for to clime.
Whiche after trial shal betide, to those that suffre smarte:
For: he doth yll deserue ye swæt, yt tasteth not ye smarte
Which argueth those yt for a while, doth bide ye brūt of pain
To be the owners of good hap, when Fortune turnes again
Whose nūber, I beseech the Gods your self may furnish out,
And that his eies may see you plaste, amid that happi rowt
Whose great good wil shal neuer dy: althogh the wāt of time
Hath don me wrong, & euer doth: in shortning of my rime.

Your most louyng Cosyn. G. VV.

IS. VV. beyng wery of writyng, sendeth this for Answere.

No lesse then thankes, I render vnto you,
What though it be a Beggers bare rewarde
Accept the same: (for Cosyn; this is true,
Tis all I haue: my haps they are so hard:
A one hearteth lyfe, is so from Fortune bard,
But

Famyliar and friendly Epistles,
But this I know, and hope it once to finde
God can, and wyl, exalt the humble minde.
This simple verce: content you for to take
for answer of your louing letter large,
For now I wyll my writting cleane forsake
till of my griefes, my stomack I discharg:
and tyll I row, in Ladie Fortunes barge.
God Cosin write not nor any more replye.
But geue mée leaue, more quietnes to trye.
Your Cosin IS. VV.

The Aucthour (though loth to leaue the Citie) vpon her Friendes procurement, is constrained to departe: wherfore (she fayneth as she would die) and maketh her VVYLL and Testament, as foloweth: VVith large Legacies of such Goods and riches which she moste aboundantly hath left behind her: and therof maketh LONdon sole executor to se her Legacies performed.

A comunication which the Auctor had to London, before she made her VVyll.

The time is come I must departe,
from thee ah famous Citie:
C.ii. I neuer

Fig. 13 The last of Whitney's letters to friends and her "Communication" to London, *Nosgay* (1573).

and London, it shows him being turned away by court after court because, as the refrain notes, "for lacke of money I may not spede."[26] In the process, Lackpenny, like Whitney, passes the merchants and peddlers at "Chepe," "London stone," "Canywike," "Estchepe," "Cornhill," and "Billingsgate," all eager to offer him goods—until they see he has no money. Finally, after making his way across the city, the narrator returns to his plow in Kent. He prays to Jesus to save London and its lawyers, "for he that lacketh money, wt them he shall not spede." Whitney's will records her own extended search for help from an everywhere-indifferent city that grants hospitality only to the wealthy. By following in Lackpenny's literary footsteps, Whitney imports not only plot into her text but also the force of an entire tradition of complaint literature.

Whitney also drew on the long-standing mock will tradition, in which the speaker, unlike Lackpenny, "feigneth to die." This included social satires like the testament of the hare, whose distribution of his body parts condemned the aristocratic hunt and the social ills it symbolized.[27] There were comic wills narrated by cheerful drunkards like Colin Bloball; by carnival troublemakers like Jack o' Lent, about whom Bishop Grindal complained; by underdog tricksters like Jack Splinter, who outmaneuvers a rich convent of greedy nuns; as well as by the devil himself, who satirized the clergy. Typically these wills exposed human error, whether literal folly such as drinking oneself to death or the Erasmian folly of doing good without reward. Like Whitney's, some wills even left bequests of ironically appropriate London neighborhoods. Colin Blobul's legacy to the abbess of "Bacchus Temple" (who was "always swining liquor"), for example, is his land in Southwark, the stews, with special provisions about quitrent for his confessor.

The one Whitney seems to have followed most closely is Robert Copeland's "Wyl of Jyl of Braintford." Jyl, a descendant of Elinor Rumming, is a clever alewife who has succumbed to a grievous stomach disorder. Apparently dying, she dictates her will to the priest, one of the friends gathered around her. Jyl leaves twenty-six and a half of her farts to the several fools in the room who richly deserve them, an apt comeuppance that surprises even the priest, who receives the last bequest for foolishly not charging her a fee. Jyl recovers at the end of her story, having had it both ways: she was allowed a last dying insult all around without actually having to die. Although Whitney's will does not resurrect her as Jyl's did, Whitney does inherit some of Jyl's self-confidence. Whitney's will, under the seemly veil of comic irony, expresses the resentment she had not voiced before.[28]

Like Jyl, Whitney bides her time. Never raucous or passionate, the will begins gently, building only slowly to her typically ironic criticism of the city's cruelty. Only as it proceeds does Whitney begin to refer more to herself and her complaints. Divided into three sections, the will opens with affectionate bequests to London and its people. Here Whitney makes London and its people seem attractive ("Wyll," 21–134). She surveys London's brave buildings, its fair streets, its goodly store of people, its streets, and its many shops with food, clothing, and adornments. This is the section in which Whitney is most evenly balanced between connection to and separation from the city: "I there was bred" ("Wyll," 26), but "I little brought" and "nothing from thee took" ("Wyll," 131–32). The only small irony that qualifies her beneficence is suggested by Whitney's gift of the city's Mint to those who need money (as if London would ever let them have any of it!) and then at the end when, without comment, Whitney leaves unseemly recreations for London's citizens and lets the implications speak for themselves: wine, proper "Gyrles" for the prentices who cannot wed, and baths "so to prevent / infection of the ayre" ["Wyll," 117, 123–24]).

Section 2 ("Wyll," 135–252) is more pointed as it turns from bequests to London's "people" to gifts for its "poore" ("Wyll," 133, 135—an ironic distinction?) and those on the literal margins at its gates and in suburban Smithfield, Bedlam, and Bridewell's. Whitney has moved from London's central streets, where people move freely, to the prisons, hospitals, and workhouses in which they are confined. The colorful wares in the shops earlier are here replaced by the punishments on offer in the prisons, among which she distinguishes like a connoisseur: the Counter, Newgate, Holborn, the Fleet, and Ludgate. Pointedly, Whitney leaves prisons to "honest men…whose coyne is very thin" as well as lawbreakers (definitely ironic here).

This section is more personal as well as more ironic than the first. It introduces Whitney's ties to both London and her audience. We learn that her parents dwelt at Smithfield and that Bedlam "was oft my walke" ("Wyll," 26). When Whitney makes her bequest to the "youthful roote" at the Inns of Court ("Wyll," 239), she may have young men like Plat and her brother in mind. To them she leaves books, tennis courts, players, and dancing schools for recreation. These are the pastimes Plat describes in two of his poems arguing that scholars should take breaks and have fun like everyone else.[29] Additionally, one passage in the section on London's prisons deals for the first time with Whitney's own poverty. At this point Whitney suddenly speaks to the reader for the first time:

> What makes you standersby to smile
>   And laugh so in your sleeve:
> I think it is because that I
>   To Ludgate nothing give.
>   ("Wyll," 174–77)

Her direct address to "you standersby" accuses them of laughing because she had not given anything to Ludgate. "I did reserve that [Ludgate] for myself," she says, if ever she came in debt ("Wyll," 179). But, she goes on with a straight face, no one would ever lend her enough credit to run up any debt, so she decides to leave Ludgate to the bankrupt after all. The irony evokes a smile, even if the reader was not quite laughing up her sleeve before.

A last personal touch in this section is perhaps unintended but interesting, because it is the will's only reference to marriage, a topic that is central to Whitney's poems in *Copy* and alluded to elsewhere in *Nosgay*. After the last of the prisons, Whitney mentions a part of London that really was her territory: her printer and the other bookbinders at Paul's. To them she leaves a bequest of customers and then immediately moves on to an apparently unconnected bequest, leaving partners to bachelors and maids:

> Amongst them [booksellers] all, my Printer must,
> have somwhat to his share:
> I wyll my Friends there Bookes to bye
> of him, with other ware.
> So, Maydens poore, and Widdoers ritch,
> do leave, that oft shall dote,
> And by that meanes shal mary them,
> to set the Girles aflote.
> And wealthy Widdowes will I leave,
> to help young Gentlemen.
>   ("Wyll," 199–206)

Whitney had juxtaposed writing and marriage before, in the letter she had written to her married sister:

> Had I a husband, or a house,
> and all that 'longs thereto
> Myself could frame about to rouse,
> as other women do:
> But till some household cares me tie.
> My books and Pen I will apply.[30]
>   (*Nosgay*, "To Misteris A.B.," 25–30)

Perhaps here too the mention of her writing reminded her of marriage.

The final section of the will is almost entirely devoted to Whitney and her last words to her friends. Her admonishment, when it finally comes, is low-key. As she had told London in her "communication," despite its cruelty "yet am I in no angry moode" but rather, "in perfect love and charytie. / My Testament here write" ("Communication," 27–30). After Whitney has disbursed everything (and, of course, nothing) to London, she simply asks London in return to give her a shroud and a simple burial. Then, almost sweetly, she adds, "And though I nothing named have, / to bury me withal,/ Consider that above the ground, / annoyance bee I shall" ("Wyll," 263–64). The joke is that Whitney's delicate reference to her decomposing body as "annoyance" is blackmail, and she uses it to extract help from London after all. The writer who apologized for the borrowed posies she offered in the first part of the book now makes her own unapologetic request in the second.

In the last lines Whitney turns her attention finally to her friends:

> To all that aske what end I made,
>   and how I went away:
> Thou answer maist like those which heere,
>   no longer tary may.
> And unto all that wysh mee well,
>   or rue that I am gon:
> Doo mee commend, and bid them cease
>   my absence for to mone.
> And tell them further, if they wolde,
>   my presence styll have had:
> They should have sought to men my luck;
>   which ever was too bad.
>   ("Wyll," 293–304)

Tell them, she says, if they miss me and wonder where I'm gone, they should have helped me when I needed it. Her ironic judgment is understated, but as with her instructions to London to bury her, it is unmistakable and unarguable. The last words of the will are followed only by the book's (and Whitney's) final "FINIS. by Is. W."

Whitney's riches-to-rags story moves away from the model of elite miscellanies like Plat's to the less formal mode of private letters, and finally to the plainspoken mode of comic complaint and satire. She puts each of these conventions—individually and together—to her own use, transforming often impersonal forms in order to construct a lively narrative about her particular abandonment by her former employers, her family, and her friends.

These claims for *Nosgay*'s narrative liveliness and autobiographical detail, however, are not meant as claims for its factual accuracy. Although there is no reason to doubt the general situation Whitney describes, *Nosgay*'s narrative sequence seems so carefully planned in its details that it suggests artful rearrangement of the facts. Whitney's typical mid-Tudor poetic style makes it hard to distinguish from that of other writers, She may well have created some of the friends' letters in order to supply such a nicely varied set of answers to her appeals. But if facts are slighted in the text's content, the emotional realities of the situation are made very clear. Whitney successfully conveys her efforts to remain a good servant, sister, and friend despite despairing over her bad fortune. With her departure from Plat and her quiet irony—her narrating "I"—she also conveys the irritation and disapproval that she does not put into the content, the story about "me." As a whole *Nosgay* shows her movement between the two stances she describes in her "Communication" with London, when she asks "Whether it best be more to mell [accept peaceably], or bitterly defy."

Nosgay suggests that despite those who find hardly any autobiographies in the sixteenth century, by the 1570s even ordinary people had a variety of easily available examples to guide them in writing autobiographically. And a savvy printer like Richard Jones thought that readers would be willing to pay for them.

CHAPTER 8

Erasing an Author's Life: *George Gascoigne's Revision of* One Hundreth Sundrie Flowres *(1573) in His* Posies *(1575)*

> I doe here protest unto you (reverend) even by the hope of my salvation, that there is no living creature touched or to be noted thereby.
> GEORGE GASCOIGNE, *Posies* (1575)

George Gascoigne's 1573 miscellany *A Hundreth Sundrie Flowres* presents itself as a collection of fashionable verse by a number of witty young authors, written on various occasions and printed without their knowledge. The initial group of linked poems, "Adventures of Master F.J.," insists provocatively on its adulterous secrets and hidden identities, and other poems allude more quietly to concealed identities. Apparently some of the book's first readers responded to the provocation. As Gascoigne later explained in his revised edition, *The Posies of George Gascoigne* (1575), *Hundreth* had been accused not only of wantonness but also of slandering important people. Gascoigne claimed that the new edition of 1575 was "gelded from all filthie phrases" and "corrected in all erroneous places," but in the end it was recalled without explanation by the Queen Majesty's Commission.[1]

The book, Gascoigne's censorship of the second edition, and the recall that it suffered nonetheless all raise questions about Gascoigne's life.[2] What had he been hiding in *Hundreth*'s "Adventures"? Who supplied the "busie conjectures" that led to attacks on it ("To the reverende Divines," [362, P1.38–39])? Why? Unfortunately, the early search for a key to the historical truth behind characters like F. J. and Elinor in "Adventures" (were they Leicester and the queen? Gascoigne and his already-married wife?) left critics wary about biography. Biographical questions do remain: Was Gascoigne really hiding something in *Hundreth* or just teasing? Did he really "geld" the offensive material in *Posies*, or was he being ironic, making only a few superficial changes and thumbing his nose at the very critics to whom he pretended to apologize?[3] Answers to the questions differ: Gascoigne may have been questioning the possibility of humanist education, exploring the nature of interpretation, or interrogating the very possibility of meaning and presence.[4] But one of the few things critics agree about is that autobiography is not important to them.

The turn from biography, however, is almost always based on isolated texts and analysis of content only. But if autobiography is located in the "I" of the narrator, as well as in the content, then Gascoigne is a primary example of the autobiographer describing and revising his past. I will argue here, first, that, as in all occasional poetry, there is much straightforward autobiographical content in *Hundreth*—perhaps more than we thought. More interesting than Gascoigne's role in the book's content—the "me"—however, is his role as its narrator/editor—the "I" in and behind the book. The two Gascoignes are best traced not only in one or two of the book's most provocative texts but rather in the entire history of *Hundreth*'s composition, from the original process of preparing the selections to the publications of the revised edition two years later. Finally, Gascoigne's sophistication, rather than precluding autobiography, as has been claimed, depends on it. The rewritten *Posies* is disappointing because it was as "gelded" of autobiography as it was of wantonness and slander. The chapter ends with an argument that, like Whythorne's and Tusser's texts, *Hundreth* was not only based on its author's experience, it was also conceived in part as an exchange with people Gascoigne knew, especially his patron, Arthur, Lord Grey of Wilton.

George Gascoigne (ca. 1539–77)

The Gascoignes were a wealthy family from Bedfordshire.[5] George Gascoigne, eldest son of Sir John Gascoigne, member of Parliament and sometime participant in court ceremonies, had been born with many advantages. He seems to have had access to private tutoring before moving on to Cambridge and then Gray's Inn. His father's influence made it possible for him to take part in the queen's coronation, where, he says, he was seduced by "the glistering court" and immediately determined to "hoyste up sayle to catch a Courtly grace" (728, 61.2, 22).

But Gascoigne's prodigality, irresponsibility, love of bad company, failure to take a degree at Cambridge, and stubborn sense of entitlement rapidly destroyed his court-bent hopes along with much of his inheritance. Even his marriage in 1561 to Elizabeth Bacon, a promisingly rich widow, only made things worse. After the wedding Gascoigne discovered Bacon's earlier disputed wedding to Edward Boyes—who promptly sued Gascoigne for bigamy, arranged a court order to prevent him from seeing Bacon, and continued to fight for control of her and her wealth. Henry Machyn's diary records a fight at her house, presumably when Gascoigne returned illegally to see her. A number of Gascoigne's poems seem to deal with their separation and his combined longing for her and fear that she might betray him. Legal conflicts with Boyes continued half a dozen years after the wedding and returned to haunt Gascoigne later, when new questions arose about his misuse of his stepsons' inheritance. Meanwhile his time at the Inns of Court was interrupted by creditors, who drove him from London. His various attempts to make a living—as a tenant farmer, as a lawyer, as a soldier—all failed.

By the winter of 1572–73 Gascoigne's problems had grown serious. He had spent time in prison and continued to face suits by family, tenants, and neighbors. He had managed to secure a seat in Parliament, a position that would have protected him from creditors. But he never got to claim it, most likely because of the letter sent to the Privy Council accusing him not only of the usual debts but also of atheism, spying, writing attacks on great men, and manslaughter: "Item he is a defamed person and noted as well for Manslaughter as for other greate crymes / Item he is a common Rymer and a deviser of slaunderous Pasquelles against diverse personnes of greate calling / Item he is a notorious Ruffianne and especiallie noted to be bothe a spie; an Atheist and godlesse personne."[6] Before leaving the country to avoid repercussions, Gascoigne, in a last attempt to improve his position, turned to writing, the one area in which he had been successful. He had recently written a masque for Lord Montacute that, it is thought, had secured him the Parliament seat, and in 1572 "Gascoigne's Woodsmanship" had gained favor with Lord Grey.[7] Now he decided to publish a volume that would further advertise his skills to all potential patrons. The result was the 1573 edition of his collected work, *A Hundredth Sundrie Flowres*.

The book, partly the product of desperation, seems also, however, to have appealed to Gascoigne's pride in his literary ability. He delighted in his powers of invention and in showing them off. As he says in the revised edition, "Although I challenge not unto my selfe the name of an English Poet," he was proud that he "coulde as well persuade with Penne, as pearce with launce" (362, P1.16–17 and note). His literary skill remained his best hope and ultimately would gain him at least a modicum of "courtly grace" and government assignments.

A Hundreth Sundrie Flowres: Gascoigne's "Me"

The separate editions of Gascoigne's book, like Tusser's, have usually been treated as a single composite text. Gascoigne himself referred only to a single volume, "my thryftlesse booke of Posyes," as did his friend and elegist, George Whetstone.[8] But the two versions draw on his experience in different ways. Each edition shows Gascoigne under a different set of pressures and writing with different motives. Although individually the differences seem small, their combined implication for the development of autobiography is important enough to consider in more detail.[9]

Hundreth's title page does not mention Gascoigne's name, but it does include his motto, "Meritum petere, grave" ("to seek reward is a serious matter," or "to seek reward is painful"). After its three introductory letters, the book is divided into two parts. The first, consisting of Gascoigne's two plays, *The Supposes* and *Jocasta*, openly identifies him as translator or co-translator. The second, longer, part is more autobiographical although less open about it. It claims to be a miscellany of verse by "sundry Gentlemen," of whom "master Gascoyne" is only one. G. T., who collected the poems, provides commentary on them, starting in his introductory letter.

G. T.'s miscellany format immediately raises autobiographical expectations because it recalls Tottel's *Miscellany* (1557) and the imitations by Barnabe Googe, Thomas Howell, George Turberville, and Hugh Plat. These all include occasional poems about the author's experience of friendships, courtships, partings, and so on. True, George Turberville tells readers that *his* love poetry is not autobiographical: but his disclaimer still implies autobiographical truth as the norm.[10] Poets might at times lie, play games, or flatter untruthfully in a particular poem. Henry Howard, earl of Surrey, did so in his politely complimentary love poem to Geraldine Fitzgerald, who was in reality too young to be courted, although old enough to receive his homage to her family. But on the whole, poets were assumed to speak from their own experience. G. T. takes it for granted that the verse in *Hundreth* is autobiographical. His praise of the poets' wit depends on knowing the personal occasion for which the poems were written: none of the verse he collected was so barren but "had in it *Aliquid Salis*" or touch of wit, he says, "especially being considered by the very proper occasion whereupon it was written (as they [the authors] them selves did always with the verse reherse unto me the cause that then moved them to write)" (145.1–4).

G. T.'s commentary extends throughout the anthology, as Baldwin's does in *Mirror for Magistrates*, providing his own perspective on the work. That perspective dominates the opening group of poems by "F.J.," written during the young poet's adulterous romance. G. T.'s supposedly literary commentary is just as interested in the titillating historical background for F. J.'s verse. His gossipy comments on "The Adventures of Master F.J.," as he calls it, make the narrative cruder. His attempts to protect identities make even the dullest reader alert for slander, as in his reference to "a gentlewoman of the company whom I have not hitherto named, and that for good respects, lest hir name might altogether disclose the rest" (191.1–3). On the other hand, readers are prodded into seeing beyond G. T.'s own voyeuristic sentimentality along with F. J.'s idealism. The result is a wonderfully complex treatment of love and literary tradition that transforms the novella into one of the most sophisticated of all sixteenth-century narratives.

Given G. T.'s role in *Hundreth*, the question is not about the book's hidden autobiographical dimension but rather about whose autobiography. Is it Gascoigne's? Ostensibly not. "Adventures" is about F. J., not Gascoigne. More important, Gascoigne exposes G. T.'s misguided focus on F. J. and what really happened rather than on the poetry. Yet much else in the book continually points outside itself to Gascoigne. The plays are identified as his, he is the only one of the sundry poets whose name is given, and his poems make up the final, culminating group in *Hundreth*. Additionally, despite the playful show of anonymity elsewhere, Gascoigne, as we shall see, leaves enough hints for readers to guess that he wrote the other poetry as well.

Apart from the plays, Gascoigne's acknowledged contributions are in fact quite insistently autobiographical. His poems are not only introduced as the work of "Master Gascoigne" but often include "Gascoigne" in their titles. Having saved his best work to claim as his own, Gascoigne wants to make sure of being remembered as its author. The poems do seem at times to cloak potentially embarrassing information. Accordingly, unlike the poems attributed to F. J. and others, Master Gascoigne's poems are not usually given extended informative introductions.[11]

When a poem happens to reflect especially well on Gascoigne, however, G. T. supplies copious contextual detail for it. The five poems usually called "Gascoigne's Memories" are a good example (274–82, 58–62). These, each elaborating a different moral topos, might well have been grouped by subject into five separate edifying verse lessons. But instead Gascoigne grouped them together by author, specifically by what they showed about "Gascoigne's Memory" and improvisation skills. G. T. tells us that Gascoigne wrote the poems as impromptu responses to topics proposed by friends while riding "by the way," without writing them down. "A small time for suche a taske," he says, very impressed, "neyther wolde I willingly undertake the like" [282, 62, 46.9–10]).

In addition, *Hundreth Sundrie Flowres* calls attention to his life when it advertises him as a reformed prodigal. G. T.'s opening letter praises the "worthy and famous Knight Sir Geffrey Chaucer," whose poetry began with "pretie devises" of youth but moved to serious treatment of life's "right pathway" when he got older (143, 27–30). Gascoigne follows Chaucer's path toward reformation. As he would say later in *Posies,* he had already reformed before publishing *Hundreth*: "I had written sundry things which coulde not chuse but content the learned and the Godlye Reader, that I had layde asid vanities, and delighted to exercise my penne in morall discourses."[12]

In particular, Master Gascoigne's group of poems emphasizes his biography because they give chronological evidence that he is a reformed prodigal.[13] He wrote wanton love poems in youth and recanted them later (57); he wrote courtly verse, sometimes to impressively titled figures like Lady This and Countess That (51, 52), or to two very impressive patrons indeed, Lord Montacute (71) and Lord Grey (72, 77). But finally he went on to reform and write moral lessons (58–62), social commentary, and "godly himnes and Psalmes," as the Printer calls them (4.22). Near the end of this section there are four poems called "Gascoignes gardnings" that, as G. T. tells us, reproduce posies in Gascoigne's real garden; one of them mentions his wife. They indicate the solid respectability achieved by "Master Gascoigne," now a husband and owner of house and garden. Perhaps just as important, they clearly distinguish Gascoigne from young F. J. of

"Adventures," whom we had seen visiting someone else's estate (and courting someone else's wife).[14]

The garden verse also includes what may be one hint that Gascoigne is author of the whole book. Verses like these were traditional at the end of single-author miscellanies like Whitney's and Plat's. A reader could understandably think that Gascoigne's reference to all (in "al these floures") included everything up to that page in *Hundreth*: "If thou sitte here to viewe this pleasant garden place, / Think thus: at last will come a frost, and al these floures deface" (318, 75.1–2).

There are even stronger hints elsewhere that all the anonymous work G. T. has collected can be traced to Gascoigne. *Hundreth*'s two longer narratives about "unlawful affection," as the Printer calls them in his letter, certainly point to Gascoigne: "The Adventures of Master F.J." opening the book and "Don Bartholmew of Bathe" closing it. Unlike the plays and "master Gascoynes" poems, they are not attributed to him, but they both tell about young men very like him. "Adventures" has been called a "fable of the artist as a young man," and despite subsequent challenges, it is easy see why.[15] F. J. the hero, like Gascoigne, is an author, and his story recounts poetic as well as amorous adventures: "I have heard the Aucthor saye, that these were the first verses that ever he wrote uppon like occasion" (146.21–22), G. T. says. Whether or not there really was an Elinor in Gascoigne's life, F. J.'s story about Elinor in "Adventures" is consistent with the prodigal life sketched by "Master Gascoigne" and with Gascoigne's biography. "Adventures" takes place in "a house in the north" where Gascoigne had landed connections, and it mocks F. J.'s lack of courtly skills, the same lack that Gascoigne boasted about later, in "Woodsmanship" (1572). At about the same time that Gascoigne published *Hundreth*, Thomas Whythorne was working an account of country-house adventures very similar to F. J.'s. Whythorne intended to be truthful, but given his innocently tendentious self-presentation, his use of initials to hide names, and his other indirections, the difference between Gascoigne's "fiction" and Whythorne's "truth" begins to look like one of quantity, not quality.

"Dan Bartholmew of Bathe," the concluding poem in *Hundreth*, immediately follows Gascoigne's poetry and may have been intended as part of it. But even if not, Dan Bartholmew is as much an alter ego for Gascoigne as is F. J. With its older hero, "Dan Bartholmew" can be seen as another portrait of the artist—this time as a middle-aged man, like F. J., still vulnerable to Cressida-like women and still writing poetry about it. G. T. leaves the story of F. J. "unperfect" (215.32), and the Reporter breaks off Bartholmew's tale midsentence (358, 12.68). Their tales both end ambiguously, hanging undecided, like Gascoigne's own situation in 1573.

The rest of the verse in *Hundreth* is supposedly written by authors known only by their "devises" or mottos. But it is nearly all drawn from the same pool of experience treated in Gascoigne's acknowledged poetry and in "Adventures" and "Dan Bartholmew of Bath." Gascoigne had only a limited repertoire of topics.[16] Again and again, lovers—many apparently adulterous—are separated and pine for one another as Gascoigne did for Elizabeth; or one lover fears that the other has been unfaithful; or one of the lovers dreams of reunion but wakes in disappointment (1); or one of the lovers is imprisoned behind literal or figurative walls (4, 27, 38). Still other poems are about love's defeats. They tell about the speaker's longing for an unobtainable woman, one who is married (like F. J.'s Elinor or Gascoigne's Elizabeth), who comes from a more elevated social position (Bartholmew's Ferenda), or who is interested in another (less worthy) man. Often, if a woman hasn't already rejected the speaker, she betrays him before the end of the poem.

Some poems allude quite specifically to Gascoigne's life. One benefit of distributing his verse among the other poets was that Gascoigne could deflect attention from certain poems by locating them in someone else's life. He thus isolated them not only from himself but also from each other, and thus from a single narrative backstory. Later, in 1575, when Gascoigne revised and censored his book, he was even more cautious. Most of his revisions in *Posies* were concentrated in "Adventures," which had caused most offense. But Gascoigne also quietly deleted three of *Hundreth*'s poems that referred either to his own adulterous marital history (39) or to separated pairs of lovers and thus perhaps to part of that history (1, 21).[17]

The poets themselves, insofar as they can be distinguished, are linked in other ways to Gascoigne and his alter egos, F. J. and Dan Bartholmew.[18] Two of the three poems (1 and 21) omitted from *Posies* are assigned to the first fictional poet, whose motto is "Si Fortunatus Infelix" ("If fortunate then unhappy"). This poet, identified by the initials from his motto, F. I., is linked to F. J. through the printer's convention that makes *I* and *J* identical. He is linked to Gascoigne as well, since he is assigned authorship of the group of five poems that retell F. J.'s story as "G.G"'s story—or

George Gascoigne's. The third fictional poet takes a motto made from the name of Bartholmew's beloved (and Gascoigne's and, later, the Green Knight's), Ferenda Natura. One of his suggestively adulterous poems, "An absent lover (parted from his Lady by Sea) thus compleyneth" (37), sounds like Gascoigne's other poems about separated (often adulterous) lovers. Apparently it was too suggestive for *Posies*. There it would be given a new title that removes it from the realm of human events and assigns it to gods instead: "Mars in despite of Vulcane written for an absent lover (parted from his Lady by the Sea)." The "Ferenda" poet is also assigned the poem (30) that is later recanted by Gascoigne (57), as if it were his own poem.

Finally the fourth poet, "Meritum petere grave," shares his motto with Gascoigne's title page. "Meritum" has links to several Gascoigne personas. To Gascoigne: he is assigned several poems about adulterous events very like Gascoigne's troubles after his bigamous marriage, including the third poem later cut from *Posies* (38, 39, 40). To Bartholmew: another poem claims the colors in Dan Bartholmew's flag (34), and yet another (35) would be taken from him and given to "Dan Bartholmew" in *Posies*. To F. J.: two more of "Meritum"'s poems treat the adulterous liaison between David and Bathsheba (42–43), the same topic that F. J. chose for his first poem to his paramour in "Adventures."[19]

Later in *Posies*, when Gascoigne reclaimed authorship of the poems by sundry gentlemen, he still insisted that none of them were about him. He had written them all for other men, he said. That is why he gave them different mottos. But he gave himself away when he added, "I have also sundrie tymes chaunged mine owne worde or devise. And no mervaile: For he that wandereth much in those wildernesses, shall seldome continue long in one minde" (371, P 3.15–18). The mottos were all his. The sundry devices, from this perspective, represent not different men but different aspects of Gascoigne's own "mind" as he wandered through various wildernesses, or, as F. J. might say, "adventures," external or internal.

In sum, Gascoigne protests too much. Despite trying to distance himself from the biographical implications of his youthful work, Gascoigne had filled his book with occasional poetry from his own past experience. A poem like "When stedfast friendship" clearly alludes to a particular occasion on the bank of the Thames, "When Popler walles enclos'd thy pensive mind," and "My painted shadow did thy woes revive" (21.8–9). So long as Gascoigne could claim it was about someone else, the poem could be published. In *Posies... of Gascoigne*, however, he had to cut the poem, probably because its details might betray him. His cuts suggest that Gascoigne not only wrote the poems but wrote them about himself. He was the "me" in his poetry as well as the "I," although often disguised as "he" or, perhaps, "G. G." Gascoigne's work refers to himself both in the individual poems and in the sequence of growth they illustrate—from wanton young lover to elegant courtier, to repentant youth who recants his past, to mature writer of serious verse about religion and morality.

One Hundreth Sundrie Flowres: Gascoigne's "I"

Gascoigne would almost certainly chafe at my emphasis so far on content and occasions for his verse. In 1575 he took pains to deny any reference to reality in *Hundreth*. He swore "even by the hope of my salvation, that there is no living creature touched or to be noted thereby" (363, P 1.10–12). He would have preferred a subject "which might generally have spred my commendation," he says. But autobiographical poems, unfortunately including his youthful trifles, were all he had (362, P 1.6–7). He explains that having started late and now too busy as a soldier, he must make do with what he has already written: "I must take the Foord as I finde it: Sometimes not as I woulde, but as I may" (362, P 1.8–9). Gascoigne downplayed content because, for him, the most important part of his work was "my Methode and maner of writing" (363, P 1.17–18). He was particularly proud of his gift for "invention," or special cleverness in finding and elaborating on a subject—any subject.[20] Part of what "quick capacitie" meant was the ability to make anything interesting: "the occasions of Inventions are (as it were) infinite" (455, P 34.9–10).

But my point here is that Gascoigne's inventiveness was nonetheless, if only by default, inventiveness in shaping an account of his own life. Gascoigne may not have set out to write autobiography, but as with other autobiographers, what he was doing was trying to find a perspective on the Gascoigne he describes from the past. He was, as George Gusdorf describes the autobiographical act, "call[ing] up the past in the present and for the present" and reconstructing it for his present needs: that is, his need to display his skill and make himself look good.[21]

The autobiographical interplay between the two Gascoignes, past and present, writer and subject, is precisely what defines the poet's most admired texts. A lyric like "Gascoigne's Woodsmanship" suggests how closely interwoven were Gascoigne's inventive and autobiographical impulses.[22] At first there seems to be only one person in "Woodsmanship," a man who has always "shot awrie" and missed every target he had ever aimed at—philosophy, law, the court, the military, and now, a deer on Lord Grey's estate. The second is an impersonal speaker addressing Lord Grey, who refers to the protagonist as "your wodman [woodsman]" (312, 72.2). The invisible speaker describes the woodsman in the third person.

He does not appear as a character himself until line 69, when he appeals to Grey on behalf of the poor fellow: "And sure I feare, unlesse your Lordship deigne, / To traine him yet into some better trade, / It will be long before he hit the veine" (314, 72.69–71). Only fifteen lines later does the speaker reveal that the poem is autobiographical and that he himself is the woodsman: "Then you marvell why *I* lette them go, / And never shoote" (315, 72.87–88, italics added). He then offers Grey a clever theory that turns his past worldly failures into a higher moral achievement, praises his present poetic skills ("But since my Muse can to my Lorde reherse / What makes me misse" [316, 72.125–26]), and, with his powerful "imagination," calls up in words alone an emblematic vision of the carrion deer that he shot, should not have shot, did not shoot, and, had he shot it, would have taught him finally to shoot true—all at once. The shift from "he" to "I" in the poem puts all these different truths about himself into play simultaneously. As in any autobiography, past and present perspectives move separately in parallel, until, finally, the narrator comments openly on his past self (69) and then joins his past to the present (89). He thus creates an "amended" self (189), who sucks new success from the teat of past failures by changing the way he sees them: "And when I see the milke hang in hir teate, / Me thinkes it sayth, olde babe now learne to sucke" (316, 72.145–46).[23]

The doubling of autobiographical retrospection in "Woodsmanship" is part of its point. With varying success it structures Gascoigne's longer narratives as well. In "The Adventures of F.J." and "Dan Bartholmew of Bathe" the speaker and protagonist are not literally the same man, as they were in "Woodsman." Yet each narrator is in all but name an older and wiser (or more disillusioned) self looking back on his youth. He sympathizes with but distances himself from the hero, and he makes the hero's story out of the latter's own poetry, as if he understood it as well as its author.[24] G. T. identifies vicariously with F. J.'s "Adventures," although he claims to bring a more sensible moral and more seasoned literary perspective to the story. "Dan Bartholmew"'s Reporter actually says that his tale looks back to "my youth" (329, 1.14) as well as to Bartholmew's. He speaks about his "deare familiar friend['s]" painful love (329 1.23), and while he says that "I my selfe was never paramoure" (332, 1.119), he later contradicts that by referring to his own similar suffering in love (357, 12.22–23). At times it is hard to tell which of the two is speaking. At the end of one section, for example, Dan Bartholmew wishes for death: "Alas how welcome were this death of mine, / If I had dyde betweene those armes of thine" (356, 11.13–14). The speaker in the first line of the next section begins with "fluddes of flowing teares, / so to suffise the swelling of mine eyes?" (356, 12.1–2)" and also goes on to wish for death: "would God that I were drowned" (356–57, 12.8). By the time the speaker says, "I am that man whome destinies ordeine," a reader tends to read "that man" as Bartholmew, the last man mentioned, and not—as the reader is surprised to learn soon after—the Reporter (357, 12.15).

"Dan Bartholmew" remains unfinished. Its contradictions, repetitions, and loose ends make it an unsuccessful text. But they also provide evidence for the process of separating past experience from present perspective that creates autobiography. The confusions about Bartholmew's narrator seem to derive from the story's evolution as it changed gradually from autobiography to fiction. Gascoigne probably wrote the poems to his own Ferenda in the 1560s, when he was writing much of his other love poetry. Then, as writer/editor of *Hundreth* in 1573, he gathered his existing Ferenda poems and attributed some of them to an otherwise barely defined alter ego, i.e., the poet who takes "Ferenda Natura" as his motto. Still later that year, Gascoigne decided to combine several Ferenda poems into a separate verse narrative about Ferenda's lover ("Let call his name *Dan Bartholmew of Bathe*" [330, 1.37]), in which Gascoigne remained hovering between his two roles as subject (Dan Bartholmew) and as observing Reporter/editor.

Gascoigne apparently changed his mind about whether Bartholmew was to tell his own story. The printer's letter, written early in the editing process, says that Dan Bartholmew "made" his story himself (4.16), but by the time Gascoigne composed the poem itself he invented a Reporter, although in his haste to complete the text he may not always have separated hero and Reporter.

One final level on which the play between subject and writer, past and present, can be observed is that of the book's structure. Gascoigne was not the only poet striving for invention in his occasional poems; many others wanted to "shewe the queintnes of their quil."[25] What made Gascoigne special was that he extended his inventiveness beyond the single lyric to the entire *Hundreth Sundrie Flowres*. Like Whythorne's framed collection of poetry, *Hundreth* is not just a miscellany of separate works. Gascoigne created a varied but unified, coherent work that displays the poetry from a variety of points of view—modest, proud, playful, serious.[26] He did so by adapting a structural "invention" from the serious playfulness of writers like Thomas More in *Utopia* and William Baldwin in *Beware the Cat*. More and Baldwin had used their perspective games to explore pressing questions about governance and religious belief.[27] But Gascoigne exercised his humanist skills to display his "quick capacitie." He attributed some work to other men; he wrapped even his acknowledged group of poems inside playfully misleading frames, "supposes," "cloudes" (161.5), and "unperfect" statements (215.32), in order to call attention to the fact that he could. It was a daring redeployment of style and format, not matched until Edmund Spenser published his *Shepheards Calendar* (1579) in the scholarly format reserved for classical authors and serious Continental poets.

Whatever Gascoigne says, it is likely that he wanted the reader to see through the devices and recognize him as the author of all the verse so they could appreciate his cleverness. He implies what G. T. says outright:

> Neyther can I declare unto you who / wrote the greatest part of them, for they are unto me but a posie / presented out of sundry gardens, neither have I any other names of / the flowers, but such short notes as the aucthors themselves have delivered therby if you can gesse them, it shall no waye offende / mee. (216.10–15)

His game of hide-and-seek is not funny unless you know the secret, and Gascoigne was not one to waste a good joke. When. G. T. praises Gascoigne as the most "forthcoming" of all the poets, for example, an informed reader would know that of course he was most forthcoming because the other—nonexistent—poets did not come forth with anything at all.[28] Elsewhere, G. T. apologizes for one of the anonymous poets who does "not compare to the rest." Here he seems to be having a little joke at Gascoigne's expense, because this is the poet who shares Gascoigne's own motto.

Gascoigne certainly identified himself as the author when he sent a copy of *Hundreth* to Grey, his most important patron. In any case, the hoax does not seem to have fooled Gascoigne's contemporaries. It neither protected him from their "objections" nor elicited any further apology for him. His flat-out assumption of authorship later in *Posies* without comment suggests that authorship (unlike wantonness and slander) was never an issue.

The Posies of George Gascoigne Esquire: Gascoigne's "Me" without the "I"

Having achieved so much in *Hundreth*, Gascoigne almost immediately undid it in his revised edition, *The Posies of George Gascoigne Esquire* (1575). The book's opening letter "To the reverende Divines" reports that *Hundreth* had been found not only "offensive for sundrie wanton speeches and lascivious phrases" but also "scandalous" (359, P 1.14–16). Gascoigne assures the "Divines" that he has corrected all that. The new *Posies* has been "gelded from all filthie phrases" and "corrected in all erronious places" (361, P 1.37). But unfortunately, this new edition censors Gascoigne's autobiography, just as it censors wantonness and slander. It drops the fiction of multiple authors and illegal publication. There is no unifying "G. T." in *Posies* to make a fuss about keeping the authors' identity secret—and thus to keep readers alert for clues to that identity. The narrators and reporters who take G. T.'s place comment instead about the character's identities. The authors themselves have disappeared, except for Gascoigne on the title page. The poems are now organized by moral status into three categories of "Hearbes," "Floures," and "Weedes" (367, P 2.24), as if they had no authors and no autobiographical occasions.

In addition Gascoigne distances himself from *Posies*' contents far more than G. T. had distanced *Hundreth*'s poems from their authors. True, the title page now announces Gascoigne as the book's author, and his introductory letters implicitly assume authorship when they tell readers, in effect, Read this and learn from my bad experience. But they also disown the verse: "the most part of them were written for other men" (370, P 3.32–33). There is no longer a section in the text called "Master Gascoigne's poems," with an appreciative G. T. to remark on them. Gascoigne also removes all clues, like the name of his fellow Innsman James Scudamore, that link the poems to real people associated with him.[29] As if that weren't enough, he edits the poetry from *Hundreth* in the way that Tottel had edited Wyatt's poetry in his miscellany. Many of Gascoigne's small, unannounced changes in the reprinted verse of *Posies* move it away from particulars toward general didactic statement: thus "*Gascoigne's* Recantation" in *Hundreth* becomes "The Recantation of *a Love*," just as Wyatt's "They fle from me" becomes "The Lover Showeth Himself to be Forsaken."[30] This is exactly what Gascoigne had tried to avoid before: the "customes of common writers" (455, P 34.22) who speak in commonplaces even when talking about themselves.

Finally, Gascoigne disclaims authorship not only of the revised "Adventures" but also of one of the added narratives: "The fruite of Fetters, with the complaint of the greene Knight" (439, P 29.01–0.2). Both, he says, were written by Bartello; he merely translated them (396, P 27.393). Gascoigne's is no longer a book emphasizing its authorship and production (who wrote it, found it, shared it, printed it) but its consumption: how to read it properly. The brazen, cleverly self-reflective author from *Hundreth* is silent, except in some few lines added to "Dan Bartholmew," to which I will return in a moment.

It might seem at first that the three long poems that Gascoigne added to *Posies* make the new edition more, not less, autobiographical.[31] There are two entirely new paired autobiographical works about Gascoigne's war experience: "The fruites of Warre," or "Dulce Bellum inexpertis" (398, P 28.0.1–0.2), and "The fruite of Fetters."[32] The first of the two war poems, "Fruites of Warre," is a sustained and serious account justifying Gascoigne's soldiering. The second, "Fruite of Fetters," elaborates on his failures, his vulnerability to women, and his time in prison. The third addition completes the already autobiographical "Dan Bartholmew." It too concerns martial as well as amorous exploits.

But the additions are autobiographical in a way very different from the texts in *Hundreth*, which focused on Gascoigne's role as narrator in the poems, the "I" who tells the stories. *Posies* foregrounds him, if at all, in his role as character, the "me" in the stories.[33] The distinction is, of course, not absolute; Gascoigne wrote and starred in all the poetry of both volumes, and he put his motto even at the end of Bartello's narratives. Nor does it apply to every poem in each volume; Gascoigne's two roles are both important, for example, in his "Voyage" (1572). It is a matter of emphasis. But emphasis matters. To foreground the narrator in *Hundreth* is to foreground Gascoigne's control over the material and his inventive powers. To foreground the characters—F. J., Bartholmew, the Greene Knight—is to emphasize failure, self-delusion, and a future of hopeless repetition. The characters are caught; the author can take control, in part by distinguishing himself from the character, as Gascoigne separates himself from the Woodsman.

Another way of describing the difference is that *Hundreth*'s riddles lead to one question: Who wrote this book? Is it Gascoigne? Who are the anonymous authors hiding behind mottos? Even when a character's identity is in question, as F. J.'s is, that character is also an author, the author of his own story. But in *Posies* the greatest mystery concerns the characters: Who is the Greene Knight? Who is Bartholmew? Might they really be the same person? Are they representations of Gascoigne?

The shift in Gascoigne's role is also a matter of tone. G. T.'s playfulness about the author's identity runs all through *Hundreth*. But *Posies* swings awkwardly between extremes, from seriousness about Gascoigne in "Fruites of Warre" to the almost manic mystifications about his alter egos in the other two poems. Much of *Hundreth*'s felt mystery disappeared with G. T. What mysteriousness remains in *Posies* hangs only on some added marginalia and the few added lines of verse in "Dan Bartholmew."

The new marginalia make claims about the "mistries" in "Dan Bartholmew." Mysteries there are. Who is the Admiral who called Ferenda a rover? What is the bracelet and what does it mean? But a marginal claim that "these thinges are mistical / And not to bee understoode but by / Th'auctour him selfe," cannot substitute for G. T.'s provocatively flawed cover-ups ("Dan Bartholmew," 337, 4.161, 236). Announcing that something is mysterious is like announcing that it is funny—unnecessary if true.

The riddle in the added text of "Dan Bartholmew" is similarly heavy-handed. The Reporter, having just described Bartholmew's repentance, goes on to say that Bartholmew will probably succumb to temptation once again and that he is no better than the Greene Knight. Our ears prick up if we know who the Greene Knight is. Continuing, the Reporter reveals that, indeed, Bartholmew and the Greene Knight are the same figure:

Bartello he which writeth ryding tales,
Bringes in a Knight which cladde was all in greene,
That sighed sore amide his greevous gales,

> And was in hold as *Bartholmew* hath beene.
> But (for a placke) it maye therein be seene,
> That, that same Knight which there his griefes begonne,
> Is *Batts* own Fathers Sisters brothers Sonne.
> (396–97, P 27.393–99)

A diligent reader might use these lines to deduce the connections between Dan Bartholmew, the Greene Knight, and Gascoigne. But in *Posies* the brevity of the reference in "Fruites of Warre," along with the length of the poems and the order of their presentation, all make the identification very difficult.[34] "Bartholmew" appears first. Thus, when the Reporter in "Bartholmew" first mentions the "Knight which cladde was all in greene," we have no idea who he is—until we read the following poem, "The fruites of Warre," which reveals (briefly!) that Gascoigne had been known in battle as "die groene Hopman" (423, P 28.129.2) or "the Greene knight" (423, P 28.129.4)—two lines out of more than 1500. The two poems are then separated from the Greene Knight's own poems by an entire section of poems, the "Hearbes."

Even if a reader does work out the connection between Bartholmew, the Greene Knight, and Gascoigne-the-Greene-Knight, all three identities still mark Gascoigne as the subject of a poem, not—as in *Hundreth*—as its author. Gascoigne is author only of "Fruites of Warre"; the rest are by Bartello, whose identity is never brought in question and never linked to Gascoigne within the book's fiction. In *Hundreth*, G. T. repeatedly talked about the authors—this one is not as good as the others, all of them talked to him, and so on. But the narrators and reporters who take G. T.'s place in *Posies* comment only on characters, not authors.

The new emphasis on character instead of author is nicely illustrated by comparing "Gascoigne's Woodsmanship" in *Hundreth* with the Greene Knight poems in *Posies*, two works that have been linked before because in each the speaker reviews a similar list of past failures. But there is a more fundamental similarity than content in the structure of the poems. Once this is highlighted it reveals a striking difference. The poems are alike because each begins by focusing on its subject (the woodsman or the knight), and each withholds the speaker's identity. Only later does each poem reveal the speaker's connection to his supposed subject. The important difference between the poems is that in "Woodsmanship" the speaker emerges triumphant over the woodsman, as we have seen, and thus over his own past, but in the Greene Knight poems the speaker emerges only to dissolve back into the knight, and thus into his own past failures.

"The fruite of Fetters" begins like "Woodsman" by reviewing the title character's failures, although this time in the first person: "I teare my time (ay me) in prison pent" (439, P 29.13). As in "Woodsmanship," the speaker does not reveal his presence until the character's story has already been told once. Then, surprisingly, he speaks: "So sighed the knight of whome *Bartello* writes, / All clad in Greene, yet banisht from delights" (442, P 29.95–96).[35]

In "Woodsman" the speaker finally returns late in the poem to talk about himself at greater length. The equivalent return in "Knight" occurs late too. We are well into the third of five poems before the speaker returns suddenly to say,

> But now to turne my tale from whence I came,
> I saie his lottes and mine were not unlike:
> He spent his youth (as I did) out of frame,
> He came at last (like me) to trayle the pike.
> He pyned in pryson pinchte with privie payne,
> And I likewise in pryson still remayne.
>   (449, P 31.55–60)

Both he and the Knight wasted their youth, became soldiers, and found themselves in prison. He is not literally the same man as the Knight, but he resembles and identifies with him.

In "Woodsman," by the time the speaker goes on to reveal himself as identical to the woodsman, he has redeemed and superseded the character. But in *Posies*, the speaker never redeems the knight and never escapes the knight's paralysis himself. At one point he does seem to be on the verge of finding redemption in imprisonment, when he begins a new line with a momentous "yet": "Yet some good fruite in fetters can I finde" (448, P 31.61).

But in this poem redemption never comes, even for the Greene Knight, let alone for the speaker. Yes, there are fruits of fetters. Imprisonment fosters virtues like repentance. But this fruit is not so easily plucked. Dangerous "fancies" grow among the fruits, like weeds among the flowers of grace. These fancies lead the prisoner astray and make him hope for release, pine for his love, and forget redemption. The Greene Knight tries to avoid these dangerous fantasies; he even sings a "farewell to Fansie." But blinded by self-love, he doesn't see that he still holds on to one last fantasy about his "firelocke peece," his beloved Petronella.[36]

The final lines, a warning about taking repentances like "Farewell to Fansie" seriously, can be applied to the speaker as well as to the knight, particularly because the speaker calls attention to himself one last time when, stopping short, he realizes that his muse has gone too far, said too much, should not be taken seriously:

> When Foxes preach, good folk beware your geese,
> But holla here, my muse to farre doth mell:
> Who list to marke what learned preacher sayeth,
> Must learne withall for to believe his lore:
> But what he doth, that toucheth nomans fayth,
> Though words with workes, (agreed) persuade the more,
> The mounting kite, oft lites on homely pray
> And wisest wittes, may sometimes go astray.
>   FINIS
>   Tam Marti, quam Merecurio
>   (454, P 33.7–16)

Whether he (the speaker? the Greene Knight?) misleads readers intentionally (like a "Foxe") or simply goes "astray" (like a kite, a bird of prey), readers should beware. If they want to benefit from what a learned preacher (the speaker? the Greene Knight?) says, they must not ask about what he does.

The speaker in "Gascoigne's Woodsmanship" had redeemed the erring woodsman by making his errant shooting seem heroic. Here the only woodsman is a beast of prey. The speaker has either withdrawn entirely or merged himself with the fox/kite/knight who goes astray. In "Woodsmanship," Gascoigne had identified himself redundantly outside the poem before revealing himself in the poem itself: in the title, the dedication, and the preface. Here, however, Gascoigne identifies himself as the speaker (rather than the protagonist who shares his nickname) only indirectly, at the end, by appending his new motto, "Tam Marti, quam Mercurio."

Gascoigne's Reader(s): "Thine onely prayse dyd make me venture forth / To set in shewe a thing so litle worth"

The focus on authors disappears from *Posies*. But there are many references to bad or foolish readers, largely in Gascoigne's three introductory letters and his final letter of instruction about how to read correctly. The poet blames ignorant readers for the attacks on *Hundreth*. As he tells the Divines, he had included material in *Hundreth* which "could not chuse but content the learned and Godlye Reader." Unfortunately it was not only the godly who read *Hundreth*. The other readers misunderstood the book: the "light minded" (361, P 1.12–13, 17), those full of ignorant opinions and "busie conjectures" [362, P 1.9]), the "curious Carpers" and "ignorant Readers" who "understande neyther the meaning of the Authour, nor the sense of the figurative speeches" (365, P 2.16, 36–37).

But there is one passage in *Posies* where Gascoigne describes a different sort of reader, in the "Lenvoye" to the newly completed "Dan Bartholmew." This is one of the very few places in which Gascoigne may be speaking in his own voice rather than attributing a poem to an anonymous narrator, the Reporter, or Bartello. Here he addresses Sir Salamanke, a figure whose significance, if any, has eluded scholars: "Syr Salamanke to thee this tale is told."[37] What we do know is that he was probably was in the Netherlands with Gascoigne to hear the first part of the poem—as the mention of "dyke" suggests. More important, Gascoigne calls him one of "our sect" (398, P 27.445), perhaps a writer, and he is a sympathetic reader: Salamanke had appreciated the first part of "Dan Bartholmew" when Gascoigne read it aloud ("[thou] seemdst to hearken with good wyll"). But at that time the wind had blown the poem's last pages into the "dyke," and they were lost. Gascoigne would never have taken the trouble to search "the corners of my brest" in order to rewrite the pages, he says, if Salamanke had not "seemd to lyke / The wofull words of *Bartholmews* discourse" (397–98, P 27.427–30):

> Such skyll thou hast to make me (foole) believe,
> My bables are as brave as any bee,
> Well since it is so, let it never greeve
> Thy friendly minde this worthlesse verse to see
> In print at last: for trust thou unto mee,

> Thine onely prayse dyd make me venture forth,
> To set in shewe a thing so litle worth.
>
> (398, P 27.435–41)

The "Lenvoye" may have been added in part to explain why "Dan Bartholmew" had been incomplete in *Hundreth*. But it could record an actual relationship to a sympathetic reader. If so, Gascoigne's claim that "thine onely praise" led him to publish is surely an exaggeration, but not necessarily a lie. His relation to "Sir Salamanke" suggests that the influence of a concerned and receptive reader could be important to even the most financial ventures such as *Hundreth*.

The other potentially friendly reader whose "happe hath heretofore / Bene, lovingly to read my reckles rimes" (*Steele Glas*, in *Works*, 143) was Gascoigne's primary patron, Arthur, Lord Grey of Wilton, to whom Edmund Spenser would later serve as secretary. What Gascoigne most needed from Grey was financial support.[38] But like Sir Salamanke, Grey may have provided other kinds of support.

We know that Grey was important at the beginning of Gascoigne's publishing career. Success in earning Grey's original patronage with "Woodsmanship" in October 1572 is usually seen as one motive for Gascoigne's turn to publication in 1573, and Grey is the most prominent patron in the book.[39] It is possible, indeed, that Grey's support helped make *Hundreth* the extraordinarily self-confident show of talent that it became.[40] *Hundreth* included not only "Woodsmanship" but also a second poem dedicated to Grey, "Gascoigne's Voyage," along with the original dedications to both. Even though "Voyage" was written after Gascoigne's embarrassing parliamentary ouster and flight to the Netherlands, it shows an even greater assurance about Grey's acceptance than "Woodsmanship." Here Gascoigne calls Grey "my Aldervievest Lorde" (319, 77.5); he claims that "God saved me your Lordshippes bound for ever (326, 77.286); and he looks forward to "com[ing] alone unto my lovely Lorde" (328, 77.352) to give him detailed war news. It does not occur to him that his misfortunes will offend his patron.

Adrian Weiss argues that Gascoigne had begun with a different and more prudent plan for *Hundreth*. He first approached the printer in January 1573, intending to publish only his two Inns of Court plays along with a third text, perhaps "Philomene" (the "Ovid" promised on the title page) or "Dan Bartholmew."[41] But then, in February, the printing was stopped.

Weiss suggests that Gascoigne changed plans and decided to publish all his work.[42] Instead of a staid volume of scholarly translations, he decided to substitute a showy tour de force. He left for Holland soon after and sent the rest of the material piecemeal to the printer, starting with "Adventures," the roman à clef about adultery in high places that would prove to be the most controversial text in the collection.[43]

Gascoigne had now embarked on a riskier undertaking. "Adventures" was a remarkable choice, particularly as the introductory selection in a first book. Gascoigne had just been ousted from Parliament, partly for writing slanderous "pasquelles," and whether or not "Adventures" was a pasquinade it was certainly trying hard to be seen as one. The volume's many amorous trifles were also an unwise choice for a book intended to prove Gascoigne's political skills.[44] He may have included the love poetry not realizing that it would offend.[45] But Gascoigne was known neither for discretion nor for modesty, and he may simply have assumed that he could get away with anything, especially because of the two new patrons named in *Hundreth*, Montacute and Grey. Gascoigne's sense of entitlement is suggested by two of his contemporaries. George Whetstone, speaking in Gascoigne's voice in his elegy for the latter, admits that, "begilde with self conceit, / A thought yat men would throw rewards on me."[46] Gabriel Harvey added a snippy comment about Gascoigne's sense of entitlement to his copy of *Posies*, inserting it beside Gascoigne's motto about seeking reward, "Meritum petere, grave." Harvey's response was, in effect, don't just talk about reward, do something to make sure you deserve it.[47]

For whatever reason, Gascoigne seemed to have no fear about losing Grey's support even after *Hundreth* had first been publicly criticized and after Gascoigne himself had been imprisoned following his surrender to the Spanish at Leiden ("yeelding is always a great disgrace" [433, P 28.181]). Gascoigne had sent Grey a copy of *Hundreth* in 1574, perhaps before hearing about the attacks on the book. Then, although Grey hadn't responded, Gascoigne dedicated a third poem to him, "The fruites of Warre" (398, P 28). In it he addresses Grey intimately, as he had in the 1572 "Voyage." He sounds confident about Grey's continued support despite the poet's admitted "weakness" and "rashness."[48]

But Grey must have disappointed him. Gascoigne did not dedicate anything to him for another two years. The original dedication to "Philomene" suggests that Gascoigne had at one point thought to present that poem, along with *The Steele Glas*, to Grey in April 1575.[49] But for whatever reason, neither work was presented to Grey until the following year: Gascoigne sent both in April 1576.[50]

There is no evidence about what caused the interruption to, and then the absence of, dedications to Grey. Grey had overlooked Gascoigne's early troubles.[51] But circumstances had changed: Grey's name had been prominently displayed in *Hundreth*, and he may have wanted to distance himself after any questions—whether military, financial, or literary—had been raised about the poet.[52] Or he may have lost interest or been distracted. What is certain is that despite Gascoigne's later literary and courtly success, Grey maintained his distance. He apparently did not respond to the poet's overture in 1576, and after that Gascoigne never dedicated anything to him again. In Whetstone's elegy for Gascoigne the speaker alludes to a cause "which kild my hart" and cut off the poet's due reward,[53] whatever that may have been. We will probably never know what caused the break, if break it was.

Undaunted, Gascoigne continued to seek other patrons while avoiding Grey. He dedicated *The Glas of Government* (April 26, 1575) to Owen Hopton, a distant relative, just days after he decided not to dedicate "Philomene" to Grey. In the summer of 1575 he finally achieved the courtly patronage he had been seeking for so long, and he worked on two different commissions. He helped prepare Leicester's entertainment for Queen Elizabeth at Kenilworth (July 9, 1575), and appeared before her in one of its pageants; later he published a description of the events. He contributed to Sir Henry Lee's entertainment for Elizabeth at Woodstock (1575) and later made an elaborate presentation copy for her with his self-portrait as frontispiece (fig. 14). He dedicated *The Droomme of Doomes day* (May 1576) to the earl of Bedford (after appearing as his opponent in a lawsuit), he dedicated *A delicate Diet* (August 10, 1576) to Lewis Dives of Bedfordshire, and he dedicated two later works to the queen. Meanwhile he had also begun forging other connections through his commendatory poems: Sir Humphrey Gilbert, George Turberville, Thomas Bedingfield, and Claudius Hollyband (*Works*, 561–67).

The remarkable fact about Gascoigne's dedications to these other patrons is that they almost never mention either the controversy about his *Posies* or anything Gascoigne suffered from it. There is no hint of his trouble, even in his 1575 dedication to *The Glas of Governement*, a prodigal son story that would have lent itself readily to an analogy with Gascoigne's prodigality in *Hundreth* and his reform thereafter. The two dedications

Fig. 14 Gascoigne, "Hemetes" (1575/76), frontispiece with poet and queen (© The British Library Board. All Rights Reserved [ROYAL 18 a XIVI]).

that do allude to the *Posies* controversy both play it down. The first, accompanying Gascoigne's translation of "The View of the world's Vanities" for the earl of Bedford (May, 1576), does "confess" briefly, "I finde my self giltie of much time mispent, & of greater curiositie then was convenient, in penning and endightyng sundrie toyes and trifles (*Works*, 211). For this he repents and goes on to vow reformation. But that is all. Gascoigne's reference to his *Posies* a few lines later seems almost unrelated to his reform: "I was (now almost twelve monethes past) pricked and much moved, by the grave and discreete wordes of one right worshipfull and mine approved friend, who (in my presence) hearing my thryftlesse booke of Poesyes underservedly commended, dyd say: that he lyked the smell of those Posies pretely well," but that he would "like the Gardyner better if he would employe his spade in ... Devinities or morall Philosophie" (*Works*, 211–12). The *Posies* may have been thriftless, but the "friend"—probably a politely

Erasing an Author's Life: George Gascoigne 191

distanced reference to Bedford himself—liked them well enough. These are not the words of a repentant or a traumatized man.

Gascoigne refers to *Posies* also in his dedication of *A delicate Diet, for daintiemouthde Droonkardes* to his friend Lewis Dives in August 1576. Here his main concern is to apologize for not having given Dives copies of any of his work before: "Syr, you maye possibly condempne me [for not sending any copies before].... But Syr, when my wanton (and worse smelling) Posies, presumed fyrst to peark abroade, they came forth sooner then I wyshed, and muche before they deserved to be lyked. So that... I was more combred with correction of them, then comforted in the constructions, whereunto they were subject." Since then, he has made "amendes for the lost time which I misbestowed in wryting so wantonlie" (*Works*, 453). *Posies* was simply published too soon, a subject not worth dwelling on, as indeed Gascoigne does not.

By contrast, the dedication of *The Steele Glas* to Grey on April 15, 1576, is so preoccupied with Gascoigne's unfair punishment and suffering that it hardly seems written by the same man. Unlike the urbanely self-forgiving speaker in the other dedications, Gascoigne here is alternately abject and defensive about his "youth mispent." He speaks of "mine own unworthynesse." He says, "I have misgoverned my youth, I confesse it," and with a rhetorical question he accepts reproof: "Shal I grudge to be reproved for that which I have done?" In a passage that Harvey recalled ten years later as an accurate description, Gascoigne chides himself: "I have loytred (my lorde) I confesse, I have lien streaking me (like a lubber) when the sunne did shine, and now I strive al in vaine to loade the carte when it raineth. I regarded not my comelynes in the Maymoone of my youth, and yet now I stand prinking me in the glasse, when the crowes foote is growen under mine eye" (*Works*, 135–36).[54]

But at the same time he presents himself as a victim: "I finde my selfe so feeble, and so unable to endure" (*Works*, 136). He expects sympathy for his punishment but refuses to admit that he deserved it: "Shall I yelde to mysery as a just plague apointed for my portion? Magnanimitie saith no, and Industrye seemeth to be of the very same opinion." Enough is enough: "I am derided, suspected, accused, and condemned: yea more than that, I am rygorously rejected when I proffer amendes for my harme. Should I therefore dispayre? Shall I yeelde unto jellosie? or drowne my dayes in idlenesse, bycause their beginning was bathed in wantonnesse?" (*Works*, 135). Concluding magnaminiously, he vows neither to "execute an envious revenge" nor to "sinke in idlenesse" (*Works*, 137). "Industrie" calls him to continue his work, which he here presents to Grey.

In a departure from his usual method, Gascoigne even repeats his self-pitying complaint in the text itself, in the early lines of *The Steele Glas* (*Works*, 143–47). Comparing himself there to Philomene, he says that she "hath taught my weary Muze, / To sing a song in spight of their despight" (*Works*, 143). Gascoigne is a woman, he says—not a man who would be capable of committing the crimes that Gascoigne is accused of. He is Satyra (Satire), who—like Philomene—has been "ravisht," imprisoned in a cage of Myserie, and had her tongue cut out ("with Raysor of Restraynte") for telling the truth (*Works*, 146).

Grey, Gascoigne implies, is his only hope. He begs Grey for "as gracious a regarde, as you have in times past been accustomed too beholde my travailes." With Grey's support, Gascoigne will be able to escape his enemies and even "give them al a rybbe of rost for their paynes." Grey can "cancel the sentence unjustly pronounced in my condemnation" (*Works*, 137). Without him, Gascoigne must continue away from the "shining Sunne" of "stately cowrts...in corner closely cowcht" (*Works*, 146), that is, out of the warm rays of patronage.

Only to Grey, then, did Gascoigne present this histrionic image of himself as an abject, helpless, castrated, imprisoned, miserable, abandoned victim.[55] In fact, only to Grey did Gascoigne write extended autobiographies, whether in the form of self-flattering portraits to prove himself a good investment or, like this one, a portrait of suffering to provoke Grey's sympathy. Grey's influence on Gascoigne's writing may not be as obvious as that of the Pagets on Thomas Tusser or the "good friend" on Thomas Whythorne. But it is worth noting how much more impassioned Gascoigne is toward Grey than he is to anyone else and how many of his longer, overtly autobiographical poems are dedicated to Grey. It is also interesting that the withdrawal of Grey's patronage roughly coincides with the often-described shift in Gascoigne's writing from its confident, inventive display in *Hundreth* to the more traditional didacticism of later works—and with the change in Gascoigne's verbal self-portraits (see fig. 15).

I close by returning to the Greene Knight's sad story in *Posies*, one of the self-portraits that may have been affected by Grey's withdrawal. The description of the Knight looks forward to Gascoigne's abject self-portrait for Grey in *The Steele Glas*, just as it looks backward to Gascoigne's

Fig. 15 Gascoigne, *The Steele Glas* (1587), title page verso, (self?) portrait (this item is reproduced by permission of The Huntington Library, San Marino, California [RB 59880]).

triumphant first self-portrait for Grey in "Woodsmanship." The Greene Knight is "in prison pent" (445, P 30.132), as Gascoigne in *Steele Glas* is caught in his "cage of Miserie." The Knight's rightful reward has been taken from him, he says, and "my gaines possessed by my foes, my friends against me bent" (445, P 30.131–32). In *Steele Glas*, Gascoigne complains similarly that his enemies,

> Which worke my woe, withouten cause or crime,
> And make my backe, a ladder for their feete,
> By slandrous steppes, and stayres of tickle talke,
> To clyme the throne, wherin my selfe should sitte.
>   (*Works*, 143)

In both portraits, his enemies have ruined him through slander and usurped his rightful place (and gains). In both, he is weak: the Greene Knight's "forces faile" (439, P 29.18), and Gascoigne is "feeble." Both Knight and Gascoigne regret misspending the "Maymoone" of their age (443, P 30.32). Each has worked hard since then, but neither can overcome his enemy's attack.

The important difference between these two unhappy later versions of the Woodsman is that in 1575 the Greene Knight, like Gascoigne, had no support from anyone like Grey. But by April 1576, Gascoigne was at least hopeful that he might regain that support: "And in ful hope therof, I have presumed to present your honour with this Satyre" (*Works*, 137). Perhaps if Gascoigne had had Grey's support when composing the 1575 *Posies*, the Greene Knight poems could have ended on a more hopeful note, not quite the exuberant optimism of "Woodsmanship" but at least the sense in *Steele Glas* that an appeal to sympathy might yet have an effect.

Gascoigne, like his London cohort—Churchyard, Googe, Turberville, Whythorne, Whitney—wrote occasional poetry with autobiographical content. But his poems, unlike theirs, also convey his particular attitude and point of view toward what he was writing about. As a result, the autobiographical aspects of his work include information not only about his past but also about his way of seeing it now—about how he thinks. The same doubled representation is achieved in his narrative poetry, which pairs a young hero with a narrator very like him, looking back and judging what might be his own experience, as the narrator does in any autobiographical narrative. Finally, Gascoigne's multiple frames for his work in *Hundreth* create yet another level of perspectival play. G. T., the editor, comments on all the poets and their work, hinting—but never admitting—that both they and he are representatives of Gascoigne in the present, collecting and commenting on Gascoigne in the past.

Then, when Gascoigne censored his work in *Posies*, he censored not only the content but also the exuberant perspectival play and self-display in his approach to it. He erased himself from his revised collection, both from the book's content and from its framing perspectives. Gascoigne's authorial self-erasure makes an interesting contrast to Thomas Tusser's autobiographical additions in his husbandry book. Tusser changed the content of his book. He added more information about himself to each edition until he finally included an entire "Author's Life." But Tusser's folksy, forthright style verse remained the same over the years. To today's readers, accustomed to the sort of authorial irony and authorial self-consciousness that were always absent from Tusser's poems, the change in his work is hardly noticeable. But Gascoigne's change is startling. Although he adds poems in 1575 with new information about his war experience, Gascoigne himself seems more distant and lifeless as he withdraws from the role of shaping author.

However, he had already given readers a model of self-revealing narrators in *Hundreth*. The text, especially "The Adventures of Master F.J.," remained to provide an impetus for others. Gabriel Harvey, George Whetstone, and Nicholas Grange are are only the best known of the imitators whose playfully autobiographical narratives followed not long after Gascoigne's. Some, like Harvey's "Dairymaid's Letter," leaned toward autobiography; others, like Whetstone's verse in *Rocke of Regarde* and Grange's *Golden Aphrodite*, toward fiction. But although none achieved Gascoigne's perfect balance, they all contributed to the development of autobiography as well as to Elizabethan letters.

CHAPTER 9

Autobiography in the Third Person: *Robert Greene's Fiction and His Autobiography by Henry Chettle (1590–92)*

> For that the gentleman is still living, I will shadowe his name, although I represent his follies.
> ROBERT GREENE, *Francesco's Fortunes* (1590)

> To say "I" is more habitual (and thus more "natural") than to say, "he," but is not therefore simpler.
> PHILIPPE LEJEUNE, "Autobiography in the Third Person"

The last of the autobiographies considered here is *[Robert] Greenes Groatsworth of Witte, Bought with a Million of Repentance* (1592).[1] Greene, as Gabriel Harvey said, was a notorious rakehell: "Who in London," Harvey asks, "hath not heard of his dissolute and licentious living?"[2] One reason for the notoriety was that Greene had advertised his own dissolution. It was probably not very surprising when a pamphlet claiming to be Greene's deathbed repentance appeared in 1592, soon after his death from a "fatall banquet of pickle herring." Greene had told his story one last time. It sounded just like something he would do.

The trouble is that the confession fit expectations so perfectly that it did not need Greene to write it. Most scholars now believe that Henry Chettle, the supposed editor of *Groatsworth*, wrote or was at least the primary author of the pamphlet.[3] A second pamphlet by Cuthburt Burby, Greene's *Repentance* (1592), is also at least in part a forgery. This was clearly big business, not autobiography, and "no serious history of the genre includes *Groatsworth* in its discussion."[4] Yet the *Groatsworth* hoax is a landmark in the development of autobiography. Even more than G. T.'s assumption in Gascoigne's *Hundreth Sundrie Flowres* (1573) that all poems derive from autobiographical "occasions," *Groatsworth* shows just how commonplace autobiography had become by that time. Chettle's forgery, to the degree that he got away with it, implies that expectations had changed considerably since 1553, when John Bale subordinated his autobiographical account in his *Vocacyon* to the format of a Pauline letter.[5] At that time, forty years earlier, few people thought to publish accounts of their experience for its own sake. But by the time of Greene's death in 1592, John Bale, William Baldwin, Thomas Churchyard, Thomas Tusser, George Gascoigne, and others had already set a precedent; the conventions for autobiographical writing were firmly enough established that a "Life" could be forged—not just fictionalized, either openly or with a wink, but written by someone else with intent to deceive.

For Shakespeareans the discovery of Chettle's hoax is a real loss, because *Groatsworth* includes the famous passage in which Greene warns playwrights about the upstart crow who thinks he's the only Shake-scene in a country. For many of Greene's biographers, however, "the actual authorship of *Groatsworth*...is hardly relevant."[6] They argue that Chettle would have included in *Groatsworth* only material that Greene had already talked about or that everyone already knew. No matter who wrote the pamphlet, it still contributes to the "Greene legend" that was circulating at the time and was recorded by Harvey, Thomas Nashe, and others.

But the hoax is a loss also for anyone interested in Greene's autobiography. *Groatsworth* can illuminate only the facts about Greene's past. It tells nothing about how Greene saw those facts. It provides none of the information encoded in an author's language and narrative style, at least not until we know more about what, if anything, in *Groatsworth* was really Greene's.

However, Greene did compose three quasi-autobiographical fictions in 1590–91, a period of repentance writings including prefaces and dedications along with the fictions, as well as a play coauthored with Thomas Lodge, *A Looking Glass for London* (1588–92). One of the fictions, *Greenes Vision*, purports to be a true report of a dream that Greene had; the other, a two-volume narrative, *Greenes Never Too Late* and *Francesco's Fortunes, or the Second Part of Greenes Never Too Late*, can be read as "autobiography in the third person," as Philippe Lejeune calls it.[7] Unlike other autobiographical texts in the third person, e.g., *The Education of Henry Adams*, or Simon Forman's "Boke of the life and generation of Simon," *Greenes Never Too Late* is not announced as an autobiography.[8] It goes out of its way to raise the possibility, however, in the same way that Gascoigne's "Adventures of F.J." does.[9] Although it is about a young man named Francesco who is very like Greene, it has been excluded with *Groatsworth* from histories of autobiography because it treats Greene's life only loosely and often in the third person. But whether or not *Never Too Late* and *Greenes Vision* accurately present Greene's life, they claim—or hint loudly—that they do.[10] All three publications do bear traces of the original contexts that generated them, and they provide information about the narrative "I," if not the protagonist, that links the text more closely to Greene's experience.

Robert Greene (1558–92)

Like Whythorne, Tusser, Whitney, and Gascoigne, Greene was struggling to support himself in London. Unlike them, he dedicated himself entirely to writing in order to do so, and he is known as one of the first professional writers in England. When Greene was born in 1558, his father was a Norwich cordwainer, or shoemaker, but Robert spent much of his childhood in the north with his Yorkshire gentry family, absorbing values and expectations like those that Tusser, Whythorne, Whitney, and Gascoigne had known from their early years.[11] He was proud of his Cambridge education (BA 1580, MA 1583), and the phrase "Robert Greene, *in Artibus magister*" almost always appeared as part of his identification on title pages.

Facts about the period between Greene's university days in Cambridge (1575?–83) and his establishment in London (1586?) are few. From what Harvey and Nashe report and the Greene legend echoes, Greene married a gentlewoman who bore his child, but he abandoned both wife and child when he came to London. There he was successful as a writer of pamphlets and plays, but was known for living riotously and spending everything he earned. By the end of his life Greene was in debt, had been abandoned by friends, and was living with the prostitute Nell Ball and possibly with a son, Fortunatus. Brenda Richardson, whose findings about Greene's early years have helped establish his genealogy, argues that we can also connect our Robert Greene to the Robert Greene who married Isabel Beck in

Lincolnshire in 1579 and possibly with the Robert Greene of Norwich who baptized a son, Robert, in the following year.[12] Dedications for Greene's earliest works until about 1585, Richardson points out, are to local Norwich families, and they suggest that he was still in the Cambridge/Norwich area or was at least maintaining close connection to it.

Greene's shift to more nationally known patrons in the mid-1580s, Richardson suggests, implies that he was by then in London and frequenting more cosmopolitan circles. By 1592, according to Harvey, everyone wanted to read what he wrote: "They must have *Greens* Arcadia: and I believe most eagerlie longed for *Greenes* Faerie Queene," he noted with scorn.[13] Then, within two years of publishing *Never Too Late*, Greene was dead, and the Greene legend about his last seedy weeks had taken hold.

Scholar, Writer, and Autobiographer

Greene's identity as a scholar and writer was central to him from the beginning to the end of his career, and he flaunted it long before he wrote about himself at greater length. *Mamillia*, his earliest fiction, ends with a fable about a "Scoler" who triumphs over rivals for the hand of a fair maiden; and Greene's final pseudonym at the other end of his career was "Cuthbert Conny-Catcher," a "scholler" who had studied at "Whittington College" (*The Defense of Conny Catching* [1592], 12:43).[14] Three of his texts, just before and after *Greenes Never Too Late*, were addressed to "The Gentlemen Scholars [or students] of both Universities" and identify this audience as Greene's "fellows."[15]

Greene had once signed himself "student of physick" in a dedication to the earl of Leicester, who was known for patronizing science.[16] But the usual meaning of *scholar* for Greene was writer, and he experimented with many varieties of writing before he turned to autobiography. *Mamillia* was written in the then newly fashionable style of fellow Cantabrigian John Lyly's *Euphues* (1578), and it was aimed at a similarly elite audience.[17] Greene produced three more euphuistic novels in the early 1580s, followed by several framed novella collections in a new and different mode made popular by William Painter and George Pettie.[18] He went on to try longer, less euphuistic romances like *Pandosto* (1588), the source for Shakespeare's *Winter's Tale*, and *Menaphon* (1589). His later London works are directed to a more popular audience. Greene tried a few patriotic works during the period of national enthusiasm following the defeat of the Spanish Armada, and then in the early 1590s, after a shaky start, he emerged as one of the city's most successful playwrights.[19] The repentance texts, among them the three autobiographical works of 1590, date from this period of Greene's great popularity. They were followed by Greene's cleverly varied collections of tales about London's coney-catching underworld that advertised its service to his country.[20]

Even before turning to autobiographical narratives, Greene had begun to include brief self-referential commentary in letters, dedications, and codas to his texts, starting about two years before the *Never Too Late* volumes and continuing until he died. These marginal texts, or paratexts, surrounding the central narratives provide a running, if not quite trustworthy, commentary about Greene's writing life that parallel the fictional lives in his narratives. The paratexts make up their own loose narrative. They look forward or backward to others and present themselves as contributions to an ongoing conversation between author and reader. Earlier Greene's prefaces and dedications had been notable, if at all, for their conventionality.[21] But they became a medium for claims about himself like those about the protagonists of *Never Too Late* and *Greene's Vision*. They defend his superiority to common writers and, later, apologize for his slide into writing trifles for the stage and the popular market.

The earliest of the self-referential paratexts is the letter "To the Gentlemen Readers" in *Perimedes the Blacksmith* (1588). In the book's brief framing narrative, Perimedes and his wife exchange stories over the fire, and their tales make up the bulk of the volume. Perimedes, unlike Greene's earlier aristocratic characters, is an ordinary blacksmith, and the book's language avoids the elegant euphuism associated with his earlier romances. Perhaps because *Perimedes* is one of Greene's earliest works to incorporate popular materials, he carefully surrounds it by paratexts reminding readers of his elite connections. The prefatory material to *Perimedes* is unusually defensive, apparently in response to criticism of one of Greene's plays for the popular stage: "Two Gentlemen Poets offered [it] on the Stage" but "I could not make my verses jet upon the stage in tragicall buskins" (7:7–8). "Gentlemen poets" probably refers to *Alphonsus, King of Aragon* (1587?), Greene's attempt at a Marlovian blockbuster. Miscarriage on the common stage was a particularly touchy issue for the man who signed himself "Master of Arts" on his title pages. He was being identified as a common playwright, and a bad one at that. His response in the preface was to separate himself from the general run of playwrights, the "pedling chapmen" who are "not able to make choice of [their] chaffer" and have only one skill to sell. Never mind the stage; the true "end of scollarism" (7:8), Greene says, is not in the mad poets' blank verse but rather in the elegant prose and poetry that he could write and these crude chapmen could not. Greene's "Letter to gentlemen readers" makes a similar case: "I keep my old course, to palter up some thing in Prose [i.e., not blank verse], using mine old poesie still, *Omni tulit puntum*" (*Perimedes*, 7:7). One of the verse commendations that Greene arranged for his book similarly elevates Greene by pairing him with John Lyly, "tous deux raffineurs d'Anglois" (*Perimedes*, 7:10), and making both the equals of Continental writers like Clément Marot and Boccaccio.[22]

As if the *Perimedes* preface had not presented a good enough case, Greene continues the argument in the epilogue. Here he sounds like one of the elite poets Richard Tottel rescued from the obscurity of private circulation when he published his *Songes and Sonnetes* (1557). The epilogue begins with a poem by (the unidentifiable) "William Bubb," who chastises Greene for keeping his sonnets in his desk and "not letting any but your familiars to peruse them." Bubb asks that Greene annex them to "this Pamphlet," and Greene obliges him (*Perimedes*, 7:88). What better proof of his superiority than these private sonnets? Three years later Greene took up arms again in his theatrical battle in his preface to *Farewell to Folly* (printed 1591), still scorning unlearned playwrights: "He that can not write true Englishe without the healpe of Clerkes of parish Churches will needes make himself the father of interludes" (9:233).

Meanwhile Greene's paratexts began to introduce a second form of self-reflection. In these Greene was developing a narrative about his repentance that would run parallel to his narratives about repentant heroes. As yet they remained separate. But they grew closer, and as they did so, they came closer as well to uniting the two elements of autobiography: a story about his past, told by a narrator looking back on and trying to make sense of that past. The paratextual commentary is clear in its outline but hardly original: Greene, he says, has written too many amorous pamphlets, and now he sees his error and promises to repent. Not every preface exactly fits its text.[23] Greene promises but defers repentance, stretching it over works between 1589 and 1591, like a soap opera. Nonetheless the paratexts are accurate enough about the overall movement toward reform to take into account.[24]

The first indication of repentance appears in *The Spanish Masquerado* (S.R. February 1, 1589).[25] Greene is not yet actually repentant, but he talks about change. He tells his "Gentlemen Readers" that hitherto he has written of loves, but "now least I might be thought to tie myselfe wholly to amorous conceites, I have adventured to discover my conscience in Religion."[26] The following year, in *Orpharion* (S.R. January 9, 1590), the book's narrator repents, ambiguously implying Greene's repentance as well. Having sought Venus to help him escape love's fancies, the narrator falls asleep and wakes up cured: "I...hastened away as fast as I could, glad that one dreame had rid me of fancy, which so long had fettered me, yet could I not hie so fast, but ere I could get home, I was overtaken with repentance. Robert Greene."[27]

The three autobiographical texts, *Never Too Late* 1 and 2 and *Vision*, were written after *Orpharion*, although *Vision* was not published until later. Their introduction of Greene's repentance will be discussed more fully below. At the end of the year (S.R. November 2, 1590) *Greenes Mourning Garment* clearly announced Greene's own repentance and also told the story of Philador, who is more like the biblical prodigal son than any other of Greene's protagonists; here author's and hero's repentance coincide. In *Garment*'s dedication Greene says, "[I had] overweaned with them of Ninivie, in publishing sundry wanton Pamphlets." Then, feeling his "palpable follies, and hearing with the eares of my heart Ionas crying, / *Except thou repent*," he continues, "As I have changed the inward affectes of my minde, so I have turned my wanton workes to effectuall labours" ("Dedication to George Clifford, Earl of Cumberland," 9:19–20). In the following letter to "Gentlemen Schollers of both Universities," Greene adds knowingly that "Schollers of all men"—presumably Greene among them—are by wanton love "soonest inveigled" (*Mourning Garment*, 9:123).

The repentance saga finally ends, or begins to end, with *Greene's Farewell to Folly* (printed 1591), where Greene draws his statements together. In *Farewell*'s letter "To the Gentlemen Students of both Universities," Greene recalls his last book ("I presented you alate with my Mourning garment"), admits backsliding in the present book, *Farewell to Folly*, but promises (once again!) that this is "the last I meane ever to publish of such superficiall labours" (*Farewell to Folly*, 9:229). It is also the last installment of his own repentance story: "Having therefore Gentlemen (in my opinion) mourned long enough for the misdeeds of my youth, [I have] nowe left off the intent, and am come to the effect" (9:230–31). That is, he will now actually stop talking and start doing something about his reformation. He comes close to saying farewell to real prodigality, as well as to stories about it, when he invites his fellow scholars to join him: "Such wags as have bene wantons with me, and have marched in the Mercer's booke to please their Mistris eye with their braverie, that as the frolic phrase is[,] have made to sweat with riotous expences, that have spent their wits in the courting of their sweethearts, and emptied their purses by being too prodigall, let them at last look backe to the follies of their youth."[28]

When Greene next appears in his paratexts, it is no longer as a repentant writer of trifling romances. His new motto is *Pro patria nascimur* (We are born to serve our country). He is now a patriotic writer of criminal exposés, spending time with coney-catchers only in order to expose them. By this point, his activities have invaded the texts themselves. The coney-catchers relay gossip about him to one another. Nan, the eponymous Shee-Conny-catcher in Greene's *Disputation Betweene a Hee Conny-catcher and a Shee Conny-catcher*, is worried that "R.G." will name her associates in his Black Book: "a pestilence on him, they say, hee hath there set downe my husbandes pettigree, and yours too, Lawrence" (10:225–26). Greene identified with Francesco. Now he is a character in the stories about coney-catchers. He is still writing autobiographically, if only briefly, about himself.

Never Too Late

The books at the center of these self-referential prefaces and epilogues are the two *Never Too Late* volumes about Francesco's repentance and *Vision* about his own. The former have sometimes invited autobiographical reading because their content coincides at times with Greene's biography. But more important to this discussion, in all three of these books a self-conscious narrator presents the protagonist's story. *Vision* is narrated by Greene about himself, and in *Never Too Late* the narrator evokes Greene as the hero does.

Never Too Late is the work that probably would have been mentioned in serious histories of autobiography had Chettle not run interference with *Groatsworth*. The hero is recognizable as Greene, and the book may well offer the first and fullest version of what would become the Greene legend, in which a well-born hero leaves his wife in the provinces and falls in with

London's underworld of courtesans, thieves, and players. In fact, Chettle seems to have had both volumes of *Never Too Late* open before him when he put *Groatsworth* together.[29] Greene's text coyly hints at its hero's relation to Greene. It is certainly the first of Greene's full-length narratives that is said to represent real people (Francesco "shadows" a living Englishman), the first to treat characters of Greene's social status rather than aristocrats, and the first to be set in England.

It is a version of the reformed prodigal story that Gascoigne and other Elizabethans had told, starting from Francesco's decision to make his way in life and ending with his final reform. Francesco is a promising young man just out of university. Unfortunately, his prospects are limited: although his parentage was "worshipfull, yet it was not indued with much wealth," and "his learning was better than his revenewes, and his wit more beneficial than his substance" (8:3). However, Francesco is well loved, and, "cocksure," he decides to court Isabel, the daughter of the wealthy gentleman Frangoso, even though Frangoso has warned him away because the young man has no money. After the couple's successful elopement, Francesco lives by his wit and teaches school in the country while Isabel raises their child and works as a seamstress. They spend five years in pastoral bliss according to this "Democritall methode" of earning their living (8:64), at which point they and their son are finally reconciled to Isabel's father. Francesco's downfall begins two years later, when he travels to Troynovant on business and falls in love there with the wily courtesan Infida. Torn between desire and reason, Francesco finally gives in and decides to stay in the city with Infida. Three years go by, and only after Infida throws him out because Francesco has spent all his money does he finally confront what he has done. His resulting despair leads to a renewed faith that God can save even a sinner like himself, and the book ends as Francesco resolves to go back to Isabel.

That decision might easily have marked the story's end, although Greene as usual leaves open the possibility of further adventures. But Greene carried the story further almost immediately. The second volume, *Francesco's Fortunes, or Never Too Late Part Two*, opens as the reformed Francesco realizes that he is too ashamed to return home penniless, and he abandons his earlier resolve. To survive, he falls back on his scholarship (and wit) and spends two years writing for a group of players. He has made some moral progress, as we see when Infida, hearing of his new wealth, tries to snare him again without success, but swineherd years are not over yet.

Still, after about only twenty of the volume's 108 pages, we leave both Francesco and the prodigal story and turn to Isabel, the wife he abandoned back in Caerbranck. Her adventures are based on another of Greene's biblical favorites, the story of Susannah and the elders, on which he had already based his *Myrrour for Modestie* (1584). While Francesco is in London, the mayor of Caerbranck, unsuccessful in an attempted seduction of Isabel, denounces her as a whore. She suffers greatly until her innocence and virtue are recognized. At this point the narrative returns to Francesco, when the story of Isabel's goodness, having been relayed all the way to Troynovant, becomes a topic of local gossip. Francesco overhears it and decides to return home, though not before writing some poetry about what he has learned and leaving it with his friends for their benefit. When he makes his way back to Isabel in Caerbranck, she is so moved by his penitence that she forgives him. Their story ends happily, and their reunion is celebrated with a festive banquet, an appropriate end for a prodigal's story.

From what we know about Greene's biography, Greene shared his hero's gentle heritage, his scholarship, his youthful self-confidence, his marriage and its offspring, and his abandonment of his wife when he moved from the countryside to Troynovant, or London. Once there, he shared Francesco's dissolute life among players and courtesans, his life with and impregnation of a courtesan, and the alienation from his friends. Richardson has argued that a number of other details from Francesco's story also correlate with Greene's biography. She cites several specific geographic and chronological correspondences between Francesco's story, on one hand, and, on the other, parish records, maps, and what we know about the playwright's history—including the fact that Francesco and Isabel's wedding, like Greene and Isabel Beck's, took place on a Thursday.

The mere fact that Greene keeps such unusually detailed track of chronology in Francesco's narrative is significant, for it is unusual in his work. Francesco is married for five years before being reconciled with Isabel's family and spends two years living near his wife's family and three years with Infida in London. According to Richardson's calculations, Greene's history follows an almost identical chronology, including an otherwise unnoticed connection during the mid-1580s to patrons from Anglia, Isabel Beck's native country. Greene seems unusually intent on making Francesco's position at the end of the novel equivalent to Greene's own position at the time of its composition. If Richardson is correct that our

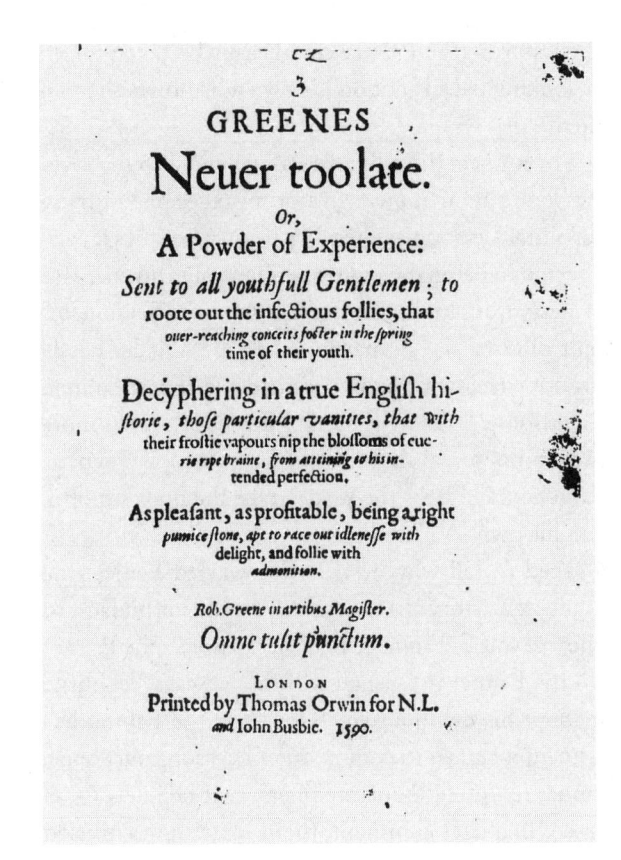

> **GREENES**
> **Neuer too late.**
> *Or,*
> A Powder of Experience:
> *Sent to all youthfull Gentlemen; to* roote out the infectious follies, that *ouer-reaching conceits fofter in the spring time of their youth.*
>
> **Decyphering in a true Englifh hi-***ftorie, thofe particular vanities, that with* their froftie vapours nip the bloſſoms of euc-*rie ripe braine, from attaining to his in-*tended perfection.
>
> As pleaſant, as profitable, being a right *pumice ftone, apt to race out idleneſſe with* delight, and follie with *admonition.*
>
> *Rob. Greene in artibus Magifter.*
> *Omne tulit punctum.*
>
> LONDON
> Printed by Thomas Orwin for N.L.
> and Iohn Busbie. 1590.

Fig. 16 Greene, *Greenes Never too late* (1590), title page (this item is reproduced by permission of The Huntington Library, San Marino, California [RB 61159]). Image published with permission of ProQuest. Further reproduction is prohibited without permission.

Greene is the Greene who married Isabel Beck in 1579, then the ten years that correspond to Francesco's ten in the first volume of *Never Too Late* would bring Greene exactly to 1589, when he was just on the threshold of writing that volume. Francesco's optimistic stance at the end of that book, when he realizes that "Numquam sera est, ad bonos mores via" (It is never too late to take the path to good), is thus suggestive of Greene's optimistic image of himself when the book was written.

The number of resemblances between Francesco's story and Greene's own history is intriguing, if often speculative. But what makes *Never Too Late* even more like the other autobiographies here is a second link to Greene that has not been noticed, in the mysterious Palmer. The Palmer tells Francesco's story to the vestigial narrator in the outermost framing story for *Never Too Late*, and, like Gascoigne's narrators who resemble the younger men in their stories, the Palmer could easily be taken for an older, wiser Francesco, looking back if not on his own adventures then on something very like them.

It may seem a stretch to connect the religious Palmer and a young lover like Francesco. But the book's anonymous narrator mistakes one of these characters for the other almost as soon as the story begins: he spies an approaching figure who seems to be "eyther some penitent pilgrim that was very religious; or some despairing lover that had bin too too affectionate" (*NTL1*, 8:13).[30] Penitent pilgrim and despairing lover are equally possible identities. The narrator's hesitation is understandable. For a palmer, he is very young and handsome: "'Adon' [Adonis] was not thought more faire." The Palmer's first words reveal that he, like Francesco, is a repentant veteran of Venus's follies, and he is the first to take the book's motto, "Numquam sera est," as his own (*NTL1*, 8:2).

In addition, when asked to tell why he is on his way to Venice, the Palmer implies that Francesco's story is a necessary prelude, or preface, to his own: "I will first rehearse you an Englishe historie," answers the Palmer (*NTL1*, 8:33). Not until the Palmer is finished with Francesco's "Englishe historie" does he talk about his own journey. Soon after the Palmer begins Francesco's story, he interrupts it to comment on London courtesans. These he pronounces more tempting than any others, as if he knew them quite as well as Francesco. In a later comment, the Palmer shows himself to be an expert on another part of Francesco's years in Troynovant, the theater. When he finishes Francesco's story, the Palmer follows it with his own, as promised. It turns out to be a verse narrative, a sort of "Palmer's Calendar" that traces his path from wanton prodigal to repentant palmer. The end of the volume brings both his story and Francesco's to their conclusions. The tale of prodigal Francesco is framed by the tale of its prodigal Palmer narrator.

Greene's treatment of the Palmer is not always consistent within the fiction. When he returns at the end of the volume, the Palmer has changed from Adonis into an old, old man. Greene may have wanted to show him aging with the progress of Francesco's tale, or perhaps he reverted carelessly to the stereotype once he shifted attention to the younger penitent, Francesco. But as a storyteller, the Palmer's connection to Greene remains constant. Unlike most palmers, his penitence is like Greene's. Rather than seeking a religious (and presumably unacceptably Catholic) shrine, the Palmer has vowed to tell his tale as a lesson for others. At the end of *Never*

Too Late the Palmer, previously identified by the gray of his clothing, perhaps puns on *green* in the last verse of his autobiography just before departing from the novel: "In greener yeares when as my greedie thoughts / Gan yield their homage to ambitious will," he begins, playing on the *g* sound in *green*. At the end he says, "Gray is the green, the flowers their beauties hides: / When as I see that I to death was borne" (*NTL2*, 8:223, 227).

Greene had already linked his prodigal hero to writing when Francesco's reformation led him to compose moral poetry for his friends. But the Palmer adds another writerly twist to the story of the prodigal son, as John Lyly did in *Euphues*.[31] The same association between a religious traveler, a reformed prodigal, and a storyteller appears again in Greene's next book, *Mourning Garment*. Its prodigal, Philador, is likened "unto some poore Pilgrime," and after he sets out for home to beg forgiveness for his prodigality, he rescues another lover by telling his story, just as the Palmer helps others with his life's story in *Never Too Late* (*Mourning Garment*, 9:184).

In turning his green young wantons into gray storytelling palmers, Greene helped develop a method for conveying the complicated self-consciousness of the autobiographical form that is thought to have appeared only much later.

Greenes Vision

Greene represented himself as both Francesco and the Palmer in *Never Too Late*. But almost nothing in the first volume of that narrative identifies Greene himself as a reformed prodigal. In fact Greene indicates the opposite in his introductory letter: "I presume to present you *as hithertoo I have done with frivolous toies*," that is, he has not changed.

But the second volume of *Never Too Late* marks a clear if unheralded turning point for Greene. He takes on a new motto, one very like the Palmer's and Francesco's "Never too late." Greene's previous motto had been "Omni tulit punctum qui miscuit utile dulci," announcing his goal of mixing pleasure and profit. The new one, "Sero sed serio" (late but seriously meant), points to repentance for the first time. Greene now promises that "for what my pen can do, look for it in *deeper matters*" (*NTL2*, 8:117, italics added). It is as if Greene had repented along with Francesco at the end of volume 1.[32]

The repentance takes place outside the narrative, in the separate text, *Greenes Vision*. *Vision*, according to its frame, was written in 1590 during the break between the two volumes of *Never Too Late*, after the anonymous *Cobbler of Canterbury* (1590) and before *Greenes Mourning Garment* (1590).[33] Although *Vision* was not published until after Greene's death, there is no reason to doubt that it was written when it says it was.

The one exception is a passage that interrupts Greene's otherwise continuous and relatively urbane discussion of his writing. The passage, the only hellfire part of the pamphlet, expresses passionate regret for Greene's sinful life. It sounds like the hellfire passages in the other supposed deathbed pamphlets, *Groatsworth* and *The Repentance of Robert Greene*, and somewhat like Faustus's last dying speech in Marlowe's *Dr. Faustus*. It was probably added to make *Vision* sound more like deathbed repentance,[34] but it is certainly unlike Greene's own repentance writings. Elsewhere Greene refers almost always to professional regret. He was sorry for wanton writing, not wanton living.[35]

Otherwise *Vision* consists of an autobiographical frame narrative that unifies its inset stories. Here the frame narrative occupies roughly three-quarters of the book's total length; there are only two insets. *Vision*'s dominant frame draws Greene's life and his fiction closer together, because it points toward both the character Francesco's repentance and Greene's promises in his paratexts to repent. Whether truthful or not, *Vision* appears like a moment of first-person autobiography in the midst of a quasi-fictional third-person autobiography that suggests how important self-reflection was in Greene's writing at this point.

Vision describes Greene's sudden doubts about his career and the dream that followed them. The catalyst for Greene's vision was an authorial comeuppance earlier that year when Londoners took him for the author of *The Cobbler of Canterbury* (1590), a "merrie worke, and made by some mad fellow." *Cobbler* was popular and sold well, but as Greene says, it was "a little tainted with scurilitie" (*Vision*, 12:213). People assumed that Greene was the sort of man who would have written it: "Because it is pleasant, and therefore mine: because it is full of wanton conceits, and therfore mine: in some places say they the stile bewraies him."[36] Although Greene denies writing *Cobbler*, the accusation, he says, made him reconsider the books that he actually had written. As a result, he begins to wonder whether these books would "redound to my ensuing credit, or my future infamie" (*Vision*, 12:213). In this "melancholy maze" Greene falls asleep and dreams about a literary trial, rather like the one John Skelton dreamed about a century before in *Garland of Laurel* (1495).

Chaucer and Gower appear to Greene and continue the debate about wanton writing that Greene has been having with himself between profit and pleasure. Chaucer begins with praise, alluding to Greene's former motto, which had tried to reconcile them. Pleasant tales best teach virtue, he says, and "it behooves a Scholler to fit his Pen to the time and persons." He cites the many moral precepts that Greene's supposedly wanton stories teach, and a modern reader finds him quite convincing. But Gower responds sternly, arguing that true scholars produce only serious and edifying works about government or philosophy or natural science; they do not write about love. Greene is convinced by Gower's argument, and he promises to follow the poet's advice. "They which helde Greene for a patron of love," he says, shall now find him a Diogenes "that will barke at every amorous pen." He asks only time to finish *Never Too Late*, and then he tells the reader, "Looke for my Morning garment, a weede I know that is of the plainest cut shall please the gravest eie" (*Vision*, 12:274).

At that moment a gorgeously robed King Solomon appears in a flash of light, and all three writers fall to their knees before his Tamberlaine-like charisma: "His stature tall, large, and hie, / Lim'd and featur'd beauteouslie, / Chest was broad, armes were strong. / Lockes of Ember passing long, / That hung and waved upon his neck, / Heavens beautie might they checke" (*Vision*, 12:275). The question is now moot. Solomon now proclaims *all* Scholarship vanity—Gower's as well as Chaucer's. "Only give thy selfe to theologie," Solomon demands; all else is worthless. Greene, awaking with "horror in my conscience, for the follyes of my Penne," vows "peremptorily to leave all thought of love" and seek after the wisdom commended by Solomon (*Vision*, 12:281). Greene's *Alphonsus* may have failed to create a Marlovian overreacher, but *Vision* wittily counters the amoral Tamberlaine with an equally heroic—and heavenly—King Solomon whom Greene chooses instead.

Vision's playful treatment of the old debate between pleasure and instruction suggests that his soul-searching should not be taken completely at face value; that is why the single passage about real moral repentance seems not to belong in it. Nonetheless, Greene's answer to complaints about his writing is complex and hardly perfunctory. He acknowledges his former triviality and promises to reject it, as indeed he soon would. Still, he excuses it cleverly, and the vision format connects his earlier performance to the greatest writers of the English poetic past. It establishes his literary credentials, just as the epilogue to *Perimedes* emphasized Greene's kinship to the circle of elite poets in Tottel's miscellany.

Despite the fact that Greene's repentance occurs in a different text from Francesco's, *Vision* implies a parallel between the two. Greene repented in *Vision* because rumors about his authorship of *The Cobbler of Canterbury* made him realize how other people saw him and his writing. He had been ignoring his faults because no one had pointed them out before: "Because that Gentlemen have *past over my workes with silence, and have rid me without a spurre*, I have (like blind Bayard) plodded forward, and set forth many Pamphlets, full of much love and little Scholarisme."[37] Francesco's change of heart in *Never Too Late* is similarly prompted when he overhears himself judged for the way he treated his wife. "At last [Isabel's fame] came to the eares of Francesco" and makes him face what he has been ignoring. He hears himself called "an unthrift" who "hath not beene with his wife these six yeares" (*NTL2*, 8:164). Stung, he decides at last to beg Isabel's forgiveness.

The important difference between the two is that while it hardly matters who brings Francesco to his senses, Greene takes special care to let readers know that it is not only popular rumor that leads him to change course. The "graver and greater sort," as he calls them, also blamed him for writing *The Cobbler of Canterbury*: "At this booke *the graver and greater sorte* repine, as thinking it not so pleasant to some, as prejudiciall to many, crossing it with such bitter invectives, that they condemne the Aucthor almost for an Atheist," *he says*, "and they father the booke upon me" (*Vision*, 12:213). Elsewhere he says that some "have given [my pamphlets] praise, but the gravest sort, whose mouthes are the trumpets of true report, ha[ve] spoken hardlie of my labours" (*Vision*, 12:273).

Patrons

The gravest judgment of all, King Solomon's in *Vision*'s dream, suggests that the grave and great, oddly enough, are concerned not so much with Greene's atheism as with carelessness about his reputation. The first thing that the "gorgeous Potentate" says to the kneeling Greene when he takes him up by the hand is "My son, they which respect their fame, are the children of wisdom: & such as feare the danger of report, shal be houlden virtuous" (12:276). Solomon does not say, "Respect theology"; he says, "Watch out for your reputation." Greene's dedications during this period make a similar point about the deleterious effects of wanton love. In *Never Too Late*, Greene's moral is that "the fraudulent effects of Venus trumperies" breed "more disparagement to the credit than content to the fancy" (*NTL1*, 8:6), and, again, that "effeminate follies are the efficient causes of dire disparagement" (*NTL2*, 8:116).[38] In *Mourning Garment* Greene warns of "the disparagement that growes from prodigall humours, the discredite that ensues by such inordinate desires: and lastly, the fatall detriment that follows the contempt of grave and advised counsaile" (8:120). It is not that love is immoral or that it makes you suffer. It ruins your reputation.

Greene was particularly worried about the discredit it produced among the graver and greater sort whose patronage he wanted. As he says in the dedication to *Mourning Garment*, he is seeking someone "at whose feete I might laie down the follies of my youth, & bequeathe to him all the profitable fruits of my ensuing age" (8:229). In these books and with his new motto, "Sero sed serio," Greene assures potential patrons that he will reform and pay more attention to their advice from now on.

In this context, Greene's choice of patron for the autobiographical *Never Too Late* is of special interest. Greene's last two texts had been written for the Lord Mayor of London and for Robert Carey, dignitaries he did not know. In *Never Too Late* his strategy is different. Both volumes are dedicated to "the right Worshipfull Thomas Burnaby esquire," the patron to whom Greene seems to have been closest. It is possible that Greene's Burnaby is related to Thomas Barnaby, a merchant who wrote to Cecil in 1552 advising him about coal exports.[39] But otherwise, external evidence about Burnaby is scarce. What we do know is that, unlike many of Greene's recent patrons, he seems to have been more wealthy than widely known; no one else dedicated anything to him, nor did he write dedicatory verses for anyone else.[40]

Greene says in the cordial dedication to the first volume of *Never Too Late* that he has been "affected" to Burnaby "in bounden duty for sundrie favors." Some of the favors were no doubt financial. But Burnaby had also contributed a dedicatory verse to *Ciceronis Amor* (1589) in his own name, and he may have written two others under pseudonyms in other books. The relationship between Burnaby and Greene seems to have gotten still closer between the two volumes, perhaps an indication that Burnaby responded well to the first volume. In the dedication of the second volume Greene is openly affectionate to Burnaby. He refers to Burnaby's "fatherly" rather than "sundrie" favors and signs himself "your adopted son" (*NTL2*, 8).

Greene's talk of fathers in an introduction to his prodigal son story is provocative. Fathers play a central role in the biblical parable, as they do in Greene's parablelike *Mourning Garment*, where the prodigal Philador needs his father's forgiveness after he repents. But *Never Too Late* is an exception. Here the father of prodigal Francesco has almost no role to play; he does not even have a name.[41] Francesco transgresses against his wife, not his father, when he abandons his family in the provinces for life with his courtesan. For this error he needs not his father's forgiveness but his wife's. The only father he disobeys is his wife's father, who opposes the marriage but forgives the couple long before Francesco sets out on the path to prodigality. At the end it is the friendly host of the inn where Isabel has been living, not either father, who organizes the celebratory banquet.

It was not Francesco but the prodigal Greene who needed a father's forgiveness.[42] He was guilty of wanton fictions that not only were trifles but also lost him the support of people whose opinion he cared about. Richardson suggests that one of those important people was Greene's now relatively prosperous father, who may have been estranged, since he did not mention Greene in his will when he died a year later. Regardless of whether Greene suspected his father's intended disinheritance, the dedication to *Never Too Late* certainly installs Burnaby in the paternal role. Greene dedicated three books to Burnaby, more than to any other patron, and all the dedications were made in the two years surrounding the death of Greene's father. After the two *Never Too Late* volumes, the third book dedicated to Burnaby was *A Quip for an Upstart Courtier, or A quaint dispute between Velvet breeches and Cloth-breeches* (1592). *Quip* is Greene's version of an estates satire against the "new men," ostensibly those like Gabriel Harvey's rope-maker father but perhaps also cordwainers-turned-innkeepers, like Greene's own newly rich father. In contrast to such money-conscious and fashion-conscious men, Greene holds up the honest, down-to-earth feudal manners of the ancient gentry. Burnaby, Greene implies, is one of the latter: "All Northamptonshire reports how you are a father of the poore, a supporter of auncient Hospitalities, an enemie to Pride, and to be shorte, a maintayner of Cloth breeches (I mean of the old and worthie customes of the Gentilitie and yeomanrie of England)" (12:210).

Burnaby's importance is suggested by his representation in *Never Too Late*'s frame narrative as well as his identification as its patron. One of the few facts that we know about the Palmer who narrates Francesco's story is that he is on his way to visit "an old friend of mine, an Englishman, to whom I have beene long time indebted, and nowe meane partely to repay with such store as I have bought with hard experience" (*NTL1*, 8:20). While traveling, the Palmer tells his story to others, but the ultimate goal of his travels is to take his hard-won "store" to his friend. Greene, like the Palmer, tells his story for an old friend, an Englishman to whom he has been indebted "in bounden duty," although he publishes it for others to read.

Of course Greene needed money. As Thomas Nashe said, with typical exaggeration, Greene did not care about "winning credit by his works," and "his only care was to have a spel in his purse to conjure up a good cup of wine."[43] In *Vision* Greene was probably trying to take advantage of *Cobbler*'s success with a popular audience whose money he did not scorn although he scorned their taste.[44] In his dedications to Burnaby he was trying to win and keep Burnaby's financial support. But was not entirely true that Greene cared nothing about "winning credit by his works." Greene resorted to popular audiences when necessary. *Never Too Late* and *Vision* suggest, however, that he also cared about a discriminating patron and good friend, one who could provide approval as well as money, and one who replaced the father in Greene's most extended autobiographical fantasy of himself as a reformed prodigal.

Groatsworth and *The Repentance of Robert Greene*

I return briefly to Greene's spurious deathbed repentances to suggest that the autobiographical structure in *Never Too Late*'s double narrative of the Palmer and Francesco may throw some light on the question of Greene's role in both *Groatsworth* and *Repentance*.

The dual stories of the Palmer and Francesco run parallel throughout *Never Too Late*. The narrative in *Greenes Groatsworth of Witte* (1592) also includes parallel stories, although its doubling is notoriously, sudden, and sequential. About one-third of the way into the text, Greene, the omniscient narrator of *Groatsworth*'s tale about Roberto, suddenly identifies himself as Roberto: "Heereafter suppose me the saide Roberto" (*Groatsworth*, 75). Richard Helgerson has called Greene's switch from narrator to hero in *Groatsworth* "one of the most remarkable passages in sixteenth-century fiction."[45] It is also one of the most notable contributions to the history of autobiography.

It is the part of *Groatsworth* that I would say is most likely to be Greene's, if any is. One important argument for acceptance of Chettle as Groatsworth's author has always been his well-known skill as a ventriloquist. If anyone could imitate Greene's style and phrasing, it was Chettle.[46] Yet Chettle hardly seems the writer to have invented the narrative switch between Roberto and the narrator. It is not that Chettle was not a good enough writer, the argument often used earlier to deny that he wrote any of *Groatsworth*, but that Chettle is known for smoothing away the joints between contributors, not emphasizing them. He was a botcher, good at filling in gaps, as he did in the "bad" quarto of *Romeo and Juliet*. He was able to subdue his own contribution to make a continuous story out of pieces from different authors, as he did in *The Book of Sir Thomas More* (1593?).[47]

Greene seems more likely than Chettle to have invented the switch. Both his pamphlets and his plays are known for their multiple perspectives and parallel plots. Just before *Groatsworth*, Greene had been experimenting in particular with the relationship between the author of the preface and the protagonist of the text and, within the text, between narrator and hero. In a text added to *A Disputation betweene a Hee Conny-catcher and a Shee Conny-catcher*, published the year Greene died, he composed a first-person account of "the wonderful life of a Curtezin, not a fiction, but a truth of one that yet lives not now in an other forme repentant" (*Disputation*, 12:201). In it, the courtesan narrator switches back and forth easily between her own story and the archetypal "inconstant life of Courtezens and common harlots" in general. At one point the narrator interrupts her description of the courtesan's underworld at large to go on with her own experience in it: "But stopping here, till occasion serve me fitter to discover the manner of Courtezins, to [turn to] my selfe, who now being brought to London..." (12:71–72).[48] The interruption moves, like the narrator's in *Groatsworth*, between third and first person, reminding the reader of the courtesan's doubled role in the text, although, unlike *Groatsworth*'s narrator, she makes no secret of her identity.

We know, too, that Greene was planning to continue the confessional mode of recent publications. The last entry Greene made in the Stationers' Register, not long before he died (S.R. August 21, 1592), is "The Repentance of a Conycatcher with the life and death of [blank] Mourton and Ned Browne, twoo notable cony catchers The one latelie executed at Tyborne the other at Aix in fraunce." Ned Browne's first-person story was published later that season as *The Black Book's Messenger* (1592), but it did not include the promised story of Mourton. In *The Black Book's Messenger* Greene explains his omission, promising that "The Conny-catchers repentance ... shall shortly be published," and he even adds a blurb describing the promised text: "It contains a passion of great importance. First how he was given over from all grace and Godlines, and seemed to have no sparke of the feare of God in him: yet neverthelesse, through the woonderful working of Gods spirite, even in the dungeon at Newgate the night before he died, he so repented him from the bottome of his hart" that he will serve as a model for all readers. The information in the two descriptions implies that the "Repentance of Conny-catcher" was intended to be, like Brown's, a histrionic first-person account of Mourton's life and repentance.

The "Repentance" never appeared. But it may have been the source for part of *The Repentance of Robert Greene* (S.R. October 6, 1592), the second of Greene's suspect deathbed confessions. This one was printed by Chettle's fellow stationer Cuthbert Burby. What matters for the argument here is that, like Chettle's *Groatsworth*, Burby's *Repentance* is essentially a two-part text, apart from some filler material. The first part of Burby's text is called "The Repentance of Robert Greene, Maister of Arts," but the story it tells does not sound like Greene's. It is narrated by someone "brought up in riot" who sounds more like Ned Browne or the mysterious Mourton than anything we hear anywhere about young Greene. Minus its title and one reference to "Robin" Greene, the section could easily be Mourton's, and is thought by some scholars to be so.[49] However, Burby's second part, "The life and death of Robert Greene, Maister of Artes," deserves to be taken more seriously as, at least in part, something that Greene could possibly have written about himself. Burby's "Life and Death" is a repetitive patchwork, including a dubious hellfire section like the one in *Greenes Vision*; it tells part of the story of Greene's life at least twice.

One of the versions seems to have been modeled partly on the Palmer's narrative of his bachelor European travels in *Never Too Late* (*NTL2*, 8). But another presents a reasonably accurate summary of externally verifiable facts in Greene's life, along with an intriguingly detailed passage about an early religious experience that Greene does not recount anywhere else (*Repentance*, 12:174–78). The passage describes Greene's encounter with a charismatic preacher, and it is both consistent with known details of Greene's life and free of the extravagant repentance that characterizes other forged deathbed messages from Greene. It has the ring of truth that invites further investigation.

If Burby was working from an original manuscript intended to be "The Repentance of a Conny catcher" named Mourton, that text was modeled, presumably, on "The repentance of Ned Browne" and would have had two parts, like Ned Browne's two. Greene seems already to have written the material for one of these, the repentance of Mourton. The question is whether Greene, unable to complete both parts of Mourton's text in his last days, attached his own "Life" to Mourton's repentance, making it a two-part text, with a dramatic switch from third- to first-person narrative. The unimaginative Burby, intent on producing a last deathbed repentance just like all the others he had seen, would simply made the few changes necessary to attribute the whole of such a document to Greene. But Chettle, if he saw it, may have found in its movement from Mourton to Greene a new model that he could use in his two-part *Groatsworth*.[50] Greene then would be responsible for *Groatsworth*'s emphasis on the act of telling the story, which thus becomes as interesting as the story itself.

Arguments about lost texts are of course speculative, although this text is perhaps not quite so lost as others: Greene had already almost, although not quite, described it in the other printed works of the last two years of his life.[51] But regardless of whether Greene played a part in *Groatsworth*, the argument suggests that future authorship studies should focus on *Groatsworth*'s structure as well as on its content, that is, on what *Groatsworth*'s author was doing as well as on what he was saying.

Finally, even if they are forgeries, *Groatsworth* and *The Repentance of Robert Greene* are useful supplements to the study of sixteenth-century autobiography. Whether truthful, lying, or something in between, they provide evidence for the multiple traditions, old and new, that nourished autobiographical writing. They have roots in impersonal genres and formulaic narratives without individual authors; they are related to popular forms like the last will and testament, *de casibus* tales, revenant ballads, tombstone poetry, last dying repentances, and Richard Tarlton's posthumous jestbook, "Newes out of Purgatorie" (1590). At the same time, they testify to the growing new market for self-conscious, supposedly individual autobiographical writing by ordinary people like Greene.

Greene's place in the history of autobiography is itself evidence of the balance between old and new. Greene's most autobiographical narrative, *Never Too Late*, bears traces of the original audience and occasion for which it was written, suggesting its roots in an earlier world of patrons and manuscript exchange. At the same time, Greene's experiments with the relation between narrator and protagonist—on which both *Groatsworth* and *Never Too Late* depend—look toward the future and the narrative self-consciousness that we associate with autobiography.

CHAPTER 10

Autobiographers: Who Were They? Why Did They Write?

The previous chapters discuss only a dozen or so writers, but they suggest a few tentative generalizations about the people who chose to write about themselves in this period and why. Much of what these writers shared was the product of their historical context. Sixteenth-century Reformation England created the "conditions for autobiography," as George Gusdorf identified them in his early study. The most important of these, he argued, was a sense of history and of how a writer's society differed from the past. That awareness was difficult to escape in the sixteenth century. The shock of changing reigns and religions was widespread. People watched as the status quo quickly became history, sometimes more than once in a lifetime. The upheavals affected even later writers like Thomas Whythorne and Thomas Tusser, as well as those, like Bale and Baldwin, caught in the early Reformation battles.

This period encouraged people's "protean ability," as Paul Delaney has called it, to "imagine themselves in more than one role" and "stand outside or above their own personality." James Amelang finds a similar "metamorphosis" common among the artisan autobiographers he traces in early modern Europe. Again, the writers treated here, part of an increasingly mobile society, were all familiar with geographic, occupational, and social dislocation. Thomas Wyatt, as King Henry VIII's ambassador, knew the languages and habits of other courts besides his own and knew how important it was to keep such difference in mind. Thomas Tusser's move from court to country, leaving him torn between ties to both, was a central fact in his life, and similar moves affected others who had emigrated to London. Churchyard and Gascoigne traveled back and forth between war and court, military and citizen life, and both wrote about the contrast.

Just as religious controversy encouraged protean skills by fostering secrecy and separating outward compliance from inner rebellion, so did the constant mingling of masters with educated, socially mobile servants in an age when service was ubiquitous. This was as true of Wyatt writing about court intrigues at the top of the hierarchy, as it was of Whitney trying to maintain her position in service to a virtuous lady lower down. It was even true of George Gascoigne and Robert Greene, who were not in service but remained desperate to find an aristocratic patron who would enlist them in service. Whether chafing at their place or hoping to rise above it through service, all witnessed the possibility of alternative roles.

The education newly available to people like them was one of the most important factors for writers. Of course, the literary and rhetorical skill that education instilled, along with the introduction to different forms of expression, were required for autobiography. But education was also one of the ways to find the patronage so often necessary throughout this period, even for those aiming at a popular market. Many of the autobiographers depended on friends who had access to wealth, power, or literary influence. Education almost certainly forged Skelton's connection to the Howards and thus to King Henry's court. John Bale's convent education made it possible for him to write the plays that attracted Cromwell's protection, and Baldwin's literary talent was the basis of his courtly connections. On a lower social level, Whitney's access to print, unusual for a woman, may have been made possible by her brother's London connections. Gascoigne's father, though a relatively minor official, gave him entry into the court social networks. Tusser looked to Lord Paget for help throughout his career, and Whythorne's apprenticeship to John Heywood seems to have helped him make connections with wealthy employers. Even Churchyard's less-than-illustrious poetic career no doubt benefited from his status as onetime soldier under Henry Howard, earl of Surrey.

Although partly determined by their common cultural context, some of the traits shared by the autobiographers set them apart from most others in their context. Other people at the time had access to education, but few went on to literary careers. For most of these writers, education is the central fact of their life. They display an unusual energy and (sometimes obsessive) devotion to observation and writing—and a tendency to write about writing. Bale, historian and antiquary, spent his life among books and manuscripts. Skelton flaunted his cunning, and even before his laureation he anticipated his title. He referred to Cambridge as his parent, and Greene, another Cantabrigian, identified himself as Master of Arts on his title pages. Many of the autobiographers depended on writing to make a living, a choice that was far more unusual than it would be today.

Yet even those who depended on writing for their existence were not entirely pragmatic about their skill. They identified themselves with the act of writing, as Skelton did when he personified his "Occupation" in his *Garland of Laurel*, or Wyatt did in his lute poems or poems about his "songs," or as Bale did in describing his "vocacyon" as preaching minister and writing apostle. Baldwin's *Mirror* frame shows him in the process of composition, and, if John King is correct, he took King Solomon, singer of songs as well as philosopher, as a model for himself. Thomas Whythorne's book culminates in a paean to the heavenly art of music, including song writing. Isabella Whitney refers to herself as a writer, mentions her printer affectionately in her mock will, and names paper, pen, and Standish (inkstand) as witnesses to that document.

Another distinguishing characteristic shared by these writers is their dramatic bent. Their protean ability to imagine alternative roles was also an ability to see through other people's eyes. Some were public performers—clergy, dramatists, people who were already accustomed to speaking before neighborhood groups and shaping their discourse for public consumption. Some wrote actual plays. Bale and Greene spent a significant portion of their energy writing for the stage. Skelton, Baldwin, and Gascoigne, though most well known for other genres, all wrote or translated and perhaps acted in plays. Additionally, some of Skelton's dream visions were probably performed as pageants for an audience of his patrons. Gascoigne too showed a histrionic gift apart from translating *Jocasta* and *Supposes* for performance at the Inns of Court. In a later contribution to the shows for Queen Elizabeth at Kenilworth, Gascoigne played a savage man carrying an uprooted oak in his hand. He startled the queen's horse and nearly caused a crisis. Then, when he reappeared as Sylvanus in the farewell show, running to keep up with the queen's horse, despite his breathlessness he improvised a comment flattering enough to earn Elizabeth's praise.

Other autobiographers wrote dramatic monologues, like the ghosts' tragedies in *Mirror for Magistrates* or Skelton's many flyting poems. For

Skelton and Bale in particular, statement seems to have been inseparable from debate. There is drama too in the way Baldwin juxtaposes multiple perspectives on his ghosts' complaints and moves suddenly from Plato's eternal wisdom about magistrates to his fellow writers' idiosyncratic perspectives. Gascoigne's collected poems in *Hundreth* are attributed to five poetic alter egos, and yet another fictional persona, "G. T.," provides the frame that introduces and comments on them all.

It is probably not surprising that many of the writers had a strong sense of themselves, as far as one can tell at this distance. Many were known as eccentric (Skelton), stubborn (Bale), overly self-conscious (Whythorne), or prone to display (Greene) or to a sense of entitlement (Gascoigne). They not only wrote about themselves but commissioned portraits of themselves, or (in Gascoigne's case) drew them. Several had themselves portrayed more than once and spent care on their visual as well as verbal self-representation. (See appendix.)

The writers discussed here were not composing memoirs or leaving a record of their time and place, as King Edward VI did in his journal. While many later autobiographers studied by Amelang described newsworthy public events, these authors wrote about what concerned them personally. Bale mentions King Edward's death because it affected him and nearly got him killed, not because it was worth reporting in itself. Others like Whythorne and Tusser, who were affected by the death, did not mention it, perhaps from discretion or perhaps because it didn't belong in their stories. Whitney was writing during the wars in the Netherlands, on which Churchyard and Gascoigne reported, but apart from one puzzling reference to war, she writes as if she knew nothing about the world of politics.

Many of the texts here are provoked by loss or disappointment; writing was often a way of assuaging it. Some, like Whitney, were asking for money or, like Gascoigne, patronage. Others wrote in self-justification, as Skelton did in his outraged "Ware the Hawk," Tusser did in his gentler apologia, and Bale and Munday did when defending their year-long stays among the papists in *Vocacyon* and *English Roman Life*. Some, like Greene, wrote to justify themselves and to appeal for help at the same time. Even without hope of a pragmatic solution to their problems, some, like Whythorne, wrote simply "to ease my mind." As Whitney says in her letters, "Cause of griefe compels me to complayne." Whythorne feared betrayal. Wyatt's meditative poems were often prompted by his sense of being betrayed, whether by king or by mistress. Similar motives can be seen in early modern autobiographies not discussed here. Anne Clifford's diary was begun in part to help her win back her proper, but contested, inheritance. Simply bearing witness was an important part of justifying oneself. Amelang tells of one diarist who recorded every offense committed by his neighbors over the course of twenty-three years. Simon Forman's autobiography consists partly of a jestbook-like sequence of confrontations with various enemies—hardly an impartial account.

Some texts come out of a period of enforced leisure, during which other, less writing-obsessed individuals might have turned to something more pragmatic and outward-looking. Whitney and Tusser had recently lost their jobs when they wrote. She had been fired before writing *Nosgay*, and Tusser had been forced to give up his land when he wrote the first edition of his husbandry book. Wyatt was exiled in the country when he composed his autobiographical verse epistles; "Whoso list his wealth and ease retain" (CLXXVI) may have been written behind a prison grate. Similarly, Surrey's moving autobiographical reminiscence about Richmond was written while he was held in Windsor Castle. Several poets were prisoners of war when they wrote: Churchyard's verse reports from the front tell of imprisonment and may have been written while he was imprisoned; the same may be true of Gascoigne's "Fruite of war" and "Fruite of fetters," both published in 1575 after he was held prisoner in the Netherlands.

Between Culture and Individual

Cultural context and individual temperament both helped produce autobiographers. But it is not clear that these texts would have been written were it not for a third influential condition attributable neither to culture nor to the individual alone. One of the most remarkable facts about this group is that in writing for themselves, they were writing for others. The autobiographical act is often said to be a social and cultural practice, but among these early writers it seems to have derived not only from the widest but also from the most intimate forms of society and culture. Being part of a family, a small group of believers, or a friendship provided both a sense of both self and audience. It fostered the self-confidence to write and the understanding of other perspectives that is necessary for self-observation. A writer wrote about herself because there was someone who wanted to read about her. Writing, like language, is a form of communication as well as self-expression. Unlocking the secrets entombed in your heart was part of an exchange.

The earliest texts here usually derive from communal occasions and take for granted a public audience: a circle of fellow courtiers, a group of coreligionists or government officials. But despite the presence of the community there is still a sense of intimacy between author and audience. Skelton and Wyatt address individuals who may actually have been in their audiences. Bale directs his polemics to the entire Christian world, but he writes as if giving a sermon in his own parish and sometimes fires insults at specific enemies. Baldwin and his cowriters write for the magistrates in Queen Mary's government, but at the same time they mediate their message with a narrative about the book's composition among a small group of friendly scholars, alert to their audience's response. Elsewhere, Baldwin points to a similarly intimate storytelling circle as the origin for his *Beware the Cat*, and Whythorne describes the songs he made up, tailored specifically to entertain a particular gathering in the houses where he worked. Greene's *Perimedes the Blacksmith* identifies itself as a collection of stories exchanged by a blacksmith and his wife over an evening's fire.

Perhaps most surprising of all, even the later writers, Londoners with hopes of wide sales, often wrote for a small, intimate audience. Many of them formed their own "coteries," composed not of courtiers but of young men coming down from university and settling at the Inns of Court. The writers were part of the same networks and often knew each other in person. Their publicly marketed pamphlets were like the earlier manuscripts circulated for a private audience, as in the letters between himself and Edmund Spenser that Gabriel Harvey published, or the quarreling exchanges that Harvey, Greene, and Thomas Nashe printed in pamphlets or prefaces.

Traces of origins in intimate exchange of concerns, losses, disappointments, irritations, and hopes can still be seen in printed books on the market or intended for it. Whythorne writes for his "good friend" to share his secrets and his pride in his verse; both Tusser's autobiographical "Dedication" and his closing "Life of the author" in his 1573 *Husbandry* book take the form of friendly letters about his painful decisions to move from country to city or in the other direction. Whitney's verse letters (and the responses) about her troubles make up half of her *Nosgay*. Gascoigne writes with his patron Lord Grey's tastes in mind as well as for the public.

Greene dedicated his most autobiographical fiction, *Never Too Late*, to his patron, Thomas Burnaby, as if to convince Burnaby that it is never too late for Greene to become a worthy client. No matter how public the eventual circulation, writers were also reporting, complaining, and, as we might say, venting to and sharing with friends. Reading one after another of these often importunate texts, one wonders how many of them would have made it into print in a world of cell phones within easy reach.

I close by mentioning one trait shared by the writers that is more difficult to characterize. All of them were interested in other people. They were theologians, antiquaries, political theorists, politicians, musicians, and scholars, but they formulated their thoughts in terms of people's actions even before they wrote about their own lives. Bale's magisterial bibliography of English writing took the form of a collection of writers' lives. His ultimate goal was to rescue the nation's manuscripts before they were lost in the dissolution of the monasteries. But he always identified books by their authors, omitting anonymous texts from his bibliography. He saw the texts he rescued as martyrs he had saved from heathen fires. Baldwin too recorded the lives of important writers. His popular *Treatise of Moral Philosophy*, for which Bale later called him the English Cato, gives a local habitation and a name to wisdom by attaching moral precepts to the philosophers who taught them and providing a brief biography of each. Baldwin's translation of the Song of Songs, *The Canticles or Ballads of Solomon* (1549), is similarly anchored in its author. Whythorne's history of music is also a history of great musicians, and his intense self-awareness is almost inseparable from his obsessive questions about and alertness to what other people were thinking.

The writers' interest in others, like their interest in themselves, had roots in both old and new traditions. In part, the habit reflected the older medieval tendency to organize the world by lives and generations, as in the Bible and the historical chronicles or the various hagiographic and scholarly traditions that influenced Bale and Baldwin. But it was also fostered by newer influences, such as the humanistic training in rhetoric that embodied ideas in speaking human beings who colored and reshaped them and used them to affect other people, sometimes even as weapons. Similarly the attention to other people was part of a new interest in human psychology as a causal force in history, whether in new attitudes toward legal evidence and historical writing, as in the *Mirror for Magistrates*, or in individual cases of intense self-scrutiny, like Thomas Whythorne's.

There is much still to learn about sixteenth-century autobiographers, both as they represented and as they stood apart from others who did not write about themselves. What we should expect, however—apart from the writers' training in and dedication to writing—is that the history of thinking and writing about the self is also the history of relationships to others.

Appendix: *The Portraits*

The authorial portraits in the texts treated here, as well as the texts themselves, also suggest how the writers were trying to present themselves. Even when Skelton, the earliest of the autobiographers, was writing, a tradition of generic introductory images for manuscripts and portrait frontispieces in printed books was already in place.[1] But, like publishing an autobiography, including a portrait in a relatively ordinary book was still a gesture novel enough to mark the author as unusual. Additionally, there were few enough precedents of individual likenesses that any individualizing details almost certainly reveal authorial intention. Like the texts themselves, the portraits cannot be easily categorized as either stereotyped or naturalistic representations. They authors personalize and combine old and new representational conventions in their own ways.

The two images of Skelton that appeared in his lifetime are the most conventional of the authorial portraits. They were both taken from generic woodcuts that had been used elsewhere. Neither is intended as a physical likeness, but revisions and additions bind each more closely to Skelton, who had a hand in producing the first and probably the second as well. The first portrait appears in the traditional location of title-page verso in *Garland of Laurel* (pr. 1523). The picture of "Skelton Poeta" (fig. 1) is taken from the woodcut for April in the *Kalendar of Shepherds* (1499). A delightful image of springtime and rebirth, it shows a young man in a field of flowers holding a laurel branch in his hand. Skelton makes it his own by adding "Skelton Poeta" at the top and a Latin verse at the bottom whose last line promises that "everywhere Skelton shall be remembered as Adonis," the very promise Skelton makes at the end of *Garland*'s text. By making the alterations, Skelton transformed the conventional emblem of seasonal rebirth into an emblem for his own poetic immortality. The second image, appearing first in "Agaynst a Comely Coystrowne" (1527?) and used three more times in his works (fig. 2), represents Skelton in the conventional pose of a preacher/orator at a lectern, reading a book. However, the added verse, "Yield, all kinds of trees, to the green laurel," places the image unmistakably with Skelton's many verbal proclamations—and the earlier visual one—of his laureate status.

Bale's three portraits are conventional primarily in representing "the outer man," as Whythorne called it, in emblematic dress.[2] Otherwise, they are remarkably naturalistic for the period. The earliest image shows a thoughtful, bearded Bale, solidly enough established to be wearing a ring and a robe with a fur collar, holding a book (fig. 4). The second is one of only two authorial portraits in Bale's authoritative catalog of British writers, *Illustrium* (1548). This one shows Bale in a typical scholar's pose and cap, a generic pose with only small differences from the portrait of Wycliffe earlier in Bale's book. Yet stereotypical as this portrait is, Bale makes original, purposeful use of it here in order to emphasize his claim, in the text, that Wycliffe is Bale's spiritual and intellectual ancestor.[3] Bale's third portrait, from *Catalogus* (fig. 5), shows him at age sixty-two, again in scholar's clothing but now surrounded by the more formal, quasi-architectural frame usually found on title pages (compare Baldwin's title page, fig. 9).

Bale incorporated two other images of himself, both showing him presenting his 1548 *Illustrium* to King Edward (figs. 7 and 8). The first, on the title page, shows him kneeling conventionally before the king's throne and holding out his book, while another man looks out from the curtain in the background. The second image is a close-up, showing only Bale and Edward. Bale is standing in the foreground while the king sits reading at a desk in front of a barely visible throne, as if he were Bale's student at school. Like his *Vocacyon*, Bale's illustrations convey a mixed message. One presents an appropriate impression of humility, but the other, albeit less obviously, implies Bale's importance even in relation to the king.

Whythorne had no fewer than four likenesses taken of himself to record his physical changes over the years. Whythorne balances convention and individuality, as he does in his text (fig. 10). Naturalistic portrayal dominates the one extant portrait, but its background includes Whythorne's emblematic coat of arms and motto. The portrait was later redone as a woodcut frontispiece for his 1571 book of music, and copies were reused for his 1590 music book and the autobiographical manuscript (fig. 9). As usual, Whythorne is explicit about his motives for including the portrait in his books. First, he wants readers to see what he looked like as well as what he was called. Because his books are his children and bear his name, he says, "I could do no less than set in every one of them, their father's picture...the form and favor of their parent" (175). In this, although he does not say so, he may have been guided by his mentor, John Heywood, one of the few contemporary authors whose portrait had been included in his text.[4] Whythorne's concern with his individual physical likeness, however, is accompanied by a more conventional desire to show "myself to be [a gentleman] as well in the outward marks, as in the outward man" (175). The marks of his social standing are his choice of dress and the inclusion of his coat of arms and motto framing the woodcut.

Gascoigne too made good use of convention to further his self-image. For a presentation copy of "Hermetes the Heremyte" to Queen Elizabeth (1575/6), he drew himself in the traditional kneeling posture of one offering a book to a prince. But the humbleness of this gesture is belied by its setting (fig. 14).[5] The queen, suspiciously alone with Gascoigne, is canopied in the lower left quadrant of the image: the other three sides of the chamber open to an outward vista, another room, and a mysterious tunnel into the ceiling or heavens, as if showing the endless possibilities that the gift (or Gascoigne) promises. A laurel halo hovers above Gascoigne's head, and an inexplicable arm descends from the opening over it, bearing Gascoigne's motto, "Tam Marti quam Mercurio." Gascoigne includes a second image in *The Steele Glas* (1576), in the usual title-page verso location (fig. 15). Austen makes a good argument that the "intense stare, and especially the slight misalignment of the eyes" make it "almost certain that this is a self-portrait, done in front of a mirror."[6] While the poet's own personality dominates the picture, however, it is framed by the conventional emblems of Mars (weapons) on one side and Mercury (a bookshelf) on the other. Individual portrait and generic emblem are paired, just as the complicated man is summed up by his reductive motto.

Notes

CHAPTER ONE

1. Wayne Shumaker's *English Autobiography: Its Emergence, Materials, and Form* (Berkeley: University of California Press, 1954) was the first work in English to treat English autobiography as a genre separate from biography, and it was limited to autobiographies "in the modern mode," beginning after the sixteenth century. Most studies of English autobiography begin in the seventeenth century or after. Paul Delaney's excellent study *British Autobiography in the Seventeenth Century* (London: Routledge & Kegan Paul, 1969), begins in the seventeenth century, although he recognizes a new spirit appearing in the sixteenth. Others do as well: Margaret Bottrall, *Every Man a Phoenix: Studies in Seventeenth-Century Autobiography* (London: J. Murray, 1958); John Morris, *Versions of the Self: Studies in English Autobiography from John Bunyan to John Stuart Mill* (New York: Basic Books, 1966); Joan Webber, *The Eloquent 'I': Style and Self in Seventeenth-Century Prose* (Madison: University of Wisconsin Press, 1968). Patricia Spacks begins later in *Imagining a Self: in Autobiography and the Novel in Eighteenth-Century England* (Cambridge, MA: Harvard University Press, 1967); Michael Mascuch mentions texts written as early as 1591, but he argues that autobiography did not appear until the seventeenth century and proper autobiography not until still later, in *Origins of the Individualist Self: Autobiography and Self-Identity in England, 1591–1791* (Stanford, CA: Stanford University Press, 1996).

Recent interest in writings by early modern women, as well as scholarly debates about subjectivity, textuality, and their relation have also led to several collections of essays analyzing early texts. See Mike Pincombe on Thomas Sackville and Helen Wilcox on John Donne in *Sixteenth-Century Identities*, ed. Amanda Piesse (Manchester, UK: Manchester University Press, 1999); Henk Dragstra, Sheila Ottway, and Helen Wilcox, eds., *Betraying Ourselves: Forms of Self-Representation in Early Modern English Texts* (Houndmills, Hampshire, UK: Macmillan, 2000), includes essays on

John Gower, Thomas Nashe, John Bale, and Thomas Whythorne. Other anthologies do not deal with sixteenth-century texts, but their essays are useful in thinking about all autobiography: Elspeth Graham et al., eds., *Her Own Life: Autobiographical Writings by Seventeenth-Century Englishwomen* (London: Routledge, 1989); Thomas F. Mayer and D. R. Woolf, eds., *The Rhetorics of Life-Writing in Early Modern England: Forms of Biography from Cassandra Fedele to Louis XIV* (Ann Arbor: University of Michigan Press, 1995); Roy Porter, ed., *Rewriting the Self: Histories from the Renaissance to the Present* (London: Routledge, 1997); Brigitte Glaser, *The Creation of the Self in Autobiographical Forms of Writing in Seventeenth-Century England* (Heidelberg: Universitatsverlag, 2001; and David Booy, ed., *Personal Disclosures: An Anthology of Self-Writings from the Seventeenth Century* (Aldershot, UK: Ashgate, 2002).

2. John Kerrigan, introduction to William Shakespeare, *The Sonnets and A Lover's Complaint* (Harmondsworth, UK: Penguin, 1986), 11. Most of the important early studies of autobiography have been broadly focused on the whole Western tradition, especially its most admired texts. They often begin with Augustine and concentrate on later figures like Jean-Jacques Rousseau and Johann Wolfgang von Goethe, with few stops between the two. From their perspective, sixteenth-century English autobiographical writing is of relatively minor importance. English texts enter only with the Puritans and self-searching spiritual autobiographies of the seventeenth century. Georg Misch did incorporate all sorts of texts in his extraordinary survey of all Western literature, but he hardly got beyond the early Renaissance. Some of his study was published in English as *The History of Autobiography in Antiquity* [1907], trans. E. W. Dickes in collaboration with Misch (Cambridge, MA: Harvard University Press, 1951). Other studies omitting the earliest English texts are Anna Robesun Burr, *The Autobiography: A Critical and Comparative Study* (Boston: Houghton Mifflin, 1909); E. Stuart Bates, *Inside Out: An Introduction to Autobiography* (New York: Sheridan House, 1937); Roy Pascal, *Design and Truth in Autobiography* (London: Harvard University Press, 1960); Georges Gusdorf, "Conditions and Limits of Autobiography," trans. James Olney, in *Autobiography: Essays Theoretical and Critical*, ed. James Olney (Princeton, NJ: Princeton University Press, 1980); James Olney, *Metaphors of the Self: The Meaning of Autobiography* (Princeton, NJ: Princeton University Press, 1972); Karl Joachim Weintraub, *The Value of the Individual: Self and Circumstance in Autobiography* (Chicago: University of Chicago Press, 1978). One reviewer, surveying several studies from the 1970s, concludes that according to these as well, autobiography "is largely a modern phenomenon (since the eighteenth century)" (Gay Wilson Allen, "Autobiography or Artifact?" *Georgia Review* 35 [1981]: 411).

For a recent survey of approaches to autobiography see Laura Marcus, *Auto/biographical Discourses: Theory, Criticism, Practice* (Manchester, UK: Manchester University Press, 1994). The most wide-ranging, well-informed, and persuasive treatment of autobiography, and the one I have learned most from, is James S. Amelang, *The Flight of Icarus: Artisan Autobiography in Early Modern Europe* (Stanford, CA: Stanford University Press, 1998). Amelang's bibliography of secondary texts and introductory essays should be essential reading for anyone working on any form of early modern autobiography. However, his study is both more general than this one (covering several centuries and all of Europe) and more specific (focused only on artisan autobiographies). It treats none of the sixteenth-century texts covered here, although it includes Simon Forman's sixteenth-century autobiography in its bibliography of primary texts, which is an extremely valuable source for scholars.

3. Philippe Lejeune, "The Autobiographical Pact," in *On Autobiography*, trans. Katherine Leary (orig. 1973; Minneapolis: University of Minnesota Press, 1989), 3–30. Pascal, for example, is interested only in "autobiography proper" (*Design and Truth*, 3, and he distinguishes the few "genuine" autobiographies in the Middle Ages from the great mass of autobiographical writing, 24).

4. Kerrigan, introduction to Shakespeare's *Sonnets and A Lover's Complaint*, 11.

5. Three early essays did list pre-1600 autobiographies or proto-autobiographies in England, although without treating them at length: Donald Stauffer, "The Autobiography," in *English Biography before 1700* (Cambridge, MA: Harvard University Press, 1930); James M. Osborn, *The Beginnings of Autobiography in England* (Los Angeles: William Andrews Clarke Memorial Library and University of California Press, 1959); and Rudolf Gottfried, "Autobiography and Art: An Elizabethan Borderland," in *Literary Criticism and Historical Understanding: Essays from the English Institute*, ed. Phillip Damon (New York: Columbia University Press, 1967), 109–34. More recently, Elizabeth Heale has discussed sixteenth-century poetic autobiographies in *Autobiography and Authorship in Renaissance Verse* (Houndmills, Hampshire, UK: Palgrave Macmillan, 2003). Medievalists, unlike early modernists, tend to locate the beginnings of autobiographical writing (and/or subjectivity) earlier than early modernists do. See David Aers, "A Whisper in the Ears of Early Modernists, or Reflections on Literary Critics Writing the 'History of the Modern Subject,'" in *Culture and History, 1350–1600: Essays on English Community, Identities, and Writing* (Detroit: Wayne State University Press, 1992), 177–202; and Lee Patterson, *Chaucer and the Subject of History* (Madison: University of Wisconsin Press, 1991).

6. Theorists who have argued for a definition of autobiography that could accommodate historical change include Elizabeth Bruss, *Autobiographical Acts: The Changing Situation of a Literary Genre* (Baltimore: Johns Hopkins University Press, 1976), and William Spengeman, *The Forms of Autobiography* (New Haven, CT: Yale University Press, 1980). Spengeman's excellent extensive annotated bibliography of secondary material, with Amelang's, should be consulted especially by anyone interested in the history of approaches to the topic or in ways of subdividing the general topic of "autobiography."

7. However, I do exclude diaries. Although they should be taken into account in any complete history of how people wrote about themselves, diaries are less useful for my purpose because they aim at what one diarist has called the "perpetual middle" of existence. They do not presume a retrospective view that separates the writer in the present from her experience in the past. They are, as Samuel Richardson said of Pamela's letters, "written under the immediate Impression of every Circumstance which occasioned them," rather than being recollected later in tranquillity (or otherwise). Many diaries, like Pepys's, it is true, turn out to be retrospectively transcribed from notes. But they still take the form of (almost) real-time discontinuous entries, and they leave the writer less scope to organize, rather than simply record, experience.

8. Anthony Low, *Aspects of Subjectivity: Society and Individuality from the Middle Ages to Shakespeare and Milton* (Pittsburgh: Duquesne University Press), traces the historical development of interest in inwardness (ix–x).

9. Alastair Fowler, *Renaissance Realism: Narrative Images in Literature and Art* (Oxford: Oxford University Press, 2003), esp. 1–34.

10. Richard Helgerson, *The Elizabethan Prodigals* (Berkeley: University of California Press, 1976).

11. William Baldwin, *Epistola* Aiv, cited by Stephen Gresham, "William Baldwin: Literary Voice of the Reign of Edward VI," *Huntington Library Quarterly*, 1981, 110. On such distinctions and the various terminologies used for them, see H. L. Levy, "As myn auctour seyth," *Medium Aevum* 12 (1945): 25–39; William Nelson, *Fact or Fiction: The Dilemma of the Renaissance Storyteller* (Cambridge, MA: Harvard University Press, 1973), Judith K. Anderson, *Biographical Truth: The Representation of Historical Persons in Tudor-Stuart Writing* (New Haven, CT: Yale University Press, 1984); Barbara Shapiro, *A Culture of Fact: England, 1550–1720* (Ithaca, NY: Cornell University Press, 2000).

12. Robert McMahon, "Autobiography as Text-Work: Augustine's Refiguring of Genesis 3 in His Conversion Account," *Exemplaria* 1 (1989): 337–66.

13. Laurence de Looze, *Pseudo-Autobiography in the Fourteenth Century: Juan Ruiz, Guillaume de Machaut, Jean Froissart, and Geoffrey Chaucer* (Gainesville: University Press of Florida, 1997). The phrase "the great fourteenth-century introspective writers" is taken from Albert N. Mancini, "Writing the Self: Forms of Autobiography in the Late Italian Renaissance," *Canadian Journal of Italian Studies* 14 (1991): 11–22, esp. 12. See also Evelyn B. Vitz, "The 'I' of the *Roman de la Rose*," trans. Barbara DeStephano, *Genre* 6 (1973): 49–75.

14. Gottfried, "Autobiography and Art," 109–34.

15. Judith H. Anderson, *The Growth of a Personal Voice: "Piers Ploughman" and "The Fairy Queene"* (New Haven, CT: Yale University Press, 1976).

16. Natalie Zemon Davis, *Fiction in the Archives: Pardon Tales and Their Tellers in Sixteenth-Century France* (Stanford, CA: Stanford University Press, 1987).

17. For fictional confessions in the period, see Matthias Schaaber, *Some Forerunners of the Newspaper in England, 1476–1622* (Philadelphia: University of Pennsylvania, 1929), 196.

18. Reprinted by the Early English Text Society, nos. 9 and 15 (London: EETS, 1898), 67–73 for the walking mort.

19. Jonathan Goldberg, "Cellini's *Vita* and the Conventions of Early Autobiography," *Modern Language Notes* 89, no. 1 (1974): 71–83.

20. J. W. Saunders proposed the existence of a "stigma of print": "From Manuscript to Print," *Proceedings of the Leeds Philosophical and Literary Society*, 1951, 507–28, and "The Stigma of Print: A Note on the Social Bases of Tudor Poetry," *Essays in Criticism* 1 (1951): 139–64. Saunders's argument is still widely accepted as fact, although its validity has been persuasively questioned several times, e.g., by Stephen W. May, "Tudor Aristocrats and the Mythical 'Stigma of Print,'" in *Renaissance Papers 1980*, 1981, 11–18, and by Nita Krevans, "Print and the Tudor Poets," *Reconsidering the Renaissance: Essays from the Twenty-first Annual Conference*, ed. Mario Di Cesare (Binghamton, NY: Medieval and Renaissance Texts and Studies, 1992), 301–13, who lists other critics who have taken part in the debate (301).

21. Krevans, "Print and the Tudor Poets," 306, lists examples: John Bourchier, Baron Berners (1524), Henry Parker, baron of Morley (1539), Queen Catherine Parr (1546 and 1548), Edward Seymour, duke of Somerset (1550). I would add Richard Neville, the younger son of Baron Latimer, who published a less serious work, "The Castell of Love" (1518).

22. For a good summary and review of the evolution of Lejeune's theory as he moved from a restrictive to an almost open-ended formulation, see John Paul Eakin's foreword to Lejeune, *On Autobiography*, viii–xxvii.

23. Eakin traces Lejeune's continued effort to define and determine "intention" in ibid., ix–xv. Scholars in other fields have also sought a viable compromise between two extreme positions: (1) naively accepting the author's stated intention at face value and (2) concluding that authorial intention is unknowable within the text and thus irrelevant to it. For various attempts at solutions, see Michael Baxandall, *Patterns of Intention: On the Historical Explanation of Pictures* (New Haven, CT: Yale University Press, 1985); David Newton-de Molina, ed., *On Literary Intention: Critical Essays* (Edinburgh: Edinburgh University Press, 1976); *Rationality*, ed. Bryan R. Wilson (Evanston, IL: Harper and Row, 1970); Richard Wollheim, *Painting as an Art*, A. W. Mellon Lectures 1984 (Princeton, NJ: Princeton University Press, 1987).

24. Ernest Renan, preface to *Souvenirs d'enfance et de jeunesse* (orig. 1884; Paris: n.p., n.d.), ii–iii, cited by Gusdorf, "Conditions and Limits," 28–48, 42.

25. See, e.g., Ulric Neisser and Robyn Fivush, eds., *The Remembering Self: Construction and Accuracy in the Self-Narrative* (Cambridge: Cambridge University Press,

1994); David C. Rubin, *Remembering Our Past: Studies in Autobiographical Memory* (Cambridge: Cambridge University Press, 1996); Luisa Passerini, "Memory: Resumé of the Final Session of the International Conference on Oral History, Aix-en-Provence, 26 September, 1982," *History Workshop Journal* 15 (1983): 195–96.

26. In this Misch followed his teacher Wilhelm Dilthy and was followed by his student Joachim Weintraub, *Value of the Individual*. Paul Lehman, working with a similar assumption that autobiography and human consciousness develop in lockstep, explains the appearance of autobiographies in the Middle Ages (when his theory of human consciousness would not have predicted them) to "the spasmodic awakening of consciousness of personality" before its time. Lehman, "Autobiographies of the Middle Ages," *Transactions of the Royal Historical Society*, 5th ser., 3 (1953): 41–52, esp. 47. Similarly, Shumaker attributes the later multiplication of autobiographies to the fact that "the orientation of consciousness to experience was undergoing a fundamental transformation" (*English Autobiography*, 20).

27. George Kane, *The Autobiographical Fallacy in Chaucer and Langland Studies*, Chambers Memorial Lecture (London: University College London, 1965), 3–20.

28. Paul Zumthor, "Autobiography in the Middle Ages?" *Genre* 6 (1973): 29–43 (35); Stephen Greenblatt, *Renaissance Self-Fashioning from More to Shakespeare* (Chicago: University of Chicago Press, 1980): "Wyatt's poetic individuality is not something uncovered, disclosed as by the lifting of a veil, but something put on, created by the brilliant assimilation of literary materials" (122); Tom Webster, "Writing to Redundancy: Approaches to Spiritual Journals and Early Modern Spirituality," *Historical Journal* 1 (1996): 33–56: "I want to consider the phenomenon of diary writing as a 'technology of the self,' a means by which the godly self was maintained, indeed constructed, through the action of writing" (40); Michael Mascuch, *Origins of the Individualist Self: Autobiography and Self-Identity in England, 1591–1791* (Stanford, CA: Stanford University Press, 1996).

29. For discrepancies among theories about the origins of modern subjectivity, see Katharine Maus, *Inwardness and Theater in the English Renaissance* (Chicago: University of Chicago Press); and A. C. Spearing, *Textual Subjectivity: The Encoding of Subjectivity in Medieval Narratives and Lyrics* (Oxford: Oxford University Press, 2005), 31–34.

30. On Skelton, see A. R. Heisserman, *Skelton and Satire* (Chicago: University of Chicago Press, 1961); on Wyatt, see Greenblatt, *Renaissance Self-Fashioning*; on Bale, see Thomas Betteridge, *Tudor Histories of the English Reformations* (Brookfield, VT: Ashgate, 1999), 16–17; on Whythorne, see David R. Shore, "The Autobiography of Thomas Whythorne: An Early Elizabethan Context for Poetry," *Renaissance and Reformation* 17 (1981): 172–86, esp. 172, and, similarly, A. Mousley, "Renaissance Selves and Life Writing: The Autobiography of Thomas Whythorne," *Forum for Modern Language Studies* 26 (1990): 228: Whythorne's text "of his life should not be taken as an

indication of a new concern with 'the self' so much as an intensified preoccupation among men of his economic class with status and role."

31. R. G. D'Andrade, "Cultural Meaning Systems," in *Cultural Theory*, ed. R. A. Schweder and R. A. LeVine (Cambridge: Cambridge University Press, 1984. See also, e.g., Mel Spiro, "Collective Representations and Mental Representations in Religious Symbol Systems," in *On Symbols in Anthropology*, ed. J. Maquet (Malibu, CA: Udena, 1982); Fitz John Porter Poole, "Socialization, Enculturation and the Development of Personal Identity," in *Companion Encyclopedia of Anthropology: Humanity, Culture, and Social Life*, ed. Tim Ingold (London: Routledge, 1994), 831–60.

32. John Morton, *Godly Learning: Puritan Attitudes toward Reason, Learning, and Education, 1560–1640* (Cambridge: Cambridge University Press, 1986), 3. In women's history too, as Laura Gowing argues, women's voices have been studied, but what has been overlooked is the indirectly conveyed "corporeal experience before it has been shaped and given expression by cultural conditioning." Laura Gowing, *Common Bodies: Women, Touch, and Power in Seventeenth-Century England* (New Haven, CT: Yale University Press, 2004).

33. James Olney, *Metaphors of the Self*, 20, 22; Pascal, *Design and Truth*.

34. Gusdorf, "Conditions and Limits," 44.

35. A. C. Spearing, *Textual Subjectivity: The Encoding of Subjectivity in Medieval Narrative and Lyrics* (Oxford: Oxford University Press, 2005). Olivia Holmes has called attention to similar dimensions of what she calls "the implied author" in *Assembling the Lyric Self: Authorship from Troubadour Song to Italian Poetry Book* (Minneapolis: University of Minnesota Press, 2000). Each identifies an array of textual details that attribute far more than a minimal subject position to the "author" encoded or implied in the text.

36. Anderson, *Growth of a Personal Voice*, 3; Kerrigan, introduction to Shakespeare's *Sonnets and A Lover's Complaint*, 11.

37. Linguists have begun to explore these possibilities, often in connection with literary texts, as they continue to define the significant dimensions of communication in language, apart from its propositional content. Spearing's *Textual Subjectivity* shows how the practical application of linguistic understanding can not only illuminate individual texts but also help resolve critical stalemates, in this case, about the narrator's role in medieval and early Renaissance texts. For the linguists themselves, see Geoffrey N. Leech and Michael H. Short, *Style in Fiction: A Linguistic Introduction to English Fictional Prose* (London: Longman, 1981), esp. 187–208; Marina Yaguello, ed., *Subjecthood and Subjectivity: The Status of the Subject in Linguistic Theory* (Paris: Ophrys, 1994), esp. the article by Sylvia Adamson (193–208); Dieter Stein and Susan Wright, *Subjectivity and Subjectivization: Linguistic Perspectives* (Cambridge: Cambridge University Press, 1995), esp. the article by Sylvia Adamson, 194–224. Harold Love makes use of linguistics in efforts to identify the authors of anonymous texts in *Attributing Authorship:*

An Introduction (Cambridge: Cambridge University Press, 2002). Love cites Barbara Johnstone, *The Linguistic Individual: Self-Expression in Language and Linguistics* (New York: Oxford University Press, 1996).

38. Francis Barker's well-known claim that there was no inner life in England before the midseventeenth century depends on ignoring traces like the ones described here. Barker limits his search for inner life to a search only for *descriptions* of inner life, a doomed effort. He analyzes Hamlet's early lines in Shakespeare's play (ca. 1600/1601) in which the prince says, "I have that within which passes show" (*Hamlet* 1.2.85), and he disagrees with the numerous readers who have seen Hamlet's line as evidence of something like a modernly conceived inner life. Because Hamlet never describes what he has within, Barker argues, Hamlet does not have anything within. Readers who hear reference to an inner life, he says, are simply projecting their own concept of "within" into Hamlet's lines. Of course the trouble is that in this period traces of the sort of thing Barker means by "inner life" are seldom found in overt statements. They are found instead in the way the authors encodes himself in his linguistic choices, his contradictions, gaps, odd emphases, and so on. Barker himself reads this way when he wants to demonstrate inner life in Samuel Pepys. Had Barker read Hamlet's lines as he reads the page in Pepys's diary, he would have found as much an inner life in the one as in the other. See Barker's *The Tremulous Private Body: Essays on Subjection* (London: Methuen, 1984), chap. 1.

39. I owe the shape of this formulation to an anonymous reader for the University of Chicago Press.

40. Elizabeth Bruss's early formulation, based on theorists like J. L. Austin, P. L. Strawson, and John Searle, is still the most authoritative: Bruss, *Autobiographical Acts*. See also Janet Varner Gunn, *Autobiography: Toward a Poetics of Experience* (Philadelphia: University of Pennsylvania Press, 1982).

41. However, for an argument that local context is still important for twentieth-century texts, see Barbara Herrnstein Smith, "Narrative Versions, Narrative Theories," *Critical Inquiry* 7 (1980): 213–36.

42. Josef Isewijn, "Humanist Autobiography," in *Studia Humanitatis: Ernesto Grassi zum 70. Geburtstag* (Munich: Wilhelm Fink Verlag, 1973), 209–19. Thomas F. Mayer and D. R. Woolf expanded the list in the introduction to *Rhetorics of Life-Writing*, 13–17.

43. On confession as the origin of autobiography, see, e.g., T. Price Zimmerman, "Confession and Autobiography in the Early Renaissance," in *Renaissance Studies in Honor of Hans Baron*, ed. Anthony Molho and John A. Tedeschi (Dekalb: Northern Illinois University Press, 1971), 121–40; James Olney, "Autobiography and the Cultural Moment," in *Autobiography*, ed. Olney, 13; and Amelang, agreeing with Olney in *Flight of Icarus*, 14. Robert Scholes and Robert Kellog, "Autobiography is either apology or confession," cited by Laura Marcus, in *Auto/biographical Discourses: Theory, Criticism, Practice* (Manchester, UK: Manchester University Press, 1994), 235.

44. Gusdorf, "Conditions and Limits," 39.

45. Sheale's ballads have been reprinted from MS Ashmole 48, in *A Collection of seventy-nine blackletter ballads and broadsides printed in the reign of Queen Elizabeth, between the years 1559 and 1597*, ed. Henry Huth (London: J. Lilly, 1867). See David C. Fowler, *A Literary History of the Popular Ballad* (Durham, NC: Duke University Press, 1968), 97. See also Teresa Watt, *Cheap Print and Popular Piety, 1550–1640* (Oxford: Clarendon, 1991), on ballads either composed entirely by minstrels like Sheale (19) or personalized by them (37).

46. Philip Berry cites Renaissance painters among the precursors for Philip Sidney's self-representations in *The Making of Sir Philip Sidney* (Toronto: University of Toronto Press, 1998), 3. Tusser's poem appears in every edition of his husbandry book.

47. Jane Stevenson and Peter Davidson, introduction to *Early Modern Women Poets: An Anthology*, ed. Jane Stevenson and Peter Davidson (Oxford: Oxford University Press, 2001), xxx.

48. See James Daybell, ed., *Early Modern Women's Letter Writing, 1450–1700* (Houndmills, Hampshire, UK: Palgrave, 2001).

49. Gary Schneider, *The Culture of Epistolarity: Vernacular Letters and Letter Writing in Early Modern England, 1500–1700* (Newark: University of Delaware Press, 2005).

50. Stevenson and Davidson, introduction to *Women Poets*, xxxii.

51. On autobiography and letters, see Amelang, *Flight of Icarus*, 40.

52. For the importance of local context and the relation between speaker and audience in street ballads, one of the cultural practices that helped shape early autobiographical writing, see Natascha Würtzbach, *The Rise of the English Street Ballad, 1550–1650*, trans. Gayne Walls (Cambridge: Cambridge University Press, 1990).

53. On the importance of local context in reading any historical text, see Robert D. Hume, "Texts within Contexts: Notes toward a Historical Method," *Philosophical Quarterly* 71 (1992): 69–100, and Linda A. Pollock, "Anger and the Negotiation of Relationships in Early Modern England," *Historical Journal* 47 (2004)" 567–71. On the importance of local context specifically in early autobiography, see Amelang, *Flight of Icarus*, esp. 80–96.

54. The distinction that C. S. Lewis introduced has remained attached to lyric. For an excellent recent discussion and expansion of its implications for the genre, see Jane Hedley, *Power in Verse: Metaphor and Metonymy in the Renaissance Lyric* (University Park: Pennsylvania State University Press, 1988).

55. Erik Erikson, *Psychohistory and Religion: The Case of Young Man Luther* (Philadelphia: Fortress, 1977). See also Chris D. Ferguson, "Autobiography as Therapy: Guilbert de Nogent, Peter Abelard, and the Making of Medieval Autobiography," *Journal of Medieval and Renaissance Studies* 13 (1983): 187–212.

56. Weintraub, *Value of the Individual*, 49.

57. Fowler, *Renaissance Realism*, 7–17.

58. Thomas Whythorne, *The Autobiography of Thomas Whythorne*, ed. James M. Osborn, modern spelling ed. (London: Oxford University Press, 1962), 1.

59. See also George Gascoigne's "prefatory epistle" to Sir Humphrey Gilbert's *Discourse of a Discoverie for a New Passage to Cataia* (London, 1576). Having published the book without Gilbert's permission, Gascoigne added a note excusing its condition: "It was meant by th'autour, but as a private Letter unto his Brother for better satisfaction; and therefore his imperfections therein (if any were) are to be pardoned, since it is very likely that if he had meant to publish the same, he would with greater heede have observed and perused the worke in everie parte" (George Gascoigne, *The Complete Works of George Gascoigne*, ed. John J. Cunliffe [Cambridge: Cambridge University Press, 1910], 2:564).

60. Students of early diaries recognize the spreading practice of diary keeping among friends. Thus Elizabeth Clarke suggests, for example, that Roger Lowe's "diary-writing might stem from his acquaintance with the more famous diarist Adam Martindale." See Clarke's "Diaries," in *A Companion to English Renaissance Literature and Culture*, ed. Michael Hattaway (Oxford: Blackwell, 2000), 609–15. Similarly, first-person narratives about foreign experience multiplied "as long-distance travel became easier and more frequent" (Ferguson, "Autobiography as Therapy," 187).

61. For diffusion theory in general, see Everett M. Rogers, *Diffusion of Innovations*, 4th ed. (New York: Free Press, 1995). For specific examples of the actual spread of ideas and techniques in this period–although not discussed in terms of diffusion theory–see, e.g., F. J. Levy, "How Information Spread among the Gentry, 1550–1640," *Journal of British Studies* 21 (1982): 11–34; Richard Cust, "News and Politics in Early Seventeenth-Century England," *Past and Present* 112 (1986): 60–90; and Bruce M. Campbell, "The Diffusion of Vetches in Medieval England," *Economic History Review*, 2nd ser., 41 (1988): 193–208. For a modern example of diffusion of style in art, see Leah A. Lievrouw and Janice T. Pope, "Contemporary Art as Aesthetic Innovation: Applying the Diffusion Model in the Art World," *Knowledge: Creation, Diffusion, and Utilization* 15 (1994): 277–309.

62. Amelang, *Flight of Icarus*, 51.

63. Lejeune, *On Autobiography*, 131, cited by Eakin, foreword, xiv.

CHAPTER TWO

1. Robert Graves, "The Dedicated Poet," in *Oxford Addresses on Poetry* (Garden City, NY: Doubleday, 1962); W. H. Auden, "John Skelton," in *The Great Tudors*, ed. Katharine Garvin (London: Ivor Nicholson and Watson, 1935), 55–67 ("no poetry is more 'outer' than Skelton's" [62]); Ivor Winters comments on the sincerity in "The Sixteenth-Century Lyric in England: A Critical and Historical Reinterpretation," *Poetry* 53 (1939): 258–72, 320–22.

2. On Skelton, see John Holloway, "Skelton," in *Proceedings of the British Academy* 44 (Oxford: Oxford University Press, 1958), 83–102; and Stanley Eugene Fish, *John Skelton's Poetry* (New Haven, CT: Yale University Press, 1965), 91–112. On Wyatt, see note 40. The descriptions of both poets date from the midtwentieth century, when many critics were discovering what Robert Langbaum called the "poetry of experience" (Robert Langbaum, *The Poetry of Experience: The Dramatic Monologue in Modern Literary Tradition* [New York: W. W. Norton, 1963]).

3. J. A. Burrow coined the term *conventional fallacy* to balance frequent warnings about the "autobiographical fallacy," in "Autobiographical Poetry in the Middle Ages: The Case of Thomas Hoccleve," in *Proceedings of the British Academy* 68 (Oxford: Oxford University Press, 1983), 389–412, esp. 394.

4. Roland Greene, "The Colonial Wyatt: Contexts and Openings," in *Rethinking the Henrician Era: Essays on Early Tudor Texts and Contexts*, ed. Peter C. Herman (Urbana: University of Illinois Press, 1994), 243.

5. The quotation about Skelton's reliance on earlier work is from Norma Philips, "Observations on the Derivative Method of Skelton's Realism," *Journal of English and Germanic Philology* 45 (1966): 24, who dismisses "the old, standard, biographical snares" (22) and is arguing only against Skelton's status as a realistic poet. See A. R. Heisserman's summary of the medieval-Renaissance debate and the inadequacy of the terms on which it was based in *Skelton and Satire* (Chicago: University of Chicago Press, 1961), 19.

6. H. A. Mason, *Humanism and Poetry in the Early Tudor Period: An Essay* (London: Routledge, 1959); see also John Stevens, *Music and Poetry in the Early Tudor Court* (Lincoln: University of Nebraska Press, 1961).

7. C. S. Lewis, *English Literature in the Sixteenth Century, Excluding Drama* (Oxford: Clarendon, 1954), 230; Stephen Greenblatt, *Renaissance Self-Fashioning from More to Shakespeare* (Chicago: University of Chicago Press, 1980).

8. Elizabeth Heale, *Wyatt, Surrey, and Early Tudor Poetry* (London: Longman, 1998), 87.

9. Although the skeptics' arguments do not take account of them, Raymond Southall, *The Courtly Maker: An Essay on the Poetry of Wyatt and His Contemporaries* (New York: Barnes and Noble, 1964), 7–11, and Patricia Thomson, *Sir Thomas Wyatt and His Background* (Stanford, CA: Stanford University Press, 1965), 111–24, had addressed the earlier doubts about Wyatt's autobiographical sincerity.

10. Thomas Whythorne, *The Autobiography of Thomas Whythorne*, ed. James M. Osborn (London: Oxford University Press, 1962).

11. Thomson, *Sir Thomas Wyatt*, 27.

12. As in the recent fuss about James Frey's *Million Little Pieces*, a supposed autobiography that was exposed as largely fictional.

13. G. K. Hunter, "Drab and Golden Lyrics of the Renaissance," in *Forms of Lyric: Papers from the English Institute*, ed. Reuben Brower (New York: Columbia University

Press, 1970), 8; Mason, *Humanism and Poetry*, 198; Alicia Ostriker, "The Lyric I: The Poetry," in *English Poetry and Prose, 1540–1674*, ed. Christopher Ricks, 91–106 (Harmondsworth, UK: Penguin, 1993); Joel Fineman, "Shakespeare's Perjur'd Eye," *Representations* 7 (1984): 5–86. The terms *ritual* and *fiction* are from Greene's essay "Sir Philip Sidney's Psalms, the Sixteenth-Century Psalter, and the Nature of Lyric," *Studies in English Literature* 30 (1990): 19–40, but see also his excellent "The Lyric," in *The Cambridge History of Literary Criticism*, vol. 3, *The Renaissance*, ed. Glyn P. Norton, 216–28 (Cambridge: Cambridge University Press, 1989).

14. Unless otherwise noted, all quotations from Skelton's poetry are taken from *The Complete Poems of John Skelton*, ed. Philip Henderson (London: J. M. Dent, 1964), and will be identified in the text by page number (Henderson does not include line numbers) as well as by title where necessary. The lines just cited are on 104. Henderson's notes on the same page identify St. John's collation as the commemoration of St. John's beheading, and he translates the Latin as "At the time of vespers, but not according to the Bishop of Sarum." An anonymous reader has suggested the more Skeltonic comic translation of "not according to the liturgy as laid out in the 'Sarum Missal,'" i.e. (roughly), "not kosher."

15. For a brief summary and review of commentary on Wyatt's formal innovations, see, e.g., Michael R. G. Spiller, *The Development of the Sonnet: An Introduction* (London: Routledge, 1992), 83–92. On his unique use of the refrain, see Hallett Smith, "The Art of Sir Thomas Wyatt," *Huntington Library Quarterly* 4 (1946): 342–45.

16. See Elizabeth Heale's account, in *Autobiography and Authorship in Renaissance Verse: Chronicles of the Self* (Houndmills, Hampshire, UK: Palgrave Macmillan, 2003), 80–85.

17. This poem is number CLXXVI in *The Collected Poems of Sir Thomas Wyatt*, ed. Kenneth Muir and Patricia Thomson (Liverpool, UK: Liverpool University Press, 1969), 219. All quotations from Wyatt's verse are taken from this edition, and poems are identified in the text by their numbers in it, followed by line numbers where appropriate.

18. See A. C. Spearing, "Prison, Writing, Absence: Representing the Subject in the English Poems of Charles D'Orleans," *Modern Language Quarterly* 53 (1992): 83–99.

19. The standard sources for biography are H. L. R. Edwards, *John Skelton: The Life and Times of an Early Tudor Poet* (London: Jonathan Cape, 1949), and Maurice Pollet, *John Skelton: Poet of Tudor England* (Lewisburg, PA: Bucknell University Press, 1971), translation of *John Skelton: Contribution a l'histoire de la prerenaissance anglaise* (1962). Nan C. Carpenter first suggested the chorister background in "Skelton and Music: *Roty bully joys*," *Review of English Studies*, n.s., 6 (1955): 369–84.

20. "Replicayon," cited in Edwards, *Skelton*, 258n4.

21. Early biographers placed it later, but several have since argued persuasively for the earlier date. See Melvin J. Tucker, "Setting in Skelton's *Bowge of Court*: A

Speculation," *English Language Notes* (1970): 168–75, as cited in F. W. Brownlow, "The Date of *The Bowge of Courte* and Skelton's Authorship of 'A Lamentable of Kyng Edward the IIII,'" *English Language Notes* (1984): 12–20.

22. On the portraits, see Mary C. Erler, "Early Woodcuts of Skelton: The Uses of Convention," *Bulletin of Research in the Humanities* 87 (1986–87): 17–28. Of "Philip Sparrow," John Scattergood says, "It is fairly clear from the envoys that Skelton added to the poem that his original readers found it too difficult to understand. In a characteristically pugnacious way, Skelton defends his method. . . . But it is obvious from the shift to a plainer more direct style . . . that the charges of obscurity worried him." The "more pugnacious style" refers to Skelton's addition of a Latin curse beginning "Luride, cur, livor, volucris pia funera damnas?" (Why, Green Envy, do you condemn the sacred funeral rites of a sparrow? [*Collected Poems*, 100]). "The Early Annotations to John Skelton's Poems," *Poetica* 35 (1992): 53–63, esp. 56.

23. Lewis, *English Literature*, 143.

24. Holloway, "Skelton," 93.

25. Fish, *John Skelton's Poetry*, 23–24; Graves, "Dedicated Poet," 20.

26. Comparison with Hawes is frequent in Skelton commentary. See, e.g., Holloway, "Skelton," 92–93.

27. Auden, "John Skelton," 62.

28. The phrase "camera eye" is Fish's in his study of the poet, *John Skelton's Poetry*.

29. See A. C. Spearing's excellent discussion of Skelton and the tradition in *Medieval Dream-Poetry* (London: Cambridge University Press, 1976), 197–202, 211–18.

30. Heisserman, *Skelton and Satire*, 19, 25–27.

31. Roy Pascal, *Design and Truth in Autobiography* (London: Harvard University Press, 1960), 16.

32. Stephen Dicky argues in illuminating detail for the continuity between the two poems and for the importance of Skelton's poetic calling, in "Seven Come Eleven: Gambling for the Laurel in *The Bowge of Courte*," *Yearbook of English Studies* 22 (1992): 238–54.

33. F. W. Brownlow's extensively annotated edition should be consulted: *The Book of the Laurel* (Newark: University of Delaware Press, 1990). His introductory essays are essential reading on the poem, its contexts, and particularly its astrological and numerical patterns.

34. Later Skelton will use the ship metaphor to describe his own poetry as part of a religious experience (*Garland*, 364).

35. Julia Boffey, "'Withdrawe your hande': The Lyrics of 'The Garland of Laurel' from Manuscript to Print," *Trivium* 31 (1999): 73–85.

36. Janet Wilson, "Skelton's 'Ware the Hawk' and the 'Circumstances' of Sin," *Medium Aevum* 58 (1989): 143–257.

37. Kenneth Muir's is still the standard biography: *The Life and Letters of Sir Thomas Wyatt* (Liverpool, UK: Liverpool University Press, 1963).

38. Muir and Thomson's note on the poem in *Collected Poems* describes the question about authenticity (*Collected Poems*, 422–23).

39. For Wyatt and the too often ignored *Court of Venus*, see Thomas Wyatt, *The Court of Venus*, ed. Russell A. Fraser (Durham, NC: Durham University Press, 1955), 27–46.

40. Muir finds a "coherent personality" in the Edgerton MS poems (*Life and Letters*, 224); Southall explores it in detail in "The Personality of Sir Thomas Wyatt," *Essays in Criticism* 14 (1964): 43–64.

41. Wyatt, like Skelton, recited and sang poetry while the ladies sewed. But the activity was as fraught for Wyatt as it was restorative to Skelton. See Wyatt's "She sat and sowed that hath done me the wrong" (LIV).

42. The process is described, e.g., by Thomson in arguing for the continued importance to Wyatt of "quiet of mind" (*Sir Thomas Wyatt*), and by Donald M Friedman, "The 'Thing' in Wyatt's Mind," *Essays in Criticism* 16 (1966): 375–81.

43. For Wyatt's relation to his predecessors, see Thompson, *Sir Thomas Wyatt*, esp. 79–140.

44. The characteristics of Wyatt's style have been described in increasing detail and there has been much agreement from Smith's 1946 essay forward. "Dramatic touch" is E. M. W. Tillyard's phrase in *Sir Thomas Wyatt and Some Collected Studies* (London: Sidgwick and Jackson, 1933). Thomas A. Hannen points to a related aspect of the verse when he says it has a quality of "thinking out loud": Hannen, "The Humanism of Sir Thomas Wyatt," in *The Rhetoric of Renaissance Poetry from Wyatt to Milton*, ed. Thomas O. Sloan and Raymond B. Waddington (Berkeley: University of California Press, 1974), 47.

45. Southall cites the "bell towre" example ("Personality," 44). Wyatt's characteristic "movement of the mind," as Southall calls it (47), from external event to internal reaction is Wyatt's most often observed characteristic. Nancy Leonard, in "The Speaker in Wyatt's Lyric Poetry," *Huntington Library Quarterly* 41 (1977): 1–8, esp. 2–5, describes this movement in useful detail; John Kerrigan calls it Wyatt's "selfish style" in "Wyatt's Selfish Style," *Essays and Studies* 34 (1981): 1–18.

46. Both Anne Ferry and Stephen Greenblatt see Wyatt's failure to describe his inwardness as a sign that he had none in the modern sense. Ferry, however, excepts Wyatt's sonnets, where she finds a new use of language that does indeed describe modern "inwardness," as opposed to Wyatt's language elsewhere. Anne Ferry, *The Inward Language: Sonnets of Wyatt, Sidney, Shakespeare, Donne* (Chicago: University of Chicago Press, 1983), 1–30; Greenblatt, *Renaissance Self-Fashioning*, 131–32.

47. See Jonathan Kamholtz's seminal essay "Thomas Wyatt's Poetry: The Politics of Love," *Criticism* 20 (1978): 350. For another change that may well have been intended to disguise personal reference, see Smith, "Art of Sir Thomas Wyatt," 328.

48. This use of the phrase is derived from a part of one of Emile Benveniste's essays in *Problems in General Linguistics*, trans. Mary Elizabeth Meek (Coral Gables, FL: University of Miami Press, 1971), 226.

49. Ben Jonson, *Discoveries*, in vol. 8 of *Ben Jonson*, ed. C. H. Herford and Percy and Evelyn Simpson (Oxford: Clarendon, 1947).

50. Greenblatt describes Wyatt as a "superior performer of cliché" (*Renaissance Self-Fashioning*, 120). Richard Harrier had previously argued that "there is a notable increase in the skill with which Renaissance writers render their *personae*. This greater effectiveness of vocal tonality and expression should not be confused, however, with autobiographical sincerity, an idea which may be inseparable from romantic realism." But Harrier, like Greenblatt, provides no examples. Richard Harrier, "Invention in Tudor Literature," in *Philosophy and Humanism: Renaissance Essays in Honor of Paul Oskar Kristeller*, ed. Edward P. Mahoney (New York: Columbia University Press, 1976), 374. However, for more detailed and persuasive warnings against facile autobiographical readings of personas, see David Lawton, "Skelton's Use of Persona," *Essays in Criticism* 30 (1980): 9–28; and A. C. Spearing's *Textual Subjectivity: The Encoding of Subjectivity in Medieval Narratives and Lyrics* (Oxford University Press: Oxford, 2005).

51. Desiderius Erasmus, *The Praise of Folly*, trans. Hoyt Hopewell Hudson (Princeton, NJ: Princeton University Press, 1941), 7. Joel B. Altman discusses Erasmus's Folly along with other examples of *ethopoeia*, or mimetic speech, and *prosopopoeia*, or personification, in *The Tudor Play of Mind: Rhetorical Inquiry and the Development of Elizabethan Drama* (Berkeley: University of California Press, 1978), 48, 54–59.

52. Other citations of "decorum" also suggest that it was far too limited a technique to achieve everything Harrier attributes to it in Wyatt. A writer in *A Mirror for Magistrates*, for example, invokes decorum to defend the monologue written for King Richard III's ghost when others objected to its meter. In response, the writer argues that "cumlynes [comeliness] called by the Rhetoricians *decorum*, is specially to be observed in al thinges. Seyng that kyng Rychard never kept measure in any of his doings, seing also that he speaketh from Hel, whereas is no order: it were agaynst the decorum of his personage to use eyther good Meter or order" (William Baldwin, *A Mirror for Magistrates*, ed. Lily B. Campbell [Cambridge: Cambridge University Press, 1936], 371). Baldwin himself may be a bit dubious here about the power automatically attributed to decorum. In any case, decorum's power to express character seems limited to a modern ear, given that Richard sounds like this: "But God, nature, dutie, allegiaunce al forgott, / This vile and haynous acte unnaturally I conspired: / Which horrible deede done, alas, alas, got wot / Such terrors me tormented, and so my spyrytes fyred / As unto such a murder and shameful deede requyred" (361, lines 36–40).

53. Henry Howard, Earl of Surrey, *Poems*, ed. Emrys Jones (Oxford: Clarendon, 1964), 2.

54. Joost Daalder, "Wyatt and Tottel: A Textual Comparison," *Southern Review* 5, no. 9 (1972): 3–12, makes the point about Wyatt's birds.

55. Even here Surrey has softened the conflict in his Petrarchan model. See Patricia Thomson's comparisons of Surrey's with Wyatt's translations of Petrarch in "The First English Petrarchans," *Huntington Library Quarterly* 22 (1959): 85–105, esp. 92, 102–5.

56. Much of what follows was inspired by Sam Hines in a class he taught many years ago. Daalder's "Wyatt and Tottel" is the best description of Tottel's tactics that I have seen. He not only demonstrates the kinds of changes Tottel made but suggests that the changes were made to make Wyatt sound more like the most admired poets of the time, particularly Surrey. Since writing this I have read Anne Ferry's excellent discussion of Wyatt's and Tottel's two versions of "They fle," in her *Tradition and the Individual Poem* (Stanford University Press: Stanford, CA, 2001), which makes some of the same points.

57. I believe this is Kenneth Burke's phrase, but I cannot locate it.

58. Elizabeth Heale claims, for example, that Tottel "misread the poetry as self-expressive and autobiographical." As a result, Wyatt's witty political (that is, nonautobiographical) commentaries were mistaken for sincere (that is, autobiographical) love plaints. Heale, *Wyatt, Surrey*, 193–95; see also her "Songs, Sonnets, and Autobiography: Self-Representation in Verse Miscellanies," in *Betraying Ourselves: Forms of Self-Representation in Early Modern English Texts*, ed. Henk Dragstra et al. (Houndmills, Hampshire, UK: Palgrave, 2000).

59. Daalder, "Wyatt and Tottel," 8–9.

60. Readers disagree about whether the speaker is conscious of the discrepancy. See, e.g., Leonard Nathan, who finds even Wyatt unaware of it, in "Tradition and Newfangleness in Wyatt's 'They Fle from Me,'" *English Literary History* 32 (1965): 15; and Michael McCanles, who disagrees, in "Love and Power in the Poetry of Sir Thomas Wyatt," *Modern Language Quarterly* 29 (1968): 155.

61. Tottel's lover clarifies spatial as well as temporal relationships. Tottel regularizes the meter in the second line so that "They" who were "With naked fote stalking in my chamber" are now more smoothly, iambicly, and exactly placed, "With naked fote stalking within my chamber."

62. On Wyatt's use of time, see David Rosen, "Time, Identity, and Context in Wyatt's Verse," *Studies in English Literature* 21 (1981): 5–20.

63. Even the actions that "they" performed earlier are often less concrete because diluted into mere verbals–either participles like "stalking" or infinitives like "to take." Once again, the dream is made to stand out from the rest of the poem because its action, unlike that preceding it, is concrete: she "did."

64. Interestingly, Skelton's female guide, Occupation, asks him a comparable question in *Garland* after leading him into the enclosed Edenic "herber." Where Wyatt's mistress asks, "How like you this?" ("They fle," 14) Occupation asks, "How say ye? Is

this after your appetite?" (*Collected Poems*, 370). Both Skelton's and Wyatt's visions of paradise, one poetic and one erotic, are discovered to the passive poet by a powerful female, and her question to each combines maternal concern with seductive teasing. Both draw on the iconography of Dame Fortune. But Skelton uses the stock allegorical figure of Fortune as a new allegory for his "occupation," while Wyatt has more thoroughly humanized the figure to represent an actual woman, fickle as Fortune but not quite allegorical. On Wyatt's treatment of the medieval allegorical figure of Fortune, see Smith, "Art of Sir Thomas Wyatt," 351–52.

65. Tottel regularized the line into more logical speech: "It was no dreame: for I lay brode awaking."

66. *Oxford English Dictionary.*

67. Similarly, while Tottel's title announces that the lover definitely "enjoyed" such as hath forsaken him, Wyatt's speaker never explicitly admits that he had "enjoyed" anything.

CHAPTER THREE

1. All quotations from *Vocacyon* are taken from *The Vocacyon of Johan Bale*, ed. Peter Happé and John N. King (Binghamton, NY: Medieval and Renaissance Texts and Studies / Renaissance English Text Society, 1990).

2. Donald A. Stauffer, *English Biography before 1700* (New York: Russell and Russell, 1964), 178.

3. Important exceptions are Leslie P. Fairfield, "*The Vocacyon of Johan Bale* and Early English Autobiography," *Renaissance Quarterly* 24, no. 3 (Fall 1971): 327–40; Fairfield, *John Bale, Mythmaker for the English Reformation* (West Lafayette, IN: Purdue University Press, 1976); John N. King, *English Reformation Literature: The Tudor Origins of the Protestant Tradition* (Princeton, NJ: Princeton University Press, 1982); and the introduction to the edition of *Vocacyon* edited by Happé and King. See also the introduction to *The Complete Plays of John Bale*, ed. and trans. Peter Happé, 2 vols. (St. Edmunds, Suffolk, UK: D. S. Brewer, 1985).

4. Sources for information about Bale's life are W. T. Davies, "A Bibliography of John Bale," in *Oxford Bibliographical Society Proceedings and Papers* (Oxford: Oxford University Press, 1939), 5:201–79; Honor McCusker, *John Bale: Dramatist and Antiquary* (Bryn Mawr, PA: Bryn Mawr College, 1942); Thora Balslev Blatt, *The Plays of John Bale: A Study of Ideas, Technique, and Style* (Copenhagen: Gad, 1968); Fairfield, "*The Vocacyon*" and *John Bale, Mythmaker*; King, *English Reformation*.

5. On the early generation of reformers, see Theodore Dwight Bozeman, *To Live Ancient Lives: The Primitivism Dimension in Puritanism* (Chapel Hill: University of North Carolina Press, 1988), 3–50.

6. John Bale, "The Examination of Master Willard Thorpe," in *Select Works of John Bale*, ed. Henry Christmas for the Parker Society (Cambridge: Cambridge University

Press, 1849), 75. On the reformers, see Ritchie D. Kendall, *The Drama of Dissent: The Radical Poetics of Nonconformity, 1380–1590* (Chapel Hill: University of North Carolina Press, 1986), who studies the effect of Tyndale's advice on later martyrs, 126–27; and John R. Knott, *Discourses of Martyrdom in English Literature, 1563–1694* (Cambridge: Cambridge University Press, 1993).

7. Knott, *Discourses of Martyrdom*, 48.

8. *Illustrious mayors Britannia scriptorium Summarium* (Ipswich, UK: John Overton, 1548); Blatt, *Plays*, 6–7.

9. Rainer Pineas, "William Tyndale's Influence on John Bale's Polemical Use of History," *Archiv für Reformationsgeschichte* 52 (1961): 79–96.

10. Fairfield, "*The Vocacyon*," 332–34.

11. For Bale "constructed by" his text, see Thomas Betteridge, *Tudor Histories of the English Reformations, 1530–83* (Brookfield, VT: Ashgate, 1999), 16–17. For Bale as "readerly" text, see Andrew Hadfield, "Translating the Reformation: John Bale's Irish Vocation," in *Representing Ireland: Literature and the Origins of Conflict, 1534–1660*, ed. Brendan Bradshaw, Andrew Hadfield, and Willy Maley (Cambridge: Cambridge University Press, 1993), 46.

12. Rainer Pineas, "John Bale's Non-dramatic Works of Religious Controversy," *Studies in the Renaissance* 9 (1962): 227–29.

13. Blatt, *Plays of John Bale*, 19.

14. McCusker, *John Bale*, 111, 115.

15. Davies, "Bibliography," 210, 106.

16. Ibid., 210.

17. Kendall argues for the inherent theatricality of Lollard discourse, with Thorpe's account prominent in it, and for the influence it had on later dissent literature (*Drama of Dissent*, esp. 50–67). Knott makes an equally persuasive, though somewhat different, argument about the "drama of martyrdom" in *Discourses of Martyrdom*, chap. 2.

18. Kendall, *Drama of Dissent*, 67.

19. Knott, Discourses of Martyrdom, 53.

20. *Scriptorum Illustrium Maioris Britanniae . . . Catalogus*, 2 vols. (Basel: Joannes Oporinus, 1557–58).

21. Anne Hudson describes the treatment of anonymous manuscripts in "Visio Baleii: An Early Literary Historian," in *The Long Fifteenth Century: Essays for Douglas Gray*, ed. Helen Cooper and Sally Mapstone, 313–39 (Oxford: Clarendon, 1997), 317. For Bale's parallel between himself and the queen, see Christopher Warner, "Elizabeth I, Savior of Books," in *John Foxe and His World*, ed. Christopher Highley and John N. King (Aldershot, UK: Ashgate, 2002), 95.

22. Paul Whitfield suggests the possibility of Bale's doubling as God, "Drama 'in the Church': Church-Playing in Tudor England," *MaRDiE* 6 (1993): 28, and doubling

as the vice Infidelity in his *Theatre and Reformation: Protestantism, Patronage, and Playing in Tudor England* (New York: Cambridge University Press, 1992), 2.

23. Knott, *Discourses of Martyrdom*, 58.

24. John Bale, "The Examination and Death of Lord Cobham," reprinted in *Select Works of John Bale*, ed. Christmas, 1:53–54.

25. *The Image of Both Churches* (1545); cited in Davies, "Bibliography," 214.

26. John Bale, *The Expostulation or complaynte agaynst the blasphemys of a Frantick Papyst* (1552), C4. The 1551 *Apologie to a Rank Papyst*, addressed to a man whose chaplain had offended Bale, is more impersonal, but Bale speaks directly to him at the end: "Thus have I answered (right worshipfull) your popyshe chaplayne.... If it is more sharpe than ye looked for, ye shall the lesse blame me, because God is in your writing so deeply dyshonored" (n.p.).

27. Apart from his *Vocacyon* Bale left three manuscript autobiographical sketches and one in print: Bodleian Library MS. Selden supra 41, fol. 195–195v; British Museum MS. Harley 3838 (*Angelorum Heliades*), fols. 111v–112v; *Summarium*, fol. 242. The longer *Catalogus* sketch quoted here is from *Catalogus* 1:702.

28. See the Reverend Canon G. V. Jourdan, "Reformation and Reaction," in *The History of the Church of Ireland*, ed. Walker Alison Phillips, 3 vols. (London: Oxford University Press, 1934), 2:228–92, esp. 271–78.

29. James Cancellar, *The Pathe of Obedience* (London, 1556), sigs. D3r–7r, reprinted in *Vocacyon*, ed. Happé and King, 129–31.

30. Ibid, 130.

31. Ibid.

32. On Paul's epistolary style, see James A. Fischer, C.M., "Pauline Literary Forms and Thought Patterns," *Catholic Biblical Quarterly* 39 (1977); and John L. White, "Saint Paul and the Apostolic Letters Tradition," *Catholic Biblical Quarterly* 45 (1983): 433–44.

33. For a brief summary of current conclusions about 2 Corinthians, see note to 2 Corinthians 11:16–33 in *The New Oxford Annotated Bible: The Holy Bible*, ed. Herbert G. May and Bruce M. Metzger (New York: Oxford University Press, 1973). For more extended commentary, see Victor Paul Furnish, *2 Corinthians*, Anchor Bible 32A (New York: Doubleday, 1964), 44–54, 498.

34. Bale omits Paul's earlier and more typically humble "boasts" ("Let him who boasts, boast of the Lord" [2 Corinthians 10:17]).

35. Also unlike Paul, Bale wants his enemies to overhear him: "And as for my cruel enemyes the papistes / if I make them sorye in the rehearsal of my delyveraunce/ I am not yll apayde thereof" (72–74).

36. Martin Luther, *Works*, vol. 28, ed. Hilton C. Oswald (St. Louis, MO: Concordia Publishing House), 1973), 61.

37. Fairfield and Davies suggest that Bale took notes while in Ireland but wrote them later (Fairfield, "*The Vocacyon*," 331; Davies, "Bibliography," 225).

38. Bale's preface had announced only a story showing God's "deliveraunce" of the faithful from "depe daungers" (15–16, marginal comment). But in the concluding lesson Bale pairs his deliverance with martyrdom as alternatives, again drawing a parallel between himself and the martyrs he had written about. He tells the brethren that the Lord "will delyver them / eyther from tyrannouse molestacyouns / as he hath done me / eyther else into martirdome" (260–62).

39. King, *English Reformation Literature*, 73. The book's title page had emphasized the weakness of the lamblike "English Christian." This one, like Askew's, suggests the martyr's paradoxical strength. Both images are accompanied by the same lines from Psalm 116, "Veritas domini manet in aeternum."

40. Bale will go on to cite other miracles God performed for him: God gave him strength to conduct services during another sickness, gave him a safe passage to Ireland (miraculous in this season, he says), and made a Catholic priest (and potential enemy) fall ill the whole time Bale was ashore so that he could do no harm to Bale, an accident much remarked on by the people.

41. Bale's presentation coincides neither with the king's letter describing the visit to Southampton, which made no mention of it, nor with the Privy Council's apparent indifference to the appointment. Although a council memorandum had noted the need to find someone after Turner refused the position, there is no mention of Bale's appointment. *The Chronicle and Political Papers of King Edward VI*, ed. W. K. Jordan (London, 1966), 138–39.

42. W. K. Jordan, *Edward VI, the Threshold of Power* (London: George Allen and Unwin, 1970), 368.

43. Ibid. Bale's friend John Philpott, in the room with King Edward at Southampton, seems to have been the one immediately responsible for the appointment, although Bale does not make this clear when he describes the scene in *Vocacyon*.

44. *The Examinations of Anne Askew*, ed. Elaine V. Beilin (New York: Oxford University Press, 1996), 280, 311–14.

45. Ibid., 1002–9.

46. The difference between Askew's and Bale's narrative had already emerged in Bale's commentary on her text (1548). There, when she had responded to a priest's question with another question and had been told that such a reply was against the order of schools, she deftly escaped his trap without overt defiance: "I tolde hym, I was but a woman, and knewe not the course of scoles." Bale's name-calling commentary on the exchange is typically cruder and less revealing: "Beastlye was that question, and of a more beastlye braine propounded" (*Examinations*, 34).

47. Luther, *Works*, 28:68, 69.

48. Ulric Neisser and Robyn Fivush, eds., *The Remembering Self: Construction and Accuracy in the Self-Narrative* (Cambridge: Cambridge University Press, 1994); David C. Rubin, *Remembering Our Past: Studies in Autobiographical Memory* (Cambridge:

Cambridge University Press, 1996); Luisa Passerini, "Memory: Resumé of the Final Session of the International Conference on Oral History, Aix-en-Provence, 26 September, 1982," *History Workshop Journal* 15 (1983): 195–96; and discussion in chapter 1.

49. Inga Clendinnen, *Ambivalent Conquests: Maya and Spaniard in the Yucatan, 1517–1570*, 2nd ed. (Cambridge: Cambridge University Press, 1987), 119–23. My brief summary cannot do justice to the nuances that make Clendinnen's interpretation so effective.

50. Pineas, "John Bale's Non-dramatic Works," 226.

51. Fairfield, "*The Vocacyon*," 335.

52. The reference to Barrett is in Bale's brief autobiographical sketch at the end of "Heliades." The reference to Lord Wentworth is in the sketch at the end of *Catalogus* (1557), 1:702–4.

53. Martin Luther, "Preface to Latin Writings," in *Luther's Works*, vol. 34, ed. Lewis W. Spitz (Philadelphia: Muhlenberg, 1960), 333–34. Later in the essay Luther says that his own conflicts left him with sympathy for others "who cling too pertinaciously to the papacy" (334). Perhaps Bale's denial of all uncertainty is related to his total lack of sympathy for papists.

54. The passage quoted is from the facsimile reproduction edited by William G. Crane (Gainesville, FL: Scholars' Facsimiles and Reprints, 1954), 150–51.

55. *Complete Plays*, Happé, I, 147–48.

56. Bale, *Catalogus*, 1:702–4, trans. Peter Happé.

57. Natalie Zemon Davis, "Boundaries and the Sense of Self in Sixteenth-Century France," in *Reconstructing Individualism: Autonomy, Individuality, and the Self in Western Thought*, ed. Thomas C. Heller, Morton Sosna, and David E. Wellbery (Stanford, CA: Stanford University Press, 1986), 56. Davis cites others who see a relationship between group identity and self-expression, 53n1.

58. On Bale's use of Skelton, see Andrew Hadfield, "John Skelton's Influence on John Bale," *Notes and Queries* (March 1994): 19.

CHAPTER FOUR

1. William Baldwin, *Epistola* sig. A1v, cited in Stephen Gresham, "William Baldwin: Literary Voice of the Reign of Edward VI," *Huntington Library Quarterly* (1981): 111.

2. The 1563 *Mirror* was reprinted in 1571 (rev.), 1574 (rev., enlarged, and retitled *The Laste Parte of the Mirour for Magistrates: Newly Corrected and Amended*), 1575 (rev.), 1578 (rev.), and 1587 (rev. and enlarged). For details of publication history, see *A Mirror for Magistrates* (1559 and 1563), ed. Lily Campbell (Cambridge: Huntington Library, 1936), 3–60; *Parts Added to "The Mirror for Magistrates" by John Higgins and Thomas*

Blenerhasset, ed. Campbell (Cambridge: Huntington Library, 1945), 3–28; and Frederick Kiefer, "*A Mirror for Magistrates*," in *Sixteenth-Century British Nondramatic Writers*, 3rd ser., ed. David A. Richardson, vol. 167 of *Dictionary of Literary Biography* (Detroit, MI: Gale Research, 1996), 116–27.

3. As in Tottel's *Songes and Sonnetes*, published two years before the *Mirror*'s first edition, the presence of an aristocrat among the authors—Surrey in *Tottel* and Sackville in *A Mirror* (Lord Vaux participated in both)—was part of the text's appeal, but in both there were many other authors as well (like Churchyard, who appeared in both).

4. Judith H. Anderson, *The Growth of a Personal Voice: "Piers Ploughman" and "The Fairy Queene"* (New Haven, CT: Yale University Press, 1976), 3. The continuities she finds between Langland and Spenser are not always the same as those between *A Mirror* and later self-writing, but they effect the same *kind* of connection: one that is less a formal or even a generic resemblance than a "way of organizing and conceiving experience." See also Anderson's *Biographical Truth: The Representation of Historical Persons in Tudor and Stuart Writing* (New Haven, CT: Yale University Press, 1984).

5. For biographical information, see John N. King, *English Reformation Literature: The Tudor Origins of the Protestant Tradition* (Princeton, NJ: Princeton University Press, 1982); Honor McCusker, *John Bale: Dramatist and Antiquary* (Bryn Mawr, PA: Bryn Mawr College, 1942); King's entry for "William Baldwin" in *Dictionary of National Biography* (Oxford: Oxford University Press, 2004), 3:479–80; Stephen Gresham, "William Baldwin: Literary Voice of the Reign of Edward VI," *Huntington Library Quarterly* 44 (1981): 101–16; Nancy A. Gutierrez, "William Baldwin," in *Dictionary of Literary Biography Sixteenth-Century Non-dramatic Writers* (Detroit, MI: Gale Research: 1993), 132:19–26.

6. King, *English Reformation Literature*, 77.

7. John Stowe, *Historical Memoranda*, cited by David Scott Kastan, "The Death of William Baldwin," *Notes and Queries*, December 1981, 516.

8. For Baldwin's framing and typography, see Terrence N. Bowers, "The Production and Communication of Knowledge in William Baldwin's *Beware the Cat*: Toward a Typographic Culture," *Criticism* 33 (1991): 1–29; Edward T. Bonahue Jr., "'I know the place and the persons': The Play of Textual Frames in Baldwin's *Beware the Cat*," *Studies in Philology* 91 (1994): 283–300; Sherri Geller, "What History Really Teaches: Historical Pyrrhonism in William Baldwin's *A Mirror for Magistrates*," in *Opening the Borders: Inclusivity in Early Modern Studies*, ed. Peter C. Herman (Newark: University of Delaware Press / Associated University Presses, 1999), 150–84.

9. Robert Copeland, *Poems*, ed. Mary Carpenter Erler (Toronto: University of Toronto Press, 1993).

10. *A Mirror*, ed. Campbell, 68. All quotations from the 1559 *Mirror* are taken from Campbell's edition and will be identified in the text with the page number from that

edition. All quotations from the 1563 *Mirror* are taken from *Parts Added*, ed. Campbell, and will be identified in the text by the short title and pages from that volume.

11. For the canceled *Mirror* edition and theories about Baldwin's prior enmity to Gardner, see Eveline I. Feasey, "William Baldwin," *Modern Language Review* 25 (1925): 413–14; Lily B. Campbell, "Humphrey Duke of Gloucester and Elinor Cobham His Wife in *A Mirror for Magistrates*," *Huntington Library Bulletin* 5 (1934), and "The Suppressed Edition of *A Mirror for Magistrates*," *Huntington Library Bulletin* 6 (1934); Scott Campbell Lucas, "The Suppressed Edition and the Creation of the 'Orthodox' *Mirror for Magistrates*," *Renaissance Papers* 1994 (1995): 31–54.

12. For other examples of writers' acknowledging their ventriloquist roles, see *Mirror*, 71, 81, 91, 101, 120, 132, 142, 154; there is also the "oracion which mayster Skelton made in his [Edward IV's] name" (235).

13. Barbara J. Shapiro, *A Culture of Fact: England, 1550–1720* (Ithaca, NY: Cornell University Press, 2000), esp. 189–207.

14. The customary distinction is between Fortune (with its random turns of the wheel, indifferent to human desire or behavior) and Providence (with its morally appropriate rewards and punishments for behavior). It is often assumed that medieval texts invoke Fortune while the more modern texts invoke Providence to explain events. But as commenters have periodically pointed out, the distinction is not always clear in any given text, and both kinds of explanation can be found even in Boccaccio. For a summary of commentary on this much-discussed issue, see the works listed in Jerry Leath Mills, "Recent Studies in *A Mirror for Magistrates*," *English Literary Renaissance* 9 (1979): 345–46, and Kiefer, "Mirror for Magistrates," 126–27.

15. King, *English Reformation Literature*, 326, 339–40; Judith H. Anderson, *The Growth of a Personal Voice: "Piers Ploughman" and "The Fairy Queene"* (New Haven, CT: Yale University Press, 1976), 3.

16. Scottish dream visions may have influenced Baldwin as well, e.g., King James I of Scotland's *Kingis Quaire* (1424?).

17. The frame segment identifying the vision of Richard as a dream, included in both Baldwin's editions (1559 and 1563), is omitted from all later editions (Campbell, 180n).

18. Baldwin, *Epistola* sig. A1v.

19. Not only in *Cat* but in Baldwin's translations (*The canticles . . . of Salomon* [1549]; *Wonderfull newes of the death of Paule the. iii. . . .* [1552?]) and in his collection of moral philosophy (*A treatise of morall phylosophie* [1547]). Additionally, the *Short Title Catalogue* identifies Baldwin as the author of the multiply framed (and fascinating) edition of Davy Dikal/Cammel's argument, *Western Wyl* (ca. 1552), although King does not mention it among his list of Baldwin's works in *English Reformation Literature*.

20. See also Jessica Winston's interesting comment in "*A Mirror for Magistrates* and the Political Discourse in Elizabethan England," *Studies in Philology* 101 (2004): 395.

21. Alwin Thaler discusses many of the *Mirror*'s poetic concerns mentioned here. See his argument that Baldwin was one of Britain's earliest literary critics: "Literary Criticism in *A Mirror for Magistrates*," *Journal of English and German Philology* 49 (1950): 1–13.

22. On decorum in "Richard III," see n. 52 in chapter 2.

23. I am persuaded by Campbell that Baldwin was making an offensive as well as defensive move in his text (51). Campbell's claim about his poetic ambition, however, does not take account of the confusion between history and poetry (and omits earlier bards who had chronicled their lords' achievements). King notes more generally that Baldwin was part of a wider pre-Sidney Reformation defense of fiction (*English Reformation Literature*, 319).

24. Richard Helgerson, *Self-Crowned Laureates: Spenser, Jonson, Milton, and the Literary System* (Berkeley: University of California Press, 1983).

25. Campbell (1938, 48; 1946, 35) and E. M. W. Tillyard saw the *Mirror* as a conservative warning to magistrates to respect the established political hierarchy. Tillyard, "*A Mirror for Magistrates* Revisited," in *Elizabethan and Jacobean Studies Presented to Frank Percy Wilson*, ed. Herbert Davis and Helen Gardner (Oxford: Clarendon, 1959), 1–16, esp. 8. David Norbrook, too, finds the *Mirror* relatively conservative compared to other more "prophetic" reformist poetry. Norbrook, *Poetry and Politics in the English Renaissance*, rev. ed. (New York: Oxford University Press, 2002), 50. Other readers, however, noting that the warning implied an attack on contemporary magistrates, see it as radical: Lucas, "Suppressed Edition," 51–54; Paul Budra, *A Mirror for Magistrates and the "De Casibus" Tradition* (Toronto: University of Toronto Press, 2000), 23–26; cf. Annabel Patterson, *Reading Holinshed's Chronicles* (Chicago: University of Chicago Press, 1994), 244–45.

26. Budra, *Mirror for Magistrates*, 35.

27. Alan T. Bradford, "Mirrors of Mutability: Winter Landscapes in Tudor Poetry," *English Literary Renaissance* 4 (1974): 17.

28. Arthur F. Marotti and others argue that Tottel misread the manuscript lyrics he went on to print, because he read them outside their original social context. He therefore mistook—and encouraged his readers to mistake—them as private, autobiographical communications rather than as social and political commentary. Marotti, "Love Is Not Love: Elizabethan Sonnet Sequences and the Social Order," *English Literary Renaissance* 49 (1982): 396–428, esp. 396.

29. Although its title sometimes appears on lists of predecessors of autobiography, presumably because of the ghosts. Marie Schutt, *Die englische Biographik der Tudor-Zeit* (Hamburg: Friederischen, de Gruyter, 1930), 158; Michael Mascuch, *Origins of the Individualist Self: Autobiography and Self-Identity in England, 1591–1791* (Stanford, CA: Stanford University Press, 1996), 64.

30. A. S. G. Edwards, "The Influence of Lydgate's *Fall of Princes*, c. 1440–1559: A Survey," *Medieval Studies* 39 (1977): 435.

31. The *Mirror*'s first two tragedies are each devoted to a pair of ghosts, but the collection soon moves to individual speakers.

32. In addition Mortimer appears "full of woundes, miserably mangled, with a pale countenaunce, and grisly looke" (119), and Owen Glendower comes "oute of the wilde mountaynes like the image of death ... so sore hath famine and hunger consumed hym" (120). Mike E. Pincomb is the only one who comments on the humor. See his "Sackville *Tragicus*: A Case of Poetic Identity," in *Sixteenth-Century Identities*, ed. A. J. Piesse (Manchester, UK: Manchester University Press, 2001), 112–32. But see Jim Ellis, who takes the gore very seriously and argues that the gruesome details in the text show the authors'—and the period's—anxiety over changing property relations: "Embodying Dislocation: A Mirror for Magistrates and Property Relations," *Renaissance Quarterly* 53 (2000): 1032–53.

33. Shapiro, *Culture of Fact*, 63–85.

34. The phrase "minutely discriminate spatio-temporal world" comes from N. W. Visser, "The Generic Identity of the Novel," *Novel*, 1978: 111.

35. An anonymous reader suggests that the distinction made here between dedication and letter should also take account of Joel B. Altman's discussion of apthonian rhetoric in Altman's *The Tudor Play of Mind: Rhetorical Inquiry and the Development of Elizabethan Drama* (Berkeley: University of California Press, 1978). That is, the two passages are different in part because each has been shaped by a different rhetorical form or task (e.g., proving a thesis versus creating speech appropriate for a particular character type). Contemporary linguists might see yet other distinctions at work in addition to the semantic, syntactic, and suasive aspects defined by classical rhetoric.

36. Geller, "What History Really Teaches," 150–84.

37. Donald A. Stauffer's chapter on autobiography in his *English Biography before 1700* (Cambridge, MA: Harvard University Press, 1930) has been the starting point for later studies of early autobiographical writing in England. Stauffer identifies ten early autobiographies: Bede, Gerald de Barri, Lydgate, and Hoccleve before 1600 and George Gascoigne, Thomas Tusser, Thomas Churchyard, Robert Greene, John Bale, and James Melville after. James Marshall Osborne adds an eleventh, Thomas Whythorne, now widely accepted as the first true or "modern" autobiographer. With Sackville and Higgins added (Churchyard is already included), *Mirror* authors make up three of the total of thirteen autobiographical writers (four of fourteen writers if we add Munday). See Osborne, *The Beginnings of Autobiography in England* (Los Angeles: William Andrew Clarke Memorial Library, University of California, 1960).

38. Sackville's poem, although composed about 1566, was not published until 1989. R. Zim and M. B. Parkes, eds., "'Sacvyles Olde Age': A Newly Discovered Poem by Thomas Sackville, Lord Buckhurst, Earl of Dorset (c. 1536–1608)," *Review of English Studies*, n.s., 40 (1989): 1–25, esp. 2–3.

39. In the introduction to her edition of Buckingham's tragedy, *The Complaint of Henry, Duke of Buckingham* (New Haven, CT: Yale University Press, 1936), 5–9, Marguerite Hearsey reports allusions not only to translations of *The Aeneid* by Gawain Gavin Douglas and Surrey but also to *The Romance of the Rose*, Chaucer's *Hous of Fame*, and Lydgate's *Fall*. Sources are also discussed in Jacobus Swart, *Thomas Sackville: A Study in Sixteenth-Century Poetry* (Groningen, Netherlands: J. B. Wolters, 1948), 25–43; and in Normand Berlin, *Thomas Sackville* (New York: Twayne, 1974), who follows Swart but suggests additional sources (32–44).

40. A comparison with the *Mirror*'s first tragedy, "Tresilian," the corrupt justice under Richard II, makes clear the difference between Sackville's and the other more didactic tragedies. Like Tresilian, Buckingham trespassed against the law to follow an evil prince, in his case Richard III. But whereas Tresilian ends his confessional monologue by describing his punishment and regretting his sin, Buckingham barely acknowledges guilt and moves quickly toward self-pity and defense.

41. Bradford, "Mirrors of Mutability," 18.

42. Pincomb, "Sackville *Tragicus*," 126.

43. The editors of "Sacvyles Olde Age" set 1566–74 as the limits of composition and provide information on the historical context, identifying its addressee, "fraunces...flowre off physcike," as Dr. Thomas Francis, Regius Professor of Medicine at Oxford when Queen Elizabeth, possibly accompanied by Sackville, heard him debate there. Their text and discussion is the basis of discussion of the poem here, although they are not concerned with any similarity between the manuscript and *A Mirror* besides verbal echoes. See Zim and Parkes, "Sacvyles Olde Age," 1–25, esp. 2–3.

44. "Sacvyles Olde Age," lines 11–12.

45. Ibid., lines 159–60.

46. Ibid., lines 55–64.

47. Ibid., 190–96.

48. See the notes in Zim and Parkes, "Sacvyles Olde Age," for other sources.

49. "Tragicall Discourse" appeared in Churchyard's miscellany, *The firste parte of Churchyardes chippes, contayning twelve severall labours* (London, 1575), but it may have been written a few years earlier.

50. Burleigh begins defiantly: "Am I of blud, or yet of byrth, so base, / O Baldwin! Now that thou forgetst my name?" (Churchyard, "Tragicall Discourse," 103). Allusions to *A Mirror* may begin even earlier in *Chippes*, in the preface, where Churchyard describes his troubles with pirated works. This is probably an allusion to his well-known troubles with "Shore's Wife," which had been reprinted in the 1571 *Mirror* without its former attribution to him.

51. Churchyard, "Tragicall Discourse," lines 10–11.

52. Ibid., lines 449–55.

53. Ibid., line 49.

54. Ibid., lines 73–76.

55. Ibid., line 587.

56. Churchyard claims that he wrote "Shore's Wife" during Edward's reign, which would have put it among the earliest *Mirror* tragedies, but it did not appear until the second edition in 1563. Churchyard also published several first-person poems in a complaint format like that of "Shore's Wife" and "Tragicall Discourse" (1566). A number of his autobiographical war reports appeared in the late 1570s, and in 1580 he published a second lengthy and also disowned autobiographical narrative, "A Story Translated out of French," in *A Light Bundle of Lively Discourses Called Churchyard's Charge* (1580). See the entries for "Churchyard" in *DNB* and *DLB*.

57. Campbell, introduction to *Parts Added*, 13.

58. *Parts Added*, 129, lines 8–11.

59. Ibid., 9. *A Mirror*'s extensive influence on later "complaints" and related works (starting as early as Jasper Heywood's preface to his translation of *Thyestes* [1560]) has been studied by, e.g., W. F. Trench, *A Mirror for Magistrates: Its Origin and Influence* (Edinburgh, 1898), 106–xxx; Willard Farnham, *The Medieval Heritage of Elizabethan Tragedy* (Berkeley: University of California Press, 1936), and Louis Ralph Zocca, *Elizabethan Narrative Poetry* (New Brunswick, NJ: Rutgers University Press, 1950). See Hallett Smith, *Elizabethan Poetry: A Study in Conventions, Meaning, and Expression* (Cambridge, MA: Harvard University Press, 1952), for discussion of the complaint. In *Motives of Woe: Shakespeare and Female Complaint—A Critical Anthology* (Oxford: Clarendon, 1991), John Kerrigan has made a separate study of the female complaint. Other edifying voices from beyond the grave appear, e.g., in poems by Barnabe Googe (Dometa in the fourth eclogue) and Hugh Plat.

CHAPTER FIVE

1. All quotations from Whythorne are taken from Thomas Whythorne, *The Autobiography of Thomas Whythorne*, ed. James M. Osborn, modern spelling ed. (London: Oxford University Press, 1962), and will be cited in the text and notes by page number. Quotations from Osborn's editorial introduction, however, are taken from his original-spelling edition, *The Autobiography of Thomas Whythorne*, ed. Osborn (Oxford: Clarendon, 1961), xii–lxv. The latter work will appear in notes as "Osborn, introduction to *Autobiography*."

2. Barnabe Googe (1567, 1576), Thomas Howell (1568), Isabella Whitney (1567, 1573), Hugh Plat (1572), and others.

3. Osborn, introduction to *Autobiography*, liv. See also David R. Shore, "Whythorne's Autobiography and the Genesis of Gascoigne's *Master F. J.*," *Journal of Medieval and Renaissance Studies* 12 (1982): 159–78, esp. 161.

4. Whythorne is drawing on two merged traditions, the measurement of a life in terms of seasons and the "ages of man." See J. A. Burrow, *The Ages of Man: A Study in Medieval Writing and Thought* (Oxford: Clarendon, 1988); and Samuel C. Chew, "The Path of Life," chap. 6 in *The Pilgrimage of Life* (New Haven, CT: Yale University Press, 1962), 144–73, esp. 156.

5. Anne Ferry, *The Inward Language: Sonnets of Wyatt, Sidney, Shakespeare, Donne* (Chicago: University of Chicago Press, 1983), 37.

6. Andrew Mousley, "Renaissance Selves and Life-Writing: The Autobiography of Thomas Whythorne," *Modern Language Studies* 26 (1990): 222–30, esp. 228.

7. Katharine Hodgkin writes about "mastery" and the conflict over control in "Thomas Whythorne and the Problems of Mastery," *History Workshop Journal* (1990): 20–41, esp. 21–22. Elizabeth Heale identifies a different anxiety-producing conflict that Tottel brought from court to bourgeois readers, between the need to appear wise and controlled and the need to display the courtly *sprezzatura* of a lover (71). See her "Songs, Sonnets, and Autobiography: Self-Representation in Sixteenth-Century Verse Miscellanies," in *Betraying Ourselves: Forms of Self-Representation in Early Modern English Texts*, ed. Hank Drengstra, Sheila Ottway, and Helen Wilcox (New York: St. Martin's, 2000), 59–75.

8. Osborn suggests that the composition began after 1569 and was completed by about 1576. The finished draft, probably composed in ordinary spelling, was then copied over in its entirety and translated into Whythorne's eccentric orthography (Osborn, introduction to *Autobiography*, lxiii). Additionally, the manuscript's later sections refer to books published after 1576, so Whythorne must have continued to make additions after that year.

9. Whythorne thinks of another motive as well while he describes the exchange: by making explicit the cause and meaning of his poems for his friend, he says, he may also "be the better occasioned to remember and consider of some dangers past, and also thereby put in remembrance to Pray to God to guide me so with his grace, that I may shun the like" (2).

10. Natalie Zemon Davis, "Boundaries and the Sense of Self in Sixteenth-Century France," in *Reconstructing Individualism: Autonomy, Individuality, and the Self in Western Thought*, ed. Thomas C. Heller, Morton Sosna, and David E. Wellbery (Stanford, CA: Stanford University Press, 1986), 56. Davis cites others who see a relationship between group identity and self-expression, 53n1.

11. Theorists disagree about how closely letter exchanges reproduced face-to-face conversation in general, and, of course, exchanges varied depending on participants and the situation. See, e.g., Lynne Magnussen, *Shakespeare and Social Dialogue: Dramatic Language and Elizabethan Letters* (Cambridge: Cambridge University Press, 1999); and Susan M. Fitzmaurice, *The Familiar Letter in Early Modern English: A Pragmatic Approach* (Amsterdam: John Benjamins, 2002).

12. Cited in John Pope-Hennessy, *The Portrait in the Renaissance* (New York: Pantheon, 1966), 97–98.

13. Maddox's portrait was painted by John Bettes, possibly Whythorne's friend "B. the P.," who had painted Whythorne's portraits. See note 25.

14. David R. Shore, "The *Autobiography* of Thomas Whythorne: An Early Elizabethan Context for Poetry," *Renaissance and Reformation* 17 (1981): 81–82. But the only earlier example of a cover letter used in roughly this way is "G.T."'s fictional letter introducing the book of George Gascoigne's poems, which is thought to have influenced Whythorne. There are important differences between G.T.'s and Whythorne's letters, however: G.T. is chatting about other people's verse; Whythorne speaks very seriously about his own. In addition, Whythorne had already framed his earlier poems with individual explanatory discourses, and he had already exchanged verse life-stories with friends. Even if he took some hint from G.T., his tone is completely different. Writing about his own poems, so close to his own secrets, is a vital innovation that added to the possibilities for autobiography. George Turberville did preface his miscellany with a letter. But Turberville, unlike Whythorne, uses it to avoid responsibility for publication; his letter is recognizable as a formal convention. It is an extra ornament that remains prefatory, and unlike Whythorne's address to his friend, Turberville's disappears when the poems begin. See George Gascoigne, *A Hundreth Sundrie Flowres*, ed. George Pigman III (New York: Oxford University Press, 2000, 560, note to 144.23.

15. *Secretum*, ca. 1347.

16. Osborn (introduction to *Autobiography*, xlix–l) and Mousley ("Renaissance Selves," 223) speculate that the friend might be the woman he ultimately married, but many of the examples of direct address are to "sir."

17. See John Kerrigan's fascinating discussion of good and bad secrecy in Shakespeare's *Twelfth Night*: "Secrecy and Gossip in *Twelfth Night*," *Shakespeare Survey* 50 (1997): 65–80.

18. Thomas Breme, *The Mirrour of Friendship: Both How to Knowe a Perfect Friend, and How to Choose Him*, 2nd ed. (London, 1584), cited in Harriet Andreadis, "Reconfiguring Early Modern Friendships: Katharine Philips and Homoerotic Desire," paper presented at meeting of the Early Modern Reading Group, Rice University, Houston, October 2005.

19. Osborn, introduction to *Autobiography*, lii–liii.

20. David C. Price, *Patrons and Musicians of the English Renaissance* (Cambridge: Cambridge University Press, 1980), 25, 37.

21. Ibid., 70–71.

22. Osborn says that some of his early poetry is like Wyatt's (introduction to *Autobiography*, liv). Whythorne mentions Wyatt's "John Poyntz" as a source for his belief about "seeming" (35).

23. Describing how embedded Tudor verse was in daily life, Shore likens it to a "form of thought" ("*Autobiography*," 75).

24. Hodgkin, "Thomas Whythorne," 39.

25. Whythorne refers twice to "B.," noting that B. was a friend as well to the court lady (*Autobiography*, 85, 89), and he refers once to his friend "B. the P." (89). The senior Bettes, probably a follower of Holbein, is far better known. For both, see Karen Hearn, "Bettes, John the Elder," in *Dictionary of National Biography* (Oxford: Oxford University Press, 2004).

26. Osborn, introduction to *Autobiography*, xxxv.

27. Ibid., xxvi–xxx, 70n1, 71.

28. Walter Darell, *A Short discourse of the life of Servingmen, plainly expressing the way that is best to be followed* . . . (London, 1573), Ai.

29. Laura Gowing, *Common Bodies: Women, Touch, and Power in Seventeenth-Century England* (New Haven, CT: Yale University Press, 2003), 64.

30. He does the same with other moralizing set pieces on, for example, "seeming" (3, 12, 33, 52, 59, 124, etc.).

31. G. K. Hunter, "Elizabethans and Foreigners," in *Dramatic Identities and Cultural Traditions: Studies in Shakespeare and His Contemporaries* (Liverpool, UK: Liverpool University Press, 1978), 9.

32. Whythorne moves from topic to topic in his narrative, without any external indication of chapters or sections, although Osborn inserted chapter titles and divisions in his editions. The opening of the "adolescency" passage, referred to here, tells how Whythorne's delight at his new independence after childhood is interrupted when he discovers the responsibilities that independence brings. He suddenly realizes that, as an independent man, he will have to "have a care of mine own credit and estimation . . . and to keep myself without penury." He deals with his "perplexity" by writing an admonitory poem that ends with a moralizing summary: "But now I see, more than before . . . & etc." (10).

33. Later Whythorne will have his mistress's portrait rather than Terpsichore's painted with his (38).

34. Osborn, introduction to *Autobiography*, xxiii; see also his appendix on the portraits (305–6).

35. *Vanitas* portraits like Whythorne's that placed the individual image in eternal context were quite popular. One pair depicting a gentry couple painted not long after Whythorne's (1566) had inscribed beneath the husband's image, "Why vantist thowe thy changing face or hast of hyt such store / To forme anew or none thou hast or not lyke as before," and an appropriate answer beneath the wife's. See Elizabeth Honig's discussion of the pair in "In Memory: Lady Dacre and Pairing by Hans Eworth," in *Renaissance Bodies*, ed. Lucy Gent and Nigel Llewellyn (London: Reaktion, 1990), 60–85.

36. The first of the three poems warns against telling secrets to dissemblers. The other two warn only against male flatterers, i.e., against the flatterer who "shapes *himself*" like your shadow and sets you up "for *his* purpose" (italics added). The poems offer a clue about why Whythorne told his heart's secrets only to a friend who could be trusted: as he says at the end of the second poem, "Therefore the faithful heart retain / That holds thy heart and secrets dear." However, none of the blandly moral poems provide any clue about the fear of women that initiated them, nor even about the women.

37. For claims about the general "erotics of service" prevailing in estates like those where Whythorne worked, see Mary Ellen Lamb, "Tracing a Heterosexual Erotics of Service in *Twelfth Night* and the Autobiographical Writings of Thomas Whythorne and Anne Clifford," *Criticism* 40 (1998): 1–25.

38. Hodgkin, "Thomas Whythorne," 36; Heale, "Songs, Sonnets," 69–70.

39. Interestingly, only after this story does Whythorne reveal the end of the adventure, which he had known all along but kept to himself. Despite saying that she would never marry, Whythorne says, the widow was "hot in the sear," and she soon married an ostler, who now "doth lubber leap her." The ostler had so much money that he "bleared the widows' eyes" and "shrouded her under a horseturd" (170–71). Whythorne's descent to scatology from his usual politeness indicates more feeling than his narrative usually does. It suggests the ill will that his previous barrage of platitudes may have been warding off.

40. See Carol Thomas Neely, *Distracted Subjects: Madness and Gender in Shakespeare and Early Modern Culture* (Ithaca, NY: Cornell University Press, 2004), 155–58; and Arthur Marotti, *Manuscript, Print, and the English Renaissance Lyric* (Ithaca, NY: Cornell University Press, 1995), 76–82.

41. Robert Greene's is a much shorter, less vivid, and more perfunctory version: "amongst many scorpions thou lookst for one eele": Robert Greene, *The Fortunes of Fortunado, or The Second Part of Greene's Never Too Late*, in *The Life and Complete Works . . . of Robert Greene*, ed. Alexander Grosart, 15 vols. (London: Huth Library, 1881–86), 8:219; see also *Greenes Vision*, 12:268.

42. "Those that want Friends to open themselves unto, are cannibals of their own Hearts." Bacon, "Of Friendship," in *The Essayes or Counsels, Civill and Morall*, ed. Michael Kiernan (Oxford: Clarendon, 2000), 80–87, 83. Cited by Kerrigan, "Secrecy," 72.

CHAPTER SIX

1. Laura Caroline Stevenson, *Praise and Paradox: Mechanicals and Craftsmen in Elizabethan Popular Literature* (New York: Cambridge University Press, 1984), 140–41.

2. Quotations from the original 1557 edition of Tusser's *A Hundreth Good Points* are taken from the reprint of the British Museum copy in the edition of William Payne and Sidney J. Herrtage (London: English Dialect Society, 1878) and identified by stanza number. Quotations from all other editions are from EEBO texts (1570 and 1573 are based on Huntington originals; 1574 is from one in the British Library). Quotations from Tusser's marginal comments are taken from EEBO's 1580 text (Folger), where they are fullest. Quotations are identified by folio number as it appears in the edition being quoted, except for quotations from the 1573 "Life," which are identified by stanza number.

3. Edward Doughty, "Unpublished Elizabethan Verse in a Huntington Manuscript," *English Literary Renaissance* 34 (2004): 22–41.

4. Andrew Macrae, "Husbandry Manuals and the Language of Agrarian Improvement," in *Culture and Cultivation in Early Modern England: Writing and the Land*, ed. Michael Leslie and Timothy Raylor (Leicester, UK: Leicester University Press, 1992), 48; and *God Speed the Plough: The Representation of Agrarian England, 1500–1660* (New York: Cambridge University Press, 1996).

5. Elizabeth Heale, *Autobiography and Authorship in Renaissance Verse* (New York: Palgrave Macmillan, 2003), 59–62.

6. John Norden, *Essex Described* (London: Camden Society 1840), 7, cited in Lord Ernle, *English Farming, Past and Present*, 6th ed. (Chicago: Quadrangle, 1961), 97.

7. Donald McDonald, *Agricultural Writers from Sir Walter of Henley to Arthur Young, 1200–1800* (orig. 1903; reprint New York: Burt Franklin, 1968), 23. Apart from Tusser's "Life," the sources for his biography are McDonald, *Agricultural Writers*, the *Dictionary of National Biography*, and the introductions to the editions of the husbandry book by William Mavor (1812, and by Payne and Herrtage (1878).

8. "Enclosure" did not refer only to the conflict over fencing previously common-use land for pasture. Tusser, like others, used it to refer to different ways of dividing agricultural fields. For Tusser, the two alternatives were "champion," open-field farming with scattered strips divided among owners, or "severalty," the "newer fashion of exchanging strips by mutual agreement, so that all a man's land lay together." M. E. Seebohm, *The Evolution of the English Farm* (Cambridge, MA: Harvard University Press, 1927), 208. See also "Enclosing and Engrossing," in *The Agrarian History of England and Wales*, gen. ed. H. P. R. Finberg, vol. 4, ed. Joan Thirsk (London: Cambridge University Press, 1967–2000).

9. McDonald, *Agricultural Writers*, 23.

10. L. G. Black, "Some Renaissance Children's Verse," *Review of English Studies* 24 (1973): 1–16.

11. It has always been assumed, I believe incorrectly, that Tusser left court in 1556 or 1557 and thus took up the "pen as soon as the plough" (McDonald, *Agricultural Writers*, 24).

12. Henry Peacham, *Minerva Britanna, or, a garden of heroical devices: furnished and adorned with emblemes and impresa's of sundry natures* (London: Walter Dight, 1612).

13. George Gascoigne, *A Hundreth Sundrie Flowres* (1573), ed. George W. Pigman III (Oxford: Oxford University Press, 2000), 452, 279.

14. Joan Thirsk writes about the importance of the classical tradition in shaping early modern landowners' attitudes toward working the land. See, e.g., "Making a Fresh Start: Sixteenth-Century Agriculture and the Classical Inspiration," in *Culture and Cultivation in Early Modern England: Writing and the Land*, ed. Michael Leslie and Timothy Raylor (Leicester, UK: Leicester University Press, 1992), 15–33. Alistair Fowler has argued to backdate the English georgic poetic tradition to the early modern period (e.g., in "Country House Poems: The Politics of a Genre," *Seventeenth Century* 17 [1986]: 3–14). Nineteenth-century scholars placed Tusser in this tradition, calling him "the English Varro" and attributing to him "the simplicity of Hesiod" (James Davies, *Hesiod and Theogonis* [Philadelphia: Lipppincott, 1880], 119–20). But not everyone agrees. Macrae argues that Tusser's origins were in popular, radical, and individualistic movements rather than in conservative elite classicism. Anthony Low sees both sides of Tusser, saying that he "oscillates between anxiety to preserve the ancient hierarchies and concern for making a quick profit." Anthony Low, *The Georgic Revolution* (Princeton, NJ: Princeton University Press, 1985), 32.

15. Tusser was consulted and appreciated for years. His book was reissued in parts monthly (*Tusser Redivivus*, 1710), and according to Anthony Clyne, in 1723 Lord Molesworth advised that Tusser's book "should be taught to the boys, to read, to copy, and to get by heart." Clyne, "The Poet of Husbandry," *Estate Magazine* 24 (1924): 801–3.

16. E.g., George Edwin Fussell writes, "This book, however, is hardly a severely practical book on farming" rather than a series of farming and domestic advice (*The Old English Farming Books from Fitzherbert to Tull, 1523–1730* [London: Crosby Lockwood], 8).

17. Macrae, "Husbandry Manuals," 45.

18. *The Book of Husbandry* (1534), ed. Walter W. Skeat (London: English Dialect Society, 1882), 1–2.

19. Tusser may also be referring to his readers' social status in the 1557 edition of *A Hundreth Good Points* when he tells the good "huyswyfe" how to please her "laboring man," apparently meaning her husband, though it is possible that he is referring to her servant. I take it that Tusser continues to address the same level of audience in later editions. But in the 1570 and 1573 editions, although Tusser continues to refer to "husbands" in this verse, he changes the reference from "gentiles" to "some": "Though *some* have a pleasure, with hawk upon hand, / Good husbands get treasure, to purchase their land" (16v).

20. Fitzherbert, *Boke*, fols. 44r–44v.

21. The quotation about style is from Chilton Latham Powell, *English Domestic Relations, 1487–1653* (New York: Russell and Russell), 110. Quotations from Whitford are taken from *Werke for Householders* (London, 1531), facsimile of the Bodleian Library copy, ed. Malone (London, 1834), 28–30.

22. *Captain Cox, His Ballads and Books, or Robert Laneham's Letter*, ed. Frederick J. Furnivall (Hertford, UK: printed for the Ballad Society by S. Austin, 1890). Laneham includes Cox in his description of the entertainments for Queen Elizabeth I at Kenilworth (1575) and includes the list of Cox's books.

23. Robert Copland, *The Kalendar & Compost of Shepherds*, ed. G. C. Heseltine (London: Peter Davies, 1931), 6.

24. Bernard Capp, *English Almanacs 1500–1800: Astrology and the Popular Press* (Ithaca, NY: Cornell University Press, 1979), 30 (Capp gives no further information about Hughbright). In a probably separate—but intriguingly parallel—development, many of the almanac authors later began to include images of themselves in their books (23).

25. Edmund Spenser, "December," in *The Shepheardes Calender* (1579).

26. Susan Snyder, *Pastoral Process: Spenser, Marvell, Milton* (Stanford, CA: Stanford University Press, 1998), 24.

27. George Watson, *The New Cambridge Bibliography of English Literature* (Cambridge: Cambridge University Press, 1974), 1:2277.

28. Gabriel Harvey, *Pierces Supererogation, or A new Prayse of an old asse: A preparative to certaine larger discourses*, ed. John Payne Collier (reprint London: Collier, 1870), 194.

29. Henry Hitchings, *Defining the World: The Extraordinary Story of Dr. Johnson's "Dictionary"* (New York: Farrar, Straus and Giroux, 2005), 105.

30. I assume that *Hundreth Goode Pointes of Huswyferie* was originally dedicated to Lady Paget because the "Huswyferie" section is dedicated to her in all extant later editions. Tusser is not known to have changed any of his other reprinted dedications. Additionally, in all later editions one of the stanzas of Lady Paget's dedication exactly parallels a stanza in the 1557 dedication to Lord Paget, suggesting an originally paired composition. I have not been able to see this edition. *Huswyferie* is listed in the Stationer's Register, but scholars assumed that it was lost. However, an anonymous reader reports that one copy is held in Norwich (STC 24372.5). It is not yet available on EEBO, and I have not been able to consult it.

31. Economic status was more complex than a simple opposition between landlords and tenants might suggest. Tenant farmers ranged from gentry younger sons to yeomen to middling tenants to the poorest of cottagers. See Joan Thirsk, *Agricultural Regions and Agrarian History in England, 1500–1750* (London: Macmillan, 1987), 15–16.

32. For bibliographic history, see note 7.

33. It was later included in the enlarged 1573 edition of *Five Hundred Points of Good Husbandry*.

34. I have not been able to look at the 1561 edition, but this letter seems to have been carried over intact to the next edition (1570). The 1570 letter celebrates the marriage of Tusser's husbandry and housewifery books as if it had just taken place, a stance more appropriate to 1561 than to 1570. Additionally, when Tusser says in the 1570 preface that he offers his book to "such as wive and fain would thrive" (fol. 3), he echoes the poem on wyving and thriving that he had published in 1561, when the first "married" edition had come out.

35. McDonald, *Agricultural Writers*, 24.

36. Ibid.

37. It is possible, in fact knowing Tusser it is likely, that he had begun the "Life" in some form at an earlier period in the country and then later tweaked it to serve for this book. Either way, it is an example of his make-do, good-enough style.

38. Heale also finds resignation in the "Life" (although she dates it 1570) and a similar resignation in the other "narratives of experience" (*Autobiography*, 61). But Macrae sees Tusser as voice of the increasingly confident economic individualist on the way up ("Husbandry Manuals," 35–62).

39. Tusser seems to have his son in mind elsewhere in this edition, addressing him in passing, e.g., in "Good husbandly lessons" (fol. 8a).

40. There is no record of remarriage; in fact, he was still married to Amy Moon when he wrote his will in 1580.

CHAPTER SEVEN

1. Both are reprinted in *"The Floures of Philosophie" (1572) and "A Sweet Nosgay" (1573) and "A Copy of a Letter" (1567) by Isabella Whitney*, ed. Richard J. Panofsky (Delmar, NY: Scholars' Facsimiles and Reprints, 1982). The *Copy* attribution rests on the initials "Is.W." on the title page, but I follow the majority of scholars in taking both works to be hers. For other poems attributed to Whitney with less certainty, see *The Poets*, ed. Susanne Woods, Betty S. Travitsky, and Patrick Cullen, vol. 10 of *The Early Modern Englishwoman: A Facsimile Library of Essential Works*, ed. Betty S. Travitsky and Patrick Cullen, ser. 1, pt. 2 (Aldershot, UK: Ashgate, 2001), x.

2. J. W. Martin, *Religious Radicals in Tudor England* (London: Hambledon, 1989); see also his article "Miles Hogarde: Artisan and Aspiring Author in Sixteenth-Century England," *Renaissance Quarterly* 34 (1981): 359–83.

3. Most scholars agree in identifying Isabella as the younger sister of Geoffrey Whitney of the Cheshire Whitneys, author of *A Choice of Emblems* (1586). The family lived at some point in London: Whitney says, "my parents there [Smithfield] did dwell" ("Wyll," 218); and see Rev. Henry Green, introduction to his *Whitney's "Choice of Emblems": A Facsimile Reprint with an Introductory Dissertation, Essays Literary and Bibliographical, and Explanatory Notes* (London: Lovell Reeve, 1886); *Floures*,

ed. Panofsky, 17–18; Robert J. Fehrenbach, "Isabella Whitney, Sir Hugh Plat, Geoffrey Whitney, and 'Sister Eldershae,'" *English Language Notes* 21 (1983): 7–11.

4. All quotations for Whitney's and Plat's works are taken from *Floures*, ed. Panofsky (unlineated), and reproduce Panofsky's page layout, in which each line of Whitney's letter "to the Reader" is broken and printed as two lines. Panofsky's facsimile does not always include identifying marks for pagination; Plat's text is, in fact, reprinted from two separate originals, so that what page numbers there are not always continuous. I have instead identified quotations from Whitney's works, where possible, by title and line number as reprinted in *Isabella Whitney, Mary Sidney, and Aemilia Lanyer: Renaissance Women Poets*, ed. Danielle Clarke (Harmondsworth, UK: Penguin, 2000), 1–28.

5. Only the first three poems are indicated on the title page. The men's poems are parallel to, although not styled as direct replies to, the gentlewoman's, and the one mentioned on the title page is sometimes taken to be Whitney's. The final poem, though similar in subject matter, is different in style. I assume that Whitney is not responsible for either.

6. The printer's "uncredible" claim in his preface, however, may mean merely that Whitney used mythological figures along with human beings.

7. Plat dedicated his book to Lady Anne, countess of Warwick, sister-in-law to Robert Dudley, earl of Leicester, to whom Geoffrey would dedicate his *Choice of Emblems*. For information about Plat and the Whitneys, see *Floures*, ed. Panofsky, xx–xi.

8. Paul A. Marquis notes literary precedents for Whitney's speaker in *The Copy*, in "Oppositional Ideologies of Gender in Isabella Whitney's *Copy of a Letter*," *Modern Language Review* 90 (1995): 314–24, esp. 15nn4–5.

9. Louise Schleiner, *Tudor and Stuart Women Writers* (Bloomington: Indiana University Press, 1994), 6.

10. See Panofsky on the text, *Floures*, ix.

11. See Anne Ferry, *Tradition and the Individual Poem: An Inquiry into Anthologies* (Stanford, CA: Stanford University Press, 2001), 69–79.

12. Panofsky, in *Floures*, xv.

13. This seems to be Whitney's own concern and may be related to the spiteful gossip that, she implies, cost her her job. Plat does not mention envy in his request to the countess for protection.

14. See Panofsky on narrative in Whitney, *Floures*, xii.

15. Elaine V. Beilin, *Redeeming Eve: Women Writers of the Renaissance* (Princeton, NJ: Princeton University Press, 1987), mentions the possibility of dream vision (95).

16. Tusser, "Life," st. 31.

17. Ian Sutherland, "When Was the Great Plague? Mortality in London, 1563 to 1665," in *Population and Social Change*, ed. D. V. Glass and Roger Revelle (London: Edward Arnold, Crane Russak, 1972), 287–320. Sutherland quotes Trevalyan on plague

and riversides. He mentions seeing evidence for an epidemic in 1573 but does not specify whether it consists of plague orders, the removal of the court to a "place of 'safety,'" or the arrangements for the installation of the Lord Mayor (312, 293n9). See also the review essays in P. Clark, ed., *The Cambridge Urban History of London*, vol. 2 (Cambridge: Cambridge University Press, 2000), especially those by Jeremy Boulton, "London 1540–1700," on the riverside parishes that were crowded with the poor (328), and Griffiths et al., "London Demography," on endemic diseases in the seventeenth century ("Smallpox claimed hundreds, and sometimes thousands, of lives every year in the last quarter of the century" [203]).

18. Harvest time varied but is identified as August according to Thomas Tusser's almanac, and it is likely that Whitney would have been thinking about being "serviceless" near Michaelmas, the end of September, which was the conventional time for renewing tenancy and labor contracts. The Indian summer period between August and the end of September was also the most dangerous time for epidemics and infections.

19. The fourth poem of *The Copy* was added in this way. Its title page announced only three. It is possible that *Nosgay*'s title page unified the two parts of Whitney's book. But unfortunately the only extant copy of *Nosgay* is missing its first three leaves.

20. Two of the letters ignore her current plight. One, "To her Cosen F. W.," was written from the country, not from London like the others. In it Whitney asks, "When you to Cuntry come / or thither chaunce to send: / Let me you see, or have some scroll, that shall of you be pend." The other is the marital warning "To my Friend Master T. L. whose good nature: I see abused."

21. The letters in *Copy* about being abandoned were written at about the time that Geoffrey left home for Cambridge (1567). In writing poems for that earlier book, might Whitney have been drawing in part on her own feelings about losing his company?

22. Presumably advice such as Isabella gave her younger sisters might not have been appropriate for one who was married.

23. This last appeal is not included, but the answer is titled "An other Letter sent to Is.W. By one: to whom she had written her infortunate state."

24. Whitney's earlier letter to Dido, who had also fixed her fancy on the wrong lover, gives similar advice about time: you will forget. "So might thy cares in time, / be banished out of thought: / His absence might well salve the sore, / that erst his presence wrought" ("A careful complaint by the unfortunate Author").

25. The will of "Dan Bartholomew of Bathe" in Gascoigne's *Hundreth Sundrie Flowres* (1573) is sometimes cited as a model, but that book was very probably printed in November, after *Nosgay*. See chapter 8.

26. Eleanor Prescott Hammond, *English Verse between Chaucer and Surrey* (Durham, NC: Duke University Press, 1927), 237–39.

27. Ebner Carle Perrow, "Last Will and Testament as a Form of Literature," *Transactions of the Wisconsin Academy of Sciences, Arts, and Letters* 17 (1913): 682–753; W. H.

Rice, *The European Ancestry of Villon's Satirical Testaments* (New York: Corporate, 1941); Julia Boffey, "Lydgate, Henryson, and the Literary Testament," *Modern Language Quarterly* 53 (2002): 41–56; Edward Wilson, "'The Testament of the Buck' and the Sociology of the Text," *Review of English Studies*, n.s., 65 (1994): 158–84.

28. However, Whitney may have been following Robert Copeland, who wrote, printed, and introduced Jyl's testament, as well as the testament itself. Like Copeland, Whitney frames her will with a narrative in which it plays a role. Copeland says that he came across Jyl's testament accidentally while mourning the death of a friend, and he tells how its comedy helped cure his melancholy. See Robert Copeland, *Poems*, ed. Mary Carpenter Erler (Toronto: University of Toronto Press, 1993), 164–86.

29. "A defence of scollers pastimes in riding abroade at Christmas times" ("Why should not we have our delight / as eache man hath beside" [140–43]), and "Howe necessarie the intermission of studie is for Scholers" (130–50).

30. The marriages described in Whitney's will—the proverbially unwise unions between (1) maids and rich widowers or (2) fortune-hunting young gentlemen and rich widows—were part of the traditional folly literature. Jyl included a similar pair of requests in her will: "A widdowe that once, hath been in the brake, / And careth not whome that she dooth take / Shall have a fart, though mine arse ake / A maid that marrieth, not caring whome / And doth repent whan she commeth home / Shall have a fart to by her a come" (Copeland, *Poems*, 171). Whitney herself had warned her friend "T. L.," apparently not for the first time, to guard against prospective wives who "wold fleece you much" ("To my Friend Master T. L. whose good nature: I see abused").

CHAPTER EIGHT

1. The quotations are taken from George Gascoigne's introductory letter to *Posies*, "To the reverende Divines," in *A Hundreth Sundrie Flowres*, ed. George Pigman (Oxford: Oxford University Press, 2000), p. 361, poem 1, line 37. See also Pigman's introduction to *Hundreth*, liii. The edition, although primarily devoted to *Hundreth*, includes the material added to it in *Posies*. All following quotations from both Gascoigne's works are taken from Pigman's edition. *A Hundreth Sundrie Flowres* will be referred to in the text as *Hundreth* and *The Posies of George Gascoigne Esquire* (1575) as *Posies*. Quotations from *Hundreth* will be identified by page number and then poem number and line number(s) in Pigman. Quotations from *Posies* will be identified by page number in Pigman, followed by "P," and then, as in Pigman, poem number and line number(s). Thus the citation for the quotations referred to in this note would read, "361, P 1.37."

2. Biographical questions were among the first addressed by modern critics. In addition to C. T. Prouty, *George Gascoigne: Elizabethan Courtier, Soldier, and Poet* (New York: Benjamin Blom, 1942), see, e.g., Leicester Bradner, "The First English Novel: A

Study of George 'Gascoigne's 'Adventures of Master F.J.,'" *PMLA* 45 (1930): 543–52; Robert P. Adams, "Gascoigne's Master F.J. as Original Fiction," *PMLA* 73 (1958): 315–26; Richard Lanham, "Narrative Structure in Gascoigne's F.J.," *Studies in Short Fiction* 4 (1966): 42–50.

3. For a good summary of the debates about Gascoigne's "reform," see Gregory Kneidel, "Reforming George Gascoigne," *Exemplaria* 10 (1998): 329–70, esp. 329–33.

4. For the claim that "Adventures" is a critique of humanist interpretive and educational strategy, see Arthur F. Kinney, *Humanist Poetic: Thought, Rhetoric, and Fiction in Sixteenth-Century England* (Amherst: University of Massachusetts Press, 1986): 89–117. For claims that "Adventures" explores the nature of interpretation, see George E. Rowe Jr., "Interpretation, Sixteenth-Century Readers, and George Gascoigne's 'The Adventures of Master F. J.," *English Literary History* 48 (1981): 271–289, and Susan C. Staub, "'According to My Source': Fictionality in *The Adventures of Master F.J.*," 1990 ("The Adventures ... is only incidentally about F.J.'s affair with Elinor; story-telling is the real subject of the tale" [117]). For a claim that "Adventures" deconstructs the poets of real presence and threatens "to unravel the very idea of an authoritative author," see Elizabeth Heale, *Autobiography and Authorship in Renaissance Verse: Chronicles of the Self* (New York: Palgrave Macmillan, 2003), 132–44.

5. Sources for the biographical sketch in the following paragraphs are Prouty, *George Gascoigne*, and Pigman, introduction to *Hundreth*.

6. Prouty, *George Gascoigne*, 61.

7. Ibid., 56, 121.

8. Gascoigne's reference to his *Posies* is in the dedication of *The Droomme of Doomes day* (1576) to Lord Bedford, in *The Complete Works of George Gascoigne*, ed. John W. Cunliffe (Cambridge: Cambridge University Press, 1910), 211. All quotations from poems in *Complete Works* will be cited in the text from here on parenthetically as *Works*, [page number]. Whetstone refers to Gascoigne's "layes," which he explained (in a footnote) as "poysies": George Whetstone, "A Remembrance of the Wel imployed life, and godly end of G. Gascoigne, Esq.," in *Londoniquod . . . Remains, Aungervyle Society*', 4th ser. (Edinburgh, 1886), 5–18.

9. Pigman provides a concise but thorough textual history in his introduction to *Hundreth*, xlv. His extraordinarily informative notes make an extended comparison between the two editions feasible for the first time, and I am indebted to his edition throughout this chapter.

10. George Turberville, "The Authors excuse for writing these and other fancies, with promise of graver matter hereafter," in "Epitaphes and Sonets," appended to *Tragical Tales translated by Turberville* (1576?); reprinted in George Turberville, *Epitaphes, Epigrams, Songs, and Sonets (1567) and Epitaphes and Sonnettes (1576)*, ed. Richard J. Panofsky (Delmar, NY: Scholars' Facsimiles and Reprints, 1977), 455–58.

11. In M. Gascoigne's section, the poems without introductions are 50, 53–57, and 63–65. Apart from these, only two of *Hundreth*'s love poems appear without introductions, and like the ones in M. Gascoigne's section, both of them turn out to be attributable to Gascoigne. Poem 21 does not even have a title, let alone an introduction. It is identified only by G. T.'s demurral: "This Sonet of his shal passe (for me) without any preface." This is one of the three poems that Gascoigne later omitted from *Posies*, presumably because it was too revealing. The second poem without introduction, "A straunge passion of another Author" (30), is attributed to another poet, but Gascoigne later includes it among those he recants as if it were his to recant (57).

12. Gascoigne adds that "the same should serve as undoubted proofe, that I had layde aside vanities, and delighted to exercise my penne in morall discourses, at least the one passing (cheeke by cheeke) with the other, muste of necessities persuade both the learned, and the light-minded, that I could aswell sowe good graine, as . . . draffe" (361. P "To the reverende Divines," 13–18).

13. Richard Helgerson included Gascoigne's work among the quasi-autobiographical "reformed prodigal" fictions he treats in *Elizabethan Prodigals* (Berkeley: University of California Press, 1977), although he is not interested what he sees as Gascoigne's unreformed work in *Hundreth*. Helgerson notes that, apart from Robert Greene, "no Elizabethan writer talks so much about himself" (44).

14. These garden poems would have ended Gascoigne's section, but "Gascoigne's Voyage" follows them, perhaps because the latter was written after the printer had already set up the rest. See Adrian Weiss's argument about the stages in which *Hundreth* was printed: "Shared Printing, Printer's Copy, and the Text(s) of Gascoigne's *A Hundreth Sundrie Flowres*," *Studies in Bibliography* 45 (1992): 71–104.

15. M. R. Rohr Philmus, "Gascoigne's 'Fable of the Artist as a Young Man,'" *Journal of English and Germanic Philology* 73 (1974): 13–31. See also Prouty, *George Gascoigne*, 190–98.

16. Scenes from Ariosto's *Orlando Furioso*, especially its description of separated lovers, also turn up frequently in Gascoigne's poems. The bracelet that makes Bartholmew suspicious of his Ferenda may be a reference to the bracelet that signaled Orlando's betrayal by his beloved. Gascoigne's fondness for "allegory" (i.e., analogy) encourages repetitive treatment of scenes. On Gascoigne and allegory, see Pigman's note (588, note to 189.13).

17. Pigman lists the three poems removed from the revised edition (1, 21, 39), although he links only one of them (39) to Gascoigne's bigamous marriage. For the revisions to 37, see Pigman's note (249, note to 37.0.1.).

18. For an excellent study of Gascoigne's personas, see Gillian Austen's dissertation, "The Literary Career of George Gascoigne: Studies in Self-Presentation," D.Phil. thesis, University of Oxford, 1997.

19. The second poet, "Spreta tamen vivent," is not connected as directly to Gascoigne, but he does write to a woman who rejects him for a base rival—as did F.J.'s, Dan Bartholmew's, and Gascoigne's women.

20. In *Posies*, the power of "invention" is an entirely admirable skill. Later Gascoigne appears to describe the same skill as "curiosity," when he admits that in penning *Hundreth* he was guilty of "greater curiositie then was convenient." "Dedication to the Earl of Bedford," in *The Droomme of Doomes day* (1576), in *Works*, 211. *Curiosity*, like *invention*, was used primarily to denote a positive trait, a care that "produced perfection" (*OED* online, s.v. "curiosity"). But as Gascoigne discovered when his book was criticized, the term could be mildly derogative. *Curiosity* could mean care "carried to excess" or even a "disposition to inquire too minutely into anything" (*OED* 1.5), a disposition Gascoigne was accused of displaying in "Adventures."

21. See chapter 1.

22. "Woodsmanship" has invited many readings. Most of them concur in noting the importance of multiple perspectives or voices, although their interpretations differ. For three good essays, see Jane Hedley, "Allegoria: Gascoigne's Master Trope," *English Literary Renaissance* 11 (1981): 148–64; Richard C. McCoy, "Gascoigne's *Poemata castrata*: The Wages of Courtly Success," *Criticism* 27 (1985): 29–55; Kneidel, "Reforming George Gascoigne," 349–55.

23. Cf. Leicester Bradner, "Point of View in Gascoigne's Fiction," *Studies in Short Fiction* 3 (1965): 16–22. Some of the short poems also create a dynamic of doubled points of view when they set opposing aspects of the narrator against each other, as in "Gascoigne's Lullabie" (56). There an older Gascoigne tells himself to "sing lullabie" to his still-wakeful youthful years, his gazing eyes, his wanton will, and his "little Robyn" (56), all of whom are fighting sleep.

24. This is also, of course, exactly what G. T. does in the retrospective collection of Master Gascoigne's verse, although he uses much less commentary to link them than he used in linking F. J.'s poems in "Adventures."

25. Turberville, *Epitaphes*, 458.

26. On the effects of gathering individual works into one new work, see Richard C. Newton, "Making Books from Leaves: Poets Become Editors," in *Print and Culture in the Renaissance*, ed. Gerald P. Tyson and Sylvia S. Wagonheim (Newark: University of Delaware Press, 1986), 246–64; and, specifically on Gascoigne, Anne Ferry, *Tradition and the Individual Poem: An Inquiry into Anthologies* (Stanford, CA: Stanford University Press, 2001), 69–72. I am indebted to Carol Neely for the latter reference.

27. Cf. Kinney, who argues that Gascoigne's text continues the tradition of serious humanist commentary, albeit more cynically (*Humanist Poetic*, 117).

28. G. T. also singles out one nameless poet whose ambition (the "clyming of an Eagles neast" is attributed to him), along with other details, may point to Gascoigne:

> For otherwise / I shall not onely provoke all the aucthors to be offended with / mee, but further shall leese the opertunitie of a greater matter, / halfe and more graunted unto mee alreadie, by the willing consent / of one of them. And to be playne (with you my friend) he hath / written (which as farre as I can learne) did never yet come to the / reading or perusinge of any man but himselfe: two notable workes. / The one called, the *Sundry lots of love*. The other of his owne / invencion entituled. *The clyming of an Eagles neast*. These thinges / (and especially the later) doth seeme by the name to be a work / worthy the reading. And the rather I judge so because his fantasie / is so occupied in the same, as that contrary to his wonted use, he / hath hitherto withhelde it from sight of any of his familiers, untill / it be finished, you may gesse him by his Nature. And therfore I / requier your secresie herein, least if he hear the contrary, we shall / not be able by any meanes to procure these other at his handes. (144.17–32)

29. Pigman, note on *Hundreth*, 625n48.
30. Pigman, introduction to *Hundreth*, lii.
31. Hughes, "Gascoigne's Poses," 3, sees the autobiographical additions, especially the "mistries" Gascoigne points to in "Dan Bartholmew," as a purposeful distraction that calls attention to Gascoigne's supposed secrets and thus prevents readers from finding slander about anyone else.
32. "The fruite of Fetters" (439, P 29), "The complaynt of the green Knight" (442, P 30), "The continuance of the Author upon the fruit of Fetters" (448, P 31), and "The Green Knight's Farewell to Fansie" (452, P 32), with "Epilogismus" (453, P 33).
33. I have not seen the distinction between the two aspects of Gascoigne, Gascoigne-author and Gascoigne-character, made before. Pigman, for example, equates all references to Gascoigne that link him to Bartholmew or the Greene Knight, without regard to whether they are linked as writers or, on the other hand, as characters in someone else's writing (Pigman, commentary on *Hundreth*, 551).
34. The reader's experience of the poems in Pigman's edition is very different, because all three poems are printed in sequence, along with notes and critical apparatus pointing out the links among them.
35. Both poems thus distance reader from character, although "Fruite of Fetters" more so because it introduces an unexpected author, Bartello, along with the unexpected speaker.
36. Compare Dan Bartholmew's similarly blatant flaw of blind, unshakable, wanton love: "whose face is plainer seene, / than he which thinks he walketh in a net?" (358, 12.57–58). Gascoigne distanced himself from the flaw of wanton love in *Hundreth* (or thought he did!), but in *Posies* he comes close to admitting the worse flaw of self-love.
37. The name is perhaps associated with the Salamanca in Spain or in Ireland, and thus perhaps with Catholicism. Gascoigne's friend Bartholmew Withypoll visited

Spain in 1562 but was dead by the time *Hundreth* appeared (Pigman, commentary on *Hundreth*, 454), but the figure is otherwise mysterious.

38. For another view of Grey's importance to Gascoigne, see Gillian Austen, "George Gascoigne and the Transformations of Phylomene," in *Elizabethan Literature and Transformation* (Tübingen: Stauffenburg Verlag, 1999), 107–19.

39. A second patron, Lord Montacute, had rescued him from debt with the parliamentary appointment in 1572, apparently awarded for his writing. But there is no further evidence of the relation to Montacute and good reason to think that it was severed when Gascoigne lost the seat in Parliament that Montacute had procured for him. The accusations that unseated Gascoigne may well have embarrassed Montacute, his sponsor. Gascoigne did not seem to be too concerned about Catholic Montacute's response to the book, because he included in it anti-Catholic material that he would later edit out of *Posies*, including the name of James Scudamore.

40. See McCoy on the book's extraordinary self-confidence, something decidedly missing from later work ("Gascoigne's *Poemata*," 30).

41. Weiss, "Shared Printing," 96. Pigman, however, is cautious—"the original plans for the book remain obscure"—although he does suggest that the third of the original texts was "Philomene" (introduction to *Hundreth*, lvii, lxi).

42. Weiss, "Shared Printing," 62.

43. Weiss believes that the printer misunderstood Gascoigne's instructions and simply printed the materials in the order in which he had received them. That is why Gascoigne's two plays, which the printer already had in his possession, were set, as noted, at the beginning of the book rather than after "Adventures," where Gascoigne intended them to be placed (ibid., 99). The second installment to the printer consisted of (Gascoigne's disowned) poetry attributed to "sundrie gentlemen." The exemplary body of poems "by Master Gascoigne" arrived next, followed still later by two more of his pieces that were either just finished or not quite finished (ibid., 96–97).

44. Heale sees the love poems as the aspect of *Hundreth* most destructive to the image of himself that Gascoigne was trying to create (Heale, *Autobiography*, 23–29).

45. He really may have thought that, as he argued in *Posies*, *Hundreth*'s moral poetry would satisfy potential critics. Or he may have thought that a simple gesture toward propriety, like "cover[ing] all our names," was enough to prevent the "losse of my familier friends," as G. T.'s friend explains in *Hundreth* (142.31–32).

46. Whetstone, "Remembrance," 188.

47. Pigman in *Hundreth*, 466, note to 1.9. For Harvey's Latin note see *Gabriel Harvey's Marginalia*, ed. G. C. Moore Smith (Stratford-upon-Avon: Shakespeare Head, 1913), 167. Prouty, agreeing with Harvey's assessment, translates it thus: "In other words, if Gascoigne had done more to deserve reward and had thought less of what was due to him as the elder son of a good family, he would have achieved far more than he did" (Prouty, *George Gascoigne*, 279).

48. "So hope I yet that your good Lordshippe wyll rather wink at my weakenesse in generallitie, then reprove my rashnesse in perticularitie. And because I would bee glad, to drawe your Lordshippe into forgetfulnesse thereof, by freshe recorde of some more martiall matter, as also for that I would have your Honour perceave that in these lyngering broyles, I doe not altogeather passe over my time in ydlenesse: I have therefore thought meete nowe to present you with this Pamphlete" (399, P 28.0.16–0.23). The poem was "[B]egon / at Delfe *in* Hollande" (398, P 0.3–0.4). If Gascoigne knew about the "busie conjectures" and criticism of *Hundreth* when he wrote this dedication, he was not very upset about them.

49. Chronological evidence consists solely of what Gascoigne tells us, and that is neither completely clear nor entirely trustworthy. That said, if we take him at his word in the original dedication to "Philomene" (*Works*, 207), Gascoigne wrote *The Steele Glas* just before April 3, 1576; he compared himself in its "Exordium" to Philomene, and that sent him back to his old "Philomene" poem from twelve or thirteen years previously; he then finished it on April 3, 1576. Apparently he did not present "Philomene" separately to Grey (or if he did there is no extant dedication) but instead wrote a single dedicatory letter for both works, dated April 15, 1576 (*Works*, 137): "Ryght noble, when I had determined with myself to write the *Satire* before recited (called the '*Steele Glas*') and had in myne 'Exordium' (by allegorie) compared my case to that of fayre *Philomene*, abused by the bloudy king hir brother by lawe: I called to minde that twelve or thirteen yeares past, I had begonne... the Complainte of *Phylomene*.... The which I presume with the rest [presumably *Steele Glas*] to present unto your honor" (*Works*, 177).

50. Given the uncertainty about *Posies'* publication date, "1575," however, all accounts of chronology must remain tentative. The date 1575 may refer to a day between January and December 1575, in agreement with the dating of the book's prefatory letters. But it could also refer to any day as late as March 1576, i.e., 1575 old style. A later date for *Posies* would explain why the Queen's Privy Council did not act to recall the book until fall 1576. But it complicates any effort (like mine) to integrate Gascoigne's relations to patrons (with dates made explicit in dedicatory letters) and the publication of *Posies*.

51. Grey was hardly a model of dignified aristocratic behavior himself. Lawrence Stone singles him out as an example of the violent behavior countenanced among nobility at the time.

52. Such an attitude may explain the little poem, "Ultimum vale to Amorous verse" (386, P 25), which Gascoigne added to introduce *Posies*, as if to placate a patron like Grey. It is an odd poem because instead of promising not to write amorous verse, it promises only not to publish it. Gascoigne does not promise to be moral, only to seem moral in public—where he might otherwise embarrass a patron.

53. Whetstone, "Remembrance," 192.

54. *Gabriel Harvey's Marginalia*, 167.

55. The dedication is also unusual in being accompanied by three commendatory poems, as if Gascoigne felt a need to prove his worth here, the way he did in *Posies*. The published version of *Steele Glas* (1576) includes a woodcut of Whythorne on the title verso (fig. 15).

CHAPTER NINE

1. All quotations from Greene's works (actual or forged), except for *Greenes Groats-worth of Witte*, are taken from *The Life and Complete Works in Prose and Verse of Robert Greene*, ed. Alexander Balloch Grosart, Huth Library, 12 vols. (London, 1827–99), and will be cited in the text with volume and page number from Grosart. Quotations from *Groatsworth* are taken from *Greene's Groatsworth of Wit Bought with a Million of Repentance* (1592), ed. D. Allen Carroll (Binghamton, NY: Medieval and Renaissance Texts and Studies, 1994).

2. Gabriel Harvey, *Foure Letters and Certaine Sonnets*, ed. G. B. Harrison (1922; reprint New York: Barnes and Noble, 1966). Harvey calls him "rakehell" in his first letter (12), and in the second he describes the banquet (21) and asks the question (19).

3. For a thorough review and analysis of the arguments about authorship, see Carroll's introduction to his edition of *Greene's Groatsworth*, 21–31. See also Carroll's two articles: "The Badger in *Greenes Groats-worth of Witte* and in Shakespeare," *Studies in Philology* 84 (1987): 471–82; and "The Player-Patron in *Greene's Groatsworth of Wit* (1592)," *Studies in Philology* 91 (1994): 301–12. John Jowett also argues for Chettle, citing evidence from Chettle's background as a compositor, in "Johannes Factotum: Henry Chettle and *Greene's Groatsworth of Wit*," *Papers of the Bibliographic Society of America* 87 (1993): 453–86.

4. Carroll, introduction to *Greene's Groatsworth*, 9.

5. Scholars (e.g., Jowett, "Johannes Factotum," 474–75) have argued that Chettle's forgery was discovered immediately, and they cite a number of contemporary comments about the pamphlet as evidence. This is not the place to make a full argument, but it should be noted in any account of the book's reception that contemporary attacks on *Groatsworth* can be explained as well, if not better, by seeing them as attacks only on the passages of the text that were considered slanderous, not on the whole pamphlet. The public did not show much sign of caring about forgery per se; unless there was an angry author to reclaim his own, forgeries could pass unnoticed. The problematic passages in *Groatsworth* were the two scathing attacks, first, on Shakes-scene and the playwrights and, second, on Burleigh in "Lamia's Fable." (On "Lamia's Fable" and Burleigh, see Carroll, appendix C in *Greene's Groatsworth*, 107–13.) According to Chettle, the letter to the playwrights is what was "offensively by one or two of [play-makers] taken," as he says in his preface to *Kind-Hart's Dream* (1592). In other words, Chettle was arguably suspected only of adding to Greene's text, not of writing the

whole thing. Chettle's claim, later in the *Kind-Hart* preface, that *Groatsworth* was "all Greenes" can be understood as denying that he *added* anything: "I put something out, but in the whole booke [*Groatsworth*] not a word in, for I protest it was all Greenes" (*Kinde-Harts Dreame*, ed. G. B. Harrison (1592; reprint London: Bodley Head, 1923), 6–7.

6. Sandra Clark, "Robert Greene (July 1558–3 September 1592)," in *Dictionary of Literary Biography*, vol. 167, *Sixteenth-Century Nondramatic Writers*, 3rd ser., ed. David A. Richardson (Detroit: Gale Group, 1996), 61–76.

7. Philippe Lejeune, in "Autobiography in the Third Person," *New Literary History* 9 (1977): 27–50, argues that the determining factor in how we read a third-person narrative—whether as fiction or autobiography—is not just the particular pronoun but also the prior pact between author and reader about the text's status. Once the author gives clues that he is writing autobiography—despite using the third person to refer to the hero—"the blurring of the enunciation becomes a fact of the enunciation" (28). In other words, the distancing between narrator and hero becomes part of the story. The distance can be used in different ways—e.g., for internal distancing and confrontation, or for miming a social confrontation that the author affirms or mocks, and so on. The third person, however, is not really a special case: "It is another way of realizing, in the form of a *doubling* [*dedoublement*] what the first person realizes in the form of a *confusion*: the ineluctable duality of the grammatical 'person.' To say 'I' is more habitual (and thus more 'natural') than to say, 'he,' but is not therefore simpler" (29).

8. *The Autobiography and Personal Diary of Dr. Simon Forman*, ed. James Orchard Halliwell (London, 1849), 1.

9. "The Adventures of Master F.J." is the first of the works collected by G. T. in George Gascoigne's *Hundreth Sundrie Flowres* (1573).

10. Important studies of the 1590 texts include John Clark Jordan, *Robert Greene* (New York: Columbia University Press, 1915), and René Pruvost, *Robert Greene et ses romans* (Paris: Belles Lettres, 1938). Two excellent later discussions are Thomas W. Cobb's introduction to his edition of *Groatsworth* ("A Critical Edition of Robert Greene's *Groatsworth of Wit*," PhD diss., Yale University, 1977), and Charles W. Crupi, *Robert Greene* (Boston: Twayne, 1986). Unfortunately, the early studies, accepting the doubtful deathbed confessions as factual, use them as the historical standard against which to match the 1590 texts.

11. For Greene's biography, see Jordan, *Robert Greene*; Pruvost, *Robert Greene*; Crupi, *Robert Greene*, esp. chap. 1; and Brenda Richardson, "Robert Greene's Yorkshire Connections: A New Hypothesis," *Yearbook of English Studies* 10 (1980): 160–80.

12. Scholars have largely come to accept Richardson's claim that Greene came from the relatively wealthy family of Robert Greene, cordwainer, rather than from the poorer saddler with the same name who never improved his situation. But see

now Arata Ide, "Robert Greene *Nordovicensis*, the Saddler's Son," *Notes and Queries*, December 2006, 432–35.

13. Harvey, *Foure Letters*, 41.

14. *Mamillia*, Stationers' Register, October 3, 1580. The Stationers' Register will hereafter be cited in the text and notes as S.R. Greene announced Cuthbert's attack in his *Second Part of Conny-Catching* (1592): "Marry the Goodman Cony-catchers, those base excrements of dishonesty, report they have got one ( ) I will not bewray his name, but a scholler they say he is, to make an invective against me." "Whittington College" refers to "Newgate [prison] builded by one Wittington," according to the marginal note in *Defense*. The discrepancy between Cuthbert's and Greene's typical claims to education is, of course, part of the joke. Greene is not identified as the author of Cuthbert Cony-Catcher's (otherwise anonymous) *Defense of Conny Catching* (1591), but many critics have argued for his authorship. See Crupi's account of the debate, *Robert Greene*, 18–19. The articles by Haviland Miller listed in Crupi's bibliography are especially persuasive in arguing for Greene's authorship.

15. *Menaphon* (1589), *Greenes Mourning Garment* (1590), and *Greenes Farewell to Follie* (1591).

16. *Planetomachia* (1585).

17. Greene's Cambridge classmate Brian Melbancke (d. 1600) printed his Euphuistic *Philotimus* in 1583, the same year that saw the publication of the two volumes of Greene's *Mamillia*. See Johnstone Parr, "Robert Greene and His Classmates at Cambridge," *PMLA* 77 (1935): 542.

18. *Gwyndonius* (S.R. April 11, 1584), *Morando* (1584?), *Planetomachia*, *Penelope's Web* (S.R. June 26. 1587), *Euphues, His Censure* (S.R. September 18, 1587), *Perimedes the Blacke-smith* (S.R. March 29, 1588), *Alcida* (S.R. December 9, 1588).

19. The patriotic texts, dedicated to important city officials (*The Spanish Masquerado* [1589], *The Royal Exchange* [1590]).

20. Critics generally agree in describing the phases of Greene's style. See, e.g., Crupi, *Robert Greene*, 39–70.

21. There are exceptions. Greene is the only one I know of, for example, whose earliest preface comments on what he discovered about the genre while reading through other prefaces. He had several standard dedications; the one for patriotic works differs from the one for his amorous tales. Each was repeated when appropriate. In two of the works dedicated to women, Greene repeats several lines word for word (*A Maiden's Dream* [1591], dedicated to Elizabeth Hatton, and *Philomela*, dedicated to Lady Fitzwater).

22. For a somewhat different interpretation of the preface allusions, see T. W. Baldwin, *On the Literary Genetics of Shakespeare's Plays, 1592–1594* (Urbana: University of Illinois Press, 1959), 1–4.

23. For example, in the conclusion to *Mourning Garment*, Greene refers to the pamphlet ambiguously as "the first fruites of my new labours, and the last farewell to my

fond desires" (9:221), and he says, "As this is the first of my reformed passions, so this is the last of my trifling Pamphlets" (9:222). Since Philador's story, as Greene says, is clearly "a divine Historie" (9:125), his reference to "trifling pamphlets" has been interpreted as merely an excuse to keep the repentance going. But Greene has been distinguishing carelessly among several categories of "trifle," and he may have been contrasting all stories about love, even ones that show its problems, with more philosophical or divine writing.

24. Critics assume that Greene's talk of repentance went on longer than intended because it proved more popular (and thus more profitable) than Greene had expected. Another suggested economic motivation was that Greene was clearing his desk of old, thus wanton, works before he moved onto the next stage (Crupi, *Robert Greene*). Economics were important, of course. Nonetheless, as Crupi says, such talk was initiated by Greene and clearly compelling for him (*Robert Greene*). Motives are seldom one-dimensional.

25. A Stationers' Register entry of June 11, 1587, lists Greene's *Farewell to Folly*. The title suggests that Greene may have already been thinking as early as that year of changing his subject matter. He may, however, have been referring only to a protagonist's farewell rather than to his own. We have no way of knowing because *Folly* did not appear, unless the book with that title printed later in 1591 is the same one, as most scholars believe. See Crupi, *Robert Greene*, 88-90. The quotation is from Greene's letter "To the Gentlemen Students," in *Farewell to Folly*, 9:233.

26. *Spanish Masquerado*, 5:16. See Crupi's discussion of the work of this period in *Robert Greene*, 84–91.

27. *Orpharion*, 12:94. *Orpharion* was written earlier and promised but not published until 1590.

28. The distinction between the two sorts of folly is ambiguous, though. Greene seems uncertain about the admission, far more so here than in *Never Too Late* (*Farewell to Folly*, 9:231–32).

29. Carroll, introduction to *Groatsworth*, 22–31.

30. From here on, cites for quotations from *Never Too Late* 1 and 2 will use *NTL1* and *NTL2* to refer to the two volumes of the text.

31. See Cobb, "Critical Edition," cclxxii, for the connection between reformed prodigals and writing.

32. The very last sentence of volume 1 similarly implies change: "Looke for *Francescoes* further fortunes, and after that my *Farewell to follie*, and then adieu to all amorous pamphlets" (8:109).

33. William Baldwin had set up a similar time scheme in *Mirror*, smoothing over a seven-year break between the first two editions with a fictional break of about a week between composition of the volumes. But Greene's description in *Vision* corresponds to publication records.

34. Since *Doctor Faustus* was revived at about the time of Greene's death, the deathbed pamphlets may in fact have been influenced by it.

35. The possible exception is in *Farewell to Folly*, as noted above, where he refers to spending too freely in pursuit of love. But even here the tone is not nearly as histrionic as in the *Vision* passage.

36. It is amusing to think that Greene suffered or envisioned the same cross-examination undergone by *Groatsworth* so many centuries later.

37. *Mourning Garment*, 9:221, italics added. In the prefaces he had stressed his gentle readers' silence, taking it as a sign of approval: "Gentlemen, I dare not step awrye from my wonted method, first to appeal to your favorable courtesies, which ever I have found (howsoever plawsible) yet smothered with a mild silence" (*Perimedes*, 7:7).

38. To "disparage" was to "degrade," "dishonor," or to "discredit," even to "vilify" (*OED*). In Greene's *Discovery of Cosenage* (1592), the coney-catcher is "discredited" by his cheating tricks. He is "either driven to run away or to live in discredit for ever." The line is cited by the *OED* to illustrate the primary meaning of *discredit*.

39. The letter is cited in Douglas Campbell, *The Puritan in Holland, England, and America* (New York: Harper, 1892), 388.

40. Franklin B. Williams Jr., *Index of Dedications and Commentary Verses in English Books before 1641* (London: Bibliographic Society, 1962).

41. See Derek Alwes, *Sons and Authors in Elizabethan England* (Newark: University of Delaware Press, 2004), who reworks Richard Helgerson's theory about the "Elizabethan Prodigals," George Gascoigne, John Lily, Philip Sidney, Thomas Lodge, and Robert Greene. Helgerson argues that the prodigal fictions re-create the writers' own conflict between obeying paternal authority and obeying their wanton desires, associated with wanton fiction (*The Elizabethan Prodigals* [Berkeley: University of California Press, 1976]). Alwes argues that in Greene, however, the relation between heroes and fathers is more oedipal than prodigal (*Sons and Authors*, 15–18, 22–27).

42. Alwes suggests that Thomas Burnaby plays the role of forgiving father lacking in Francesco's story: "In Greene's late works the merciful father is not totally excluded from his fiction; he is recast as a supporter of Greene's work, thereby relieving Greene of any guilt about not having lived up to paternal expectation" (*Sons and Authors*, 23).

43. *Strange Newes, of Intercepting Certaine Letters*, in *The Works of Thomas Nashe*, ed. Ronald McKerrow, 5 vols. (Oxford: Oxford University Press, 1958), 1:330.

44. For various implications of Greene's redirection of his work to popular topics, modes, and audiences, see Lawrence Manley, *Literature and Culture in Early Modern London* (New York: Cambridge University Press, 1995), 320–24, 341–52; Carmine di Biasi, "The Decline of Euphuism: Robert Greene's Struggle against Popular Taste," in *Critical Approaches to English Prose Fiction, 1520–1640*, ed. Donald Beecher (Ottawa: Dovehouse, 1998); and Alwes, *Sons and Authors*.

45. Helgerson, *Elizabethan Prodigals*, 80.

46. For debates about *Groatsworth*'s author, see note 3.

47. Sidney Thomas, "Henry Chettle and the First Quarto of *Romeo and Juliet*," *Review of English Studies*, n.s., 1 (1950): 8–16.

48. After *Groatsworth*, Chettle did emphasize the narrative switch from one plot to another in his *Englandes Mourning Garment* (London, 1603), but not before it.

49. Although the authorship of *Repentance of Robert Greene* has generated less attention (computer studies, for example, have focused on *Groatsworth*), it too has been debated. For details about it and its relation to the "Repentance of a Conny-catcher" and other texts, see Crupi, *Robert Greene*, 34, and Jowett, "Johannes Factotum," 453–66.

50. *The Repentance* appeared after *Groatsworth*, but Burby and Chettle could have seen each other's work; in fact, Jowett argues that "Chettle must have seen it" ("Johannes Factotum," 8).

51. The Stationers' Register, *Black Book's Messenger*, and *Defense of Conny Catching* (1592) all refer to it.

APPENDIX

1. The interesting exceptions are the Ellesmere manuscript illustrations for *The Canterbury Tales*, which are unusual in being both relatively detailed and faithful to the text. For this fact and others below about the history of frontispieces and portraits, see Elizabeth Salter and Derek Pearsall, "Pictorial Representation of Late Medieval Poetic Texts: The Role of the Frontispiece or Prefatory Picture," in *Medieval Iconography and Narrative*, ed. Flemming B. Andersen (Odense, Denmark: Odense University Press, 1980), 100–123, and, about Skelton in particular, Mary C. Erler, "Early Woodcuts of Skelton: The Uses of Convention," *Bulletin of Research in the Humanities* 87 (1986–87): 17–28.

2. Bale also had precedent for having new portraits made for later books written when he was older, although this practice became most common later. See Margery Corbett and Ronald Lightbown, *The Comely Frontispiece: The Emblematic Title-Page in England, 1550–1660* (London: Routledge & Kegan Paul, 1979), 44.

3. The *Illustrium* portrait is described by Thora Balslev Blatt (*The Plays of John Bale: A Study of Ideas, Technique, and Style* [Copenhagen: Gad, 1968], 7–8), who includes illustrations of both Bale's and Wycliffe's images. She cites *Illustrium* as its source without providing further details except the fact that the portrait does not appear in all copies. W. T. Davies ("A Bibliography of John Bale," in *Oxford Bibliographical Society Proceedings and Papers* [Oxford: Oxford University Press, 1939], 5:201–79) is in accord: he lists an issue of *Illustrium* differing from the last only in the addition of a leaf with a portrait of Bale, "aetatis suo anno LIII" on its verso. I have checked only about ten of the many extant copies, and none of them included the portrait.

4. Heywood's portrait, cast like Skelton's in the traditional preacher/orator format, is more conventional.

5. For analyses of Gascoigne's portraits, see Gillian Austen, "The Literary Career of George Gascoigne: Studies in Self-Presentation," D.Phil. thesis, University of Oxford, 1997, and her "George Gascoigne and the Transformations of Phylomene," in *Elizabethan Literature and Transformation* (Tübingen: Stauffenburg Verlag, 1999), 107–19, as well as Richard C. McCoy, "Gascoigne's *Poemata castrata*: The Wages of Courtly Success," *Criticism* 27 (1985),): 29–55.

6. Austen, "Transformations of Phylomene," 115.

Index

Abelard, 1
Adams, Robert P., "Gascoigne's Master F.J. as Original Fiction," 271n2
Adamson, Sylvia, 239n37
additive autobiography, 11–12. *See also* process, autobiographical
Aers, David, "A Whisper in the Ears of Early Modernists," 235n5
affective linguistics, 37, 239n37
allegory, 30, 157
Allen, Gay Wilson, "Autobiography or Artifact?" 234n2
almanacs, 138–39, 266n24, 269n18
Altman, Joel B., *The Tudor Play of Mind*, 247n51, 257n35
Alwes, Derek, *Sons and Authors in Elizabethan England*, 281nn41–42
Amelang, James, 13–14, 220, 223, 224, 235n6, 240n43; *The Flight of Icarus*, 235n2
Anderson, Judith, 8, 74; *Biographical Truth*, 236n11; *The Growth of a Personal Voice*, 236n15
Askew, Anne, 52, 55, 60–61, 62, 252n39, 252n46

Auden, W. H., 27; "John Skelton," 242n1
audience, for autobiographer, 9, 22, 220–27; Bale, 54, 58, 59, 62, 64; Baldwin, 73, 95, 97; Gascoigne, 169, 187–95; Greene, 200–201, 215, 218, 241n52, 265n19, 281n44; Skelton, 31, 33; Tusser, 133, 136, 146, 147, 148; Wyatt, 39; Whythorne, 83, 85, 101, 102, 103, 107; Whitney, 157, 164. *See also* family; friends
Augustine, Saint, 1, 3, 9–10, 103
Austen, Gillian, 231; "George Gascoigne and the Transformations of Phylomene," 275n38; "The Literary Career of George Gascoigne," 272n18, 283n5
autobiography. *See* audience; autobiography, history of; content; convention; family; friends; historical accuracy; "I" and "me"; intention; language; memory; narrator; occasion; patrons; process; style; subjective world
autobiography, history of, 1–2, 14–15, 98–99, 149–50, 167, 198, 218–19, 220–27

Bacon, Francis, 122; "Of Friendship," 263n42

Baker, Robert, 23
Baldwin, T. W., *On the Literary Genetics of Shakespeare's Plays, 1592–1594*, 279n22
Baldwin, William, 3, 4, 13, 73–97, 130, 198, 220–27; *Beware the Cat*, 80, 180, 225; *The Canticles or Ballads of Solomon*, 226; *Epistola*, 236n11, 253n1; *A Mirror for Magistrates*, 16, 73–97, 136, 222, 226, 247n52, 253n2, 254n3, 256n25, 257nn31–32, 258n40, 280n33; *Treatise of Morall Phylosophie*, 107, 226
Bale, John, 6, 8, 11, 13, 16, 49–72, 101, 198, 220–27, 230, 251n27; *Apologie to a Rank Papyst*, 251n26; *Catalogus*, 50, 53, 54, 68–70, 253n52; "The Examination and Death of Lord Cobham," 251n24; "The Examination of Master Willard Thorpe," 249n6; "Expostulation to a Frantik Papist," 62; "Heliades," 253n52; *Illustrious mayors Britannia scriptorium Summarium*, 52, 53, 62, 250n8; plays, 10, 54; *Scriptorum Illustrium Maioris Britanniae*, 63, 250n20, 282n3; *Three Laws*, 50; *Vocacyon*, 8–9, 49–68, 70, 71–72, 223, 225, 252nn38–39, 252nn40–41
ballads, 10, 218, 241n45, 241n52
Barker, Francis, *The Tremulous Private Body*, 240n38
Bates, E. Stuart, *Inside Out*, 234n2
Baxandall, Michael, *Patterns of Intention*, 237n23
Beilin, Elaine V.: *The Examinations of Anne Askew*, (ed.), 252n44; *Redeeming Eve*, 268n15
Benveniste, Emile, *Problems in General Linguistics*, 247n48
Berlin, Normand, *Thomas Sackville*, 258n39
Berry, Philip, *The Making of Sir Philip Sidney*, 241n46

Betteridge, Thomas, *Tudor Histories of the English Reformations*, 238n30
Biasi, Carmine di, "The Decline of Euphuism," 281n44
Blatt, Thora Balslev, *The Plays of John Bale*, 249n4, 282n3
Boccaccio, Giovanni, 75, 79, 83, 84–85, 202, 255n14; *De casibus*, 79
Boffey, Julia: "Lydgate, Henryson, and the Literary Testament," 270n27; "'Withdrawe your hande,'" 245n35
Bonahue, Edward T., Jr., "'I know the place and the persons,'" 254n8
Booy, David (ed.), *Personal Disclosures*, 234n1
Bottrall, Margaret, *Every Man a Phoenix*, 233n1
Boulton, Jeremy, "London, 1540–1700," 269n17
Bowers, Terrence N., "The Production and Communication of Knowledge in William Baldwin's *Beware the Cat*," 254n8
Bozeman, Theodore Dwight, *To Live Ancient Lives*, 249n5
Bradford, Alan T., "Mirrors of Mutability," 256n27
Bradner, Leicester: "The First English Novel," 270–71n2; "Point of View in Gascoigne's Fiction," 273n23
Breme, Thomas, *Mirrour of Friendship*, 103–4, 261n18
Brownlow, F. W., *The Book of the Laurel*, 245n33
Bruss, Elizabeth, *Autobiographical Acts*, 235n6
Burby, Cuthbert, 217–18, 279n14; *Repentance of Robert Greene*, 197, 210, 215, 217–18, 282nn49–50

Burckhardt, Jacob, *The Civilization of the Renaissance in Italy*, 71, 101
Burr, Anna Robesun, *The Autobiography*, 234n2
Burrow, J. A.: *The Ages of Man*, 260n4; "Autobiographical Poetry in the Middle Ages," 243n3

Cambridge Bibliography of English Literature, 139
Cambridge University, 24, 34, 53, 70, 100, 108, 129, 151, 169, 199, 222
Campbell, Bruce M., "The Diffusion of Vetches in Medieval England," 242n61
Campbell, Douglas, *The Puritan in Holland, England, and America*, 281n39
Campbell, Lily, 82, 96; "Humphrey Duke of Gloucester and Elinor Cobham His Wife in *A Mirror for Magistrates*," 255n11; *A Mirror for Magistrates*, (ed.), 247n52; *Parts Added to "The Mirror for Magistrates" by John Higgins and Thomas Blenerhasset*, (ed.), 252–53n2; "The Suppressed Edition of *A Mirror for Magistrates*," 255n11
Cancellar, James, 56–57, 65, 66; *The Pathe of Obedience*, 251n29
Capp, Bernard, *English Almanacs, 1500–1800*, 266n24
Cardano, Gerolamo, 1, 98–99
Carpenter, Nan C., "Skelton and Music," 244n19
Carroll, D. Allen: "The Badger in *Greenes Groats-worth of Witte* and in Shakespeare," 277n3; *Greene's Groatsworth of Wit Bought with a Million of Repentance*, (ed.), 277nn1–2; "The Player-Patron in *Greene's Groatsworth of Wit* (1592)," 277n3

Castiglione, Baldassare, *Book of the Courtier*, 103
Cavendish, George, *Metrical Visions*, 77
Cavendish, Margaret, 14
Cavyl, *Mirror*, 75–76
Cellini, Benvenuto, 1, 4, 98–99
Chaloner, Thomas, *Mirror*, 75–76
Chaucer, Geoffrey, 3, 6, 14, 20, 35, 173; *The Canterbury Tales*, 79, 80, 83, 282n1; dream poems of, 79; *Hous of Fame*, 258n39
Chettle, Henry, 14, 198, 204–5, 216, 218, 277–78n5; *The Book of Sir Thomas More*, 216; *Englandes Mourning Garment*, 282n48; *Kind-Hart's Dream*, 277–78n5
Chew, Samuel C., *Path of Life*, 260n4
Churchyard, Thomas, 23, 73–74, 75–76, 91, 99, 195, 198, 220–27, 254n3; *The first parte of Churchyardes chippes*, 258nn49–50, 259n56; *A Light Bundle of Lively Discourses Called Churchyard's Charge*, 259n56; "Shore's Wife," *Mirror*, 94, 95, 258n50, 259n56; "A Tragicall Discourse of the Unhappy Mans Life," 94–96, 258nn49–50, 259n56
Clark, Sandra, "Robert Green" (*DLB*), 278n6
Clarke, Danielle, *Isabella Whitney, Mary Sidney, and Aemilia Lanyer*, 268n4
Clarke, Elizabeth, "Diaries," 242n60
Cleland, John, *Institution of a Young Nobleman*, 103
Clendinnen, Inga, 66–67; *Ambivalent Conquests*, 253n49
Clifford, Anne, 224
Clyne, Anthony, "The Poet of Husbandry," 265n15
Cobb, Thomas W., "A Critical Edition of Robert Greene's Groatsworth of Wit," 278n10

Cobbler of Canterbury, The, 210, 212, 215
Coleville, Elizabeth, *Ane Godlie Dreame*, 14
complaint, 14, 20, 73, 77, 91, 97, 161–62, 223, 259n56, 259n59; comic complaint, 166
content, versus style or personal voice, 6, 7, 8, 41, 167, 177, 195, 218
convention, versus individuality, 5–7, 16, 17, 20–22; and Bale, 49, 60; and Baldwin, 89; and Gascoigne, 180; and Greene, 201, 211, 218; and Skelton, 28, 32; in Thomas Tusser's "Life," 145, 146, 147; and Whitney, 150, 151, 153, 156, 158, 166; and Wyatt, 34–35, 39–40, 41, 43; and Whythorne, 99–101, 102–3, 105, 110–12, 114–15, 120–21, 124, 198, 231. *See also* group versus individual identity
Copeland, Robert, 75; *The Seven Sorowes That Women Have When Theyr Husbandes Be Deade*, 75; "Wyll of Jyl of Braintford," 3, 4, 75, 163, 270n28, 270n30
Corbett, Margery, *The Comely Frontispiece*, 282n2
Crupi, Charles W., *Robert Greene*, 278n10, 279n14
Cullen, Patrick (ed.), *The Poets*, 267n1
Cunliffe, John (ed.), *The Complete Works of George Gascoigne*, 271n8
Cust, Richard, "News and Politics in Early Seventeenth Century England," 242n61

Daalder, Joost, "Wyatt and Tottel," 248n54
D'Andrade, R. G., "Cultural Meaning Systems," 239n31
Daniel, Samuel, 14, 139
Dante, 1, 3, 83, 99; *Comedia*, 79

Darell, Walter, *Short Discourse of the Life of Servingmen*, 109, 262n28
David, psalms, 99
Davidson, Peter (ed.), *Early Modern Women Poets*, 241n47
Davies, James, *Hesiod and Theogonis*, 265n14
Davies, W. T., 282n3; "A Bibliography of John Bale," 249n4
Daybell, James (ed.), *Early Modern Women's Letter Writing, 1450–1700*, 241n48
de casibus tradition, 78, 89, 218
decorum, 39, 42, 81, 247n52
dedications, 76, 86–87, 90, 131–34, 140, 146–47, 198, 199, 257n35; George Gascoigne's, 188, 189–93, 271n8, 276nn48–49, 277n55; Robert Greene's, 198, 200, 201, 203, 213–14, 226; Hugh Plat's, 153, 268n7; Thomas Tusser's, 225, 266n30, 130, 131–35, 140, 143, 146–47; Geoffrey Whitney's, 268; Isabella Whitney's, 152, 154
Delaney, Paul, 220; *British Autobiography in the Seventeenth Century*, 233n1
diaries and diarists, 6, 15, 120, 170, 224, 236n7, 238n28, 242n60
Dicky, Stephen, "Seven Come Eleven," 245n32
Dolman, *Mirror*, 75–76
Donne, John, 14
Doughty, Edward, "Unpublished Elizabethan Verse in a Huntington Manuscript," 264n3
Douglas, Gawain Gavin (trans.), *The Aeneid*, 258n39
Dragstra, Henk (ed.), *Betraying Ourselves*, 233n1
drama, dramatic monologue, dialogue, and autobiographer, 222–23

dream vision, 4, 77, 78, 149, 268n15; Baldwin and, 79–80, 82, 83, 93; Churchyard and, 95; Higgins and, 96; prefaces to, 10; Sackville's, 93; Scottish, 255n16; Skelton and, 25, 27–31, 32, 33, 222; vision literature, 79; Whitney and, 154–55, 158. *See also* Baldwin, William: *A Mirror for Magistrates*; Gascoigne, George: "Phylomene"; Greene, Robert: *Greenes Vision*

Eakin, John Paul, 237n22
education and autobiographer, 13, 220–27; Skelton, 24; Wyatt, 34–35; Bale, 52–53; Baldwin, 57; Whythorne, 105–6; Tusser, 129–30; Whitney, 150; Gascoigne, 169–70; Greene, 199–200
Edward IV, 20, 25, 27
Edward VI, 9, 61–62, 70, 71, 74, 223, 230; court of, 130; death of, 49, 108, 223; title page images of, 63
Edwards, A. S. G., "The Influence of Lydgate's *Fall of Princes*," 256n30
Edwards, H. L. R., *John Skelton*, 244n19
Edwards, Philip, 105–6
Elizabeth I, Queen, 54, 190, 191, 222, 231, 258n43, 266n22
Ellis, Jim, "Embodying Dislocation," 257n32
envy, slander, and autobiographer, 154, 245n22, 268n13
Erasmus, 39, 102; *Adagia*, 107; *Moriae Encomium*, 80; *The Praise of Folly*, 39, 247n51
Erikson, Erik, *Psychohistory and Religion*, 11, 241n55
Erler, Mary C.: "Early Woodcuts of Skelton," 245n22, 282n1; *Robert Copland, Poems*, (ed.), 254n9

Fairfield, Leslie, 52; *John Bale, Mythmaker for the English Reformation*, 249n3; "*The Vocacyon of Johan Bale* and Early English Autobiography," 249n3
family, autobiographer's, 102, 138, 224; of John Bale, 52, 59, 70; of George Gascoigne, 169–70, 175, 221; of Robert Greene, 199–200, 206, 281n41; of Thomas Sackville, 94; of John Skelton, 19, 24; of Thomas Tusser, 128, 129, 136–38, 141–43, 144, 146, 267n40; of Isabella Whitney, 150, 151, 159–61, 221, 269n22, 267n3, 268n7; of Thomas Whythorne, 102, 103, 105, 117, 129; of Thomas Wyatt, 20, 34
Farnham, Willard, *The Medieval Heritage of Elizabethan Tragedy*, 259n59
Feasey, Eveline, "William Baldwin," 255n11
Fehrenbach, Robert J., "Isabella Whitney, Sir Hugh Plat, Geoffrey Whitney, and 'Sister Eldershae,'" 268n3
Ferrers, George, *Mirror*, 75–76, 80, 88, 89
Ferguson, Chris D., "Autobiography as Therapy," 241n55
Ferry, Anne, 99; *The Inward Language*, 246n46; *Tradition and the Individual Poem*, 248n56
fiction. *See* historical accuracy
Finberg, H. P. R., *The Agrarian History of England and Wales*, 264n8
Fineman, Joel, 22; "Shakespeare's Perjur'd Eye," 244n13
Fish, Stanley, 27; *John Skelton's Poetry*, 243n2
Fischer, C. M., "Pauline Literary Forms and Thought Patterns," 251n32
Fitzherbert, John, 135–36; *The Boke of Husbandry*, 135–36, 265n18

Index 289

Fitzmaurice, Susan M., *The Familiar Letter in Early Modern English*, 260n11

Five Hundred Points of Evil Husbandry, 126

Fivush, Robyn (ed.), *The Remembering Self*, 237n25

Forman, Simon, 224; *The Autobiography and Personal Diary of Dr. Simon Forman*, 278n8; "Life and Generation of Simon," 14, 235n2

Fowler, Alastair: "Country House Poems," 265n14; *Renaissance Realism*, 236n9

Fowler, David C., *A Literary History of the Popular Ballad*, 241n45

Foxe, John, *Acts and Monuments of the Christian Church*, 52, 98

Fraser, Russell (ed.), *The Court of Venus* (Wyatt), 246n39

Friedman, Donald M., "The 'Thing' in Wyatt's Mind," 246n42

friends, and autobiographer, 11, 28, 102, 171, 224–27, 263n42; Bale, 67, 71; Churchyard, 96; Greene, 215; Tusser, 127, 134, 144–47; Whitney, 152, 156, 159, 160–61, 165–66; Whythorne, 16–17, 100–104 passim, 107, 108, 125. *See also* audience; letters

Furnish, Victor Paul, *2 Corinthians*, 251n33

Fussell, George Edwin, *The Old English Farming Books from Fitzherbert to Tull*, 265n16

Gascoigne, George, 4, 10, 13, 17, 23, 99, 109, 130, 139, 153, 168–96, 191, 194, 198, 220–27, 231, 272n12, 272n17, 273n20; *A delicate Diet, for daintiemouthde Droonkardes*, 190, 192; *The Droomme of Doomes day*, 190, 271n8; *The Glas of Governement*, 190–91; "Hermetes the Heremyte," 231; *Hundreth Sundrie Flowres*, 99, 109, 168–69, 170–85, 187–90, 195–96, 198, 271n4, 271n23, 272n11, 272n14, 273n23, 274nn35–36, 275nn44–45, 278n9; *Jocasta*, 6, 222; "Phylomene," 189, 193, 276n49; *The Posies of George Gascoigne*, 168–69, 173, 175–77, 180–88, 190–92, 193–95, 270n1, 274n36, 276n50, 276n52; prefatory epistle, 242n59; *Steele Glas*, 189–90, 192–94, 195; *The Supposes*, 6, 222; "The View of the World's Vanities," (trans.), 191; *The Whole Woorkes*, 194; "Woodsmanship," 170, 174, 178, 184–86, 188, 195, 273n22. *See also* Burby; Chettle

Gascoigne, George, alter egos of, 223, 274n33; Dan Bartholmew, 174–75, 176, 179; F. I., 175–76; F. J., 172, 173–76, 178–79, 183, 199; G. T., 171, 172, 173–75, 176–77, 178, 180, 184, 195, 261n14, 273n24

Geller, Sherri, "What History Really Teaches," 254n8

genre, 100, 135–40, 166–67. *See also* individual genres

georgics, 135

Glaser, Brigitte, *The Creation of Self in Autobiographical Forms of Writing in Seventeenth-Century England*, 234n1

Godwin, Francis, 4

Goldberg, Jonathan, "Cellini's Vita and the Conventions of Early Autobiography," 237n19

Googe, Barnabe, 10, 135, 152, 171, 195, 259n59; *Eglogs, Epytaphes, and Sonettes*, 153

Gottfried, Rudolf, "Autobiography and Art," 235n5

290   *Index*

Gowing, Laura, *Common Bodies*, 239n32
Graham, Elspeth, *Her Own Life*, 234n1
Grange, Nicholas, 196; *Golden Aphrodite*, 196
Graves, Robert, 27; "The Dedicated Poet," 242n1
Green, Rev. Henry, *Whitney's "Choice of Emblems,"* 267n3
Greenblatt, Stephan, 6, 20, 246n46, 247n50; *Renaissance Self-Fashioning from More to Shakespeare*, 243n7
Greene, Robert, 4, 10, 13, 14, 17, 73, 120, 197–219, 221, 222, 223, 225, 226, 272n12; *Alphonsus, King of Aragon*, 201, 211; *Black Book's Messenger*, 216–17; *Ciceronis Amor*, 213; *The Defense of Conny Catching*, 200, 279n14; *Discovery of Cosenage*, 281n38; *A Disputation between a Hee Conny-catcher and a Shee Conny-catcher*, 216; *Greenes Farewell to Folly*, 202, 203–4, 280n25, 281n35; *Greenes Mourning Garment*, 203, 209, 213, 214, 279–80n23; *Greenes Vision*, 198–99, 201, 204, 210–13, 215, 280n33; *A Maiden's Dream*, 279n21; *Mamillia*, 200, 279n17; *Menaphon*, 200; *Myrrour for Modestie*, 206; *Never Too Late*, parts I and II, 17, 198–99, 201, 203, 204–9, 212, 213–14, 218–19, 263n41; *Orpharion*, 203, 280n27; *Pandosto*, 200; *Perimedes the Blacksmith*, 201–2, 212, 225, 281n37; *Philomela*, 279n21; *A Quip for an Upstart Courtier*, 214; *Second Part of Conny-Catching*, 279n14; *The Spanish Masquerade*, 203
Greene, Roland, 20, 22; "The Colonial Wyatt," 243n4; "The Lyric," 244n13; "Sir Philip Sidney's Psalms, the Sixteenth-Century Psalter and the Nature of Lyric," 244n13

Gresham, Stephen, "William Baldwin," 236n11
Griffiths et al., "London Demography," 269n17
Grimald, Nicholas, 23, 105–6
Grosart, Alexander (ed.), *The Life and Complete Works . . . of Robert Greene*, 263n41, 277n1
group versus individual identity, 5–6, 16–17, 220–24; and Bale, 50–52, 70–71; and Whythorne, 101–2
Gunn, Janet Varner, *Autobiography*, 240n40
Gusdorf, George, 7, 10, 177, 220; "Conditions and Limits of Autobiography," 234n2
Gutierrez, Nancy A., "William Baldwin," 254n5

Hadfield, Andrew: "John Skelton's Influence on John Bale," 253n58; "Translating the Reformation," 250n11
Hakluyt, Richard, *Principall Navigations*, 23
Hall, John, 10
Halliwell, James Orchard (ed.), *The Autobiography and Personal Diary of Dr. Simon Forman*, 278n8
Hammond, Eleanor Prescott, *English Verse between Chaucer and Surrey*, 269n26
Hannen, Thomas A., "The Humanism of Sir Thomas Wyatt," 246n44
Happé, Peter (ed.): *The Complete Plays of John Bale*, 249n3; *The Vocacyon of Johan Bale*, 249n1
Harman, Thomas, *Caveat or Warning for Common Cursetors*, 4
Harrier, Richard, "Invention in Tudor Literature," 247n50

Harrison, G. B. (ed.): *Foure Letters and Certaine Sonnets* (Harvey), 277n2; *Kinde-Harts Dreame* (Chettle), 278n5

Harvey, Gabriel, 14, 99, 139, 189, 192, 197, 198, 199, 200, 214, 225; "Dairymaid's Letter," 196; *Foure Letters and Certaine Sonnets*, 277n2; *Pierces Supererogation*, 266n28

Hawes, Stephen, 27, 245n26

Heale, Elizabeth, 127, 248n58, 275n44; *Autobiography and Authorship in Renaissance Verse*, 235n5, 271n4; "Songs, Sonnets, and Autobiography," 248n58; *Wyatt, Surrey, and Early Tudor Poetry*, 243n8

Hearn, Karen, "Bettes, John the Elder," 262n25

Hearsey, Marguerite, *The Complaint of Henry, Duke of Buckingham*, 258n39

Hedley, Jane: "Allegoria," 273n22; *Power in Verse*, 241n54

Heisserman, A. R., *Skelton and Satire*, 238n30

Helgerson, Richard, 3, 83, 215, 281n41; *The Elizabethan Prodigals*, 236n10; *Self-Crowned Laureates*, 256n24

Henderson, Philip (ed.), *The Complete Poems of John Skelton*, 244n14

Henry VII, 20, 25, 34

Henry VIII, 20, 25, 34, 67, 220

Heywood, Jasper, 10; *Thyestes*, (trans.), 259n59

Heywood, John, 106, 108, 139, 221, 231; *Dialogue Conteyning the Nomber in Effect of All the Proverbs in the Englishe Tongue*, 107

Higgins, John, 74, 91, 96–97; *First Part of the Mirroure*, 91, 96–97

Hines, Sam, 248n55

historical accuracy: versus convention, 21, 22–23, 32, 146–47, 151, 167; versus fiction, 3, 16, 17, 61, 73–74, 77–84, 98, 198–99

Hitchings, Henry, *Defining the World*, 266n29

Hoccleve, Thomas, 14

Hodgkin, Katharine, "Thomas Whythorne and the Problems of Mastery," 260n7

Hogarde, Miles, 149–50; "A Mirroure of Myserie," 149–50

Holland, Hugh, *Pancharis*, 14

Holless, Elizabeth, 11

Holloway, John, 27; "Skelton," 243n2

Holmes, Olivia, *Assembling the Lyric Self*, 239n35

Honig, Elizabeth, "In Memory," 262n35

Howell, Thomas, 171

Hudson, Anne, "Visio Baleii," 250n21

Hughes, Felicity, "Gascoigne's Poses," 274n31

Hume, Robert D., "Texts within Contexts," 241n53

Hunter, G. K., 22, 111; "Drab and Golden Lyrics of the Renaissance," 243n13; "Elizabethans and Foreigners," 262n31

"I" and "me," 7, 16; Baldwin, 82, 85, 86; Gascoigne, 169, 171, 178, 182; Greene and autobiography in the third person, 198–99, 216; "I" and "he," 7, 16, 38, 93, 96; Skelton, 24, 37; Whitney, 167; Whythorne, 113. *See also* narrator

Ide, Arata, "Robert Greene *Nordovicensis*, the Saddler's Son," 279n12

intention, autobiographer's, 5, 15, 55–58 passim, 101, 176–77, 220–27; and unintended revelations, 2–3, 9, 56, 67, 123–24, 165

292 Index

invention, poetic, 77, 177, 180, 193, 273n20
Isewijn, Josef, "Humanist Autobiography," 240n42

James I, King, *Kingis Quaire*, 255n16
Johnstone, Barbara, *The Linguistic Individual*, 240n37
Jones, Emrys (ed.), *Poems* (Surrey), 247n53
Jones, Richard, 149, 151, 152, 167
Jonson, Ben, 37, 83; *Discoveries*, 247n49
Jordan, John Clark, *Robert Green*, 278n10
Jordan, W. K.: *The Chronicle and Political Papers of King Edward VI*, (ed.), 252n41; *Edward VI, the Threshold of Power*, 252n42
Jourdan, Rev. Canon G. V., "Reformation and Reaction," 251n28

Kalendar and Compost of Shepherds, 138, 143, 229–30, 266n23
Kamholtz, Jonathan, "Thomas Wyatt's Poetry," 246n47
Kane, George, 6; *The Autobiographical Fallacy in Chaucer and Langland Studies*, 238n27
Kellog, Robert, 240n43
Kempe, Margery, 4, 14
Kempe, William, 14
Kendall, Ritchie, *The Drama of Dissent*, 250n6
Kerrigan, John, 1, 2, 8, 9, 41, 99, 115, 234n2; *Motives of Woe*, 259n59; "Secrecy and Gossip in *Twelfth Night*," 261n17; "Wyatt's Selfish Style," 246n45
Kiefer, Frederick, "A Mirror for Magistrates" (*DLB*), 254n2
King, John, 74, 222; *English Reformation Literature*, 249n3; *The Vocacyon of John Bale*, (ed.), 249n1

Kinney, Arthur F., 273n27; *Humanist Poetic*, 271n4
Kneidel, Gregory, "Reforming George Gascoigne," 271n3
Knott, John R., *Discourses of Martyrdom in English Literature*, 250n6
Krevans, Nita, "Print and the Tudor Poets," 237n20

Lamb, Mary Ellen, "Tracing a Heterosexual Erotics of Service in *Twelfth Night* and the Autobiographical Writings of Thomas Whythorne and Anne Clifford," 263n37
Landa, Diego de, *Relacion de la cosas de Yucatan*, 66–67
Laneham, Robert, 138; *Captain Cox, His Ballads and Books*, 266n22
Langbaum, Robert, *The Poetry of Experience*, 243n2
Langland, William, 20, 254n4; *Piers Ploughman*, 4, 79
language: Bale's, 67–68, 71; Whythorne's, 99; Wyatt's, 21, 37, 39, 41, 44, 246n46
Lanham, Richard, "Narrative Structure in Gascoigne's F.J.," 271n2
Lawton, David, "Skelton's Use of Persona," 247n50
Lazarillo de Tormes, 4
Leech, Geoffrey N., *Style in Fiction*, 239n37
Lehman, Paul, "Autobiographies of the Middle Ages," 238n26
Lejeune, Philippe, 2, 5, 15, 199, 237n23; "The Autobiographical Pact," 235n3; "Autobiography in the Third Person," 278n7; "On Autobiography," 237n22
Leonard, Nancy, "The Speaker in Wyatt's Lyric Poetry," 246n45

Index 293

letters, 10–11, 225–26; Baldwin (letter to the reader), 75–76; Bale (and Paul's Epistles), 58–60; Greene (letters to the reader), 201–4; Whitney, 158–61; Whitney (letter to the reader), 154–58; Whythorne, 101–3

Levy, F. J., "How Information Spread among the Gentry," 242n61

Levy, H. L., "As myn auctour seyth," 236n11

Lewis, C. S., 20, 25, 241n54; *English Literature in the Sixteenth Century*, 243n7

Lievrouw, Leah A., "Contemporary Art as Aesthetic Innovation," 242n61

Lightbrown, Ronald, *The Comely Frontispiece*, 282n2

liturgy, 22

Looze, Laurence de, *Pseudo-Autobiography in the Fourteenth Century*, 236n13

Love, Harold, *Attributing Authorship*, 239n37

Low, Anthony, 135, 265n14; *Aspects of Subjectivity*, 236n8; *The Georgic Revolution*, 265n14

Lowe, Roger, diarist, 242n60

Lucas, Scott Campbell, "The Suppressed Edition and the Creation of the 'Orthodox' *Mirror for Magistrates*," 255n11

Luther, Martin, 60, 62, 67; "Preface to Latin Writings," 253n53; *Works*, 251n36

Lydgate, John, 79, 83, 90; *Fall of Princes*, 75, 76, 84–85, 258n39; "London Lickpenny," 161–62

Lyly, John, 202; *Euphues*, 200, 209

Lyndsaye, David, "Tragedye of Father David," 77

lyric, 4, 7; sonnet, 14, 20, 22, 35–36

Machyn, Henry, diarist, 170

Macrae, Andrew, 127, 135; *God Speed the Plough*, 264n4; "Husbandry Manuals and the Language of Agrarian Improvement," 264n4

Maddox, Richard, 102

Magnussen, Lynne, *Shakespeare and Social Dialogue*, 260n11

Mancini, Albert N., "Writing the Self," 236n13

Manley, Lawrence, *Literature and Culture in Early Modern London*, 281n44

Marcus, Laura, *Auto/biographical Discourses*, 234n2

Marlowe, Christopher: *Dr. Faustus*, 110; *Tamburlaine*, 111, 201

Marotti, Arthur F.: "Love Is Not Love," 256n28; *Manuscript, Print, and the English Renaissance Lyric*, 263n40

Marprelate, Martin, 14

Marquis, Paul A., "Oppositional Ideologies of Gender in Isabella Whitney's *Copy of a Letter*," 268n8

Martin, J. W.: "Miles Hogarde," 267n2; *Religious Radicals in Tudor England*, 267n2

Martindale, Adam, 242n60

Mary, Queen (Tudor), 49, 73, 74, 127, 149

Mason, H. A., 20; *Humanism and Poetry in the Early Tudor Period*, 243n6

Mascuch, Michael, 6; *Origins of the Individualist Self*, 233n1

Maus, Katharine, *Inwardness and Theater in the English Renaissance*, 238n29

May, Stephen W., "Tudor Aristocrats and the Mythical 'Stigma of Print,'" 237n20

Mayer, Thomas F. (ed.), *The Rhetorics of Life-Writing in Early Modern England*, 234n1

294   Index

McCanles, Michael, "Love and Power in the Poetry of Sir Thomas Wyatt," 248n60

McCoy, Richard, "Gascoigne's *Poemata castrata*," 273n22, 283n5

McCusker, Honor, *John Bale*, 249n4

McDonald, Donald: "Agricultural Writers" (*DNB*), 264n7; *Agricultural Writers from Sir Walter of Henley to Arthur Young, 1200–1800*, 264n7

McKerrow, Ronald (ed.), *The Works of Thomas Nashe*, 281n43

McMahon, Robert, "Autobiography as Text-Work," 236n2

Melbancke, Brian, *Philotimus*, 279n17

Melville, Sir James, 14

memory, 5, 66–67; Bale, 92; memorization, 130, 138; remembrance, 45, 66, 107, 117, 124; Whythorne, 110, 124; Wyatt, 43–44, 47; memoirs, 15, 102

Mills, Jerry Leath, "Recent Studies in *A Mirror for Magistrates*," 255n14

miscellany, 10, 97, 100, 104, 105–6, 110, 139, 153

Misch, Georg, 5–6, 238n26; *The History of Autobiography in Antiquity*, 234n2

More, Sir Thomas, 102; "Ruefull Lamentation," 77; *Utopia*, 4, 80, 180

Morris, John, *Versions of Self*, 233n1

Morton, John, 7; *Godley Learning*, 239n32

Mousley, Andrew, 99, 261n16; "Renaissance Selves and Life Writing," 238n30

Muir, Kenneth: *The Collected Poems of Sir Thomas Wyatt*, (ed.), 244n17; *The Life and Letters of Sir Thomas Wyatt*, 246n37

Munday, Anthony, 74; *English Roman Life*, 223; *Mirror of Mutability*, 73, 91

music and autobiographers, 24, 105–6, 130, 132, 134–35

narrator: and author, 5, 19, 151, 158, 167, 207–9; Bale, 66–68; Baldwin, 82, 85, 86–88; Gascoigne, 171–78; Greene, 202–3, 210, 212, 215–18; narrator's choices, 8, 9, 103, 158; and protagonist, 7–8. *See also* style

Nashe, Thomas, 14, 198, 199, 215, 225; "Sommer's Last Will," 157; *Strange Newes of Intercepting Certaine Letters*, 281n43

Nathan, Leonard, "Tradition and Newfangleness in Wyatt's 'They Fle from Me,'" 248n60

Neely, Carol Thomas, *Distracted Subjects*, 263n40

Neisser, Ulric (ed.), *The Remembering Self*, 237n25

Nelson, William, *Fact or Fiction*, 236n11

Newton, Richard C., "Making Books from Leaves," 273n26

Newton-de Molina, David (ed.), *On Literary Intention*, 237n23

Norbrook, David, *Poetry and Politics in the English Renaissance*, 256n25

Norden, John, 128; *Essex Described*, 264n6

occasion, for autobiography, 9–11, 220–27; and Baldwin, 146–48; and Bale, 52, 54, 55; and Gascoigne, 170–71; and Skelton, 27, 31; and Tusser, 144, 146–48; and Whitney, 152, 154; and Whythorne, 101, 104, 107

Olney, James, 7; *Autobiography*, (ed.), 234n2; *Metaphors of the Self*, 234n2

Osborn, James, 108, 260n8, 261n16, 261n22, 262n32; *The Autobiography of Thomas Whythorne*, (ed.), 242n58, 259n1; *The Beginnings of Autobiography in England*, 235n5

Ostriker, Alicia, 22; "The Lyric I," 244n13

Index 295

Oswald, Hilton C. (ed.), *Works* (Luther), 251n36
Ottway, Sheila (ed.), *Betraying Ourselves*, 233n1
Ovid, 3, 9
Oxford University, 24, 75, 106, 152

Painter, William, 80, 200
Panofsky, Richard J. (ed.): *Epitaphs, Epigrams, Songs and Sonets (1567) and Epitaphes and Sonnettes (1576)* by George Turberville, 271n10; *"The Floures of Philosophie" (1572) and "A Sweet Nosgay" (1573) and "A Copy of a Letter" (1567) by Isabella Whitney*, 267n1, 268n4
Parkes, M. B. (ed.), "'Sacvyles Olde Age,'" 257n38
Parson, Father Robert, *Memorial for the Reformation of England*, 14
Pascal, Roy, 7; *Design and Truth in Autobiography*, 234n2, 235n3
Passerini, Luisa, 5; "Memory," 238n25
passion (emotion), 27, 37, 39, 62, 101, 115–25
patrons, 29, 61–62, 221–25; and Bale, 53–55 passim, 62, 67, 69–71, 74; fictional, 214; and Gascoigne, 169, 170, 173, 177–78, 181, 187–95, 275nn38–39, 276n49, 276n51; and Greene, 200, 206, 212–15, 219; and Skelton, 24, 25, 29, 71; and Tusser, 127–35, 140, 145, 146–47, 266n30; and Whitney, 150–54 passim; and Whythorne, 106, 198
Patterson, Annabel, *Reading Holinshed's Chronicles*, 256n25
Patterson, Lee, *Chaucer and the Subject of History*, 235n5
Peacham, Henry, 139; *Garden of Eloquence*, 68; *Minerva Britanna*, 265n12

Pearsall, Derek, "Pictorial Representation of Late Medieval Poetic Texts," 282n1
Pepys, Samuel, *Diary*, 236n7, 240n38
Perrow, Eber Carle, "Last Will and Testament as a Form of Literature," 269n27
Petrarch, 1, 3, 35, 99, 103; *Rime Sparse*, 35
Phaer, Thomas, *Mirror*, 75–76
Pettie, George, 80, 200
Philips, Norma, "Observations on the Derivative Method of Skelton's Realism," 243n5
Philmus, M. R., "Gascoigne's 'Fable of the Artist as a Young Man,'" 262n15
Pigman, George, III, 274n33, 275n41; *A Hundreth Sundrie Flowres* (Gascoigne), (ed.), 261n14, 270n1, 274n34
Pincombe, Mike, "Sackville *Tragicus*," 233n1, 257n32
Pineas, Rainer: "John Bale's Nondramatic Works of Religious Controversy," 250n12; "William Tyndale's Influence on John Bale's Polemical Use of History," 250n9
plague and epidemics, 156–57, 268–69n17, 269n18
Plat, Hugh, 152, 171, 259n59; *Floures of Philosophie*, 152, 153–54, 155–56, 157–59, 270n29
Platter, Thomas, memoirs, 102
Plutarch, 9, 34
Pollet, Maurice, *John Skelton*, 244n19
Pollock, Linda A., "Anger and the Negotiation of Relationships in Early Modern England," 241n53
Poole, Fitz John Porter, "Socialization, Enculturation and the Development of Personal Identity," 239n31

Pope, Janice T., "Contemporary Art as Aesthetic Innovation," 242n61
Pope-Hennessy, John, *The Portrait in the Renaissance*, 261n12
Porter, Roy (ed.), *Rewriting the Self*, 234n1
portraits, 2, 229–31; of Bale, 50, 52, 62, 63, 282nn2–3; 102, 223, 229–31, 282n1, 282–83nn2–5; of Gascoigne, 194, 191, 231, 283n5; of Skelton, 25, 26, 282n1; of Whythorne, 102, 106, 112–13, 114, 262n33, 261n13, 262n35
Powell, Chilton Latham, *English Domestic Relations*, 266n21
Price, David C., *Patrons and Musicians of the English Renaissance*, 261n20
print, print culture, and printers, 9, 11, 12–15, 220–27; Baldwin, 74–77, 87–88; Catholic, 75, 76; Gascoigne, 188–89, 272n14, 275n43; Protestant, 74, 75; stigma of print, 4, 237n20; Whitney, 149, 165, 222; Wyatt, 34
process, autobiographical, 9, 220–27; additive autobiography, 11–12, 17; Bale, 51, 60, 68–72; Gascoigne, 170–86 passim, 179, 181–84, 188–89; Skelton, 27; Whythorne, 100–101, 104, 110–25 passim
prodigal and prodigal son, 173, 174, 190, 272n12, 203, 205, 206, 208, 209, 214, 215, 280n31
Prouty, C. T., *George Gascoigne*, 270n2, 275n47
Pruvost, René, *Robert Greene et ses romans*, 278n10

Redford, John, 129
Renan, Ernest, 5; *Souvenirs d'enfance et de jeunesse*, 237n24
repentance and confession, 4, 9, 14, 220–27, 240n43; Greene, 191, 197, 198, 201, 202–4, 208–10, 212, 216–18, 237n17, 280n24
Rice, W. H., *The European Ancestry of Villon's Satirical Testaments*, 269–70n27
Richardson, Brenda, 199, 206, 214; "Robert Greene's Yorkshire Connections," 278nn11–12
Robinson, Richard, 10
Roman de la Rose (de Lorris and de Meun), 157, 258n39
Rogers, Everett M., *Diffusion of Innovations*, 242n61
Rosen, David, "Time, Identity, and Context in Wyatt's Verse," 248n62
Rowe, George E., Jr., "Interpretation, Sixteenth-Century Readers, and George Gascoigne's 'The Adventures of Master F. J.,'" 271n4
Rubin, David C., *Remembering Our Past*, 238n25

Sackville, Thomas, 4, 73–74, 75–76, 91–94, 96, 254n3; "Sacvyles Olde Age," 91, 92–94, 257n38, 258n43; "Tragedy of Buckingham," 76, 81, 83, 92
saint's lives and martyrologies, 1, 50, 52, 54, 55, 58, 60, 72, 98
Salter, Elizabeth, "Pictorial Representation of Late Medieval Poetic Texts," 282n1
satire, 25, 27–28, 32, 64
Saunders, J. W., "From Manuscript to Print," 237n20
Scattergood, John, "The Early Annotations to John Skelton's Poems," 245n22
Schleiner, Louise, *Tudor and Stuart Women Writers*, 268n9
Schneider, Gary, *The Culture of Epistolarity*, 241n49
Scholes, Robert, 240n43

Index 297

Schutt, Marie, *Die englische Biographik der Tudor Zeit*, 256n29
Seagar, *Mirror*, 75–76
seasons of a life, 110–12, 114–15, 138–40, 144, 208
Seebohm, M. E., *The Evolution of the English Farm*, 264n8
self, the (abstraction), 2, 5–6, 7, 8, 12, 13, 16, 18; and Baldwin, 86, 91; and Bale, 52; and Gascoigne, 178, 224, 227, 238n28–29; and Whythorne, 99, 102, 105, 113; and Wyatt, 37, 41, 43, 46, 47
sense of self as writer, autobiographer's, 220–27; Baldwin, 80–82, 86; Bale, 52–53, 55; Gascoigne, 171, 177–81; Greene, 200; Skelton, 24–25, 29–31; Tusser, 131–32, 134, 144; Whythorne, 105, 106–8; Wyatt, 34
sermon, 1, 9, 32; style of, 225
Shakespeare, William, 14, 78, 120; *Hamlet*, 240n38; *A Midsummer Night's Dream*, 21; *Othello*, 109; *The Winter's Tale*, 200
Shapiro, Barbara, *A Culture of Fact*, 236n11
Sheale, Richard, minstrel, 10, 241n45
Shore, David R., 262n23; "The Autobiography of Thomas Whythorne," 238n30; "Whythorne's Autobiography and the Genesis of Gascoigne's Master F. J.," 259n3
Short, Michael H., *Style in Fiction*, 239n37
Shumaker, Wayne, *English Autobiography*, 233n1
Sidney, Sir Philip, 79, 107–8, 139, 152, 241n46; *Apologie for Poesie*, 3; sonnets, 14
Skeat, Walter W. (ed.), *The Book of Husbandry* (Fitzherbert), 265n18

Skelton, John, 4, 6, 10, 11, 13, 16, 19–20, 21, 22, 23–34, 71, 82, 106, 155, 220–27, 246n41; *Against a Comely Coystrowne*, 26, 230; *Bouge of Court*, 24, 27–29, 30, 32, 33, 79; "Calliope," 24; flyting poems, 25; *Garland of Laurel*, 24, 26, 27, 29–31, 107, 222, 229, 248n64; "King Edward the Forth," 77; "On the Death of the Noble Prince, King Edward IV," 25; "Philip Sparrow," 25, 245n22; portraits of, 26, 229–30; "The Replycation,"; "Tunning of Elinour Rumming," 27; "Ware the Hawk," 24, 27, 31–33, 223
Smith, Barbara Herrnstein, "Narrative Versions, Narrative Theories," 240n41
Smith, G. C. Moore (ed.), *Gabriel Harvey's Marginalia*, 275n47
Smith, Hallett: "The Art of Sir Thomas Wyatt," 244n15; *Elizabethan Poetry*, 259n59
Snyder, Susan, *Pastoral Process*, 266n26
Solomon, 138, 211, 222; Song of Songs, 226
Southall, Raymond, *The Courtly Maker*, 243n9
Spacks, Patricia, *Imagining a Self*, 233n1
Spearing, A. C., 8; *Medieval Dream-Poetry*, 245n29; "Prison, Writing, Absence," 244n18; *Textual Subjectivity*, 238n29
Spengeman, William, *The Forms of Autobiography*, 235n6
Spenser, Edmund, 14, 83, 188, 225, 254n4; *The Faerie Queen*, 139
Spiller, Michael R. G., *The Development of the Sonnet*, 244n15
Spiro, Mel, "Collective Representations and Mental Representations in Religious Symbol Systems," 239n31
Spitz, Lewis W. (ed.), *Luther's Works*, 253n53

Staub, Susan C., "'According to My Source,'" 271n4
Stauffer, Donald, 49; "The Autobiography," 235n5; *English Biography before 1700*, 249n2, 257n37
Stein, Dieter, *Subjectivity and Subjectivization*, 239n37
Sternhold, Thomas, 130
Stevens, John, *Music and Poetry in the Early Tudor Court*, 243n6
Stevenson, Jane (ed.), *Early Modern Women Poets*, 241n47
Stevenson, Laura Caroline, *Praise and Paradox*, 263n1
Stowe, John, 74; "Historical Memoranda," 254n7
style (personal voice), 3–4, 8–9, 12, 20–3; of Bale, 64, 66, 74, 89–90; of Baldwin, 74, 86–88, 225; of earl of Surrey, 39; of Greene, 198, 200, 216, 279n20; of Skelton, 22, 25; of Tusser, 195, 267n37; of Whitney, 161–63; of Whythorne, 99, 115; of Wyatt, 20, 24, 37–48, 246nn44–45. *See also* narrator
subjective world, 23; Bale, 68–72; Gascoigne, 175; Skelton, 27–29, 33; Whythorne, 100, 114–15; Wyatt, 26;
Surrey, Henry Howard, earl of, 7, 23, 39–40, 41, 83, 221, 248n55, 254n3; *The Aeneid*, (trans.), 258n39; love poem to Geraldine Fitzgerald, 171–72; *Poems*, 247n53; "The soot season," 39–40
Sutherland, Ian, "When Was the Great Plague?" 268n17
Swart, Jacobus, *Thomas Sackville*, 258n39

Tarlton, Richard, 73; "Newes out of Purgatorie," 218
Taylor, John, 4
Teresa of Avila, Saint, 1, 98–99

Thaler, Alwin, "Literary Criticism in *A Mirror for Magistrates*," 256n21
Thirsk, Joan: *Agricultural Regions and Agrarian History in England, 1500–1750*, 266n31; "Making a Fresh Start," 265n14
Thomas, Sidney, "Henry Chettle and the First Quarto of *Romeo and Juliet*," 282n47
Thomson, Patricia, 244n17; *The Collected Poems of Sir Thomas Wyatt*, (ed.), 244n17; "The First English Petrarchans," 248n55; *Sir Thomas Wyatt and His Background*, 243n9
Thorpe, Willard, 51, 54, 55, 62
Tillyard, E. M. W., 86; "*A Mirror for Magistrates* Revisited," 256n25; *Sir Thomas Wyatt and Some Collected Studies*, 246n44
Tottel, Richard, 38, 40–43, 44, 46, 47–48, 140, 202, 248n58, 254n3, 260n7; changes made by, 248n56, 248n61, 249n67; as printer, 140, 256n28; *Songs and Sonnetes*, 23, 41, 73, 84, 97, 99, 100, 152, 171, 202
travel narratives, 1, 4, 14, 86, 242n60
Travitsky, Betty S. (ed.), *The Poets*, 267n1
Trench, W. F., *A Mirror for Magistrates*, 259n59
Tucker, Melvin J., "Setting in Skelton's *Bowge of Court*," 244n21
Turberville, George, 23, 171, 190, 195, 261n14; "Epitaphes and Sonets," 271n10; *Heroides* (Ovid), (trans.), 97, 152
Tusser, Thomas, 17, 24, 106, 109, 126–48, 151, 195, 198, 220–27; "Author's Life," 12, 17, 126–27, 128–31, 139, 143, 144–48, 156, 195, 225; and classical tradition, 265n14; Catewald (farm), 131; Fairstead (farm),

Index 299

Tusser (*cont.*)
129, 141; on fencing, 264n8; *Five Hundreth Good Points of Husbandry*, 12, 17, 126, 128, 131–48, 265nn15–16; *A Hundreth Good Points of Husbandry*, 11, 126, 131–32, 264n2, 265n19, 267n34; *A Hundreth Goode Pointes of Huswyferie*, 140, 141, 266n30; introductory poem, 10, 241n46

Tuve, Rosamund, 157

Tyndale, William, 51, 52, 55, 71

Udall, Nicholas, 129

Vaux, Lord, *Mirror*, 89, 254n3
Virgil, *Aeneid*, 79, 258n39
Visser, N. W., "The Generic Identity of the Novel," 257n34
Vitz, Evelyn B., "The 'I' of the *Roman de la Rose*," 236n13

Warner, Christopher, "Elizabeth I, Savior of Books," 250n21
Watson, George (ed.), *The New Cambridge Bibliography of English Literature*, 266n27
Watson, Thomas, 14
Watt, Teresa, *Cheap Print and Popular Piety*, 241n45
Webber, Joan, *The Eloquent "I,"* 233n1
Webster, Thomas, 6; "Writing to Redundancy," 238n28
Weintraub, Karl, 11; *The Value of the Individual*, 234n2
Weiss, Adrian, 188–89, 275n43; "Shared Printing, Printer's Copy, and the Text(s) of Gascoigne's *A Hundreth Sundrie Flowres*," 272n14
Whetstone, George, 99, 130, 171, 189, 190, 196; "A Remembrance of the Wel imployed life, and godly end of G. Gascoigne, Esq.," 271n8; *Rocke of Regarde*, 196

White, John L., "Saint Paul and the Apostolic Letters Tradition," 251n32
White, Paul Whitfield: "Drama 'in the Church,'" 250–51n22; *Theatre and Reformation*, 250–51n22
Whitford, Richard, *Werke for Householders*, 136, 138, 266n21
Whitney, Isabella, 4, 11, 13, 14, 17, 99, 149–67, 195, 220–27; *The Copy of a Letter*, 149, 151, 159, 161, 268n5, 269n19, 269n21; and sisters, 109, 151, 159–60, 165, 269n22; *A Sweet Nosgay, or Pleasant Posy*, 17, 149, 150, 151–67, 225, 269nn19–20, 269n24; "Wyll," 157, 161–66, 270n28, 270n30
Whythorne, Thomas, 6, 10, 11, 12, 16–17, 24, 98–125, 127, 129, 139, 153, 174, 195, 220–27, 260nn8–9, 261n14, 261n22; portraits of, 113, 114, 230–31; "songs and sonnets," 20–21, 98–125, 238–39n30, 262n32, 263n36, 263n39
Wilcox, Helen: *Betraying Ourselves*, (ed.), 233n1; on John Donne, 233n1
Williams, Franklin B., Jr., *Index of Dedications and Commendary Verses in English Books before 1641*, 281n40
wills, 3, 4, 10, 13, 75, 157, 161–66, 218, 222, 267n40, 270n28, 270n30; mock will tradition, 162–63
Wilson, Bryan R. (ed.), *Rationality*, 237n23
Wilson, Edward, "'The Testament of the Buck' and the Sociology of the Text," 270n27
Wilson, Janet, "Skelton's 'Ware, the Hauke' and the 'Circumstances' of Sin," 245n36

Winston, Jessica, "*A Mirror for Magistrates* and the Political Discourse in Elizabethan England," 255n20

Winters, Ivor, "The Sixteenth-Century Lyric in England," 242n1

Wollheim, Richard, *Painting as an Art*, 237n23

Woods, Susanne (ed.), *The Poets*, 267n1

Woolf, D. R. (ed.), *The Rhetorics of Life-Writing in Early Modern England*, 234n1

Wright, Susan, *Subjectivity and Subjectivization*, 239n37

Wright, Thomas, *Passions of the Mind*, 103

Würtzbach, Natascha, *The Rise of the English Street Ballad*, 241n52

Wyatt, Thomas, 4, 6, 13, 16, 19–20, 21, 22–24, 34–48, 51, 83, 120, 145, 220, 221, 222, 223, 224, 225, 238n28, 246n41, 247n50; *Collected Poems*, 23, 34, 35, 36–39, 40–47; *Court of Venus*, 10, 34, 246n39; "They fle from me," 40, 43–47, 120, 182, 249n64

Yaguello, Marina (ed.), *Subjecthood and Subjectivity*, 239n37

Zemon-Davies, Natalie, 4, 5, 71, 102; "Boundaries and the Sense of Self in Sixteenth-Century France," 253n57; *Fiction in the Archives*, 236n16

Zim, R. (ed.), "'Sacvyles Olde Age,'" 257n38

Zimmerman, T. Price, "Confession and Autobiography in the Early Renaissance," 240n43

Zocca, Louis Ralph, *Elizabethan Narrative Poetry*, 259n59

Zumthor, Paul, 6; "Autobiography in the Middle Ages," 238n28

Index 301